D0034655

WITHDRAWN
UTSA LIBRARIES

PIETRO MASCAGNI AND HIS OPERAS

PIETRO MASCAGNI
AND HIS OPERAS

Alan Mallach

Northeastern University Press
Boston

Advisor in Music to Northeastern University Press
Gunther Schuller

Northeastern University Press

Copyright 2002 by Alan Mallach

All rights reserved. Except for the quotation of short passages for the purposes of criticism and review, no part of this book may be reproduced in any form or by any means, electronic or mechanical, including photocopying, recording, or any information storage and retrieval system now known or to be invented, without written permission of the publisher.

Library of Congress Cataloging-in-Publication Data
Mallach, Alan.
Pietro Mascagni and his operas / Alan Mallach.
p.   cm.
Includes bibliographical references and index.
ISBN 1-55553-524-0 (cloth : alk. paper)
1. Mascagni, Pietro, 1863–1945.   2. Composers—Italy—Biography.   I. Title.
ML410.M39 M25 2002
782.1′092—dc21
[B]   2001059191

Designed by Judy Arisman

Composed in Weiss by G&S Typesetters, Austin, Texas
Printed and bound by Thomson-Shore, Inc., Dexter, Michigan.
The paper is Supple Opaque Recycled, an acid-free stock.

MANUFACTURED IN THE UNITED STATES OF AMERICA
06   05   04   03   02   5   4   3   2   1

Library
University of Texas
at San Antonio

Contents

Illustrations

Acknowledgments

A biography, especially when it is the first English-language biography of the subject, is an expedition into unknown territory. I have been fortunate to have had the help of many guides to the territory, without whose help this book could not have been written. Edoardo and Guia Farinelli, Mascagni's great-grandchildren, and Edoardo's wife, Stefania Deon, have been constantly helpful, making information readily available without reservations or pre-conditions, and offering their moral support and their hospitality. I am also particularly grateful to Father Francesco Bonello of Bagnara di Romagna, the devoted custodian of the composer's letters to Anna Lolli, and to the generous hospitality of the people of Bagnara di Romagna. I have also benefited from the insights and suggestions of Nedo Benvenuti, Julian Budden, Mario Morini, Cesare Orselli, Alessandro Valenti, Peter Warren, William Weaver, and the late David Stivender. I am grateful to Pia Tassinari, who shared her memories of Mascagni with me shortly before her death, and to Aldo Dente, a passionate *mascagnano* and collector, for his encouragement and enthusiasm.

Marcella Previti of the Museo Mascagnano in Livorno, Nandi Ostali of the Casa Musicale Sonzogno, Renata Vercesi of Il Trovatore, and Anna Giusti Gallini of the Libreria Musicale Gallini in Milan provided access to valuable information, as did the many dedicated and helpful staff I found at the New

York City Library of the Performing Arts, the Pierpont Morgan Library in New York, the Library of Congress, the Biblioteca Comunale Sormani in Milan, the Biblioteca Livia Simoni of the Museo Teatrale alla Scala in Milan, the Cineteca Italiana in Milan, the Raccolta Stampe Bertarelli in Milan, the library of the Conservatorio "G. Verdi" in Milan, the library of the Conservatorio "G. Rossini" in Pesaro, and the Biblioteca Labronica in Livorno.

I would also like to thank Bruce Burroughs, William Ashbrook, and Thomas Glasow, editors of *The Opera Quarterly*, for giving me the opportunity during the 1990s to publish some of my earlier investigations into Mascagni's life, while other commitments forced me to postpone work on the book itself for nearly a decade. My thanks also go to William Frohlich and his assistant, Sarah Rowley, at Northeastern University Press, for their encouragement as I laboriously cut my manuscript down to publishable length. My errors and omissions, of course, are my own.

Finally, my deepest gratitude goes to Robin, whose enthusiasm and support for this project never flagged over fifteen years, who accompanied me along Italy's byways in my search for Mascagni, and whose companionship and moral support has always sustained me. It is to her that this book is dedicated.

Preface:
In Search of Pietro Mascagni

Browsing in a record store in Italy in 1984, my eye fell on a recording of an opera bearing the incongruous title of *Guglielmo Ratcliff*, by Pietro Mascagni, a composer I knew for his *Cavalleria rusticana* and little else. I had never heard of it. More out of curiosity than anything else, I brought it back with me to the United States and, once home, listened to it. What began with curiosity ended with awe. I was overwhelmed by *Ratcliff*, a grand romantic opera, thoroughly in the mainstream of late nineteenth-century romanticism yet imbued with a passionate voice all its own. Having listened to it, my curiosity now extended to his other operas and to Mascagni himself, the man who had written this magnificent work, clearly by the same composer as *Cavalleria* yet utterly different in spirit and character. Over the next few years I was able to familiarize myself with many of his other operas largely through private recordings, discovering a wealth of musical riches of which I had hardly been aware. The man behind the operas, however, remained a mystery.

Other than brief entries in opera guides and dictionaries and passing references in books devoted to Puccini or other aspects of Italian opera, Mascagni barely existed in the English opera literature. He is generally dismissed as having written a single effective but tawdry opera, and few writers have seen any need even to investigate his life or works beyond *Cavalleria*. Moreover, the accounts of his first twenty-six years leading up to the premiere of *Cavalleria*, which even the most disdainful writers acknowledged to be worth retelling, were wildly inconsistent. While most agreed on the broad outlines of the story, there were few details about which the sources could agree. As I learned more about Mascagni, I realized that most of the accounts of his life, even in the most authoritative publications, were riddled with simple factual errors, not to mention questionable and tendentious interpretations.

I then set about learning Italian, on the not unreasonable assumption that the literature on Mascagni in Italian would be more extensive, and that definitive information on his life and works would certainly be available in his native language. Those assumptions turned out to be only partially correct. It was true that there is a vast literature on Mascagni in Italian. There was, however, little that was definitive about it. Much of what was published during his lifetime in Italy fell into the category of hagiography, rather than either biography or criticism, while four decades after his death both Mascagni's life and his operas still had the ability to stir controversy in Italy. Perhaps the only significant exception, from the vantage point of 1985, was the work of Mario Morini, particularly his superb 1964 two-volume collection of essays and documents on the composer. To my surprise, however, in the forty years since his death, no Italian writer or scholar had ventured to write a biography of Mascagni. At some point during the mid-1980s, then, my interest in reading a biography of Mascagni gradually changed to a strangely persistent desire to write such a biography, and in the process come to understand, as best I could, a man who had come to intrigue me deeply.

Mascagni, I discovered, bred controversy and contention. During his lifetime, his fans were so many and so passionate in their devotion that the term *mascagnano* was recognized as a common noun by major Italian dictionaries. For fifty years after being propelled to worldwide fame by *Cavalleria*'s electrifying debut in 1890, he was an overpowering presence on the Italian musical scene. He was everywhere, composing operas, conducting, teaching, lecturing, fighting, and litigating. He rarely avoided a confrontation. With a strange and quixotic combination of integrity, innocence, and arrogance, he marched off time and again to do battle on behalf of his vision of Italian music and Italian art, and above all, what he saw as *italianità*, the elusive notion of what it meant to be Italian. Passionately patriotic, he was bitterly opposed to his country's involvement in both world wars; a political naïf, he was denounced as a Bolshevik in 1920 and as a Fascist in the aftermath of World War II.

He was quick to mount crusades against abuses and inequities—real or imaginary—in the musical world of his time, and with his sharp tongue and caustic wit made as many enemies as he had admirers. Driven by the need to maintain his extravagant lifestyle and to support the many families dependent on him, he maintained a killing schedule of concert and operatic appearances into his late seventies, long after his contemporaries had died or gone into comfortable retirement. Drawn to opulence and display, to the end there remained a part of him that wanted nothing more than a simple plate of spaghetti, a glass of vermouth, and a card game with old friends in a haze of cigar smoke.

For all his frenetic activity in other spheres, though, being a composer was Mascagni's life work. More specifically, he was a composer of *operas*, who, once his student days were over, devoted little time or energy to music in any other form. To Mascagni, opera was an art form that made up, in some not entirely clear metaphysical sense, part of the spiritual essence of the Italian soul. Writing operas, therefore, was far more than a craft, more even than the expression of his creative spirit. It was a calling. That calling demanded that every opera he wrote was not only a personal challenge but also a battle on behalf of the Italian opera tradition. That battle became more pronounced from the 1910s onward, as his every new opera became part of a struggle on behalf of *italianità*, against the winds of modernism sweeping in from France and Germany, a never-ending attempt to prove that the tradition of Rossini, Bellini, Donizetti, and Verdi was still a dynamic force in the world of music.

His combative, restless temperament meant that every new opera became a search to reinvent himself and his muse, a challenge to extend further the boundaries of his talent. For him, to repeat himself was a form of artistic death. His greatest years were between 1898 and 1913, when his creative spirit was at its most adventuresome. During those fifteen years, beginning with *Iris* and culminating with *Parisina*, through such varied works as the opera buffa *Le Maschere* and the mystical, expressionistic *Isabeau*, he exploited his gift to its fullest, taking Italian opera into new, barely explored territory. *Parisina*, the climax of his creative trajectory, although ultimately undone by its inordinate length and its paucity of dramatic action, is a work of rare power and poignancy. One of the most important Italian operas of the last hundred and more years, it inhabits a realm far removed from that of the operatic melodramas being written by his Italian contemporaries.

Drama in the conventional sense was of little interest to him. In contrast to Puccini, who commented after hearing *Parisina*, "In the theater one doesn't want words, one wants action," Mascagni needed words, not just any words, but the words through which he could find the music that would illuminate his characters and their innermost drives and motivations. It was the interplay between the characters that drove him, the desire to find the moment in each work when drama, psychology, words, and music fused into a transcendent whole. For all his fundamentally Italian spirit, and the intensely Italian character of his musical language, his vision of opera placed him in many respects closer to composers from across the Alps—Wagner, whom Mascagni all but worshiped from his student days, Richard Strauss, and even the Debussy of *Pelléas et Mélisande*—than to his peers in the Italian opera world.

His works often fail to live up to his visionary aspirations. Mascagni's music is uneven. Even in his finest works, sandwiched between passages of great beauty and emotional power, one finds incongruous moments, awkward transitions, and effects that do not quite come off. He wrote in haste, like a man possessed, working all night, sleeping little if at all. His first drafts differ in only the most trivial details from his final, exquisitely calligraphic manuscripts. There is little doubt that Mascagni suffered all his life from a manic-depressive condition, and his operas are almost archetypal products of the manic state, their characteristics aptly, if cruelly, captured in one description from the psychological literature:

> *The driving energy of mania produces large-scale, intense, powerful, and sometimes crude work. Because mania is the enemy of restraint, the work often contains an excess of ideas and material, unnecessary elaboration, and elements that do not belong. The manic has a preference for exaggeration, overemphasis, and dramatic effects.*

Yet for all the exaggeration and overemphasis, Mascagni's music has a power and intensity that, along with the composer's extraordinary melodic gift, give it a unique place in Italian opera of the late nineteenth and twentieth centuries. No Mascagni opera after *Cavalleria*, taken as a whole, can be said to work as well as do most of Puccini's, yet well into the 1930s, respectable voices in Italian musical criticism continued to maintain that, for all his defects, Mascagni was the greater composer. It is unlikely that anyone would still take that position today, but the fact that it was credibly argued should give today's critics pause.

In the late 1980s, as I was beginning the research that led to this book, a modest Mascagni revival can be said to have begun in Italy. Works such as *Guglielmo Ratcliff* and *Le Maschere*, hardly heard since the 1950s, were revived and began to gain a following, if not a place in the repertoire. The year 1985 saw the first of a continuing series of symposia on Mascagni held in Livorno under the sponsorship of the Casa Musicale Sonzogno, shedding fresh light not only on the familiar *Cavalleria* but also on neglected but important works such as *Iris* and *Il Piccolo Marat*. In 1987 a modest biography of the composer by Roberto Iovino appeared. While far from definitive, Iovino's was the first book to bring to wider attention the story of the composer's thirty-five-year love affair with Anna Lolli, adding a remarkable and hitherto unknown romantic dimension to his life.

By 1989 I had come far in my search for Mascagni. I had traced his steps to Cerignola, the provincial town in southern Italy where he had written *Cavalleria,* and read his letters to his childhood friend Gianfranceschi in the hush of the secluded library attached to the La Scala museum in Milan. I had paged through the original manuscripts of his operas at the small but beautifully laid out Mascagni museum in his hometown of Livorno, and spent weeks reading about him in old newspapers and magazines, feeding spool after spool into the microfilm reader in Milan's cavernous public library. As I followed the newspaper accounts of his doings in the public eye, I realized that his life was almost too well documented. As one of the premier celebrities of the early days of mass media, rotogravure, and Sunday supplements, his every word was news, his steps routinely followed by the cameraman and the inquiring reporter.

Finally, pursuing the hints in Iovino's book, I traveled to Bagnara di Romagna. Bagnara di Romagna is a modest cluster of houses, stores, and workshops huddled around a church and a fourteenth-century castle, nestled among the flat, green fields of the Po Valley, twenty-five miles east of Bologna. A prosperous but tiny village of no more than a thousand souls, it is a peaceful, almost enchanted place, far from the bustle of Rome or Milan. Anna Lolli had been born in Bagnara di Romagna in 1888; before her death in 1973, she offered everything she had saved from her years with Pietro Mascagni to create a museum in the parish church of the tiny village that had been her first home. After some soul searching, the church had accepted her gift, hired a local librarian to put the material in a rudimentary sort of order, and installed it in two rooms on the top floor of the rectory.

If there is a place in the world where Pietro Mascagni's spirit still resides, it is in those two rooms filled with photographs, books, letters, sketches and drafts, newspaper clippings, everything that could be accumulated over more than thirty-five years of unbroken extramarital devotion. In more than 4,200 letters that he wrote Anna between 1910 and 1943, Mascagni poured out not only his love but also every detail of his personal and professional life, from his love for his children and his frustration with their wayward behavior, his despair over the vagaries of politicians, bureaucrats, and singers, to his delight in a successful performance of one of his operas or a good evening's card game with his friends.

The hospitable parish priest had a work table and chair set up for me in the middle of one room, and I spent the summer of 1989 at that table, reading every single letter, reading every one of the hundreds of newspaper articles that Lolli had cut out and laboriously pasted onto huge sheets of heavy black paper, even playing Mascagni's music on the upright piano he had bought for Lolli's apartment, now sitting in a corner of the room. As I sat there reading, I was never unaware of the presence of the two guardian spirits of the room, in the form of two enormous oil portraits of Mascagni and Lolli, painted by Bruno Croatto in the 1930s, hanging behind me on the wall. By the end of the summer, when I returned to the United States and began to write, I had far more material than I would ever be able to use. It was time to sum up and start writing.

Thrust by *Cavalleria* into sudden fame at twenty-six, Pietro Mascagni spent the rest of his life pursued by the relentless shadow of that opera. Driven by his vision of a transcendent fusion of words and music, he devoted his life to creating a body of operas that, for all their power and beauty, could not but fall short of the exalted goals he set himself. It was his fate, though, to be remembered not for the operas, such as *Iris* or *Isabeau*, in which he pursued those exalted goals, but for a single work, dashed off as a desperate bid to escape poverty, that, however remarkable, reflected neither his aspirations nor his deepest creative drives. Despite the vagaries of posterity, though, Mascagni's remarkable oeuvre remains, ready to be discovered anew by future generations of lovers of Italian opera.

PIETRO MASCAGNI AND HIS OPERAS

1. *Becoming a Composer,*

1863—1882

The Mascagni family was of old Tuscan stock, linked in family tradition to grandees of medieval and Renaissance Florence, and to distinguished figures such as Paolo Mascagni, a famous eighteenth-century anatomist. By that time, Mascagni's immediate family were modest artisans and small tradesmen in San Miniato, a picturesque but impoverished hill town overlooking the Arno River, midway between Livorno and Florence. In 1850 the composer's grandfather Antonio Mascagni, a baker, moved to Livorno looking for opportunity. His sons Stefano and Domenico went with him, while two more sons and a daughter stayed behind in San Miniato. Ten years later, Domenico Mascagni, the composer's father, married a young Livornese woman named Emilia Rebua, opened his own bakery shop on the ground floor of a tenement building on the Piazza delle Erbe, and began to raise a family in rooms over the shop. His older brother Stefano found a job in a bank but never married.

The Piazza delle Erbe had long been the principal market square of old Livorno. Only one block from the formal Piazza Grande with its government buildings, it inhabited another world. Ringed by grim five-story tenements, their peeling stuccoed walls punctuated by narrow windows, it was noisy, crowded, and raucous, full of the sounds and smells of a meat, fish, and vegetable market. Most of the tenements are long since gone, replaced by modern apartment buildings. A plaque, first mounted in 1931 and now set in the wall of one of those buildings, marks Pietro Mascagni's birthplace: "On December 7, 1863, Pietro Mascagni, who gave his inspired and original melodies to people everywhere, and with his immortal operas made his own Livorno— as already were Pesaro, Catania, and Busseto—famous throughout the world, was born in this house." Here the future composer of *Cavalleria rusticana* was born, at six-thirty in the morning on December 7, 1863, to the noises of the market coming through the bedroom windows.

LIVORNO

When Pietro Mascagni was born in Livorno in 1863, Italy was hardly a country. Although the kingdom of Italy, with Vittorio Emanuele II at its head, had been established two years before, that nebulous entity meant little to most Italians. Few had been touched by the Risorgimento, the combination of martial episodes and backroom deals that had made a motley collection of kingdoms, duchies, and captive provinces into a nation. Then even more than now, Italians' first allegiance was to their family, and then to their town or city.

Livorno, known as Leghorn to the English-speaking world, is neither old nor beautiful by Italian standards. Its history begins in the sixteenth century, when the Medici dukes of Florence decided to convert an insignificant fishing village into a major trading center. Although as time went on it built its own cultural institutions and traditions, Livorno was first and foremost a commercial city. Its character was determined in 1593, when Grand Duke Ferdinand issued the famous Livornina, the charter of the city, in which "men of the East and West, Spaniards and Portuguese, Greeks, Germans, Italians, Hebrews, Turks, Moors, Armenians, Persians, and others" without regard to race, religion, or nationality were invited to settle in Livorno and make it prosper. From then on, "the malcontents and compromised of all nations," as one writer put it, flocked to the new city. Jews, in particular, found in Livorno not only economic opportunity but also a place where they could live with a dignity rare in Christian Europe.

Livorno became the middleman of the Mediterranean. Manufactured goods were imported from England, France, and Switzerland, then sent throughout Italy and on to the Levant; cotton was imported from Egypt and sent on to England, France, and Belgium; cowhides were imported, processed, and exported again; coral was turned into jewelry and exported to Russia, China, and India, where it was bartered for diamonds. During the nineteenth century, though, Livorno's mercantile role declined. When the city regained its economic vitality during the latter years of the century, it was as a city of foundries, steel mills, and shipyards. It also became a more conventionally Italian city, as much of the polyglot population that had given Livorno its special character left with the decline in the city's foreign trade.

The Livorno of Mascagni's youth was a city in transition. It was a gritty city, but a city of waterfront esplanades set off by green hills as well as a city of grimy docks and warehouses. Its people were known throughout Italy for their frank speech and sharp minds, their unreconstructed radical republican sentiments, and their readiness for a fight. A hotbed of revolutionary activity in 1848, it kept alive a militant tradition, which boiled over regularly into strikes and demonstrations. For all its prosperity, it was an overcrowded city in which much of the population was packed into unsanitary tenements. It had one of the highest death rates from tuberculosis in Italy, as well as one of the highest suicide rates.

Livorno stamped Pietro Mascagni with its mark. Although he lived most of his life elsewhere, his bond with his native city remained a deep one; at eighty, an invalid in his Rome hotel room, he would exclaim to a visitor, "You, a fellow Livornese, can only imagine how deeply I feel nostalgia for our city."

EARLY YEARS

Domenico Mascagni's first son, Francesco, was born in 1862, and Pietro, the second of four sons and a daughter, followed a year later. As a baker and proprietor of his own modest shop, Domenico Mascagni fell into the uncomfortable middle of the Livornese socioeconomic milieu, closer both in means and lifestyle to the working class than to the merchants or professional classes, but socially part of a class of artisans and small proprietors that was neither one nor the other. As an immigrant, he was largely uninvolved in the powerful political currents that washed through the city. No radical, he was a devout man and a diligent churchgoer. He could read and write, an unusual achievement for an artisan of his generation, and had ambitions for his family. Those ambitions focused on young Pietro, who showed more aptitude for book learning than his older brother. Domenico Mascagni decided that Francesco would learn the family trade and inherit the bakery, while Pietro would become a lawyer.

Lawyers in late nineteenth century Italy were part of the upper middle class, a class that was gradually supplanting the aristocracy as the ruling class of the young nation. While the practice of law was not in itself particularly lucrative—there were far more lawyers than the legal profession required—

it opened many doors in government service, in parliament, and in business to an energetic young man. It was a wildly ambitious goal, however, for a working-class father. To enter the university, a classical education was required: after the five years of elementary school, five years in the *ginnasio*, or middle school, and three more years in the *liceo*, or classical high school. The substantial fees involved rendered education beyond the fifth grade, theoretically open to all, the preserve of an exceedingly small elite.

Domenico Mascagni decided to raise the money. Propelled by his father's sacrifices, Pietro Mascagni entered the *ginnasio* after finishing elementary school at the age of ten. Once inside its doors, he became part of a world that would mold the way he saw himself and his nation for his entire life. Although secondary school students were few in number, they were perceived by the young nation's leaders as Italy's future elite, and were indoctrinated with what Martin Clark has called "a constant, relentless dose of patriotism."

Italian patriotism was not a reflection of strongly held traditions but an effort to force-feed a reluctant nation with a sense of its identity. Secondary school graduates of Mascagni's generation spent their lives trying to reconcile the idealized country of their schooling with the ambiguous reality of their adult experience. For Mascagni, although a political naïf, to be Italian was never a simple matter. The search to discover what it meant to be Italian, and the pursuit of the elusive idea of *italianità*, a term much used in later years, was for him a lifelong struggle.

The same year the young Mascagni entered the *ginnasio*, his mother, who had been ailing for years, died of tuberculosis at thirty-three, leaving her husband with five small children. Her loss changed her son's life both inwardly and outwardly. Outwardly, her absence left the family home uncomfortably in the hands of his harsh and demanding father. Inwardly, his mother remained for the rest of his life a romantic, idealized figure, to whose grave he would find himself drawn in later years at moments of emotional upheaval. He never recovered from the loss that her death meant to him, a loss that is reflected vividly in his choice of themes and subjects for his operas, from *Cavalleria rusticana* to the 1921 *Il Piccolo Marat*.

A year later, at the age of eleven, his father sent him to the Schola Cantorum at the nearby church of San Benedetto, where he sang and learned solfège from its director, a retired singer named Emilio Bianchi. The Schola Cantorum had been formed only three years earlier by San Benedetto's zealous parish priest to combat the anticlerical temper of the times and indoctrinate the neighborhood's youth. More than a chorus, it was an environment in which worship, religious education, and sophisticated choral singing were combined; it was chosen by his devout father more probably for religious rather than musical reasons. Studying in this devotional setting, and still shaken by his mother's untimely death, Mascagni was much given to manifestations of preadolescent religious fervor, building a miniature church in his bedroom and enlisting his brothers' help to conduct imaginary services, accompanying himself on a toy piano and making up Paternosters and Kyries for the imaginary congregation.

Quick and intelligent, and a good student when he put his mind to it, he was known in school and at home as a troublemaker, the sort of child who enlists his classmates to do mischief, a child who shouted back at his teachers when they shouted at him, rather than accepting punishment as the natural order of things. Despite his troublesome streak, he studied well enough to graduate from the *ginnasio*. Although his heart seems to have been only intermittently in his studies, he nonetheless absorbed a firm foundation of Italian culture and a lifelong love of art and literature while mastering a clear, vivid Italian writing style.

Not long after entering the Schola Cantorum, he began piano lessons with Antonio Biagini, a local church organist. To encourage his son's musical activities, which he may have considered a suitable hobby for a future attorney, his father bought a used upright piano. "No harm done for a young man to learn the piano," Mascagni in later years imagined his father thinking, going on, "but God help me, had he imagined the rest!"

FIRST STEPS IN MUSIC

Pietro changed dramatically as he reached his thirteenth birthday. Until then he had appeared to be a typical boy, energetic and mischievous, with a taste for music not excessive for an intelligent Italian child. From the age of thirteen, however, his interest in music became an obsession. Little else mattered to him but studying, playing, and above all, writing music. From this point accounts of his life become more detailed, but also far more treacherous, as the facts become more and more interwoven with elaborate and inconsistent anecdotes and recollections. Mascagni himself, who enjoyed storytelling and was not fastidious about details that interfered with his narrative flow, often told varying and even contradictory tales over the years about the same episodes of his early life.

In 1942, when Mascagni told his life story to the young Livornese journalist Salvatore De Carlo, he described how he had decided to write an opera at thirteen. In the stock of a pushcart vendor he found a libretto called *Zilia*, written by Felice Romani, a prominent librettist of the early nineteenth century. As Mascagni remembered this venture many years later, "It was called *Zilia*, after the name of a woman, but it was really about Christopher Columbus. . . . Columbus, on his way back from discovering America, ran into a storm, and was shipwrecked on an island full of savages, and captured along with his son."

Columbus, in a familiar plot device, predicts a solar eclipse, and is freed by the dumbstruck savages. In Mascagni's account, after having written most of the opera, "[his] father, hearing his son's singing all day at home, and hearing the grating sound of the toy piano, one fine day took the libretto and burned it." Never again, he went on, was he able to find another copy of the libretto. Some of the themes from *Zilia*, however, he claimed, ended up in his opera *Guglielmo Ratcliff*.

This may have happened. Romani did write such a libretto, although it is called *Colombo* rather than *Zilia*, the name of its heroine. The composer's accounts of his childhood written closer to the events, however, fail to include anything like this story. The elderly composer was prone to spinning yarns, particularly to an impressionable young man like De Carlo.

The young Mascagni soon found an outlet for his all-consuming musical passion in a new music school that had just been established in Livorno. First called the Istituto Musicale Livornese, and renamed the Istituto Luigi Cherubini in 1879, it was founded and directed by Alfredo Soffredini, a young Livornese musician and a recent graduate of the famous Milan conservatory. While there had been singing schools in Livorno such as the Schola Cantorum, Soffredini's was the first in Livorno to offer a more comprehensive musical education, including composition and music theory as well as instruction on a variety of instruments.

Soffredini, whose "enormous gold-rimmed glasses and plump round face gave him the look of a monk, who spoke in a great hurry, breaking words down into syllables, punctuating each word," as one of Mascagni's contemporaries described him, became the dominant figure in Mascagni's early musical life. It was Mascagni's great fortune to fall into the hands of someone far above the level of the typical provincial music teacher. Soffredini was a first-rate musician who later had a respectable career both as an operatic composer and as a popular writer on musical subjects. Only nine years older than Mascagni, Soffredini immediately recognized the youth's talent. As he described his first encounter with Mascagni's compositions:

> *After three or four [piano] lessons, the young man, without the least timidity, pulled out a sheet of music paper and told me: "Look, Maestro, I've written a Kyrie." I looked at him, not at the Kyrie. "Are you crazy? A Kyrie?" "That's right," he said,*

"and I want to have it performed in a church." . . . *my condescending smile was swept away by my surprise: that modest . . . page of music . . . was a revelation. It was only a concept, an idea; but that concept was a thousand times more interesting than the concepts that go into the Kyries of plenty of musical old fogies.*

Soffredini added lessons in harmony and counterpoint to Mascagni's musical diet and set him to copying out Cherubini's *Treatise on Counterpoint.*

Mascagni's father soon realized that his dream for his son was in jeopardy, and he reacted vehemently. Accounts differ, however, as to precisely how and when this took place. According to one, Mascagni began to study with Soffredini after school on his own, without letting his father know, and his father exploded when he learned what his son was doing. In another version, the young Mascagni began his studies with Soffredini with his father's permission, and the rupture took place some time—perhaps a few months—later, when Domenico Mascagni first learned from the teacher not only that his son had musical talent but that with Soffredini's encouragement he planned to become not a lawyer but a professional musician.

Musicians in Italy, other than the handful blessed with great genius, ranked poorly both socially and economically. A musician was a journeyman eking out a meager living, in some cases predictably as a music teacher or church organist, but more often irregularly as a member of one of the innumerable little bands or orchestras that dotted the Italian landscape. In the late nineteenth century, this picture had just begun to change. As Italy's conservatories grew stronger, music was becoming more professional, while Italy was slowly and hesitantly absorbing the romantic idea of the Artist from the lands to the north, imbuing composers and virtuosos with glamour and social status, as well as earning capacity. The status of musicians had been raised as well by the example of the great line of nineteenth-century opera composers, from Rossini to Verdi, and by the iconic role that Verdi played in Italy's political culture.

Verdi was Verdi, however, and the Italian people's love for his music meant little to the poor devils who held forth in the piazza. Musicians were almost a national symbol of poverty and improvidence. As lawyers were becoming the new aristocracy of power and patronage, few musicians could even aspire to the stability of a full-time municipal or church appointment, let alone recognition as a composer. The hand-to-mouth existence of a composer was the opposite of the respectable and prosperous life that Domenico Mascagni wanted for his gifted but troublesome son. Ignoring Soffredini's pleas, he forbade Pietro to continue his musical studies, locking him in the family apartment to keep him from sneaking out to his music lessons.

At this point a deus ex machina entered the picture. Soffredini appealed to the senior Mascagni family member in Livorno, Mascagni's bachelor uncle Stefano, who was already aware of his nephew's musical aspirations. Through Soffredini's intervention, Mascagni's uncle now arrived on the scene, telling Domenico Mascagni, as his nephew retold the story many years later:

> *Listen, Domenico, your son, my nephew Pietro, wants to study music. I've talked to his teachers. They all say he has talent, and will do well. . . . Now, I'm all by myself. I'm getting old. . . . I'll take him with me. You'll see him all the time; after all, both of us are in Livorno, you in one street, me in another. . . . It's useless [to argue]; . . . he's determined, and there's no point trying to stop him.*

His uncle then proceeded to move Pietro into his home. The excitement of this sudden turn of events is still vivid in Mascagni's account years later:

> *My uncle said to me . . . "I'll give you a key to the house and subscriptions to all the theaters . . . you go to the theaters, and I'll see you back home whenever you feel like." For me, this was a dream come true. Still just a kid, I was free to live the life I wanted. I played [the piano] from morning to evening, I went to my piano teacher, and I went to . . . Soffredini.*

It was a heady existence for a boy in his early teens. Livorno offered a rich operatic diet, with three different theaters at which one could hear frequent performances. In 1878 alone Livorno heard *Rigoletto, Il Trovatore, Nabucco, Un Ballo in maschera, Faust, Il Barbiere di Siviglia, Norma,* and Pacini's *Saffo.* Meanwhile, in Livorno's theaters, frequent stops for Italy's touring companies, Mascagni developed his lifelong taste for the legitimate theater, and for the drama of the spoken word.

A FEVER FOR MUSIC

Although still enrolled in the *ginnasio,* from which he did not graduate until the summer of 1879, Mascagni was now devoting most of his waking life to music. At the Istituto Cherubini he studied harmony and counterpoint, piano and organ, string instruments, including the double bass, and the history of music, while reading through Soffredini's collection of orchestral scores. Every free moment he composed music. His speed and facility were little short of phenomenal. By the fall of 1879, now concentrating entirely on music, he was producing scores in great profusion.

Leaving aside the possibly apocryphal Kyrie and the most probably apocryphal desert island opera, his first documented composition is a song,

"Duolo eterno!" (Eternal sorrow!), dated July 5, 1878, dedicated to his father, perhaps as a gesture of appeasement or reconciliation. He was fourteen at the time. A more substantial effort was a Symphony in C Minor, "for small orchestra with piano," which was performed by the students of the Istituto Cherubini in December 1879, on the eve of his sixteenth birthday. Most of his teenage compositions, however, took the form of sacred choral music, for which the many churches of Livorno created a steady demand. Mascagni wrote a mass together with a fellow student named Barbini; when it was performed, he remembered, "at a certain point people started to clap their hands and applaud just like in the theater, to the great indignation of the priests and the dignitaries present."

Late in 1880, after having turned out a host of religious pieces, and a few short instrumental works, he embarked on a second symphony, in F major. The symphony is a substantial work, more than a hundred manuscript pages, containing an Allegro with a slow introduction, followed by a Larghetto, Minuetto, and Allegro Molto, all written during November 1880. The third movement was a minuet for strings composed earlier in the year, but the remaining three movements, all substantial in scale, were composed in little more than three weeks. While close to the classical models of Haydn and Mozart and, at its most advanced those of Schubert and Mendelssohn, it is nonetheless an impressive achievement. It has both individual character and a high level of technical control, comparable to much of the work done by the early romantic masters at the same age. Furthermore, in contrast to what one might expect knowing Mascagni's subsequent operatic career, it is conceived and executed in symphonic terms, rather than being a collection of tunes cobbled together and more or less arbitrarily called a symphony.

Mascagni's symphonic models were the classical and early romantic composers, available to him only through Soffredini's small collection of scores and through performance on the piano. At sixteen, Mascagni had never attended a symphonic concert and—except for operatic overtures and ballets played by pit ensembles—never heard music performed by a real orchestra. While the students of the Istituto Cherubini performed some orchestral works, it is doubtful that either their instrumental makeup or their training allowed them to offer more than a rough approximation of the works performed.

A comment by Soffredini not long after the first performance of *Cavalleria rusticana*, however overstated it may appear, is nonetheless apt in light of the young Mascagni's symphonic precocity: "Every strand of his music was a continuous confirmation of his inherent genius, truly phenomenal. It was impossible to keep up with his production in those days; . . . every one, I repeat, held a *promise* [emphasis in the original] even greater than shown in the in-credibly successful *Cavalleria.*" The adult Mascagni lost interest in the sym-phonic muse, however, commenting sarcastically at one point later in his life, "I try to fill my operas with music, as long as I have any . . . once I haven't any more, I'll write symphonies."

Soffredini, realizing that he had a pupil of no ordinary talent on his hands, had begun to contemplate how best to further the young man's career and perhaps, to the extent that attention would fasten as well on the prodigy's teacher, his own. With symphonies, however well crafted, of little interest to the Italian public, he prepared a text for a "dramatic cantata," *In filanda* (In the spinning mill), for his prize pupil to set to music. Mascagni began work on the cantata, a large-scale piece for soprano, tenor, and baritone soloists, mixed chorus, and orchestra, on December 2, 1880, just before his seven-teenth birthday. He completed the piano-vocal score on January 7, 1881, and the orchestral score (with the exception of a new prelude to the second part) by January 29. With its first performance that February, he moved out of the church and the salon into the heady world of the theater and the mass audi-ence. He had already begun to attract attention in Livorno. *In filanda* made him a local celebrity.

Stefano Mascagni, who had nurtured his nephew's musical career since having rescued him from his father, agreed to underwrite the performance of the new work. In a later account, Mascagni told a touching story about his uncle's role in the performance:

> Then, my uncle said to me, "I've had an idea; let's put this piece on at the Avvalorati Theater in Livorno." . . . "But, uncle, money is needed . . ." "Don't you worry about that, I'll deal with it." And that poor man, who'd never had anything to do with it before, who understood none of these things, did everything: he called the musicians and signed up the orchestra and chorus, and they performed the work under Soffre-dini's direction. . . . I said to my uncle, "Are you coming?" "No, no, I'm not coming. Imagine me in a theater!" He didn't want to come, but when I came out of the theater at midnight, after the performance, I found my uncle waiting for me outside, on the sidewalk. . . . "I hear from everybody that it went very well." [he said] "I'm very, very pleased. . . . Those few banknotes were well spent."

The work was given its first performance on February 9, 1881, in the theater of the Casino di San Marco, an elegant neoclassical 1806 structure, rather than the larger Avvalorati. The thirty-eight-member chorus included, among others, his older brother Francesco and the young woman who was the first love of his life, Giuseppina Acconci. Soffredini conducted the modest eighteen-member orchestra. Making allowances for the limited resources available, Mascagni had scored the work for strings, two flutes, and timpani, reinforced by harmonium and piano, the last played by the composer himself.

In filanda, a great success, was repeated two days later, and again on March 30 as a benefit for the victims of the recent earthquake at Casamicciola in southern Italy. It received considerable attention from the local newspapers, including *Il Telegrafo*, which wrote, "The complete success reported for this truly praiseworthy work, according to all reports, is noteworthy, also because it so rarely happens that one sees a young man of such tender years complete, with such extraordinary diligence, such a severe and thorough course of study in only three years." The Spinning Chorus and the Romanza had to be repeated, the soprano aria was applauded, and the composer and performers were called forward for repeated applause at the end. *Il Telegrafo* concluded with the prophecy that "the day will come in which Livorno will have the sweet satisfaction of having given him birth and seeing his name become famous."

A. G. Petri, writing in *Il Popolano*, commented on the event in somewhat lighter vein, with an ironic reference to the Mascagni family trade:

> *At the end, when, after having heard this Terzetto, one saw a kid come out to receive the applause, one might say, unready even for the idea of growing hair under his nose, one is almost tempted to believe the whole thing a hoax. Let us praise Mascagni, and give honor and glory to Soffredini, who raised him from a bread crumb.*

Postcards containing Mascagni's picture were sold in the streets of Livorno, for two soldi or ten centimes each.

Soffredini had Mascagni dedicate the score of *In filanda* to Amilcare Ponchielli, the composer of *La Gioconda*, professor of composition at the Milan Conservatory, and Soffredini's former teacher. After Verdi, Ponchielli was the most widely respected operatic composer of the time. While Verdi had long since adopted a reclusive style of life on his estate at Sant'Agata, Ponchielli, a generous and considerate man, had never forgotten his many frustrating years as a struggling young musician and remained eager to help young musicians of promise start their careers. Ponchielli arranged for Soffredini, Mascagni, and their forces to come to Milan and present the work at the musical competition of the Commercial Exposition late in the spring of 1881, Mascagni's first trip beyond Livorno or San Miniato. It was a highly successful excursion. Both *In filanda* and the composer's earlier Ave Maria won honorable mentions at the competition, while Mascagni met not only Ponchielli but also Arrigo Boito, then working with Verdi on *Otello*, and Carlos Gomes, an opera composer almost as popular as Ponchielli. For the young composer it was an exciting introduction to life and music outside the familiar but provincial confines of Livorno.

In filanda, the work that attracted this attention, is a straightforward work of few pretensions but considerable vitality, made up of a series of separate musical numbers in which the chorus plays a particularly large role, linked by short recitatives. Subtitled a *bozzetto lombardo* (Lombard sketch), it relocates the idyllic cliché of the happy peasant to an industrial setting, a spinning mill somewhere in rural Lombardy. There are three characters: the benevolent owner of the mill; Ninetta, a beautiful orphan; and Beppe, the handsome young man who loves her. The mill workers sing a great deal, and the owner urges Beppe and Ninetta to declare their love for one another. In the end they do, and all join in song to celebrate the young couple's wedding. Many of the numbers have a religious or at least a quasi-devotional character, in which Mascagni may have recycled some of his earlier compositions.

Mascagni's models for his cantata were his operatic forebears, in particular Donizetti and early Verdi. The tenor and soprano both receive solos, while the bass sings all the recitatives, through which the modest dramatic action moves forward. The melodies are fresh and attractive, although they show little of the distinctive flavor of the mature Mascagni. The major choral and ensemble numbers, including a large concertato finale, are ambitious and well crafted; the voice leading, the use of imitation, and the balance of soloists and chorus are all executed with a sure, confident hand. Mascagni's harmonic skills at seventeen are still well behind his highly developed choral writing abilities and his less sophisticated but still considerable skill at thematic manipulation. The harmonic language of *In filanda*, although correct, is rudimentary. Moving largely in simple triads along conventional lines, the harmony exists only to support the composer's melodic lines.

For all its limitations, *In filanda* is alive. Its modest subject was well suited to the composer's skills. It is not boring, nor is it excessive, in contrast to Mascagni's next major effort, the overambitious *Alla gioia*. It is free of rhetoric or bombast, and the young composer's sense of musical pace and proportion rarely err. While a minor work, it would be not without interest in an occasional performance.

After the success of *In filanda*, and the excitement of his first visit to Milan, Mascagni went back to his music. The Symphony in F Major was performed in June at the Istituto Cherubini, with Mascagni, who appears to have developed an affinity for that instrument, playing the double bass in the student orchestra. During the month of July 1881 he completed a *Strophe* for chorus, a *Romance* for tenor, and a *Novellina* for piano. These pieces, however, were mere preparation. By midsummer the young composer had already begun to sketch out a truly monumental composition, fueled this time not by Soffredini's efforts, but by his own ever more grandiose musical aspirations. The new piece was to be *Alla gioia*, a setting for soloists, chorus, and orchestra of Schiller's "Ode to Joy."

The seventeen-year-old Mascagni had already begun to take himself very seriously both as a composer and as a personage. During the preceding year he had received an extraordinary amount of acclaim from his fellow Livornese. Having from childhood sought the center of attention, whether in school, at play, or elsewhere, his talent and his considerable charm now enabled him to enter circles to which he could have never otherwise aspired. His sense of his own abilities and importance grew in proportion to the attention he received, and he had already begun prematurely to convince himself that his musical apprenticeship was ending and that he was ready to join the ranks of Italy's major composers.

Arnaldo Bonaventura, a childhood friend later to become a prominent musicologist, has described Pietro Mascagni at this time:

> Tall, thin, slender, clear bright eyes, thick hair—although not yet grown into that characteristic quiff that every caricaturist later immortalized—without a hair on his face . . . that was the adolescent Mascagni. A handsome young man, lively, volcanic, an easy and continuous talker even then, a shameless manufacturer of lively jokes and quips, already as wild about billiards as he later became about scopone [a card game], and even then . . . faithful to the Tuscan mezzo [a thin cigar].

The young man seen by his friends radiated vitality but showed little of the intense emotional turmoil within him; a letter he wrote Soffredini not long after the premiere of *In filanda* conveys the intensity of his ambition; "I will go on with this rugged ascent, paying no attention to those who, instead of encouraging the young artist, look only for ways of making that difficult route impossible to him." In actuality, once past the early conflict with his father, now nearly three years behind him, the course of Mascagni's creative life to this point appears to have run unusually smoothly. Inwardly, he already saw his world, as he would for the rest of his life, in wildly melodramatic terms. To him, life was always a battle, with enemies always ready to attack.

The young composer's emotional turbulence was reflected in his behavior while he was writing *Alla gioia*, about which time Soffredini wrote that "periods of zeal and prodigious fecundity were followed by moments of loss of confidence and of groundless apathy: spitefulness, tantrums, tempers." He was already given to wild mood swings, in which he would go from exaltation to utter despair, and from bouts of intense creativity to long periods of nearly total blockage and frustration. This pattern, too, would characterize Mascagni's entire life.

It was in the flush of this youthful ambition that he decided to set Schiller's famous ode, in an Italian translation by Andrea Maffei, whose translation of Heinrich Heine's dramatic ballad *William Ratcliff* was to become his first true operatic project two years later. He was well aware that this was the same text that Beethoven had used in the choral finale to his Ninth Symphony. Sixty years later, in his conversations with De Carlo, while dismissing *In filanda* as a "tiny work," he admitted that an adequate treatment of the "Ode to Joy" might well have been beyond his musical abilities, at least at that time:

> *Imagine that a great musician, the greatest musician ever, had set Schiller's "Joy," namely, Beethoven. . . . Then, another great composer who is very dear to me, the Russian Tchaikovsky: at thirty-five he realized he was born to write music . . . and then wrote [a setting of] the "Ode to Joy" as well. This, however, I learned later. As far as I was concerned, it cost me more than one tongue-lashing from Soffredini.*

Alla gioia is an oratorio in three large parts, divided in turn into a total of fourteen separate sections for vocal quartet, chorus, and orchestra. It was put on at the Avvalorati Theater, a substantially larger hall than the San Marco, on March 27, 1882. The forces assembled for this performance were considerably grander than those a year before. Soffredini conducted a forty-member orchestra and a chorus with sixty-four singers. With the untimely death of Mascagni's uncle Stefano the previous June, the performance of *Alla gioia* was underwritten by Count Florestano De Larderel, a wealthy Livorno industrialist and arts patron, to whom Mascagni dedicated the work.

Although only slightly more than half of the score of *Alla gioia* has survived, it is more than enough to show that this is a far grander piece, in conception and execution, than *In filanda*. While the earlier work was restricted by its sentimental subject matter to a narrow musical and emotional dimension, *Alla gioia* addresses the entire range of human and spiritual existence. From its opening bars, Mascagni speaks with a powerful new voice. The opening *fortissimo* chords, which become a motto theme pervading the entire work, suggestive of the Prologue from Boito's *Mefistofele*, are of an entirely different order from anything in *In filanda*. These chords set the tone for the entire work; grand and bold, with an attention to harmonic structure completely unexpected less than a year after the harmonically timid earlier work.

Throughout *Alla gioia* the harmonic structure, which provides the dynamic force in the music, is used with a boldness suggesting not only Mascagni's greater ambitions and maturity but also the powerful effect of his sudden exposure to new music during his spring 1881 visit to Milan. He attempts new and unusual progressions and modulations; although often awkward, they are occasionally effective, even striking. While his rhythmic language in *In filanda* was square and routine, with a profusion of repetitive four-bar phrases, here it begins to take on the flexibility and asymmetry that characterize his mature music.

Everything is on a grand scale. Sections are introduced by extended orchestral passages, often including elaborate cadenzas. Many are laid out on large, complex ground plans; chorales, fugato passages, and interjections of the motto theme with cries of "Gioia, gioia!" ("Joy, joy!") appear frequently. Massive tuttis clash with choral shouts, as his search for a musical grandeur worthy of the text leads Mascagni into realms well beyond the extent of his abilities.

This is, of course, the greatest difficulty with *Alla gioia*. Time after time, in his effort to reflect what he perceives to be the moral or spiritual weight of Schiller's message, or perhaps in his constant awareness of Beethoven's presence over his shoulder, Mascagni overreaches, and his best ideas dissolve in bombast and noise. Despite superb moments far better than anything *In filanda* offers, Mascagni's overall goal was far beyond his reach, certainly at eighteen, and arguably at any point in his life. It is unsurprising that perhaps the most successful single surviving section of *Alla gioia* is its most unassuming, the *coretto*, a delicate scherzando movement for chorus with minimal orchestral accompaniment, which foreshadows the delightful *cicaleccio* from his opera *I Rantzau*.

Whatever its limitations, *Alla gioia* was warmly received by the hometown audience. It was performed twice more, at the San Marco Theater on April 2 and April 27, and again during the summer of 1883 in Pisa. It was also profitable for Mascagni, raising the not insignificant sum of three hundred lire toward his future education.

These performances marked the end of Mascagni's life as a young man of Livorno. The city of his youth had no more to offer him at this point, either musically or personally. On April 14, he received a letter from Ponchielli urging him to come to Milan, and he lost no time arranging his affairs and making his plans to leave. Little more than a week after the third performance of *Alla gioia*, on April 27, Mascagni left Livorno for Milan. He was eager to become a part of the musical world he had first encountered there the previous spring, expecting that world to recognize him as a successful composer and award him the fame and fortune he had almost come to count on as his due. He was mistaken, of course, and the fame he sought would not come until many years later, and only after many bitter disappointments and frustrations. When it came, however, it would be far more dramatic and sudden than he could possibly have anticipated.

Mascagni retained close ties with the city of Livorno. As a student, he returned home to Livorno regularly, and after *Cavalleria rusticana* had made him rich and famous, one of his first actions was to purchase a mansion in the city's heart. For years he maintained a home in the city and took part in its musical life. Although the most important events of his life took place elsewhere, until the end of his life he thought of himself as being first and foremost Livornese, wherever he might actually be living. Similarly, the people of Livorno have never hesitated to claim him as a native son, to take pride in their connection with him, and to cherish his music, however much it may have fallen out of favor elsewhere.

2. *Student, Wandering Musician, and* Guglielmo Ratcliff, 1882–1887

By the spring of 1882, the eighteen-year-old Pietro Mascagni had become a celebrity in his native Livorno. Livorno, however, offered him little opportunity either to further his musical education or, more important, to win fame and fortune. There was only one destination for him: Milan, Italy's musical capital. He had three hundred lire from the performances of *Alla gioia* after the expenses had been paid, and another three hundred from the wealthy Count Florestano de Larderel, to whom he had dedicated the work. With this money in his pocket, on which he could hope to live for four or five months with careful economies, Mascagni left for Milan early in the morning of May 6, 1882.

Milan in those days was the ultimate destination of nearly every ambitious young Italian. Although second in population to Naples, it was Italy's largest manufacturing center and its financial capital; it was also a city of elegance and tradition, as the nostalgic Luigi Barzini saw it, with "old houses, old streets, old arches and ancient churches; villas surrounded by old gardens reflected in small lakes, and a hundred secret gardens in the middle of the city." It was also a city of tenements with "cracked, damp, peeling, falling down, dark, stinking walls . . . and filth-encrusted rooms," a city of sweatshops teeming with angry workers who would take to the streets in the thousands in the spring of 1898, changing the course of Italian political life.

Milan was the center of the Italian musical world, as Gallini has written: "The Milanese musical scene . . . had never been so brilliant. The appearances and the visits of Verdi at the Hotel Milan, the permanent residence of Boito, the famous conservatory with such outstanding teachers as Ponchielli, Bazzini, and Saladino; La Scala Theater with its 130-member orchestra conducted by Franco Faccio." Music was a vital part of the city's life. It was the home of Ricordi, Sonzogno, and Lucca, Italy's three major musical publishers, and all Milan read their magazines, particularly Ricordi's *Gazzetta musicale di Milano.* While La Scala was the dominant opera house, it was not the only one. Operas could also be heard at the Teatro dal Verme, where Puccini's *Le Villi* saw the light of day, and at the old Teatro Cannobbiana, which Sonzogno later bought, gave a coat of paint, and renamed the Teatro Lirico Internazionale.

Only in Milan, the only Italian city where orchestral and chamber music were regularly heard, could a young Italian musician not only hear the best in Italian opera but also study the music being written elsewhere in Europe. Instrumental concerts had begun in the 1860s, and in 1879, three years before Mascagni's arrival in Milan, Franco Faccio established the Società Orchestrale della Scala and began to offer regular seasons of orchestral concerts. In Milan one could even hear Wagner's music and study his scores. This was the city that Mascagni was determined to conquer.

Although Ponchielli had urged Mascagni to come to Milan to enroll at the conservatory, nothing was further from the young man's mind. His Livorno successes ringing in his ears, he no longer thought of himself as a student at all but as a fully prepared artist, standing on the first rung of the ladder of success. His purpose in Milan was not to study but to win recognition as the important composer he already felt himself to be. During his first months in Milan he was consumed with the thought of writing an opera and winning recognition from the Italian public; he wrote to Soffredini not long after arriving in Milan: "I must write an opera! I feel a craving . . . that won't even let me sleep. When I'm at the piano I constantly imagine myself writing an opera; I make up the prelude . . . duets . . . arias . . . finales . . . Oh, if only I had a libretto! . . . it's hopeless: I won't be well again until I've written an opera."

With neither a libretto nor the funds to obtain one, Mascagni set about trying instead to get a commission from one of Milan's three music publishers. As he made his rounds, he discovered that they had no interest in gambling on an untried young man from the provinces, as his unsuccessful interview with Giovanna Lucca showed:

> *She began by saying that she wants to help out; but she is besieged with letters of recommendation, and that it's impossible for her to satisfy everybody. Then she*

went into a rambling diatribe against the . . . music schools, which make their stu-
dents study hard and take them up to the point where they can make something of
themselves, and then, instead of arranging a way for them to have their work heard,
dump them on the poor publishers.

After his first week in Milan, the impatient Mascagni was finding the city frustrating, writing Soffredini: "So many times I tear out my hair, I bite on my handkerchiefs, I don't know what I'm doing anymore. Other times, though, I'm calm and serene. . . . the road is a tough one, and now I'm starting to see it."

Although his operatic ambitions remained unfulfilled, he continued to grow as a musician. He went to operas, concerts, and theater; he read through the operatic scores of Verdi and Wagner and heard the latter's music for the first time. He became better acquainted with the generous Ponchielli, whom he visited both in Milan and at the composer's summer home on Lake Como, and he made new friends, including a young engineering student, Vittorio Gianfranceschi, who was to become his lifelong friend and confidant.

Above all, he continued to compose. Less than two weeks after his arrival, he wrote Soffredini that he had just finished a new *preludio* "almost alla Wagner," that is, in the "Milanese style." He composed piano pieces, a motet in the Dorian mode, three pieces he called "Canzoni," short chamber works in popular style for various combinations of instruments, and songs. His songs from this period included "La tua stella," which he subsequently appropriated for *Pinotta,* and the more extended "La Stella di Garibaldi," which taps the spirit of Tuscan popular song in a personal and distinctive fashion.

For all these distractions, Mascagni's stay in Milan was a disheartening one. By the middle of July, running short of money and no closer to his goal, he returned dejectedly home, taking his new pieces with him. Having expected the musical world to welcome him with open arms, he was now back in Livorno, which looked even more provincial after cosmopolitan Milan. His dream of success seemed further away than ever.

Mascagni did not remain dejected long but plunged immediately back into the world he had left only a few months earlier. A concert nine days after his return featured his new *Canzone amorosa* for flute, violin, cello, and piano, while a nuptial chorus for the wedding of a wealthy local attorney brought him 150 lire from the appreciative bridegroom. Meanwhile, he had Giuseppina Acconci, with whom his relationship had blossomed. During the summer the young couple walked out together regularly, and it appeared that it would be only a short while before their engagement would be announced. The summer ended sadly, however, with the death of the composer's younger brother Carlo, early in September. Mascagni's sister, Maria, was also ailing and would die the following January.

AT THE CONSERVATORY

By summer's end, Mascagni's plans had become more realistic. He would return to Milan, but to enroll in the conservatory rather than continue to seek his fortune. Armed with a monthly stipend of 150 lire from the Count de Larderel, he left for Milan on the morning of October 1. The following week he walked through the conservatory's large, bare courtyard to the examination room. Two days later, he described his reception in a letter to Soffredini:

> The committee was made up of Bazzini, Ponchielli, Dominiceti, Galli, Panzini, and Palmintieri. . . . My fear and agitation kept building up, but when finally I heard them call "Mascagni," my fears went away like magic, and with a firm step I went into the room and greeted them in a clear voice. "Oh, my dear Mascagni," Ponchielli greeted me, and began to talk about me and my work. At one point Dominiceti exclaimed, "Well, is this the one who wrote Filanda?" . . . then they started throwing questions at me. What have you studied? Where did you study? With whom? . . . with which methods? . . . then they jumped on my music.

The simple counterpoint exercises that made up the examination posed little difficulty to Mascagni, who had had more training than the typical incoming student. After a proficiency exam, he was relieved of the requirement that he take piano lessons, and as a *ginnasio* graduate, he was not required to take the general education courses required of the less prepared students.

His first year's course included harmony and counterpoint, music history, and poetic and dramatic literature. More exciting, however, was the news of a competition for the best student opera. The next day, slightly anticipating reality, he wrote his father that he was "competing in an opera [competition] at the conservatory with a prize of six hundred lire. The work must be finished by May 30, 1883."

The Milan Royal Conservatory, which had been founded in 1808, was the most highly regarded institution of musical training in Italy. After having rejected Verdi fifty years earlier, it had since produced a stream of distinguished graduates including Arrigo Boito, Franco Faccio, the rising operatic star Alfredo Catalani, and Ponchielli himself. While Mascagni may initially have felt some excitement over his admission to such a prestigious institution, that soon passed, to be replaced by disappointment, frustration, and, ultimately, bitterness. Mascagni was not well suited for the pupil's role. His restless temperament, his impatience, and his awareness of the extent to which his achievements dwarfed those of most of his classmates ensured him a difficult time. He missed Soffredini's praise and the adulation of the Livornese public; when he faced the prospect of having to spend three years in a highly disciplined academic program, his frustration quickly boiled over. After only a month he wrote Soffredini's younger brother Giuseppe:

> *I'm not appreciated at all at the conservatory and I suffer terribly; I go to class and do everything that the professors give me; but that wonderful time when I composed so much, when my mind, free from any yoke or chain, burst with songs of peace and love, is no longer. . . . they have put a yoke on my brain, they have chained my heart.*

At the end of this melodramatic letter, however, he swore Beppe to secrecy, for "I have told it to nobody but you, and I want no one to know anything."

Life as a young artist and man about town in Milan made up for some of his frustration at the conservatory. Dazzlingly handsome, lavishly and often outlandishly dressed, he frequented Milan's artistic cafés, charming everyone. His magnetism and his verbal virtuosity, coupled with his vivid and restless imagination, made him a popular figure, the *enfant gâté* of Milan's artistic and intellectual circles.

As he moved gracefully through these circles, his exposure to the Scapigliatura, a movement that virtually defined the cultural avant-garde at the time, was molding his musical ideas. The Scapigliati emerged in the 1860s as a reaction to the normalization of political and social life that came with the end of the Risorgimento. As Mazzinians, protosocialists, or simply dreamers, they saw the bourgeois ethos of the new Italian nation as a betrayal of the dreams of its people; as Emilio Praga, perhaps their quintessential figure, wrote in a famous poem:

> We are the sons of diseased parents,
> Eagles whose feathers are falling off;
> We fly about aimlessly, silent, stupefied,
> Famished, above our god's death struggle.

While the Scapigliati sometimes seemed defined more by their opposition to bourgeois values and their bohemian lifestyles than by a coherent body of critical ideas, many of them, including Boito, sought to justify their opposition by proposing a new body of artistic and cultural theories to supplant the old ones that they had rejected.

They argued for the affinity and interrelationship of the arts, for poetry that would convey the sounds and smells of the world, à la Baudelaire; for

sculpture and architecture that would be "frozen music." They admired the
French decadents and revered the German romantics, particularly Heinrich
Heine. Led by Boito and Faccio, they challenged the traditional forms and
practices of Italian opera, prizing transalpine innovations both for themselves
and as a tonic for the dilapidated state of Italian musical life. Wagner's music
in particular was admired for its freedom from traditional formulas, the importance of its poetic content, and the way in which it addressed issues of social and philosophical significance beyond the trivialities of mere melodrama.

The Scapigliatura brought new ideas about opera—an openness to
Wagner's reforms, a search for continuity through orchestral texture and the
avoidance of closed forms, a greater emphasis on the meaning and poetry of
the operatic libretto, and a search for strange and exotic forms and subjects
—into Italian musical life. Much of Italian operatic activity during the last
third of the century was influenced by them, notably the operas of Catalani
and, ultimately, the one opera that most closely embodies their teachings,
Mascagni's early *Guglielmo Ratcliff*.

Although its heyday had passed by the 1880s, the Scapigliatura was still
a lively presence in Milan's cafés and salons. Through them, Mascagni was
drawn to Wagner and the "music of the future." He attended La Scala's few
Wagner performances and every concert that featured a Wagner work. On
Wagner's death in 1883 he was moved enough to rush to his room and write
an extended *Elegy* for large orchestra in his memory, completing it in less
than a week.

During Mascagni's first year at the conservatory he also met Giacomo
Puccini, who was then in his third and last year, and shared rooms with him
for the year in the Vicolo San Carlo. Puccini was from Lucca, close enough
to Livorno that the two could almost consider themselves fellow townsmen.
The life that the two struggling students shared during the course of the year
was much like that of the four starving artists in Puccini's *La Bohème*—sharing
clothes and devising endless ruses to keep importuning creditors from the
door. They took their frugal meals together at the Osteria dell'Aida, a modest nearby restaurant at which they could eat traditional Tuscan food, order-
ing cup after cup of coffee during the cold winter months in order to spend
long hours in front of the restaurant's warm stove. Although Mascagni and
Puccini lived together for less than a year, they formed a lifelong bond. In
later years their friendship would be badly strained but never broken by their
rivalry, a rivalry stoked by the press and by their respective friends and admirers, as Italy's two most prominent composers.

Although de Larderel's monthly stipend of 150 lire could provide a
single man with a modest living, the life of a young Milanese musician and

dandy was antithetical to an abstemious lifestyle. Besides food, drink, and cigars, there were concerts and operas to attend, dress clothes to wear, and music to buy. In one grandly extravagant gesture Puccini and Mascagni each put up sixty lire to buy a score of *Parsifal*. One way or another, Mascagni was often in financial difficulty; he gave up his rented piano and at one point wrote his father, in the fall of 1883, "If you could send me two lengths of cloth, I could make myself a pair of trousers, because I've found a tailor who works well and cheaply." He was always looking for ways to make ends meet; in the same letter to his father he added, "I have just been hired to play double bass at the Teatro dal Verme, at three lire an evening. I am wild with joy! Now I can send some money to Cecco [his brother Francesco]!" He joined other orchestras—playing the piano and the double bass—from time to time, coached singers, and gave piano lessons.

He continued to attend class, turning in his harmony and counterpoint exercises while constantly seeking signs that his teachers recognized his music and his talent. In April 1883 he described such an episode to Soffredini:

> After having looked over my counterpoint [exercises], the professor [Saladino] took my Romance and looked at it closely. Then, turning to me, he said frankly that it was very beautiful, and that I showed great promise. . . . Then he said, laughing, "This could give you a swelled head, you, who bring me these pieces and then don't want to study."

He described the stern contrapuntist Michele Saladino, "always so cold to me, so affected by my poor little piece, moved almost to tears."

Mascagni had put himself in an impossible position. He could not passively accept the student's role without abandoning his image of himself as a fully formed composer. At the same time that he was desperately trying to convince his professors of his true worth and make them acknowledge that he was not just another student destined to be no more than a provincial music teacher, he was fighting to keep that image alive within himself. His inattention to his lessons was not a sign of laziness or incapacity but a conscious rebellion against the subordinate, passive role that the conservatory expected him to play.

At twenty, Mascagni possessed a prodigious and still largely unexplored talent as a composer. Neither he nor his teachers had any idea of the extent to which that talent would develop and the paths that it would follow. Ponchielli and Saladino, if perhaps not Bazzini, saw him as a future composer of potentially great importance. They realized, however, far better than he did himself, how much more he needed to learn, and that his great gifts made it that much more important that he master the intricacies of harmony and counterpoint. Mascagni respected and admired his professors but could not accept, or even perhaps understand, their position. The great esteem that he felt for them, however, in light of their nearly total mutual incomprehension, only increased the emotional strain under which he labored. He desperately sought their approval and admiration, yet his own temperament and convictions made it impossible for him to behave in the only way that would win their approval, by excelling in his studies.

His drive to win recognition as a composer in his own right focused on the student opera competition. On October 16, five days after hearing of the competition, he described it in some detail to Soffredini, concluding by saying, "This year I too want to compete. But I lack a libretto." A libretto cost between one hundred and three hundred lire, and nowhere in Milan could Mascagni find a writer willing to work without pay on a student work with no visible commercial prospects.

After wasting three valuable months, in January 1883 Mascagni decided to rework his cantata *In filanda* into an opera. Soffredini reluctantly agreed to prepare a new libretto by modifying parts of his earlier text and adding a few new sections. Busy with other work, however, and less than eager to revisit his unprepossessing effort, he took his time. It was not until April, less than two months before the deadline, that Mascagni received the new libretto.

Mascagni called his new work *Pinotta* after the heroine, whom he had renamed in tribute to Giuseppina Acconci. Mascagni's exposure to the music of his contemporaries is visible on every page. The harmonies are bolder, the musical continuity is far greater, and the work abounds in imaginative touches and ingenious thematic connections that would never have occurred to the seventeen-year-old composer of *In filanda*.

Of the original nine numbers, only four were retained, all heavily reworked, while a daring new prelude, in which offstage women's voices play an important part, was added. The most impressive part of the new work, the high point of an entirely new second half, is the new finale. Instead of the elaborate but stuffy concertato of the earlier work, it is an extended lyrical scene for the young lovers, culminating in an ecstatic duet—in which a theme originally used in his Symphony in F appears—that dies away to a whispered *pianissimo* "t'amo" on the final chord. This scene, about which Soffredini wrote "the more one hears it, the more one appreciates its worth," also interpolated his song "La tua stella," written the year before.

Mascagni had high hopes for the outcome of the competition. Although the money would have been welcome, he was far more interested in the attention that he expected from the performance of the winning opera. With raised expectations, his friends and admirers in Livorno, not only his family and Soffredini but Count de Larderel as well, were all waiting daily to hear that he had been awarded the first prize.

In the end, however, Mascagni failed to complete his opera until June 8, eight days after the deadline. April and May were a hard time of year to find time to work on an opera. Not only did he have to study for his examinations, held at the beginning of June, but concerts and operas were taking place that Mascagni felt he could not miss, including a memorial concert of Wagner's works on April 4 and a mid-May concert at the dedication of a monument to Manzoni, at which Verdi's Requiem and a new cantata by Ponchielli were performed. Finally, he was ill for much of the time, suffering from an unspecified but debilitating condition, one of many such attacks that took place during these years.

After equivocating for over two weeks, the authorities finally refused to accept his belated entry, and the short season of his elevated expectations was over. Only one other student entered, and had Mascagni submitted his manuscript in time, he would almost certainly have received the prize. It is doubtful that winning the competition would have made much difference in his future. While *Pinotta* is a charming work, it lacks even the modest dramatic impetus of its near-contemporary, Puccini's *Le Villi*. It is unlikely that a publisher would have been prompted on hearing it to commission a second opera from the young student, as happened a year later to Puccini.

Although Mascagni did well in his harmony and counterpoint examinations, he failed entirely to appear for his examinations in literature and music history. Ponchielli, well aware of Mascagni's precarious situation, took the liberty of writing Soffredini without Mascagni's knowledge that their protégé had achieved the maximum score on his examinations for the year. As a result, de Larderel agreed to continue his subsidy, enabling Mascagni to return to Milan for another year. Meanwhile, Mascagni took pains to restore his eroded position with his father, sending him a resolutely upbeat letter on June 18, closing with "My first thought is to be able to help you, and with my firm will and iron courage, I have no doubt at all that I will succeed."

Despite the excitement of life in Milan, Mascagni was nonetheless relieved to be back in Livorno for the summer, writing his Milanese friends, "What air! what freshness! what perfume! I am even more convinced that Livorno is the most beautiful city in the world." Revived by his stay in Livorno, and by Giuseppina Acconci's attentions, he returned to Milan in the fall of 1883 for another year of study.

It was during his second year at the conservatory that Vittorio Gianfranceschi presented him with a thin volume containing a play, *Guglielmo Ratcliff* by Heinrich Heine. Mascagni had found the work he was determined to make his masterpiece. In July 1884, at the end of his second year, he wrote his father before leaving Milan: "I have been working on a grand opera which I should finish next year, and if things go well with me, I will take the grand prize and have it performed. . . . my opera is in a completely new style and will cause quite a stir." *Ratcliff* became an obsession for Mascagni, who lavished nearly all his attention and creative energy on it for the next three years. Although he set it aside still unfinished in 1887, he picked it up again in 1893, after *Cavalleria rusticana* had made him famous, finally conducting it at La Scala in 1895.

Guglielmo Ratcliff is a "dramatic ballad" by Heinrich Heine, written by the poet when he was himself in his early twenties; it was inspired in large measure by his unrequited love for his cousin Amalie and is full of the young Heine's straining for poetic effect and his resentment of the bourgeois conventions of his time. More than many of his mature works, it shows the traits that made Heine a hero to the Scapigliati and that attracted the ardent young Mascagni. Set in the literary Scottish Highlands of Sir Walter Scott's novels, its quasi-autobiographical central figure, William Ratcliff, is obsessed with a love that cannot be. A rebel against lawful society, he is doomed, yet he goes down railing eloquently against the forces that have ordained his downfall. All of this made his character particularly appealing to the striving, frustrated Mascagni.

Heine's play was translated into Italian during the 1870s by Andrea Maffei, a friend of the Scapigliati. Although Maffei's translation was in eleven-syllable lines difficult to set successfully to music, Mascagni fell in love with the work. As he wrote a few years later, "Maffei's verses seemed to be so beautiful . . . I declaimed them all night, walking back and forth in my room; and they set me so much on fire, and I fell in love with them so madly, that I dreamed of nothing but . . . the fantastic passion of Guglielmo [William]." Many years later, the elderly composer remarked, "*Ratcliff* was always my grand passion. . . . [It] was truly my first opera, my first child, truly the child of my love."

Mascagni devoted far more time during his second year at the conservatory to *Ratcliff* than to his studies, taking it home with him to continue work during the summer of 1884. By early 1885 he had written a substantial part of the opera, most notably the intermezzo known as "Ratcliff's Dream," which would at least in part precipitate his departure from the conservatory later that year.

Mascagni's second year at the conservatory saw the premiere of his friend Puccini's first opera, *Le Villi*, at the Teatro dal Verme on May 31, 1884, which he watched from the wings alongside the work's composer. Although Puccini's opera would have some influence on Mascagni's own musical language, its immediate effect was emotional, making Mascagni's torment even more painful, inflaming his intense desire to complete his own opera and win fame and fortune for himself. A letter he wrote not long afterward reflects his tortured emotional state:

> *Here I was watching my dearest friend reach the goal that I myself have dreamed of for so long, and I was burning with the desire to imitate him, and yet I could not see any possibility of doing so: . . . Oh, art! My beautiful art! Would I never, then, be able to reach the glory that I longed for, which I dreamed about even wide awake?*

Despite Mascagni's frustration with the rule-bound conservatory, he nonetheless learned a great deal from the course of study. He greatly respected Saladino, who taught him counterpoint, and Ponchielli, who taught composition. The conservatory encouraged its students to develop broader cultural interests, enabling Mascagni to study literature, aesthetics, and the history of music with distinguished professors such as Amintore Galli, who would become a cherished colleague in later years. Finally, he had Ponchielli's almost paternal encouragement. As he did with Puccini, Ponchielli took Mascagni into his home, introduced him to Milanese cultural circles, and watched over his progress at the conservatory, interceding on his behalf as best he could.

Still, it is more surprising that Mascagni somehow remained at the conservatory until nearly the end of the customary three-year course of study than that he ultimately left without receiving the prized diploma entitling him to be called *maestro.* His stay was prolonged by his respect for his mentors, in Livorno as well as in Milan, and by his fear of the consequences of leaving prematurely, in terms of its effect both on his strained relationship with his father and on his already doubtful economic prospects. In the end, his untimely departure was prompted not only by his resentment of the manner in which the conservatory continued to thwart his musical ambitions but also by a fortuitous opportunity suddenly given him to earn his living in the musical world without need of a diploma, from Milan or anywhere else.

BREAKING WITH THE CONSERVATORY

Students at the Milan Conservatory were not allowed to have their music performed outside the conservatory without the director's permission, a rule that Mascagni found particularly oppressive. During his years there, he had had small pieces performed at different times both by a small concert orchestra in which he played the double bass and by the salon orchestra at the popular Caffè Biffi, next to La Scala. In order to avoid openly flouting the conservatory's rules, these pieces appeared as the work of a composer named Pigmeo Sarcanti, an anagram of Mascagni's name.

The conservatory's officials, who were probably aware of Mascagni's breach of their rule, were apparently satisfied with the fig leaf of anonymity his pseudonym provided. Early in 1885, however, a conflict arose that could not be similarly sidestepped. By this point in his work on *Ratcliff*, he had finished the act 3 intermezzo known as "Ratcliff's Dream," perhaps the finest thing the young composer had done so far. Proud of his work, he showed it to Franco Faccio, conductor of the La Scala orchestra. Faccio was enthusiastic and offered to perform the intermezzo if Mascagni could get the approval of Antonio Bazzini, director of the conservatory. The elderly Bazzini's approval, however, was not forthcoming. Instead, the director savaged the piece, calling it "a madman's music." Mascagni angrily stormed out of the office, shouting, "Who are you to judge me?," and slamming the door behind him.

Even then he might have stayed on, bitter as he was, but for a chance opportunity given him at almost the same time. The summer before he had written a song for a childhood friend, the tenor Dario Acconci, Giuseppina's brother, entitled "Il Re a Napoli." Acconci, three years older than Mascagni and already well on his way to a successful career in operetta, was fond of the song and performed it often on his travels around Italy.

In 1885 Acconci was touring with the Castagnetta-Forlì operetta company through northern Italy, reaching Cremona, a short train ride from Milan, in March. Acconci decided to perform "Il Re a Napoli" at two variety nights and invited Mascagni to come to Cremona from Milan to conduct the band. Within a week, Mascagni had become attached to the company. Although he immediately wrote his father, presenting his new undertaking in glowing terms, the confidence that he was trying to convey to his father was an illusion. Only three days later, Mascagni wrote his close friend Vittorio (Vichi) Gianfranceschi, near panic, desperately seeking to undo what he had done:

> *While I was ill thousands and thousands of thoughts raced through my head, above all my one terrible fear: the thought that I won't be able to take the final exam. If I don't get the diploma this year I am ruined. . . . Listen, Vichi, if I knew I could take the exam, and if I could get [back] into the composition class at Easter, I swear that at the end of the year I'd do honor to myself and the conservatory. But look: if I don't get a promise that I can sit for the exam, I'm not budging from here.*

After baring his soul, he came to the point:

> *Professor Saladino has always liked me; go to him, tell him that I am unwell and have been in bad shape; ask him if it is possible for me to take the final exam this*

year *[emphasis in the original]. That's all I ask, just to take the exam. If it's possible, I will study with passion. Otherwise, I will stay here, conducting an operetta company. I will renounce composing forever.*

Although Gianfranceschi dutifully carried the message to Saladino, Mascagni's record was not strong enough, and his absences too numerous. Word came back that, even should he return immediately, he would not be allowed to take the examination that summer, but would have to return for a fourth year and sit for the examinations in the summer of 1886.

After returning to Milan to receive the bad news, Mascagni rejoined the Castagnetta-Forlì operetta company in Piacenza as their new assistant conductor. On April 22, as a notation on his conservatory record shows, he "withdrew of his own free will" from the institution in which he had suffered for nearly three years.

LIFE ON THE ROAD

The status of an assistant conductor of an operetta company was far removed from the exalted state about which Mascagni had so often fantasized during his years at the conservatory. Operetta in Italy, imported from France in the 1860s, was opera's struggling, scruffy stepchild. The first Italian companies were slapdash affairs, more like variety than serious operetta, with jokes, songs, and other stage business interpolated at the singers' whims.

Operetta companies occasionally booked small theaters in larger cities but more often played in towns and cities too small or too impoverished to support an opera company. Most of their repertory was not even Italian, but French operettas in translation, largely works by Offenbach, Charles Lecocq (whose *La Fille de Madame Angot* is still occasionally heard), and their largely forgotten contemporary Edmond Audran.

The status of operetta performers was much like that of the traveling theater companies of the time, of which William Weaver has written, "The expression 'strolling players' is misleading. It summons up, erroneously, a happy image of jolly vagabonds. . . . Reality, in the Italy of the mid-nineteenth century, was far less amusing. Most of the time, traveling players led lives of brutal poverty, homelessness, and humiliation." Operetta companies broke up easily and abruptly, with lives measured often in months rather than years. Bookings were uncertain, payments erratic, promoters often corrupt or irresponsible.

Time after time, after weeks of short wages or none at all, company members would be thrown on their own resources in remote provincial towns, their company dissolved and its owner gone. Meanwhile, the owner would return to Milan or Naples, raise more money, secure a booking elsewhere, recruit a new company, and start over again. For the next two years, accompanied by the valise in which he kept his precious *Ratcliff,* Mascagni lived this life. It turned out to be even more miserable, and far more uncomfortable physically, than anything he had experienced at the Milan Conservatory.

Early in May the company moved on from Piacenza to Reggio Emilia and, after a week, on to Parma, where he conducted for the first time on June 13. His debut work was the Italian version of Lecocq's *Le Coeur et la main,* a popular work that had first appeared in Paris in 1882. From Parma the company moved on to Bologna, where the company met its demise, and as Mascagni wrote later, "I packed up my stuff and went home to my family in Livorno with my tail between my legs like a whipped cur."

It was a sad end to Mascagni's dream of independence. Only three months after having left the conservatory, he was back in his father's house, humiliated, penniless, and completely dependent on him even for the roof over his head. All summer long he faced a barrage of reproaches, worst of all from Giuseppina, who made no secret of her disappointment with him and with the direction he was taking. This was to be his last visit to Livorno for many years. A year later, when he found himself in far worse straits than he had been in the summer of 1885, he did not go back, writing Gianfranceschi at one point, "I can't go back to Livorno, first because of my own self-respect, and anyway, because my father is in no position to support me."

Fortunately, the same Forlì who had earlier abandoned Mascagni invited him in the fall to join him as conductor of the new company at the respectable salary of seven lire a day. Mascagni left Livorno immediately for Naples with relief. Although Forlì's company was dissolved almost immediately, it was soon merged with that of Alfonso and Ciro Sconamiglio, where Mascagni retained his position as conductor and was reunited with his friend Dario Acconci. The Sconamiglio companies were among the more respectable of the traveling companies, known for putting on works largely as written by their composers.

After a short season in Naples, the company set off in December for an engagement in Genoa for the carnival season. As the phase of his life he would later call his "via crucis" began, he was conducting at least a performance a day. Although he was still working and being paid more or less regularly, whatever charms the world of the traveling musician had initially held had worn off; in February he described his life in a letter to Gianfranceschi from Genoa:

A mechanical existence, home and theater, theater and home, continuously going on with work that wears out body and soul, that brutalizes, that takes away even the time to think about one's own place in the world, that strangles even the thought of being able to aspire to another life . . . to another art, as if this could be called art rather than a business.

His relationship with Giuseppina Acconci had finally come to an end, victim of her growing distaste for his vagabond life and irregular existence. "Only to you," he wrote Gianfranceschi, "can I say what I've suffered from being abandoned by that woman, whom I loved to madness; what I would do to rekindle our love, no one but you can ever know." Mascagni's relationship with Giuseppina had been the center of his emotional life since his teens. Months after she had broken off their relationship, Mascagni continued to think about Giuseppina, at times sorrowfully and at other times bitterly.

The company went from Genoa to Alessandria, a small city in southern Piedmont, then southeast to Modena. Trekking from one cheap lodging to another, the company reached Ancona, a busy Adriatic port, by April 1. After a few weeks there they moved inland to the small mountain town of Ascoli Piceno. The company was following a predictable trajectory. On May 9, from Ascoli Piceno, Mascagni wrote Gianfranceschi that "things are beginning to turn sour . . . now we are on half pay, and nobody knows how we will be able to go on." By mid-May he was stranded again. Alone in a remote, unfamiliar part of the country, penniless, and suffering from a series of undefined fevers and pains, he felt his existence was hopeless.

Despite everything, he kept working fitfully on *Ratcliff*, the one remaining thread still sustaining his self-respect, finding in it temporary oblivion from the smells and sounds of cheap boarding houses and cafés. Between passages describing in detail his physical and emotional miseries, he regularly wrote Gianfranceschi long and enthusiastic descriptions of the new music he has just added to the growing pile:

Believe me, Vichi, this fourth act came out even better than I'd believed; I am madly in love with the love duet. . . . It is beautiful, it is unusual, it is powerful; it is the purest of loves mixed with the erotic, it is the perfume of Maria's virgin bedchamber, it is Guglielmo's bloodstained hair. . . . it delights me, my friend, I am in love with it.

Carrying his valise, Mascagni wandered back to Ancona, where he sold his only possessions of value—a watch, a silver chain, and a gold ring—to buy food, and sent out letters desperately looking for work. After some weeks of privation, Dario Acconci again came to his rescue, sending him a money order for a train ticket to Naples. Although reluctant to accept Acconci's charity, and perhaps suspecting that Giuseppina was somehow connected with it, Mascagni was in no position to refuse and left immediately.

Mascagni arrived in Naples in mid-June. Hired as conductor of the Cirella company, with which Acconci was singing at the time, he was assigned to prepare the company's first performance of a new work, *Il Grande Mogol* (*Le Grand Mogul*) by Audran. While the work was well received, the box office receipts failed to cover the cost of the lavish production, and the company soon folded. As the hot Neapolitan summer wore on, things became far worse. Mascagni's illnesses became still more debilitating, and had there been work, he would have been unable to take it. Even *Ratcliff* was no consolation, as Mascagni wrote: "In these days of sickness I've added a few notes to poor Guglielmo, but it's sorry stuff, sick like me." Three weeks later, on August 2, he wrote Gianfranceschi with further medical details: "I had wanted to write you long before, but a terrible illness in my hands has prevented me. . . . Awful pains in my wrists that didn't permit even the slightest movement of my hand or my arm; terrible pains that gave me no peace during the day and didn't let me sleep at night." The description suggests a sort of arthritic condition, or perhaps something like rheumatic fever. The extent of his medical problems during these years, however, for a young man who had been an apparently healthy adolescent and was to live a long healthy life afterward, remains a mystery. There is no reason to believe that they were imaginary; at the same time, it is likely that they were at least in part psychosomatic, linked to his general state of depression and his unhappiness with the routine of work in his various operetta companies. As he was a conductor, the fact that his problems appeared to affect his hands and arms most severely may be significant.

Meanwhile, Mascagni and Acconci were sharing the latter's quarters, selling Acconci's possessions one by one to be able to eat. While Mascagni continued to work fitfully on his opera between bouts of fever and miscellaneous aches and pains, neither was making any money. As the summer went on, without work, money, or expectations, Mascagni became more and more distraught, sending off letter after letter to Gianfranceschi, urging him to try to market his songs in Milan. Finally, by the end of September Mascagni gave up, striking a chastened, apologetic tone: "I got a letter from my father and my brother in which they demand that I return home, criticizing the way I've behaved toward my family and appealing to my self-respect ('if you have any left,' these are my father's words) to make up my mind once and for all 'to come home, give up music, and look for a job so you'll end up decently.'" His initial reaction was to reject his father's ultimatum, commenting with bitter bravado that "I've survived being ditched by my good Beppina, I can survive this too." By the end of the letter, however, he had resigned himself to return home: "I have already decided; I'll sell my last shirt and will get myself to Livorno, and who knows, I might just make a go of a job in some business concern. . . . After so many years, after so much money down the drain, after so much work. Enough! . . . remember your poor Pietro from time to time." It is unclear whether Mascagni actually would have abandoned his musical career. Fortunately, only a few days later he was invited by Luigi Maresca, a comedian turned operetta impresario, to join his company. He accepted immediately and within weeks was back on the road.

With Giuseppina's rejection still in his thoughts, in Naples Mascagni turned for consolation to a new relationship with Argenide Marcellina Carbognani, known as Lina, the woman who would eventually become his wife. The precise circumstances of their meeting are obscure, and romanticized versions of their encounter formed part of the many short biographies of Mascagni that appeared in Italy during his lifetime. The following is typical:

> He was unemployed, miserable, deprived of everything, and half sick. A sweet woman showed compassion for this unfortunate youth; she cared for him, she healed him, she revived him into a new life. That young woman, too, needed support; he, recognizing this, asked her if she would agree to unite their two destinies. They were married.

This is plausible, but only up to a point. Their first child was born on May 22 of the following year, placing his conception in August, while he was still lamenting Giuseppina's desertion in his letters, and suggesting that the relationship began not long after the breakup of the Cirella company and the onset of his mysterious illness. In a letter he wrote Gianfranceschi a year later, trying to explain how he could have acquired a woman—if not yet a wife—and a son, Mascagni gave his own somewhat sanitized version of their encounter. He had met her first in Genoa, "a sweet young woman, daughter of a good Parma family, exquisitely educated by the nuns, with a heart of gold." Later, in Naples, "I went through possibly the worst time of my life. I was alone, abandoned by all, without any means of support, without hope; and on top of it I was deathly ill and needed total rest. In my misery, a hand stretched out to help me." Lina nursed him through his illness, and he was grateful. "Did I love her out of gratitude?" he went on, "did I love her to get even [with Giuseppina]? . . . Do I truly love her? I don't know, and I don't care to know. I know that I vowed to keep her with me forever, to make her mine."

All of this is somewhat confusing and far from convincing. In a time and place when an unmarried woman of good family lived in the shadow of her male relatives and would not lightly undertake even a short journey unchaperoned, one must wonder how Lina came to be in exotic, dangerous

Naples, far from Parma, and how once there, she happened upon the impoverished, miserable composer. Mascagni was almost certainly being disingenuous. It is far more likely that their relationship began elsewhere, perhaps as a casual encounter either in Genoa or Parma, and that either Lina followed him to Naples or from Naples he summoned her to join him.

It is clear from her letters that Lina Mascagni was not a well-educated woman. In fact, as Mascagni only discovered eleven years later, in 1897, when he met her family for the first time in a visit to Parma, Lina's background was even more modest than his own. By that time, they had been married eight years and had three growing children. Although her father was dead by then, her mother and her brother Paolino, along with Paolino's wife and children, all lived in a small apartment above the tavern the family kept. Although it was Easter Sunday, the tavern was a rowdy place, as he wrote Lina later, "a great racket, someone singing, someone screaming, card players cursing, drunks." The Carbognanis were decent, struggling folks, though, and he got on well with them. Paolino's children, though, brought tears to his eyes. "Their poor children," he wrote, "never smile. . . . They don't even know it's Easter!" While Lina may have wanted initially to conceal from her parents that she was living with a man to whom she was not married, it is not clear why she kept her husband and her family apart for so long after they were married, and after he had become wealthy and famous.

Mascagni and Lina did not marry in Naples, nor did they in fact marry until 1889, shortly before Lina gave birth to their second son. Indeed, even after Lina had joined him in Naples, the bittersweet memory of Giuseppina Acconci still weighed more heavily on his mind than did the woman with whom he was sleeping. In mid-August, within weeks of the day on which his first son was conceived, Mascagni was still thinking of his old love, writing Gianfranceschi, "I am despised by the one I love more than myself. Ah, my friend, how this thought makes me melancholy."

Giuseppina, however, was in the past now, and Lina very much in the present. When Mascagni went on the road in late October with the Maresca company, Lina went with him. The Maresca company was playing towns even more modest than the northern and central cities in which Mascagni had performed before. From Naples the company went to Benevento, a farm market town in the hills east of Naples, and then on to Foggia, capital of the province of Puglia, a prosperous and busy city by southern standards. In December they moved on to the small nearby market town of Cerignola. Hired for the entire carnival season, they would remain in the same place for the next two months, until the middle of February.

Mascagni's arrival in Cerignola marks the end of his wandering years. The transition from wandering musician to solid citizen and paterfamilias was both eventful and rapid. Within a few months, Mascagni was to find himself a respected member of a settled community and a "serious" musician once again. The next dramatic change in his life would take place three years later, with the success of *Cavalleria rusticana* in 1890.

3. *Cerignola and the Composition of* Cavalleria rusticana, *1887–1890*

Mascagni arrived in Cerignola in December 1886. Tucked away in the Tavoliere, the fertile Apulian plain in southeastern Italy, Cerignola was little touched by the currents of cultural or artistic life elsewhere. While before Mascagni had been a marginal figure, living a transient life in cheap lodgings and cafés, in Cerignola he found himself accepted as a serious artist, welcomed by the more educated and cultured members of the community.

Cerignola was an unpretentious, dusty market town of straight streets lined with rows of modest two- and three-story buildings, its stores spread out along a straggling main street that rumbled with the coming and going of peasants' oxcarts. It boasted an attractive neoclassical theater of substantial proportions, named in honor of the Neapolitan composer Saverio Mercadante, which had opened in November 1868 with a performance of its namesake's *La Vestale*. It was a white elephant, however, hopelessly extravagant for a backward region populated largely by illiterate and impoverished peasants and workingmen. After February 1869, when the curtain fell on the last performance of its heavily subsidized opening season, the theater remained dark except for the rare operetta or band concert. By 1886 musical life in Cerignola was reduced to the elderly Prisciano Martucci, who played in the churches and led the town band in the religious processions and civic events that added variety to the routine of a provincial town.

While it is common to think of towns in southern Italy as cultural and intellectual wastelands, each southern town had its educated circles, made up of landed proprietors, bored aristocrats, professionals, and officials. Such men generally had few onerous duties and sought out one another's company to pass the time. Mascagni, with his charm, musical talent, and Milanese veneer, was a welcome addition to these circles. His new friends encouraged him to think of settling in Cerignola, rather than moving on in February. Giuseppe Cannone, the mayor and a member of one of the town's most prominent families, was particularly encouraging. He hired Mascagni to give piano lessons to his daughters and proposed to reinstitute the town's music school and orchestra, which had been disbanded ten years earlier.

Mascagni welcomed Cannone's attentions. His last few years had been hectic and disorderly. Although still young, he was tired. With memories of his miserable summer in Naples still fresh, he was ready to exchange the life of a musical vagabond for a stable existence in a community he could call his own. Cerignola was acceptable; as he wrote his father, "Cerignola is a bit primitive, but they like me a lot." By mid-January, moreover, Lina was five months pregnant and reluctant to give birth and raise a child in a series of horsecarts, third-class railway cars, and cheap rental rooms. The only obstacle was Maresca, who had heard about Mascagni's conversations, and who made it clear that he expected his conductor to go with the company to Sicily. The two had already come to blows, and Maresca began to watch Mascagni closely.

With the help of Cannone and his son-in-law, Luigi Manzari, Mascagni escaped Maresca's clutches. Before the company's last performance in Cerignola, Mascagni entrusted Manzari with his precious valise containing the score of *Guglielmo Ratcliff*. At the end of the performance, he rushed from the theater to Manzari's house, where Lina was already waiting for him. After he had changed out of his tails and the coast was clear, Manzari spirited them off into the country in the freezing February night, hiding them in a tenant farmer's cottage on his estate. The tenants, as Mascagni later wrote, "made a big fire and threw together as best they could a sorry supper; more than I was cold, I was dying of hunger. There weren't any beds, and they improvised something with slabs of tufa and sacks of beans." Two days later, Manzari came to fetch them back to Cerignola. Maresca had stayed on for a day after the company had left, combing the town for Mascagni or, failing that, his valise. Finally he too had left to join his company in Sicily.

In Cerignola, Mascagni and Lina set up housekeeping with the help of a bank loan of eight hundred lire and another hundred borrowed from Cannone. It was the first moment of peace and privacy for the young couple: "On that day when we could have our own bed and our own table, and Lina and I faced one another over that first dinner prepared in the family, and eaten in our own home . . . a sense of tenderness came over us, and, looking at one another and holding hands, we couldn't imagine the slightest cloud hanging over our uncertain future."

LIFE IN CERIGNOLA

Cannone was true to his word. Once Mascagni was settled, Cannone arranged for the reopening of the municipal music school and orchestra with Mascagni as its teacher and director. Mascagni was hired in March for one year at the modest stipend of one hundred lire per month, with the understanding that he could supplement his income by giving piano lessons to young women from well-to-do families. While he had hoped to earn as much as 150 lire per month that way, no more than twenty to twenty-five families in Cerignola, however, along with a handful in the surrounding villages, owned pianos, and as Mascagni later noted, piano lessons were an uncertain source of income. "Piano lessons," he wrote, "in that part of the country, didn't last long. Young ladies ready for marriage worked at studying the piano to add to their attractions, but as soon as they were married, good-bye piano!"

For four hours each day he gave lessons and drilled his nascent orchestra in a large, bare room with rows of wooden benches that the city had set aside for him, and the rest of the time gave piano lessons, driving a horsecart to his pupils' homes. He was soon teaching forty pupils to sing and play a variety of instruments, which posed a considerable challenge for the young musician. Though he was a highly competent pianist, violinist, and double bass player, much of his time was devoted to learning the other instruments that he was expected to teach. Staying one step ahead of his young charges, he and they made steady progress. Within a year his orchestra was able to perform a variety of works in public, including a number of his own compositions.

Evenings were spent with his circle of friends, in the cafés along the Corso Vittorio Emanuele, or in the "club" with the town's aristocracy. He never forgot, however, the musical world to the north, where new operas were being performed and discussed; a letter from Gianfranceschi describing the premiere of Verdi's *Otello* set him musing, "If I could only go to Rome, not to see the Pope, but to hear *Otello* by the Pope of all musicians. I mean Italian musicians, of course, since you know how much I esteem Wagner, as Pope of all musicians present and future." *Otello* struck him particularly strongly; after having borrowed a copy of the vocal score, he wrote his friend, "I've found in *Otello* some things so much like my *Guglielmo* that it frightens me . . . Believe me, my friend, there are things exactly alike!"

At the end of May Lina gave birth to their first son, whom they named Domenico after Mascagni's father, and who was known as Mimi. With his birth Mascagni moved his family to a small house on Via Assunta, which has since been renamed Via Mascagni. Life in Cerignola was not exciting, prompting Mascagni to write Gianfranceschi, "One doesn't live here, one vegetates," but it was full. He found unexpected joy with the woman who was his wife in all but name, and with his infant son, writing Gianfranceschi in July that "I had never expected to love [Lina] as much as I do now, as our affection for our child has brought us so much closer."

In August, though, he was summoned back from Caserta, where he had gone to purchase musical instruments, with the news that Lina was suffering from typhus. Her illness dragged on through September; once she had begun to recover, little Mimi was ill. All month he declined, and on October 2, the baby died in his father's arms. That fall Mascagni composed a Requiem Mass, his first extended work since putting his opera aside a year earlier.

Early in February 1888, after returning from a trip to Naples to see Puccini, who had come south for a performance of *Le Villi* at the San Carlo Theater, Mascagni began work on a second mass, the *Messa di Gloria*, which he completed by the end of March and performed with his students on April 22. The performance prompted a prophetic article by the writer Michele Siniscalchi in the Lucera periodical *Avanguardia*:

> *Mascagni is a true artist and composer, and not a vulgar one, to whom a brilliant future may well be destined. . . . One must right away call the orchestra, made up in large part of youths, a miracle; to become an orchestra after only a few months of school, to sound the way they sounded, to perform such delicate music, so full of difficulty, far exceeded the general expectation.*

In one important respect, Siniscalchi, who was not a professional musician, was wrong. The work is anything but difficult; on the contrary, it reflects Mascagni's uncanny ability to achieve powerful effects with a minimum of technical difficulty. Describing it a few years later to Amintore Galli, then artistic director of the Casa Sonzogno, he noted that "it was written to be performed by an orchestra made up of kids who had only found middle C a year and a half before."

The *Messa di Gloria* is an effective work whose most outstanding feature is its unflagging melodic vein and rhythmic impetus. Mascagni has created one attractive tune after another for each of the mass's seventeen sections.

Some are particularly beautiful, including the solemn "Qui sedes" taken from his earlier *Alla gioia;* the ethereal "Agnus dei"; and the contrasting major and minor themes of the "Laudamus te." Other themes, such as the bouncy "Domine deus," with its lighthearted dotted rhythms, are steeped in the flavor of operetta.

It is clear from the music that Mascagni had already written for *Ratcliff,* and would soon write in *Cavalleria,* that he was a far more sophisticated composer than the *Messa di Gloria,* with its simple harmonies and repetitive rhythms, suggests. Its achievement, instead, is that within the constraints dictated by his performers' extremely limited capabilities, he was able to create a work that sustains the listener's interest over a span of nearly an hour. Engaging as Mascagni's mass is, however, there is little about it that would make one anticipate that its composer would write *Cavalleria rusticana* a year later.

Mascagni's contract was renewed at the beginning of 1888. Aside from the continuing strain of making ends meet on his modest salary and a handful of piano lessons, his routine had become increasingly unsatisfying. Even if he had set his dreams aside for a short while, he was unable to give them up. Years later he summed up his state of mind at the time, writing, "I wanted to get out of Cerignola. . . . I was totally aware that for my artistic aspirations . . . a little provincial spot like Cerignola was the kiss of death." Provincial life, moreover, was boring for a young man raised in the streets of a bustling city. "Going out to the countryside with my friends," he wrote, "the most interesting things to do there were to go stare at the grapevines, the sheep, and the dairy cows."

The opportunity to escape this frustrating existence finally appeared from an unexpected direction. In July 1888 the Casa Sonzogno, upstart rivals to the famous Ricordi publishing firm, announced its second competition for a one-act opera by a young Italian composer. That competition would soon change not only Mascagni's life but Italian musical history.

THE COMPOSITION OF *CAVALLERIA RUSTICANA*

Edoardo Sonzogno, grandson of the founder of the Sonzogno publishing firm, was determined to become a major figure in the Italian musical industry, competing not only with Ricordi, which owned the operas of Rossini, Bellini, Donizetti, and Verdi, but also with Italy's second firm, Lucca, which controlled many lesser Italian composers' works, as well as the Italian rights to Wagner's operas. To succeed, his only recourse was to find talented new composers under contract to neither Ricordi nor Lucca.

In 1883 he decided to hold a competition for a new one-act opera.

Although the prize of two thousand lire was divided between two insignificant operas, both of which have utterly disappeared, the competition prompted Puccini to write his first opera, *Le Villi*. It is widely held that Puccini's opera failed because the judges were unable to decipher the nearly illegible scrawl in which his manuscript was written. Perhaps for this reason, the rules of the second competition specifically provided that "the full score [must be] written legibly."

The second competition was announced in Sonzogno's periodicals *Il Secolo* and *Il Teatro Illustrato* on July 1, 1888. The competition was for "an opera in one act—in one or two scenes—on an idyllic, serious, or comic subject of the competitor's choice." The first prize money had been increased to three thousand lire, more than a year's income for a struggling musician like Mascagni, while a second prize of two thousand lire would also be awarded. A separate jury was to award a prize of one thousand lire to the best libretto. Perhaps realizing that the nine months allowed in the first competition had been too short, the deadline for the second competition was set for May 31, 1889, eleven months away.

Mascagni saw this as the great opportunity for which he had been waiting. "By Jove," he remembered telling Lina, "I won't let this chance get away." It would be difficult, however, to take advantage of the opportunity. Mascagni realized immediately that he would have to write a new work. Nothing in *Ratcliff* could be suitably carved into a one-act opera, while *Pinotta* was clearly inadequate. Once again, he would have to search for a librettist.

His first efforts were unsuccessful. Siniscalchi wrote on his behalf to the poet Rocco Pagliara, who taught at the San Pietro a Maiella Conservatory in Naples. After praising Mascagni's talent, Siniscalchi came to the point, albeit somewhat misrepresenting the circumstances: "[Mascagni] has been charged by the publisher Sonzogno to write a little opera, like an idyll, a fable, or something of the sort, and he has expressed to me a strong desire that you write his libretto. It is understood that your work would not go without recompense, when the effort succeeds." Siniscalchi did not fool Pagliara. Neither he nor Ferdinando Fontana, whom Mascagni had known in Milan, were willing to work without advance payment. While Siniscalchi continued to canvass local poets, Mascagni's thoughts turned to a childhood friend, a Livornese teacher and aspiring poet named Giovanni Targioni-Tozzetti.

Targioni, occupied with his teaching duties, was reluctant to commit himself to the project. With no alternative, and unable to sway him by mail, Mascagni searched for a way to travel to Livorno to plead with him in person to prepare a libretto for his entry. The impoverished composer had a stroke of luck. With the death of Adriano Novi-Lena, a parliamentary deputy for Livorno, voters in the by-election could buy railroad tickets at a substantial discount. Stopping on the way to see the first Italian production of *Tristan und Isolde* in Bologna, Mascagni traveled to Livorno in September, where he was able to convince Targioni to prepare a libretto for him. Back in Cerignola, Mascagni sent him a long letter laying out the terms of the competition, concluding fervently, "Now it's up to you. This contest, just possibly, could be the beginning of my good fortune. Work as fast as you can, because your verses are the only thing still holding me up. . . . I place myself completely in your hands." They still had, however, to choose a subject for the new opera.

It is unclear precisely when and by whom the decision was made to set Giovanni Verga's *Cavalleria rusticana.* Although Mascagni, who had seen Verga's play in Milan in 1884, later claimed that the idea of using *Cavalleria* came to him immediately upon first hearing of the competition, like many other of his later recollections, this is doubtful. Siniscalchi's letter to Pagliara makes clear that the subject of the opera was at that point quite open, while Mascagni's first discussions with Targioni involved a story entitled "Husband and Priest" by Nicola Misasi, from which Targioni-Tozzetti had begun to outline a scenario, under the working title of *Serafina.*

Mascagni may have suggested *Cavalleria* initially, only to be discouraged by Targioni-Tozzetti, who was at that point quite unfamiliar with the play. In any event, after seeing a Livorno production, Targioni was immediately convinced of its potential as an opera. Mascagni responded directly, writing on December 14 that he "had thought of doing *Cavalleria rusticana* back when I saw it done in Milan for the first time. . . . All that I ask is that you work quickly, because time is pressing." He had, in fact, already written the first bars of what became *Cavalleria,* having written the famous intermezzo, in a piano version all but identical to the final one, two months earlier. While it was obviously not initially intended to be part of *Cavalleria rusticana,* it is unclear whether it was written for some other operatic project or simply dashed off as a piano piece, perhaps for one of his pupils.

The first lines of the libretto arrived in Cerignola on January 4, 1889, and Mascagni set to work. By now, only five months were left. To produce the libretto in time, Targioni enlisted Guido Menasci, a young Livornese poet, as coauthor. Over the next two months Mascagni received the libretto from the authors bit by bit, some installments containing as little as a few lines on the back of a postcard.

In *Cavalleria rusticana* Mascagni and his collaborators had selected a work that was far more than simply a popular story and play, but the iconic work of the school of naturalism, or verismo, in Italian literature. Giovanni Verga, author of *Cavalleria* and perhaps the most widely known author in Italy, was himself Sicilian, born in Catania in 1840. Although as a young man he had lived in Milan and Florence, writing undistinguished sentimental fiction, in his thirties he had returned to Sicily and settled in the small town of Vizzini, where he began to write the starkly realistic stories and novels of Sicilian life that still preserve his fame.

Cavalleria rusticana began as a short story, first published in March 1880. Although it was only one of a collection of stories entitled *Vita dei campi* that appeared that fall, its fame rapidly outstripped its companions. For that reason, when Verga decided for financial reasons to embark on a career as a playwright, he chose *Cavalleria* as his first theatrical project. With the assistance of the Milanese playwright Giuseppe Giacosa, better known today as one of Puccini's librettists, Verga completed his theatrical adaptation of *Cavalleria rusticana* in October 1883. The play was first performed in Turin in January 1884, with Eleanora Duse as Santuzza and the Sicilian Flavio Andò as Turridu. It was spectacularly successful and soon became a staple of the Italian theater. Duse performed it throughout the world, while innumerable companies toured with it up and down the peninsula.

Mascagni's librettists found that Verga, in creating a tight one-act play from his story, had already done much of their work. The events of the story, which may have been based on an actual incident in Vizzini, are few and simple. Turridu Macca, a handsome but idle young man, has returned from the army to discover that his former sweetheart, Lola, has married Alfio, a carter. Eager to revenge himself on Lola, he courts Santuzza. Lola is drawn back to Turridu; they become lovers, and he abandons Santuzza. When Alfio returns to the village, Santuzza tells him about Lola and Turridu. Alfio confronts Turridu, who accepts his challenge. They walk outside the village, take out their knives, and fight. A few moments later Turridu is lying dead on the ground. In the play, although not in the original story, the fateful cry is heard, "They've killed comrade Turridu!"

The story on which the play is based is a masterpiece of compressed power and vivid description, brilliantly recreating the mental world of Verga's Sicilian villagers. Despite its dramatic quality, it was not easy to bring to the stage. It is told so much from inside its characters that it gives little sense of either time or place. The story has no landscape, while the events leading up to the final confrontation take place over a period that could be weeks, months, or years. In adapting his story, rather than trying to recreate the entire tale, Verga focused on the few hours of that final confrontation, locking the story into a specific time, Easter Sunday morning, and place, Turridu's mother's wine shop facing the church. Rather than dramatizing his story, Verga actually wrote a new play based on his story, bringing his characters together in a series of Easter morning encounters that lead up to the final confrontation, each of which enhances our understanding of the characters and their relationship to one another.

In making *Cavalleria* into a play, Verga came up with a brilliant stroke that enables the play to transcend the status of crude melodrama. He created four omnipresent background figures—neighbors who, although having no role in the events of the play, are intimately involved as bystanders, witnesses of the drama being enacted. As a Greek chorus observing and even interrupting the dramatic events, their presence heightens the tension as the story moves to its inevitable conclusion. Their role, however, is more important than that. They are the personification of the village itself, as Vallora writes, "active witnesses, informers, primitive country Iagos." Their presence reminds one that in a Sicilian village there are no secrets, and that everything is already known, except perhaps to the doomed protagonists.

Although at least one standard reference refers to the libretto of *Cavalleria rusticana* as being "based on the short story rather than the drama of Verga," Targioni-Tozzetti and Menasci in fact took their libretto directly from Verga's play. In so doing, their most difficult problem was the background characters, who are so important to the play. It was clear that it would be little short of impossible to retain Verga's primitive Iagos in an operatic libretto. If no one but the major characters was to remain, however, *Cavalleria* would not only lose any sense of dramatic pace or balance in its headlong rush to its tragic end but also lose the sense of the omnipresence of the community, so fundamental a part of its reality.

The librettists' solution was to create a chorus of villagers, appearing in a series of set numbers framing the confrontations and encounters between the protagonists. While formally these numbers are the most conventional element in the libretto, including a traditional *coro d'introduzione*, they allowed the librettists to capture much of the same sense of an omnipresent community behind the drama, attributable both to the manner in which the choral numbers are interwoven with the events of the opera, and to the sheer mass of choral writing, particularly in the first half of the opera. Few operas devote so much time to choral music as *Cavalleria* and so little to the protagonists themselves.

The addition of five choral numbers was the only structural change the librettists made, retaining all of the confrontations and encounters precisely in the sequence in which they appear in the play. The weight of many encounters, however, was changed substantially. Targioni and Menasci reduce an extended scene between Lola and Turridu in the play nearly to the vanishing point, while Turridu's farewell to his mother, which Verga treats briefly and dispassionately, becomes far more important in the libretto. While both cover much the same ground, in what is, after all, an intrinsically sentimental moment, Verga maintains his distance, treating the scene as flatly as the material will allow. Targioni and Menasci, however, rather than resist the sentimental appeal inherent in the material, embrace it, magnifying it with Turridu's pathetic cry—echoing the last word's of Verdi's Otello—"Un bacio, un altro bacio."

It was inevitable that two proper young men from Livorno would soften Verga's material to some extent. The greatest softening, though, had already taken place by Verga's own hand, when he converted his story to a play meant to be a commercial venture, moving the knife fight offstage and deleting any reference to the unsporting manner of Alfio's victory. Many of the characters, particularly Santuzza, became far more sympathetic in the play than they had been in the story. The play, even more than the story, is written in conventional standard Italian.

What is notable is how much of Verga's essence the librettists retained. Turridu's farewell to his mother is the exception rather than the rule. Recognizing the different time dimension in which the sung, in comparison to the spoken, word operates, the librettists devoted much of their efforts to conveying the essence of each scene in fewer words. Santuzza's "Voi lo sapete," in particular, is a marvel of compression, in which the librettists tell the entire story of Turridu, Santuzza, and Lola in only sixty-three words. If anything, the language of the libretto is more straightforward, because more succinct. If it is occasionally unclear, that is more often a function of the nearly telegraphic character of some of the dialogue than of excessively literary tendencies. It is, however, far more pedestrian than Verga's language, with none of the imagery that adds such a distinctive quality to Verga's play. In the final analysis, however, all Menasci and Targioni-Tozzetti wanted to do was provide the words that Mascagni could set to music. For that purpose, their libretto is an effective and well-crafted effort.

Mascagni worked steadily on *Cavalleria* during the early months of 1889. By the middle of January he had completed the opening chorus and Alfio's entrance. He had no money of his own to rent a piano, but his aunt Maria in San Miniato came to his rescue, sending him a money order for 150 lire. An upright piano was laboriously transported by horsecart from Bari and delivered on February 11. On February 15 he wrote his aunt a letter full of enthusiasm: "A few lines, with a heart full of jubilation. I have the piano! . . . You can imagine how much I've yearned for one, and how happy and content I am. . . . Now I can work at my own pace; I feel truly reborn." Soon he was spending up to eighteen hours a day composing.

February 1889 was particularly momentous. On the fourth Lina gave birth to a second boy, who was also named Domenico after his grandfather. The day before, the municipal registrar had arrived at the Mascagni home and, in the presence of a few close friends of the couple, married Pietro Mascagni and Argenide Marcellina Carbognani, two years after they had arrived in Cerignola. Four days later, the couple was married again in the Cerignola cathedral by Father Antonio Caradonna. The church ceremony was a private one, attended only by the two obligatory witnesses. Pietro and Lina were already widely believed to be husband and wife, particularly by the parents of his piano students, who would have been outraged had they known an unmarried man was teaching their daughters. The wedding, if it ever became known, would have come to many of their acquaintances as quite a surprise.

Lina Mascagni remains an obscure figure; Iovino describes her as "a reserved figure, but at the same time strong-willed and possessive [; she] lived her entire life in the composer's shadow, ready, if need be, to fight on his behalf with fire and energy." Deeply superstitious and intensely jealous, she was changed little by the sudden fame and fortune that came into her life little more than a year after their marriage. As their sophisticated daughter, Emy, wrote many years later, "She remained the same frugal, domestic, woman . . . [who] went on washing her Piero's socks and handkerchiefs with her own hands, brushed his suits, and shined his shoes."

Not beautiful, perhaps, but with strong, almost chiseled features, Lina followed her husband's business affairs closely, dashing off strong, even vituperative letters to impresarios and publishers whom she believed to be cheating her Piero. Despite its unpromising beginnings and its later deterioration, their relationship was for many years a close, even passionate one; a year later, in Rome presenting *Cavalleria* to the competition jury, Mascagni could take time to write her, "I am madly in love with you and would give anything to have you here in my arms."

After the wedding, Mascagni returned to *Cavalleria*. By mid-March he had the entire libretto and wrote a long letter to his librettists raising a number of questions and suggesting numerous modifications to the text. While many of the changes were minor, other aspects of the libretto went through substantial transformations before achieving final form. The ending of the opera posed difficult problems. The librettists' first version followed Alfio's challenge with an extended concertato for Alfio, Turridu, Lola, and chorus, followed by these instructions: "Turridu and Alfio rush out. Lola remains still singing on the fatal outcome of the rustic duel. Santuzza reenters, running, and cries desperately, 'Torello is dead! Torello is dead!' The chorus falls on their knees, invoking the pity and forgiveness of God, as the curtain falls." The librettists had changed Nunzia to Lucia, presumably for greater euphony, and had at first changed Turridu to Torello, the standard Italian equivalent of the Sicilian name.

At Mascagni's request, the concertato was eliminated and replaced with Turridu's short appeal to Alfio, followed by his farewell to his mother. The end itself was still unsettled. Targioni-Tozzetti and Menasci had come up with a new version, in which the choral finale was changed to have the chorus singing after the curtain had come down. It clearly troubled the composer, who raised his concerns tactfully in a letter of March 18, suggesting the final resolution of the problem:

> *Wth your final chorus with the curtain down you have made the most intimate chords of my imagination vibrate, but at the same time you have raised a doubt in my mind: how will the jury react to something so original? So, I have decided to write two finales: one with the chorus, as you've written, the other as in Verga's original, thus: have the outcry "Torello is dead" heard twice, and after a general scream, bring the curtain down slowly.*

Later in the letter he adds, "If you are willing, couldn't he be called Turridu instead of Torello?" The librettists changed his name back to Turridu.

Mascagni subsequently returned to Verga's actual wording, "Hanno ammazzatto compare Turridu," or "They've killed comrade Turridu." He was still unsure how best to set those words. In the version of the finale submitted to the competition, the fateful words are sung rather than spoken, first by a solo voice, then by members of the women's chorus, with the notation *gridando* (shouting) written alongside. Mascagni was already looking for an equivalent to the spoken voice at this crucial point, but was not quite ready to abandon song altogether.

Perhaps the most unusual feature of the opera was not prepared by the librettists, but added by Mascagni himself—the Siciliana Turridu sings behind the curtain during the prelude, serenading Lola the night before the fateful Easter Sunday. The Siciliana is a powerful coup de théâtre. It is also the only moment in the opera at which one actually hears Sicilian dialect. It is, in fact, the composer's adaptation of a dialect poem written, or perhaps collected, by one of his Cerignola friends. Although Mascagni was convinced of its merits, he remained to the end unsure of its reception, and submitted instead a score that began with the orchestral introduction to the opening chorus. He did not unveil the "real" prelude to the jury in Rome until the following February, after he had already been chosen as a finalist in the competition.

By mid-March less than two months were left for actual composition. By the rules of the competition, a fair copy of the full orchestral score, a piano-vocal score, and a separate clean copy of the libretto had to be in the jury's hands by the end of May. Reluctantly, Mascagni abandoned plans for a second trip to Livorno to review the final version of the libretto with his librettists and continued writing frantically. By mid-May, roughly four months after he had started work, *Cavalleria rusticana* was completed.

One of the most popular anecdotes from this rags-to-riches period in Mascagni's life is the story of how the opera actually reached the competition. The following version belongs to Alfredo Jeri, a Mascagni biographer from the 1930s:

> *Now his doubts came. Oh, the jury could not possibly take a work like this seriously. Didn't he have anything better? He was thinking that he should rather send the fourth (or perhaps the third) act of* Ratcliff, *reworked into one act. He was thinking other things . . . but Lina had her vigilant eye on him. . . . She watched quietly, watched and planned. . . . One of her husband's friends (on an evening when it was raining cats and dogs) kindly accompanied her as she sent off the package with* Cavalleria *in it by registered mail. It was the very last moment.*

Pompei, Mascagni's first extended biographer, further embroiders this story, offering a vivid description of Lina rushing off with the package under her arm into the downpour, forgetting her umbrella, and being rescued by a friend. Even the relatively careful Iovino includes this story in his 1987 biography.

While the image of Lina rushing into the rain as the composer sits at home sinking into a creative postpartum depression is exciting melodrama, it is completely untrue. Indeed, in a letter to his librettists written the day after sending off the work, Mascagni provided a detailed description of his frenetic but hardly melodramatic dispatching of the opera to Milan. After a final week of sixteen- to eighteen-hour days, all the scores were completed. He prepared the fair copy of the libretto at the bindery, his dog Titania by his side, as the two scores were covered and bound. Rather than depressed, he was elated, writing to his friends in great good humor that "everything seemed rosy to me, even the binder's wife who was actually prune-colored; everything seemed happy, even the face of the poor devil cursing all the saints while binding my two sorry books." At six in the evening on May 27, the parcel, weighing 2.8 kilos (6.2 pounds), was on its way to Milan.

Mascagni's wait was far more desperate than it would have been a year earlier. Although his contract had been renewed at the end of 1888, economic conditions in the area had steadily deteriorated during the year. Inadequate rainfall, a poor harvest, and finally an outbreak of phylloxera in the Apulian vineyards, all added to Italy's disastrous "tariff war" with France, sent the local economy reeling. In August Mascagni wrote Targioni:

> I've lost all my private lessons, except for the mayor's daughter, and I will also lose the municipal contract . . . because a municipality that lays off the midwife and closes the middle school to save money cannot possibly spend money on a music master. . . . As a result, I [have] the prospect of finding myself tomorrow out in the street.

In 1889 enemies of the mayor, Mascagni's friend Cannone, started a weekly newspaper, Il Risveglio (The Awakening), devoted largely to polemics against his administration. Mascagni, as an outsider—not even a southerner, let alone a native of Cerignola—and a municipal employee, became a particular target of their venom. Throughout 1889 he was attacked for his personal as well as his professional shortcomings: the food he stole from starving people's mouths to feed his dog, Titania, the extravagance of his having ordered a basket of strawberries from Foggia for Lina, even the incompetence of his orchestra and the ugliness of the music he wrote for his students. That fall he wrote Puccini, "Find me a few lessons to give in Milan, find me a place in the Dal Verme orchestra, anything, so I can get myself out of here."

Meanwhile, the wait dragged on. Although the competition's sponsors had planned to select and perform the three operas in late fall and award the grand prize no later than December, the large number of entries made that impossible. Late in July, the jury announced that the selection of finalists from among the seventy-three entries would not take place until the end of December. For the composer, in increasingly desperate straits, this news, as he wrote his librettists, came "like a thunderclap in a clear sky."

His wait turned out to be even longer. It was not until February 20 that the finalists were selected. The next day, after nine months of anxiety and privation, Mascagni received a telegram summoning him to Rome to present his opera to the jury on February 25, four days later. After "being abandoned for five years," as he wrote Targioni and Menasci, "reading the telegram, I cried like a baby."

February 1890 marks the end of Mascagni's wanderings and the start of his climb to fame and fortune. While the full measure of his triumph would not be apparent until after Cavalleria rusticana's first performance in May, the summons to Rome represented the first recognition for the young composer since his adolescent days in Livorno, eight years before. Even in his wildest fantasies, however, Mascagni could not have anticipated the magnitude of the triumph that would unfold over the next few months.

4. *The Triumph of* Cavalleria rusticana *and the Reinvention of Italian Opera*

On Sunday, February 23, 1890, once again borrowing money from the obliging Cannone, Mascagni left Cerignola for Rome to present *Cavalleria rusticana*
to a jury whose quality reflected Sonzogno's commitment to a credible competition. Its members were Amintore Galli, professor at the Milan Conservatory and music editor of Sonzogno's newspaper *Il Secolo*; Giovanni Sgambati,
professor at the Santa Cecilia Conservatory and a prominent instrumental
composer; Filippo Marchetti, composer of the popular opera *Ruy Blas* and music tutor to Italy's Queen Margherita; Pietro Platania, director of the Naples
Conservatory; and Francesco D'Arcais, marchese of Valverde, a composer and
music critic for the Roman newspaper *L'Opinione*. All five men were established
professional musicians at the height of their reputations, only Galli having
a connection to the publisher. They were unlikely to be susceptible to the
pressures that would be brought to bear on them by the competitors, their
relatives, and their friends in high places.

On Wednesday morning Mascagni left his lodgings at the modest Albergo del Sole and presented himself to the jury at the Santa Cecilia Conservatory. After an awkward moment, Marchetti introduced himself, followed
by the others. One juror pointed to the roll of music paper that Mascagni had
tucked under his arm:

"What've you got there, under your arm?"

"It's the prelude for my opera."

"Eh? You didn't send it in?"

"Well, I sent in a sort of prelude, but this is the real one."

"How come?"

"Because I was afraid. Since it has a song sung by the tenor, in Sicilian dialect, behind the curtain, I figured you would find it too risky, and it would hurt my chances, so I didn't send it."

"And then why did you bring it now?

"If the gentlemen of the jury would care to hear it . . . you don't have to, that's understood."

"Well, let's hear it."

Mascagni was invited to sit down at the piano and perform his opera, starting with his new prelude. Unlike some contestants, he lacked the means to hire singers and instrumentalists to present his work to the jury. As he went through the opera, however, wrestling with the parts, Marchetti walked over to the piano. Leaning over Mascagni's shoulder, he took the principal vocal line in the ensembles and choruses, while the composer played the piano and filled in the secondary voices.

The performance was followed by an animated discussion; as he wrote Lina, "I received the most moving praises. . . . Sgambati [said] that he found my work *worthy of a superior mind* (his words). Marchetti stood alongside me and kept saying 'bravo, bravo, maestro,' pointing to the places he liked most." Mascagni left the jury room full of excitement. Although his competitors, congregating in the lobby downstairs, derided him for his enthusiasm, he was consoled by Galli, who sought him out and made him promise not to leave Rome before they had spoken further.

Each day, the jury heard two operas presented by their composers. On March 4 they sang and played through the four operas whose composers had been unable to come to Rome, voting the next day to select three candidates for the first prize. Their charge was not to award the prizes but to select the three best operas for public performance. After hearing the operas in the theater and observing the reactions of the audience, they would reconvene and select the first and second prize winners from among the three performed.

On March 3, planning to leave Rome that evening, Mascagni met Platania and Galli, who pressed him to wait for the jury's decision on March 5. As Mascagni had reason to hope, his opera was one of the three chosen for performance at the Teatro Costanzi. The others were *Labilia* by Nicola Spinelli and *Rudello* by Vincenzo Ferroni. Spinelli was another struggling musician, a year younger than Mascagni, while Ferroni was in his thirties. Ferroni's entry was the least successful of the three, and in later life he was more an educator than a composer, serving for many years as professor of composition at the Milan Conservatory.

On the morning of the sixth, embarrassed by his threadbare clothes, Mascagni presented himself to Sonzogno at the Hotel Quirinale. After congratulating him, the publisher commented "You live in some provincial town . . . Cerignola, eh? I must admit I've never heard of it. It's in Puglia, no?" After the hesitant Mascagni assured the publisher that his opera could be staged almost without expense, Sonzogno responded, "My dear Mascagni, I'm pleased, because I don't expect much of this opera . . . You're a fine composer, but your opera is just not theatrical." After adding, "But let the public judge for themselves," Sonzogno ushered Mascagni out.

After a few days back in Cerignola, Mascagni left for Milan to revise *Cavalleria* for performance and to supervise the copying of the parts. The musical community of Italy's cultural capital turned out to honor the return of the young man who had slipped furtively out of town five years before. At the Caffè Biffi and in the Galleria, he was the center of attention. He and Puccini spent long hours together, sharing their dreams and listening to one another's music. He paid a call on his teachers at the conservatory and played his opera for his old professor Saladino. Although enthusiastic about the work's prospects, the contrapuntist was unhappy with Alfio's aria, "Il cavallo scalpita," which he found "barbarous and strange."

The Sonzogno competition was a major event in Italy's musical world. The magnitude of the prizes and the distinction of the jury ensured respect, while Sonzogno's efforts guaranteed publicity. Moreover, the unexpected choice of Mascagni added a piquant note to the proceedings; as he wrote, "They told me in Milan that no one had thought about my winning the contest, even in error." For Milan's musicians, Mascagni was a faint memory from the past. Although he had once been part of their world, he had vanished into Italy's mysterious deep south. He had returned with an opera; not a predictable opera written by Pezzi or Bossi, on whom the Milanese had put their money, but something rumored to be new and different, something that might turn out to be far more than another well-crafted but ephemeral work.

Mascagni left Milan after a week, arriving in Livorno on the nineteenth, meeting Targioni's collaborator, Guido Menasci, for the first time. After visiting his father and his brothers and making a short trip to San Miniato to see his aunt Maria, he returned to Cerignola late in March. The next month, which he spent quietly with his wife and son Mimi, now one year old, was the last moment of anonymity he would experience before the sudden celebrity that was about to engulf him.

Mascagni had one more pressing issue to address before the opera could be performed. He had never formally obtained Giovanni Verga's permission to set *Cavalleria rusticana*. Spurred by a combination of ignorance and naïve faith in others, Mascagni had gone forward without direct contact with Verga, confident that his permission would be forthcoming, casually but inaccurately writing "with Verga's consent" on the cover of the libretto submitted to the competition.

He was not unaware that permission was needed. As early as January 1889, after receiving the first installments of the libretto from Targioni-Tozzetti, he wrote back: "You've certainly put a flea in my ear about this literary property business. I didn't think it very important; but I'd like to know, soon, what I must do. If you could write to Giannino Salvestri? I think he's a good friend of Verga's." Salvestri was a Milanese journalist, originally from Livorno, whom Mascagni had known during his Milan days and who was indeed close to Verga. Mascagni counted on Salvestri to obtain the permission he needed. Salvestri did speak to Verga, but what had materialized was a postcard from Salvestri to Mascagni, in which he wrote that "[Verga] insists that his play is not suitable for the operatic stage. A well-known poet turned it into a libretto for a first-rate musician, and their *Mala Pasqua* flopped! But if Mascagni wants to try, he can go ahead at his own risk."

Finally, on March 9, before leaving Cerignola for Milan, he took matters in hand and wrote Verga a carefully drafted letter, diffidently writing, "I await your consent; and I am certain that you would not want to interrupt the golden dream of one who sees in this the beginning of a career." After reminding the author that he "has the right to impose whatever terms he believes desirable or necessary," he closed by urging "the speediest possible comforting word."

The comforting word from Verga was waiting for him on his return to Cerignola. Verga, whose letter has not survived, apparently suggested that he would have preferred that Mascagni set his play directly, rather than have it turned into a libretto by others. In his response, Mascagni assured the author that "the libretto has reproduced almost to the letter your *Cavalleria*, preserving in every way that coloration and atmosphere that have made your work immortal." Verga responded, offering to have a contract drawn, adding, "I want nothing from the Sonzogno competition. But for later performances, since my work is worth something to you, it seems fair to me and I understand that I will be guaranteed whatever I am entitled to by law." Mascagni wrote back immediately, agreeing to Verga's terms. A contract was drawn up by Verga, who signed it on April 7, and sent to Cerignola, where Mascagni signed it two days later.

The contract between Mascagni and Verga, however each may have construed it, lacked clear financial provisions. After *Cavalleria* had triumphed beyond the dreams of either Verga or Mascagni, and Sonzogno had purchased the opera from Mascagni, the publisher made Verga an offer of 1,000 lire, which the author not unreasonably rejected. Verga brought suit against both Mascagni, with whom he had signed the contract, and Sonzogno. Bitterly contested and appealed up to Italy's highest court, the case was resolved in 1893 when Sonzogno agreed to pay Verga the substantial sum of 143,000 lire in settlement of all claims.

Mascagni arrived in Rome on the afternoon of May 2 and, after checking in at his hotel, rushed to the theater. He was now staying at the more respectable Albergo Novara, near the railway station and the Costanzi Theater. When he entered the hall, a rehearsal was under way: "As soon as [conductor Leopoldo] Mugnone had been advised of my presence, he put down his baton and ran from the stage to embrace me. The entire orchestra, on their feet, gave me a great reception. I don't know how to tell you, my dear Lina, the emotion I felt. Everybody made so much of me. It was wild."

Cavalleria was looking more and more like the only one of the three operas with much potential for popular success. *Rudello* had had to be postponed because of production difficulties, and it was rumored that Ferroni had been asked to withdraw the opera but had refused. After visiting Spinelli, Mascagni wrote Lina "He told me he'd heard *Cavalleria* in rehearsal, and it made a great impression on him. He added that his opera was much thinner than mine, and that he thanked God that it was being put on first." Sonzogno even offered to advance him as much of the the first prize award as he might need in the meantime and arranged for him to move out of the modest Novara and into the grander Hotel Massimo D'Azeglio next door. Sonzogno also suggested that he rewrite *Cavalleria* "to add some dances and divide the opera into two acts," a suggestion quickly forgotten after the first performance.

Sonzogno had engaged the husband-and-wife team of Roberto Stagno and Gemma Bellincioni to sing Turridu and Santuzza. Although neither was perhaps a great voice, both were among the more compelling operatic actors of the time. Stagno was now fifty-four and somewhat past his prime; as one writer noted, "He belonged, notoriously, to that category of singer associated with the school of . . . ardent temperament, rather than having the pure resources of a truly privileged voice." Bellincioni, only twenty-six, was just beginning her career; her fame, which would come through her success in verismo roles such as Santuzza and Giordano's Fedora, as well as Strauss's Salome, was ahead of her. Although her voice was on the thin side, with a vibrato some found excessive, she was a powerful singing actress with a winning stage presence.

Mascagni was delighted with both, particularly Stagno, writing, "One word is enough: he is sublime." Things did not always go smoothly between Stagno and Mascagni; at one point, when the composer criticized his rendition of a particular phrase, Stagno looked him in the eye and replied, "Dear maestro, you are the composer, and that is well and good, but I am Roberto Stagno, and as far as the interpretation is concerned, I will deal with it!" He continued to perform the disputed passage his way.

Mascagni's days in Rome passed quickly. With Mugnone's help, extensive modifications were made to the score of *Cavalleria*. More than two hundred bars were cut from the original, including sixty bars of choral counterpoint from "Il cavallo scalpita" and ninety-three bars from the choral parts of Turridu's drinking song. It was also most probably at this time that the crucial decision was made to remove the last vestiges of musical notation from the final cry of "Hanno ammazzato compare Turridu," allowing it to become the desperate scream that has since transfixed generations of operagoers.

Shortly after arriving in Rome, he wrote Lina, "I truly don't know whether what I am involved in—and of which I am the principal object— is real. I ask myself whether it is a dream of my imagination. My earlier successes vanish compared to what is happening to me now." The attention he was receiving might have been overwhelming for a young man fresh from the provinces, accustomed to the routine of a small-town music teacher, still wearing what the sophisticated Bellincioni called his "criminally provincial clothes." Despite sudden flashes of panic, his diffident manner, and his threadbare wardrobe, however, his confidence in the worth of his music and his mission as a composer was unshakeable.

In March, months before the first performance of *Cavalleria*, he had written his librettists, "I must work seriously: the outcome of the competition places obligations on me." To Mascagni, carrying Italian opera forward as a living art was not a business but a sacred duty. At twenty-six, he was the same man who would write in 1940, on the eve of the fiftieth anniversary of the first performance of *Cavalleria rusticana*, albeit with a rhetoric associated with that celebratory occasion, "Whether *Cavalleria* has served to keep alive and defend the tradition of our music is something that must be left to history to say: I created it with that intent, for that ideal." Although Mascagni would not have put it quite the same way in 1890, his beliefs were the same. His self-confidence as he waited for his opera's first performance stemmed not only from a simple belief that he had written a good opera, but also from a fundamental conviction that the success of his opera was part of some larger purpose, which it would be the object of his life to achieve.

Meanwhile, musical circles were coming to believe that an event of rare importance was approaching. The day of the first performance, a prophetic

article appeared, written by the Roman journalist and critic Eugenio Checchi, who wrote under the pen name of "Tom": "If I had a prophet's mantle, I
would say this: the name of Pietro Mascagni, as unknown until this morning as Carneade to Don Abbondio, will be saluted this evening by a joyous public and will obtain perhaps the most sought-after baptism of them all:
that of lasting fame." Checchi was indeed wearing his mantle when he wrote
those lines.

MASCAGNI'S TRIUMPH: THE FIRST PERFORMANCE
OF *CAVALLERIA RUSTICANA*

The first performance of *Cavalleria rusticana*, on Saturday evening, May 17,
1890, was the climax of the most remarkable success story in opera. Overnight, Pietro Mascagni was transformed from an unknown provincial musician to a celebrity whose fame quickly traveled across the world; more than a
celebrity, he became the composer on whom the Italian musical world rested
its hopes for the future of opera. The description of the performance from
one popular opera book is, for once, not even slightly overstated: "Before the
representation had progressed very far, the half-filled house was in a state of
excitement and enthusiasm bordering on hysteria. The production of *Cavalleria Rusticana* remains one of the sensational nights in the history of opera.
It made Mascagni famous in a night." The house was, at most, half full. Despite Queen Margherita's presence and the curiosity of Mascagni's fellow
musicians, few Romans wanted to spend a beautiful May evening in a stuffy
theater watching a one-act opera by an unknown composer. Those who
did were won over within moments, however, as Gemma Bellincioni wrote
afterward:

> *You cannot even have the barest idea of what happened in the hall of the Costanzi on
> that unforgettable evening. After the Siciliana the public applauded; after the prayer,
> they cried out enthusiastically; after the duet between Santuzza and Turridu they
> exploded in delirious joy. At the end of the opera the spectators seemed literally to go
> crazy. They screamed, they waved their handkerchiefs; in the corridors strangers em-
> braced. "We have a maestro! Hurrah for the new Italian maestro!"*

At the end, the performers, along with the young composer, "white as
a sheet," were called back sixty times. The critical reaction was not so much
enthusiastic as rhapsodic, as in the next day's review in *Capitan Fracassa*: "I am
still under the profound spell of an intense spiritual delight. . . . I am still under the spell of that music full of clarity and passion, so sweetly melodic,
so elegantly elaborated; I still see the young composer appear onstage, pale,

smiling, dazed by his dream of glory coming true." Francesco D'Arcais, who had served on the Sonzogno jury and was already familiar with the opera, wrote in *L'opinione:* "Of its type, in its proportions *Cavalleria* is a masterpiece. The traces of inexperience are few and easily corrected; it has the security of a proven master. Mascagni has a wonderfully abundant melodic vein: everything is spontaneous. . . . Nothing is reminiscent, it is original in character and utterly personal."

By noon the next day no tickets were left for the second performance. The Costanzi, extending its season well beyond its usual closing date, scheduled altogether fourteen performances of *Cavalleria,* each of which played to a packed house.

Nearly all of the writers reviewing the first performance of *Cavalleria* were certain that they were present at something momentous. D'Arcais began his review by noting that "it has been a long time since one has attended an artistic event of such importance." One writer who sought to define the reasons for the magnitude of *Cavalleria's* success, and the importance of its arrival on the Italian operatic scene, was the critic for *Il Diritto,* writing after the second performance:

> For too long we have been condemned to anemia in opera; elegant construction, knowledgeable application of artistic resources, dramatic intelligence, elaborate orchestration, we have had all of these from Italian composers over the past twenty years — everything that one can learn from careful study. Far too little of it has been the fruit of fervent imagination, of artistic instinct, of personal emotion. Mascagni arrives on the scene bringing us his personal note, the clarity of thought, the sincerity of art. . . . It is true music, as the technicians say, made of distinctive musical ideas, shaped clearly, developed logically; not made out of textbook exercises, patched together like meaningless babble.

Checchi, posing a few weeks later the rhetorical question, "Why do all unanimously acclaim him as the legitimate successor of the few great [masters]?," replied:

> Pietro Mascagni, with *Cavalleria* rusticana, *has solved the great problem that has fruitlessly worn out the world of music for more than a quarter of a century; he has found the perfect fusion of Italian song with the modern orchestral style; he has fulfilled the great Verdi's wish to return to the past, but a return filtered through new demands, new needs, the revitalized aspirations of art.*

Or, as the prominent critic Guido Pannain wrote fifty years later:

> It was like a door that suddenly blew open onto a sealed room. A fresh, cool wind from the country blew away the faint smell of mildew that was beginning to spread

and set the old faded tapestries trembling. It was a furious exaltation of song. The
public, which was the people, heard their voice in it and were overwhelmed.

Whatever the reasons, and they were many, it was a phenomenon never before seen in Italian opera, even in the days of Verdi's greatest triumphs. Two
days later Mascagni wrote his father. He was still in a state of shock, but not
too much to forget the importance of letting his father appreciate the material dimensions of his success:

> *I still haven't gotten over the emotions and the confusion. . . . Everybody cheered; in*
> *the boxes, in the hall, everyone was on their feet, the orchestra was on its feet. All the*
> *gentlemen, even the queen, were cheering. It was a colossal success like nobody has*
> *ever seen. Sonzogno has assigned me three hundred lire a month. My position is*
> *totally changed. I'm going crazy!*

A new life had begun for Pietro Mascagni.

"ABBIAMO UN MAESTRO": *CAVALLERIA RUSTICANA* AND THE WORLD OF ITALIAN OPERA IN 1890

On May 17, 1890, the ecstatic crowd rushed into the street, shouting "Ab-
biamo un maestro! [We have a maestro!]" While any graduate of an Italian
conservatory is entitled to be called maestro as a title of respect, the crowd
had something very different in mind. To them, a maestro was a master, a
composer in the glorious tradition of Rossini, Bellini, Donizetti, and most
of all, the incomparable Giuseppe Verdi. The influential critic Primo Levi
(L'Italico), in his review of *Cavalleria*, made both the distinction and the importance of the matter clear:

> *We have . . . thanks to their studies, and the nobility of their intentions, not a few*
> *maestri. But up to now, with every new attempt public and critics alike have had to*
> *ask, doubtful and hesitant, do we have the maestro? Do we have, that is, the man*
> *destined to remain? To extend, or better, to begin anew, the tradition of our great ones,*
> *to open it to the future? to demonstrate if there will be an opera of tomorrow, and*
> *what it will be?*

By 1890 Levi's question had become a burning one to a public watching with
growing concern the decline of Italian opera, in comparison with the seemingly vibrant operatic life of lands that once had sat in Italy's operatic shadow.
    Nineteenth-century Italy has been characterized as "a historic moment
of connection between opera and people, or better yet, nation." Opera was a
vital, popular art, and the people who made operas were important people,

not only to a small coterie of connoisseurs but to the greater part of the even moderately literate public. While opera was popular, it was far more than merely popular. During most of the nineteenth century it was an art form of iconic significance in Italy, a major factor fostering unity in an otherwise fractious and diverse nation. Other performing arts were largely seen as secondary, either as pleasant but trivial entertainment, as in the case of operetta, or as arcane esoterica for the few, as in the case of chamber music.

The importance of opera in Italian life was cemented by the extraordinary creative output of the first half of the nineteenth century. Between 1810 and 1860 masterwork after masterwork came from the pens of Rossini, Bellini, Donizetti, and Verdi, composers who were more nearly contemporary than is often remembered. When Verdi's first opera, *Oberto*, was first performed, Bellini had been dead only four years—at the early age of thirty-three—and Donizetti was still in his prime. Those fifty years encompassed the entire careers of Rossini, Bellini, and Donizetti, and Verdi's career through *Un Ballo in maschera*.

Italy was its own operatic universe. With few exceptions, Italian opera houses performed Italian operas. Operas from abroad waited decades for Italian performances, if performed at all. Italian operas, however, were in demand everywhere. The works of Rossini, Bellini, and their successors were immediately taken up by opera companies across Europe. Italian composers reaped the rich rewards of Vienna or Paris productions, but their music remained quintessentially Italian. It was not only Italians to whom it seemed during these years that the entire operatic world was fundamentally Italian.

By the 1860s things had changed. Of the four great men who had made Italian opera, only Verdi was still alive. Verdi, however, was more and more the squire of Sant'Agata and less and less the hardworking composer of earlier years. Although he had produced fifteen operas between 1839 and 1849, and eight between 1850 and 1859, only two Verdi operas appeared during the 1860s, both written for foreign opera houses. The 1870s brought only *Aida*, written for Egypt.

From the 1860s Italian theaters added foreign, mostly French, operas to their repertory, as Lucca and Sonzogno promoted foreign works to compensate for the shortage of viable new Italian operas and Ricordi's near-monopoly of the Italian classics. With each year the delay between a successful Paris premiere and the Italian production grew shorter. *Faust* reached Italy in 1862, three years after its premiere, while Meyerbeer's *L'Africaine* took only two years to reach Italy. Massenet's *Le Roi de Lahore* was performed in Italy in 1878, little more than a year after its Paris debut. By the 1870s Wagner had also arrived in Italy. *Lohengrin* was performed in Bologna in 1871, to be followed by *Tannhäuser* in 1872, *Rienzi* in 1874, and *Der fliegende Holländer* in 1877.

The lion's share of the repertory was still Italian; moreover, two of every three Italian works performed was by a living composer. That was the greater problem. By the 1870s it was abundantly clear that Petrella, Cagnoni, Ricci, and their like, talented men writing pleasant music, had nothing significant to add to Italian opera. Nothing in their music suggested any future directions that Italian opera might take, whether by assimilating or by rejecting the new waves of French and German music.

Three new composers attracted initial excitement in the 1870s—Antonio Carlo Gomes, Amilcare Ponchielli, and Alfredo Catalani—but none, in the end, offered useful answers. Gomes and Ponchielli, in particular, were little more than Verdian epigones, seeking new and superficially different ways of manipulating a vocabulary that by 1870 even the great Verdi had largely transcended. While the Brazilian Gomes had a clamorous success with his opera *Il Guarany* at La Scala in 1870, his brief turn in the Italian spotlight lasted barely a decade. Ponchielli, although he wrote one opera that remains in the repertory, had only a little more to offer. *La Gioconda* is a triumph of sheer craftsmanship, the work of a musician who has gained his operatic experience slowly and methodically. His technical mastery of the resources of the grand opera tradition, from the subtle motivic manipulation in the prelude to the massive ensembles in the first and third acts, is breathtaking. *La Gioconda* is more than mere craftsmanship, however, and reflects Ponchielli's not inconsiderable musical gifts. It is also given to bombast and hyperbole, prefiguring some of the excesses of the next generation of Italian composers.

Ponchielli is a more significant transitional figure between Verdi and the generation of Mascagni than is Gomes, who was thoroughly trapped in the earlier era. The beginnings of a new quality of dramatic intensity, a prominent feature in the music of the next generation, first appear in Ponchielli's music. His melodic lines, with their wide range and their haste to reach a dramatic climax—generally a vocal climax on a high note as well—strongly influenced the way in which younger composers thought of vocal melody. The impact of the famous "Suicidio" aria in the fourth act of *La Gioconda*, both in its dramatic potency and the wide-ranging freedom of its vocal line, is visible in both Puccini's and Mascagni's early works, including *Cavalleria rusticana*. In the final analysis, however, Ponchielli, for all his occasional departures, never escaped Verdi's shadow.

While Ponchielli sought to build on indigenous traditions, Catalani was the first Italian composer of note to consciously seek a synthesis between the Italian and German operatic traditions. His work reflects the Scapigliatura's vision of opera, with its exotic subject matter and assimilation of the musical vocabulary of the French and German composers into the Italian operatic language. His 1890 *Loreley* carries this to extremes. Phrases reminiscent of early Wagner abound, while long stretches could easily belong to a minor German composer such as Goetz or Reinecke.

Although the links between Catalani and the verismo composers are perhaps less visible than those linking Ponchielli to the younger generation, they are significant. Catalani broke new ground among Italian composers with respect to both harmonic and rhythmic freedom. Although there may be few direct echoes of Catalani in the music of Mascagni or Puccini, both of whom admired his music during their conservatory days, his efforts to stretch the boundaries of Italian opera contributed notably to making their music possible.

Much to the dismay of Catalani's small but fervent band of admirers, which included the young Arturo Toscanini, the Italian public never warmed to his music. Up to *La Wally*, he still seems to use a borrowed language not yet transmuted into a personal style. Although he began to overcome that difficulty in his last opera, that only threw into sharper relief his ultimate failure, which Julian Budden aptly summarizes: "Though he finally solved all the problems of scale and dramatic continuity and won through to a new freedom of expression, his own artistic personality emerges curiously pallid and insubstantial. . . . The direct echoes of Massenet, Wagner, Mendelssohn and Gounod have gone; but Catalani's own voice remains elusive and his ideas mostly unmemorable."

By then, Catalani, not yet forty and suffering from tuberculosis, could see his death approaching. Embittered by the success of composers whom he considered unworthy of his high standards, he poured out his bile in his last years in a long stream of bitter letters denouncing Puccini, Mascagni, and Leoncavallo. He died in 1893, having lived just long enough to realize that the fame he had sought all his life had passed him by and gone to others.

The 1880s offered little new hope. Giacomo Puccini, fresh out of the Milan Conservatory, attracted brief attention in 1884 with his *Le Villi*. This opera was another Nordic tale not unlike *Loreley*, although its music owed more to Massenet and Bizet than to Wagner. *Le Villi*, though, did not sustain its initial success, while his next opera, the massive *Edgar*, was an outright failure. Baron Alberto Franchetti, whose mother was a Rothschild, also attracted some attention with his 1888 opera *Asrael*, which has been dubbed "Wagner alla Meyerbeer." From the vantage point of 1890, however, neither Puccini nor Franchetti appeared likely to add anything significantly new to the Italian operatic scene.

The void was still there, threatening to turn into a chasm. By 1890 Verdi was seventy-seven years old and still the most creative figure in Italian opera.

For thirty years the Italian musical world had been listening to opera after opera, looking in vain for the new maestro, and becoming increasingly
dejected as every new aspirant to the title had been proven wanting. When
Cavalleria rusticana emerged on the scene, it was believed, at least for a while,
that the new maestro had indeed been found. The opera spoke with a new,
fresh voice, indisputably Italian, yet unlike any of its predecessors. Although
the mantle of Verdi would not rest long on Mascagni's shoulders, that does
not diminish the significance of *Cavalleria rusticana*. The Roman crowds of
1890 were correct to hail it as something fundamentally new and important.
It was the seminal work through which Italian opera recovered its voice and
emerged into what has aptly been called the Indian summer of Italian opera.

CAVALLERIA RUSTICANA

Cavalleria rusticana was fundamentally different from anything Italy had ever
heard before. Initiating what soon came to be known as verismo opera, it dis-
played a new power of dramatic compression and intensity, presented in a
fresh, eclectic language that borrowed equally from the grand opera tradition, from operetta, and from the popular music of the day.

Although *Cavalleria* is widely considered to have brought into being
a sort of school of verismo opera, the term is in many respects misleading.
Verismo, as a literary term, the rough equivalent of the French *naturalisme*, had
already been in use for many years by 1890. Applied to the works of Verga
and contemporaries such as Luigi Capuana and Grazia Deledda, verismo "was
inspired by the life of the . . . humble folk, the poor; it sought to uncover and
bring alive the social and environmental conditions of the different regions
[of Italy]." Verismo also aimed to eliminate the sentimental, subjective element from fiction and remove the writer as the middleman between character and reader; as Verga wrote, "the triumph of fiction [will be achieved] . . .
when the honesty of its reality will be so clear, and its manner and raison
d'être so necessary, that the hand of the artist will remain utterly invisible,
and the work will have taken on the character of reality."

This is not literally possible in music, where the composer's hand is always evident. The term *verismo* in music came to be applied more and more
loosely. The definition in *New Grove*—"[Verismo operas] introduc[ed] characters from the lower social strata, strong local color and situations center-
ing on the violent clash of fierce, even brutal passions, particularly hatred,
lust, betrayal and murder"—not only is worthless as a musical definition but
also, except for the emphasis on the lower strata, could equally be applied to

most nineteenth-century Italian opera, which is hard to imagine without large amounts of hatred, lust, betrayal, and murder.

The verismo epithet landed on *Cavalleria rusticana* at first for no reason other than its being based on Verga's famous story, the paradigmatic work of literary verismo. There is better reason to dub *Cavalleria* a verismo opera, however, not because of its reliance on lust, betrayal, and murder, but because of the manner in which Mascagni's music enhances the immediacy of the opera, making it feel more direct and unmediated, rather than extending or distancing its events in traditional operatic fashion. If it is possible for musical technique to fool an audience into believing that the hand of the composer is invisible, Mascagni has done so.

In *Cavalleria* the characters are less individuals than figures in a defining social landscape. They have no inner lives, nor do they call upon duty or higher morality, or even seek to justify their behavior in the manner typical of operatic heroes and heroines. Their significance lies not in their personalities but in the social roles they play. They are, above all, a part of a timeless community, and their roles are defined by rules ruthlessly enforced by that community, which surrounds them and in many respects is the true protagonist of the opera.

Mascagni brings the community alive through his use of the chorus. While his librettists have been criticized for replacing Verga's contrapuntal use of minor characters with stereotypical choral episodes, few writers have appreciated the extent to which those episodes, in the context of the story's dramatic action, achieve much the same effect in terms appropriate to a musical, rather than verbal, drama. Their power lies in their constant presence, not in any explicit message; as the late Stephen Oliver, in one of the most insightful essays written on *Cavalleria*, wrote:

> The brilliant stroke in all this is that nowhere in the opera is the community ostensibly threatening in the least. It celebrates every public act one can imagine—work, recreation, travel, worship, and drink—and in the pursuit of these we see it only innocently happy. . . . But the people we meet understand well enough the peril they face in defying their neighbors' conventions.

The idyllic sentiments expressed by the people of the community heighten the contrast between the conventional pieties of the Sicilian village and the drama of betrayal and murder inexorably taking place under their eyes.

From the moment the curtain rises onto the grim piazza of this remote village and the women drift onstage singing, "Gli aranci olezzano," until the very end, we are constantly aware of the village's presence. Once that chorus ends, there is time for only a momentary exchange between Santuzza and

Mamma Lucia before Alfio arrives and the chorus embarks on a second extended number. After an even briefer conversation between Alfio and Mamma Lucia, the chorus resumes again, as the villagers move toward the church, singing the Regina Coeli and the massive Easter Hymn. As everyone but Santuzza and Lucia enters the church, the opera is nearly half over, and yet, except for a few scraps of recitative of uncertain significance, no dramatic action has yet taken place. As a result, once Santuzza begins to explain matters in her famous "Voi lo sapete," the weight of the community's presence has been thoroughly imprinted on the listener's mind. Indeed, even during her confrontation with Turridu, the audience is constantly aware that the community is still present in the church facing the piazza, hovering over every word spoken outside.

The chorus, moreover, is essential to the construction of the intense dramatic tension that, more than any other single feature, defines *Cavalleria*. More than any other opera before it, the experience of *Cavalleria* is that of a single uninterrupted dramatic arc from beginning to end. That experience, more visceral than intellectual, was a new one for an 1890 audience, and was undoubtedly largely responsible for their passionate response to the work, described by one participant as "an almost orgiastic festival, an almost religious rite." It is not possible, of course, to construct a work of more than a few minutes as a continuous upward dramatic trajectory. It is the genius (a word not used lightly) of *Cavalleria* that by brilliantly building and then releasing tension in precisely measured quantities it creates the overwhelming effect of an inexorable and cumulative increase in dramatic intensity over the course of an hour and a quarter.

The chorus plays a pivotal role in this process, as does the orchestra. The three choral episodes, and the short recitatives between them, that precede Santuzza's narrative prepare the listener for the tragedy to come, not only by making the community omnipresent but also by slowly, imperceptibly building dramatic tension. Once Santuzza begins, the level of intensity moves sharply upward, through her confrontation with Turridu, until the dramatic climax of the first half of the opera, her desperate cry of "A te la mala Pasqua!" Her confrontation with Turridu, though, would be far less powerful without the interruption, simultaneously releasing and increasing tension, of the ineffable Lola. While the interruption appears also in Verga's play, its power is due entirely to Mascagni's music and the contrast between Lola's lighthearted *stornello* and the intensity of Santuzza and Turridu's duet.

The orchestra is almost another character in *Cavalleria*. It is the orchestra that both propels Santuzza's desperate cry and then brings the emotional climate down, setting the stage for her scene with Alfio, and again, with the famous Intermezzo, after Alfio has cried, "Vendetta avrò!" one last time and stalked offstage. The Intermezzo, along with the orchestral echo of the opening chorus that follows, deliberately reminds one of the community and its peaceful pursuits, magnifying the power of the final outcome of the drama of betrayal. The orchestra is not only important in its many large, self-contained passages; it is constantly intervening to accentuate the characters' words or, even more important, their silences. Those silences, where the orchestra speaks what the characters cannot, are among the most powerful moments in the opera.

These painful silences reflect another facet of the work. In contrast to conventional opera, it is in real time. There is not a single moment in *Cavalleria* when a character stops to sing of his or her emotions. There are no ensembles where time freezes and the characters express their separate feelings. Mascagni takes no more time with his characters than their live counterparts would have needed. When Turridu says, "Compare Alfio," and stops, and the cello goes on, the music of the cello is not a prelude, it is the sound of Turridu trying to figure out what to say to the man who is about to kill him.

If the sheer dramatic power of *Cavalleria* forms part of its special appeal, a second part comes from the novelty and freshness of its musical language. Mascagni's solution to the problem of giving immediacy to the rough, uneducated folk in his opera was a brilliant one. He adopted a language that mixed in operetta and popular song, the most commonplace music of the Italian people, music never heard before except as momentary bursts of color in the opera house. The popular sound of much of the music—from the coarse bandlike noises the orchestra makes in the opening chorus to the *stornello* Lola sings as she barges in on Santuzza and Turridu—plays an important role in making the social dimension of both setting and events real to the audience.

This is not local color. There is no local color in *Cavalleria*. Even if Mascagni, who had never been to Sicily when he wrote the work, could have introduced Sicilian color, he had no desire to do so. Indeed, it was part of his design to avoid anything that might be perceived as exotic or folkloric, that would put distance between the audience and the immediacy of the events taking place. Local color is distancing, and Mascagni does not want to distance his Sicilian peasants by making them seem exotic and strange to his audiences, but to make them even more real. Lola's *stornello* and Turridu's serenade are the two most vivid examples of popular song in the opera, but the one is Tuscan and the other, for all its Sicilian words, more or less Neapolitan. Both genres, however disdained by the cognoscenti, were not exotic, but familiar sounds of Italian everyday life.

The composer's success, however, lies not merely in his use of popular materials but in his success integrating them with the more formal operatic vocabulary of the rest of the opera. There is no incongruity, as there so often is with self-conscious folk-song quotations in opera, in these passages; they are all part of the rich texture of the piece. To make that possible, Mascagni has simplified his musical language, something that can easily be seen by comparing *Cavalleria* with the music he had already written for *Ratcliff*. Although not without their subtleties, scenes such as Santuzza's "Voi lo sapete" and her duets with Turridu and with Alfio, while far more intense in feeling than the choral episodes, are hardly more complex musically.

The music is tightly linked to the words, following the rule of one syllable, one note. Vocal ornamentation is all but nonexistent. Numbers are distinct and clearly differentiated. The melodic lines are spontaneous and vivid, and the harmonies for the most part straightforward, giving Mascagni ample room to unleash his extraordinary melodic gifts. While some of this can be characterized as a sort of "dumbing down" of his musical inclinations, it permitted Mascagni to create a language that fit his characters and that fed the overarching illusion that the composer's hand was indeed invisible. In one important respect, moreover, *Cavalleria* is not only not dumb but highly sophisticated. Mascagni had not spent time studying Wagner's scores in vain. *Cavalleria* is tightly organized, with the major dramatic episodes—beginning with the first bar of the Prelude—grounded in a network of leitmotifs and thematic connections that carry through to the final chords of the work, adding immeasurably to the sense of overall unity and cohesion felt by the listener.

Cavalleria is an extraordinary act of synthesis under pressure, driven by the intense time constraints under which Mascagni was working. Not surprisingly, the work contains numerous small borrowings, including echoes of his own earlier *Ratcliff* and his friend Puccini's *Le Villi*, along with such disparate works as Bizet's *Carmen* and Verdi's *Otello*. More significantly, with barely more than three months to compose the opera, leaving another month for orchestration and copying, his strategy of simplification largely determined the form and language of the opera. That strategy dictated that he write *Cavalleria* as a series of set pieces rather than as a modern opera with a continuous musical texture, although that choice flew in the face of his most cherished convictions about how opera should be written. He recreated variety numbers from his operetta days in Alfio's "Il cavallo scalpita" and in Turridu's drinking song. Finally, putting aside notions of the sort of opera one *should* write, he allowed his natural melodic vein, nurtured by popular music as much as by his Milan training, to flow freely. The result, half conscious and half fortuitous, was an opera that both reached back to the roots of the Italian opera tradition and was yet utterly new and different.

For all these reasons, *Cavalleria* stands alone in the composer's oeuvre. Much as he was urged in later years to compose another *Cavalleria*, he could not, any more than he could recreate the desperate conditions in Cerignola in 1889 that drove him to pin his hopes on the Sonzogno competition and the inexorable deadline that forced him to write the opera he did write rather than the opera he might have written without that pressure. Nor did he have any desire to do so. Although its composition had intensely engaged him, his deeper interests lay elsewhere. *Cavalleria* was a means to an end. As he awaited the jury's decision, Mascagni wrote Gianfrancheschi, "A victory in this contest will be the future. . . . Only then will our *Ratcliff* be able to have its triumph!" *Guglielmo Ratcliff* was the very antithesis of *Cavalleria rusticana*, a high-minded romantic opera in the grand tradition. While Mascagni wrote much beautiful music and many memorable operas, he never wrote another "verismo" opera, nor—except for the unfortunate 1895 *Silvano*, composed under pressure from Sonzogno—did he ever try.

Although Mascagni may have put *Cavalleria rusticana* behind him, the opera was nonetheless a seminal work for a generation of composers, not only in Italy but also throughout Europe. The least of this was the host of more or less literal imitations that were spawned over the coming years, including such forgettable works as *A Basso Porto* by his fellow competitor Spinelli, *Tilda* by Cilea, *Mala vita* by Giordano, and the sole survivor of the phenomenon, Leoncavallo's *Pagliacci*. These works imitated no more than the outward form of *Cavalleria*. No other composer ever came close to capturing its unique atmosphere; even *Pagliacci*, for all its merits, is musically far closer to Verdi and Ponchielli than it is to Mascagni.

More important by far was the manner in which an entire generation of composers such as Puccini, Giordano, and innumerable others from Alfred Bruneau to Leoš Janáček found creative liberation in Mascagni's work, releasing their own creative energies through its example and freeing themselves from the dead hand of the past with its conventions and shibboleths. *Cavalleria rusticana* was a manifesto that, whatever its composer's intentions, reinvigorated the European opera tradition.

5. *Fame, Fortune, and* L'Amico Fritz,

1890–1892

Ippolito Valetta described Pietro Mascagni at the time of the first performance of *Cavalleria rusticana:* "[He is] of medium height, slender without looking ascetic. . . . he has regular and delicate features, a high forehead capped by an unruly shock of hair; he keeps his face and lips completely clean shaven and, all in all, gives an impression of great sweetness and tranquillity. . . . Immediately sympathetic in his manner," Valetta added, "he is aware of his worth, having had a constantly burning, unquenchable faith that sooner or later his circumstances would change; he puts on no airs and talks with serene innocence."

He was strikingly handsome. Clean shaven in an age of beards and side whiskers, he personified vigorous youth wedded to poetic intensity. Articulate and witty, his youthful sweetness tempering a self-confidence falling just short of conceit, Mascagni charmed everyone. His appearance, his manner, and the many anecdotes in which he figured fanned what came to be known as the *fenomeno Mascagni.*

Italy needed a hero. Thirty years after the Risorgimento, Italians saw around them nothing but economic troubles, scandals, and a political world that was seen as "a gray, ignoble business of granting favors and buying sup-

port, of job-seeking and compromise." All of this contributed to the transformation of Pietro Mascagni, as one commentator wrote:

> *The physical appearance of [*Cavalleria's*] composer, his manner of moving and
> speaking, of reacting to his sudden glory, of dealing with the public and the news-
> papers, of announcing plans for the future, of self-promotion and repelling attacks,
> all seemed to have come to fill a void, making something happen for which just then
> everyone was waiting.*

He was to become the most widely known musician, and for a while perhaps
the most widely known individual from any walk of life, in Italy. His portrait
and scenes from his operas were on millions of postcards; his movements, his
plans, and his *mots* were front-page news throughout Italy. For the next fifty
years, however his critical standing might fluctuate, he would retain his hold
on the soul of the Italian people.

Lina had joined him in Rome after the first performance of *Cavalleria*.
After the last Roman performance and a short family visit to Livorno, they
returned to Cerignola, arriving on June 26 to a welcome never before seen
in the town's history. The town was decked with homemade banners, while
thousands of people had walked or ridden on horseback or in oxcarts to await
the composer at the railroad station, three miles outside town. As the train
pulled in, the cry of "Viva Mascagni" erupted from thousands of throats. Carrying Mascagni with them, the crowd marched and danced along the dusty
road into town and down the city streets to his home, while others threw
flowers and confetti from their balconies. Celebrations continued well into the
night, with the crowd shouting "Viva Mascagni" under the composer's window until the early morning hours.

The celebrations over, Mascagni was eager to begin work on a new
opera. Even before *Cavalleria's* debut, in mid-April he had written his librett-
tists, seeking a subject to follow that opera: "The genre? up to you. Any genre
is fine with me, as long as it has truth, passion, and above all drama, strong
drama." Later that month, Targioni-Tozzetti sent Mascagni a draft of the first
scenes of a libretto on the French Revolution entitled *Charlotte Corday*. Although he wrote Galli that "the subject seems to me to be really fine, strong,
true, full of passion and dramatic situations," he did not pursue it further.

After *Corday* was set aside, his librettists proposed a *Beatrice Cenci*, which
failed to interest the composer, and a treatment of *Vistilia*, a novel by Rocco
de Zerbi set in ancient Rome. Responding with alacrity to Mascagni's initially favorable reaction, they quickly prepared a complete libretto. Although
Mascagni began work on *Vistilia*, he soon left it for other projects. For the next
thirty years he would work on it briefly and set it aside time and again, writ-

ing much of the music but never bringing it to completion. Its performance was announced on more than one occasion, and a few reference works mistakenly include it in the list of his operas. Much of it ended up in Mascagni's last opera, the 1935 *Nerone.*

The idea of writing an opera based on Pietro Cossa's 1877 play about the dissolute Roman emperor also intrigued him. Nero was a delicate subject, however, since the Italian musical world had long been awaiting a *Nerone* from the distinguished composer Arrigo Boito. In 1892 a heedless off-the-cuff remark by Mascagni—"Yes, [I plan to compose] a *Nerone,* for which the honorable maestro Boito is allowing me plenty of time"—offended not only Boito but also, more seriously, the great Verdi. The chastened Mascagni abandoned the project, announcing that he would not compose a *Nerone* until after Boito had first presented his opera.

Mascagni showed no immediate interest in returning to *Guglielmo Ratcliff,* perhaps feeling that it would be a step backward when a forward step was required. He was not about to abandon it, however, and in September 1890, at the first performance of *Cavalleria rusticana* in Florence, signed a contract with Sonzogno's rival Giulio Ricordi for the publication of *Guglielmo Ratcliff.* Since Mascagni was already committed to provide Sonzogno with two more operas, it is clear that neither he nor Ricordi saw it as an immediate concern. He did eventually resume work on *Ratcliff* in 1893.

In July 1890 Mascagni and his librettists decided to set the play *I Rantzau (Les Rantzau)* by the French Alsatian writers Emile Erckmann and Charles Chatrian, known as Erckmann-Chatrian, a literary twosome wildly popular in their time. *Les Rantzau,* which first appeared in 1882, was a dramatization of their 1872 novel, *Les deux frères,* a variation on the timeless Romeo and Juliet story. Set in Alsace, as were most of their works, it ends happily, as the love of two cousins persuades their feuding parents to set aside their quarrel. The loss of Alsace after the Franco-Prussian War was never far from Erckmann-Chatrian's minds, and both *Les deux frères* and *Les Rantzau* are thinly veiled pleas for reconciliation of the feuding factions of a torn and bloodied France, still fighting over the 1870 debacle.

Mascagni had barely begun work on *I Rantzau* before he left Cerignola at the end of July to attend the first performance of *Cavalleria* outside Rome, in his home town of Livorno. By a pleasant coincidence, the Emanuel theater company was in Livorno performing *I Rantzau,* enabling Mascagni to see a performance of the play he had already begun to turn into an opera. The next day he wrote Lina, "The work pleased me immensely and has confirmed my impression. My choice is definite."

His welcome in Livorno was that of Cerignola writ large. Thousands of

Livornese were at the station to greet the composer, so that, as Pompei writes, "to save him from that demonstration of love and admiration, a battalion of soldiers and hundreds of police were needed." The trip from the station to the Via San Francesco, where Mascagni's family now lived, was a sea of flowers, waving handkerchiefs, and cries of "Viva Mascagni." The house was packed, and the square in front of the Goldoni Theater, Livorno's principal opera house, was filled every night of the six performances, which were done by a cast headed by Stagno and Bellincioni, direct from Rome, with Mugnone leading the local orchestra.

These performances were the first since the Roman premiere, as the Italian opera world was largely dormant from May through September. After Livorno, however, the pace of new productions of *Cavalleria* increased dramatically, as the opera "raced over the world like wildfire," in the words of Pitts Sanborn, who added that "the peoples of the earth were . . . suffering from 'an acute attack of Mascagnitis.'"

The next three years saw at least 185 productions of *Cavalleria* in 66 Italian cities and 62 cities outside Italy. By the end of 1893 *Cavalleria* had already been staged four times in Rome and in Milan, three in Buenos Aires, Saint Petersburg, and Oporto. In the year beginning with September 1890 alone, 41 Italian cities saw *Cavalleria*, not only all of Italy's major centers, but also dozens of smaller cities where opera was rarely heard, such as Lecce, Trani, Faenza, Chieti, and Udine.

"Mascagnitis" went beyond the opera stage, as Arturo Colautti wrote: "The explosive success onstage is reenacted on the drawing rooms . . . all the men turn into Turridu and all the women imitate Santuzza." Although *Cavalleria* is Italian to the core, its success in Germany and Austria equaled its success at home, amazing many contemporaries, as the sarcastic Collauti added:

> No, this grand inebriation . . . this international hysteria, this new religion, in short, is more than the product of publicity. The good Viennese have not read Amintore Galli's reviews, they do not subscribe to Teatro Illustrato. The Messrs. Hanslick, Speidel, Kalbeck, all the toga-clad critics, are far above suspicion. Edoardo Sonzogno, that nabob publisher . . . could not have poisoned the water of Johann Strauss's beautiful blue river.

The triumph of *Cavalleria rusticana* was complete.

FROM *I RANTZAU* TO *L'AMICO FRITZ*

After renting an apartment in Livorno for his family and attending the first performance of *Cavalleria* in Florence, Mascagni returned to Cerignola late in

September 1890. By now he had thoroughly enlarged and refurbished their home there, which he bought for seven thousand lire, and, with one child at home and a second expected, had acquired a German governess named Anna Dietze. During the fall he made little progress on *I Rantzau* and soon put it aside, partly from weariness after the intense strain of the previous months, and partly from his waning enthusiasm for the project. In its place, he occupied himself by dashing off a series of modest works, including a number of songs, among which "Allora ed ora" (Then and now) has a particularly appealing, nostalgic quality. Another work, written for the Christmas issue of *Il Secolo Illustrato*, is a charming piano piece entitled "Pifferata di Natale," an homage to the shepherds of the Abruzzi mountains, who still go to Rome at Christmastime, playing their shawms and bagpipes on street corners.

An alternative to *I Rantzau* appeared in January 1891. Mascagni's second son was born in Cerignola on the third. A few days later, Mascagni left Cerignola to join Edoardo Sonzogno at the Naples debut of *Cavalleria*, featuring a stellar cast led by Emma Calvé, who had first sung Santuzza in Florence, and the great tenor Fernando De Lucia. It was a great success, with thirty performances playing to full houses. On the twentieth, Mascagni, Sonzogno, and Nicola Daspuro, Sonzogno's Naples agent, boarded the train for Cerignola, where the publisher would act as godfather to Mascagni's newborn son, who would be named Edoardo in his honor.

Edoardo Sonzogno was a remarkable, complex person. Passionately dedicated to music and the theater, he turned to publishing after trying his hand as an author and actor, building the family firm into a music publisher second only to Ricordi. He was also founder and publisher of the daily newspaper *Il Secolo*, a vehicle for his radical republican views that for many years had the largest circulation of any Italian newspaper. A famous bon vivant, he entertained lavishly and maintained luxurious town houses in Milan and Paris. He was farsighted enough to commit a fortune to his one-act opera competitions and to organize those competitions at a level of probity remarkable in the corrupt musical world of the time, but he could also be mean-spirited and grasping, as he showed in his derisory offer of one thousand lire to Verga for the rights to *Cavalleria rusticana*, and in his later treatment of Mascagni and the other young composers in his stable.

The character of Mascagni's future relations with Sonzogno was set already at *Cavalleria*'s debut. While Giulio Ricordi had offered the young composer a contract immediately after the first performance, Sonzogno bided his time, telling Mascagni a few days later "not to worry [his] head about a contract," while, as Mascagni later described matters, "given my natural feelings of gratitude toward the publisher Sonzogno, who had sponsored the competition, [I] told [Ricordi] that I had already given *Cavalleria* to Sonzogno. It was a lie which I began to regret, because one performance after another went by, and there was no word from Sonzogno."

Finally, after two weeks, Sonzogno "presented [Mascagni] . . . a contract that, in return for the publication and performance rights to *Cavalleria* for the entire period permitted by law, offered no more than a percentage of 20 percent for ten years," substantially less than Ricordi's offer. After Mascagni had diffidently noted how much better Ricordi's offer was, "the shrewd publisher, almost apologizing, saying that this contract was clearly incorrect, and that it must have been a copyist's error, said he would arrange for a new contract to be drafted providing for 30 percent of gross rentals for twenty years." This manipulative style would be typical of Sonzogno's dealings with the composer.

In later years, after bearing the brunt of Sonzogno's personal and financial manipulations, Mascagni would become bitterly resentful toward the publisher. In 1891, however, he was utterly under the spell of the first of a long series of substitute father figures to whom he would attach himself. His letters to Sonzogno convey an almost abject deference, as he writes, "Oh, how I will bless your name, Signor Edoardo, and how much I will teach my children to be devoted and grateful to you!" A few months later, in the summer of 1891, following the execution of his contract with Sonzogno for *L'Amico Fritz*, he writes, "I have been treated by you like a son, and I swear that I will do everything to compensate for all of your goodness, with all of my affection." Not long afterward, Sonzogno would use his emotional sway over the young composer to force Mascagni to beg Giulio Ricordi to release him from the contract he had signed for *Guglielmo Ratcliff*.

On the train, Sonzogno turned the conversation to Mascagni's obligation to produce a new opera. Since Mascagni readily shared with him every detail of his personal and artistic life, Sonzogno was undoubtedly aware that the composer was having difficulty with *I Rantzau*. He came quickly to the point. Pompei, in his version of the popular story, describes the scene:

> "I believe I have a subject for you," Sonzogno replied.
>
> "Really?"
>
> "And what's better, I can show it to you." Sonzogno opened his valise and pulled out a thin volume. On the cover, in French, it read "L'Amico Fritz, comedy in three acts by Erckmann-Chatrian." Mascagni took the volume and began to read carefully, while Sonzogno and Daspuro went on idly chatting. Finished reading, Mascagni got up from his seat and . . . said:
>
> "I love it. It's just what I want. Let's not talk about it any more. I will set L'Amico Fritz."

By the end of the train ride, Daspuro had agreed to prepare a libretto from the Erckman-Chatrian play. This story, however, is in large part an entertaining fiction.

The publisher had actually first seen *L'Amico Fritz* as a vehicle for his protégé in June 1890, only a month after the premiere of *Cavalleria*, and had commissioned the elderly Angelo Zanardini, who had written libretti for Ponchielli and Catalani, to construct a libretto from the play. Mascagni liked the idea, but when the libretto was finally in his hands, perhaps on that same January train ride, his reaction was immediate: "I loved the subject, but the lines . . . My God, what stuff! Poor old Zanardini!—you bring Piave back to life—imagine, 'a re-greening of baby leaves, and a heart that throbs ardently with shame.'" It was at that point that Sonzogno proposed Daspuro, who was already working on a libretto for Umberto Giordano. Mascagni accepted the suggestion with enthusiasm.

After the baptism of little Edoardo on the twenty-first, Sonzogno and Daspuro left. Soon after his return to Naples, Daspuro began to send material to Mascagni, who wrote the first notes of *L'Amico Fritz* during the first half of February. Daspuro returned to Cerignola in April. Taking a room next door, he worked through April with the composer, writing the libretto as Mascagni wrote the music, as he vividly described some years later:

> In the morning, when I woke up, I took up pencil and paper and set to writing an aria, a scene, or a duet, still in bed. . . . Then I got up, copied over what I had written in pen, and took it all to Mascagni. He grabbed hold of my stuff, read it, and throwing on a bathrobe, ran and closed himself in the little room where there was a piano and a rough little table with the necessities for writing music. It wasn't thirty or forty minutes that—and he had me hear it—it was already beautifully done, alive, vibrant, complete.

Although Daspuro claimed that he completed the libretto in twelve days in Cerignola, only part of the music for *Fritz* was written before Mascagni broke off work in mid-May to travel to Orvieto, north of Rome, where he performed his *Messa di Gloria* on the occasion of the six hundredth anniversary of the foundation of the magnificent Orvieto cathedral. The *Mass* was the same work he had written in 1888 for his Cerignola students, with one change; "in response to the request of thousands of his admirers," the Intermezzo from *Cavalleria* was interpolated for the elevation of the host.

The Orvieto performance created a frenzy in the usually tranquil medieval city. As one reporter described the scene:

> It is impossible to describe the unusual excitement that took over this peaceful little town. . . . Every train that arrives . . . is jam-packed with travelers, getting off at the

station and coming into town on the cable car or even on foot. It was a sight to see
the roads, even the mule paths, where swarms of people [were] using every means of
transport from the time of Adam up to now . . . just to be able to arrive in time, and
to be able to have a chance to get into the Duomo!

The performance was wildly acclaimed, and at the end of the ceremony the local notables presented the composer with a diamond solitaire in a lavish gold setting.

From Orvieto, Mascagni traveled to Milan, where he continued to work on *Fritz*, writing Lina on June 2, "In the princely room that Signor Edoardo has set aside for me, I work with alacrity. I hope to finish in a few days." In reality, the opera was still far from finished, and its composer was becoming increasingly dissatisfied with Daspuro's libretto, particularly the grandiose ending he considered utterly out of proportion to the rest of the opera. Although he made some progress during the first part of June, his difficulties with the libretto, coupled with the strain of constant work and travel, sent him into one of his recurrent depressive states, rendering him unable to work or even contemplate the idea of work. Late in June, he wrote his aunt Maria, "During the past days, I've had a series of nervous crises that have really knocked me down. . . . They say that travel will help me, but I don't really believe it: I believe my condition is incurable and afflicts me constantly." He put his opera aside and left Milan. He traveled to Como to attend a performance of *Cavalleria*, to Siena, and finally to Livorno, reaching friendly surroundings by mid-July, where he resumed work, soon sending the first act of *L'Amico Fritz* off to Galli.

In Livorno, Targioni and Menasci began to revise Daspuro's effort, smoothing and shaping his awkward verse. Back in Cerignola, Mascagni completed the second act late in August. By September 7 Mascagni could write Galli, "This morning I sent you a registered package of music: at least two-thirds of the third act of *Fritz*. Believe me, I have worked miracles." The opera was not finished until late September, perilously close to the date already set for its first performance. As a face-saving compromise, the published libretto and score of *L'Amico Fritz* bear the title "lyric comedy in three acts by P. Suardon," an anagram for N. Daspuro.

The first performance of *L'Amico Fritz* took place on October 31, 1891, at the Costanzi Theater in Rome, scene of the triumphal premiere of *Cavalleria rusticana*. The high expectations of the evening were mixed with an element of trepidation, as Celletti suggests: "If on one hand a second masterpiece was expected of Mascagni, on the other its success was anxiously desired."

The opera was a great success. "The applause," wrote Biaggi in *La Na-*

zione, "was continuous, warm, enthusiastic; the composer, the singers, the conductor were called onstage innumerable times, and . . . no fewer than six pieces were repeated." Emma Calvé, in the role of Suzel, was particularly successful; De Lucia, who was apparently in poor voice that night, less so. Paul Lhérie, a tenor turned baritone, created the role of Rabbi David. Himself Jewish, as Celletti comments, "the credibility of his performance was accentuated, over and above his theatrical intelligence, by impeccably realistic makeup."

The Roman critics were enthusiastic about the new work, while tactfully acknowledging some of the work's limitations. *Fanfulla's* Checchi found it almost worthy of its predecessor:

> *What the new opera has in common with* Cavalleria rusticana *is genius: that is to say, written in a burst of inspiration, so spontaneous are its phrases, the modulations, and the orchestration. . . . As a musical work,* L'Amico Fritz *stands a degree above* Cavalleria. *The harmonies are more elegant, the voices better handled, the instrumentation more thoughtful and richer . . . but as a work of theater, [it] is a degree below* Cavalleria, *because it lacks the grand line.*

The second act came in for particular praise; De Barga in *Fieramosca* concluded that "this second act, by itself, is worth all of *Cavalleria*," while Primo Levi (L'Italico) was moved to write that "the second act would be enough to give [Mascagni] a place in the sublime ranks of creators from which he will never be removed, whatever failures may yet come." Although Levi had some reservations, he nonetheless concluded that "no public will fail to confirm the judgment that came sincerely and spontaneously yesterday from the thousands of spectators, showing both intelligence and good taste: in Pietro Mascagni we have, without a doubt, the maestro."

The critics' reaction to *Fritz* shows their relief that Mascagni was not going to be a one-opera phenomenon, and that his second opera had proven to be a worthy achievement, if perhaps less remarkable than *Cavalleria*. That relief may have contributed more than a little to the perhaps excessively favorable reception it received. *L'Amico Fritz* moved quickly from Rome to theaters throughout Europe. In December it appeared in five Italian cities including Naples, where it was performed with Stagno and Bellincioni as Fritz and Suzel. In January 1892 Gustav Mahler performed it in Hamburg; over the next few months there were productions in Prague, Vienna, Berlin, and a host of other German opera houses. During 1892 alone *Fritz* received nearly forty different productions.

After its fast start, however, *L'Amico Fritz* did not show *Cavalleria's* staying power. By the end of the 1890s, productions had begun to drop off, as

Celletti suggests: "First *Falstaff* [1893] and then *Bohème* [1896] pointed out to the public the true weak spot of *L'Amico Fritz:* with all its famous pages, it was neither quite amusing, nor quite moving, enough." The sheer beauty of the score has enabled it to retain a modest place in the Italian operatic world — not quite strong enough to enter the standard repertory, but too appealling to be ignored. During Mascagni's lifetime an operagoer was more likely to encounter it in the small theaters of provincial towns than in the major theaters of Milan or Rome. It still exists on the fringe of the repertory, with frequent revivals around the world.

L'AMICO FRITZ

Novel, play, and libretto all tell the simple tale of the wealthy rentier Fritz's transformation from contented bachelor to husband through the love of the beautiful young Suzel and the machinations of his friend and mentor, Rabbi David. The story in each version is the same, but the flavor is different. The novel, written in 1864, is set in Bavaria. Its exiguous plot is little more than a framework on which Erckmann and Chatrian spread a series of genre scenes depicting Bavarian country life and Jewish customs. Fritz himself is a restless creature, despite his paeans to the bachelor state, and there is a biting quality about his relationship with the older Rabbi David. Suzel is a practical peasant lass who, one suspects, marries Fritz as much for his money as for his personal qualities.

Erckmann-Chatrian turned their novel into a play in 1876, six years after the loss of their beloved Alsace. The play is set in French Alsace, before the German occupation. The genre scenes are gone, and Rabbi David has become a spokesman for their new patriotic themes. The pursuit of love and marriage is a duty to the nation, and Fritz's aimless life of good fellowship is treated as a dereliction of his patriotic obligation. As the happy couple embrace at the end, Rabbi David turns to Fritz's bachelor friends, reminding them that the first duty of all Frenchmen is to produce more men to rebuild the homeland.

The libretto follows the play closely, eliminating a number of minor scenes and adding set numbers for the principals. The patriotic theme, which would have fallen with indifference on Italian ears of the 1890s, was removed by the librettists, whose Rabbi David asserts that marriage and procreation are a moral, rather than a political, duty. In the way of opera, the characters of both Fritz and Suzel have been softened, but enough of Fritz's astringency is left to make him more than a generic tenor. Both have been given set pieces, and two scenes from act 2 of the play have been cleverly worked into operatic duets, the famous Cherry Duet between Fritz and Suzel and the nearly as fine Bible Duet between Suzel and the Rabbi. Joseph the gypsy, an insignificant figure in the play, has been renamed Beppe. He has two arias, neither drawn from the play, and both all but redundant in the opera.

Two features rescue L'Amico Fritz from its lack of overt dramatic activity: Rabbi David's powerful personality, and the sensitive depiction of Fritz's shifting emotional balance as feelings of love invade his hitherto-settled mind. As a benevolent stage manager, Rabbi David nourishes the connection between Fritz and Suzel and sees it through to its successful conclusion. He is the opera's moral center. His matchmaking may be the butt of Fritz's jokes, but it has a serious purpose, reminding the audience as well as Fritz and his friends that life is more than a recreational activity.

The gradual emergence of Fritz's feelings for Suzel is the heart of the opera. While few moments in opera depict the awakening of love more beautifully than the famous Cherry Duet, as important are short, perfectly realized moments of discovery, particularly Fritz's brief exchange with Suzel in the first act, set against Beppe's violin solo:

> Fritz: (looking at Suzel) Why are you crying, why?
> Suzel: (timidly) The music moves me. . . . forgive me. . . .
> Fritz: (whispering) For what? It moves me as well.

The words are trivial, yet in the opera, preceded by the characters' long silence as they listen to the offstage violin, they are deeply moving. For the first time, Fritz has truly seen Suzel, not as an attractive part of the scenery, but as another human being.

Mascagni deploys his musical means in keeping with his gossamer subject. The orchestral sound is almost entirely limited to strings and winds, with extended solo passages for violin and oboe. Brass and percussion are used sparingly for color and for a handful of moments of special emphasis. Although all three acts have brief choral moments, the chorus never appears, only adding atmospheric touches from behind the curtain.

The special quality of L'Amico Fritz lies in its inexhaustible flow of cantabile melody. While it reflects Mascagni's interest in complex rhythms and unusual harmonic relationships, everything is subordinated to song. Far more than in Cavalleria, Fritz seems often to be spun from a single continuous melodic line, passionate and tender by turns. Never before or after were Mascagni's powers of melodic invention as fecund as in this opera. Exquisite melodies follow one after the other, whether fragments that appear and disappear in the orchestra or the major numbers, from Suzel's "Son pochi fiori," which permeates the first act of the opera, to the lovely closing duet between Fritz and Suzel. Recurrent references to these and other melodies form the opera's texture, all coming together at the end. As Fritz and Suzel fall into each other's arms we hear first "Son pochi fiori" to recall the moment when their love began, then a few bars from the Bible Duet to recall David's role in bringing them together, and finally "O amore" as Fritz steps forward, to be joined by the others in a joyous paean to the power of love.

Mascagni recognized that cantabile melody, however excellent, can become monotonous over nearly two hours. He provides dramatic contrast through an occasional confrontation, such as Fritz's quarrel with the Rabbi at the end of the second act, and musical contrast with a series of delightful scherzando motives for Fritz's friends, which pop up delightfully at apposite moments throughout the opera. The opera's weakest link is Beppe the gypsy violinist, implausibly cast as a trouser role. Dramatically, Beppe exists only to provide the offstage violin music that provides the setting for Fritz's momentous discovery of Suzel. His two solos are both uninteresting genre pieces. In contrast to the other solos and ensembles, which are dextrously woven into both the musical texture and dramatic flow of the opera, they are self-conscious set pieces, pleasant enough but of little musical interest or dramatic purpose. In the end, though, this one miscalculation does little harm to an opera that is, within its narrow compass, a gem.

It is not clear what attracted Mascagni so strongly to the tenuous and sentimental *L'Amico Fritz*, so different not only from *Cavalleria* but also from the various subjects that the composer had been contemplating. Sonzogno's influence played a part, as did his own strong sentimental streak. Perhaps the only answer may be that from Mascagni's own account of his train ride with Sonzogno:

> *"But where will I find a libretto like* Cavalleria?*" I told him. "Anyway, even if I found one, it would be a bad idea. No, I want to take a different road, particularly seeing that too many newspapers, praising* Cavalleria, *attributed all its success to the libretto. Just for that reason I want a simple libretto, something almost insubstantial, so that the opera will be judged entirely on its music."*

If that was his objective, he was successful. As Tedeschi writes, "[Here] the historic contest between 'prima la parola' and 'prima la musica' resolves in favor of music."

I RANTZAU

With *L'Amico Fritz* well launched, Mascagni traveled to Livorno for its local premiere, which took place on December 26, with the composer receiving thirty-eight curtain calls. After spending the holidays with family and friends in Livorno, Mascagni left Lina and the children early in January to return to Cerignola. He was now ready to resume work on *I Rantzau*, which he had neglected for over a year.

During the 1890s Mascagni would frequently escape to Cerignola. The town's isolation freed him from the pressure of his fame; it was also a place where he could combine his taste for unpretentious socializing with intense bouts of creative activity, as he wrote Lina while working on *Rantzau:* "This Cerignola is a rich vein of inspiration for me. After dining with a bunch of friends . . . after having made quite a racket, I returned home and worked until morning. I've finished the woman's first-act aria, and started work on the finale of the same act."

He worked feverishly through mid-February. His ambitions for *I Rantzau* were becoming clearer; after finishing the Kyrie, a duel for contending vocal ensembles, he wrote that "it will be a fresh challenge to the writers of conventional operas, and a red flag waved at certain critics and certain musicians whose minds are closed to any sense of modernism." Although Mascagni, by the standards of the time, considered himself a modernist, he had never before set about to write self-consciously modern music. While both *Cavalleria* and *Fritz* contain passages that show Mascagni to be au courant with trends in modern music, both subordinate innovation to the untrammeled flow of impassioned song. *I Rantzau,* however, was to be something different. He was determined to make it a work composed, as he wrote Lina toward the end of the month, "according to the most audacious modern forms."

By the end of the month, Mascagni decided to return to Livorno. He was lonely and had gone as far as he could for the moment in wrestling with the ambitious project to which he had committed himself. Turning away from it, at least for the moment, before he left he wrote Lina, "Meanwhile . . . I have picked up *Ratcliff* again, my *Ratcliff*, my favorite *Ratcliff*. Would you believe that when I reread a few sections, they seemed to me really beautiful?"

The composition of *I Rantzau* did not come easily. It was nearly three more months before he finally sent Sonzogno the first two acts. By the end of June 1892 the entire opera was, in rough form, in Galli's hands. While Mascagni's scores were usually marvels of clarity and legibility, the manuscript was full of erasures and corrections, reflecting its composer's many revisions and second thoughts The score was such a mess that Galli then arranged for a copyist to make a clean copy, which was sent back to the composer for corrections and used as a basis for the opera's orchestral score. This procedure was never repeated. In the future, Mascagni, to whom the calligraphic quality of his manuscripts was a point of considerable pride, never sent his publishers anything but a clean, finished score, written in a clear, elegant hand. By the end of August, or at the latest the beginning of September, *I Rantzau*, Mascagni's most ambitious opera to date, was completed.

By the fall of 1892 a number of younger composers were winning attention, becoming known as the "young school" of Italian composers. In addition to Mascagni and Puccini, they now included Ruggero Leoncavallo, whose *Pagliacci* had appeared in May, Francesco Cilea, and Umberto Giordano. Although the latter two had not yet written the operas for which they would be remembered, each had attracted notice with works staged in 1892, Cilea's *Tilda* and Giordano's *Mala vita*.

In September Mascagni, Leoncavallo, Cilea, and Giordano were enlisted by Sonzogno to participate in an international musical exposition being held in Vienna. Aside from those three operas, the Vienna program included Mascagni's *Cavalleria rusticana* and *L'Amico Fritz*, as well as Leopoldo Mugnone's one-act opera *Il Biricchino*. The only composer missing was Puccini, whose operas belonged to Ricordi.

The Italian season at the exposition represented the debut of the "young school" and was warmly received by the Viennese critics and public. More than anything else, however, it became another personal triumph for Mascagni, as the excitement generated by his visit to the Austrian capital rivaled Livorno or Cerignola. On his first night in Vienna he was the subject of an impromptu demonstration at the opera house, where he had gone to hear Goldmark's *Die Königin von Saba*. The next day, when he went to visit the exposition, as he wrote Lina, "I saw little. The newspapers . . . had announced my visit, and a great mob was waiting for me at the entrance." Years later, he wrote, "I couldn't walk a step without people jumping up asking for autographs. Every day three or four hundred letters came for me at the hotel, mostly from women, everyone looking for a picture and an autograph."

The prominent Viennese critic Eduard Hanslick, who had already written extensively on both *Cavalleria* and *Fritz*, summarized Mascagni's appeal to the Viennese musical world in his autobiography: "We all shared the cult of his personality. One who did not know that modest and sensible young man, so open facing this fanatical spectacle, might well have spontaneously resented him. All the attention and the ovations were for him, as much for his personal warmth as for his artistic genius." Hanslick's encomium is a reminder that Mascagni appealed not only to the German-speaking masses but also to sophisticated musicians such as Hanslick and Mahler. Mahler admired Mascagni's music greatly and put on his operas first in Budapest, where he gave *Cavalleria* its second production outside Italy, in Hamburg, where he conducted both *L'Amico Fritz* and *I Rantzau*, and in Vienna. In January 1893

Mahler expressed his feelings about *Fritz* and about Mascagni in a letter to his sister Justi: "I consider *L'Amico Fritz* a decisive advance on *Cavalleria*, and I am fully convinced that once again those gentlemen, the orchestra conductors, have wrecked it by their conducting, for it is difficult to perform and full of great subtleties. With easily understandable sympathy for this unappreciated and abused composer, I dedicated all my energies to this work in order to impose it on that riffraff," adding, somewhat cryptically, "between Mascagni and myself, there are a lot of affinities."

Returning to Italy at the end of September, Mascagni began immediately to prepare for the first performance of *I Rantzau*, which took place at the Pergola Theater in Florence on November 10, 1892. The young lovers were sung by De Lucia and the young Hariclea Darclée, who later created the title roles in Mascagni's *Iris* and Puccini's *Tosca*. The important dark baritone role of Gianni, Luisa's father, was sung by Mattia Battistini, of whom Galli wrote, "He was great, first in his hatred, then in his love; he sang, he acted, he embodied the character of Gianni in a way one could not imagine done better."

I Rantzau was warmly received by the first-night audience, eager to applaud Mascagni's latest work. Six pieces were repeated, and Mascagni took thirty-seven curtain calls at the end of the performance. The critical reaction, however, was mixed, and many reviewers were more respectful than truly enthusiastic. The novelty of the music and its advanced vocabulary were widely noted, as the critic for *Fieramosca* somewhat ambiguously commented: "The abundance of new concepts and rhythms, the elevated quality, consistent throughout, of the musical ideas and forms, must necessarily produce a strong impression on the public." An even greater wariness could be found in the comment of the *Corriere Italiano*, which noted that "it is not possible, with respect to an impressive work such as that which maestro Mascagni has presented to the Florentine public, to pronounce a firm and reliable judgement on the basis of the fugitive impressions of one hearing." The critical confusion was summarized by the writer for the *Teatro Illustrato*, who wrote that "the learned critics have said so much, of so many diverse stripes; the opinions have been so disparate . . . that the public, knowledgeable or not . . . must not understand anything. Down into the dust, and up on the altar!"

The Roman premiere took place on November 26 with the composer on the podium, much to the displeasure of Arturo Toscanini, who had initially been engaged by the Costanzi to conduct the work. Although Mascagni had sought to conduct only the initial performances of the work, leaving the rest to Toscanini, a practice which Sachs describes as "not an uncommon tribute to composers in those days," Toscanini objected, taking the unusual step of writing an open letter to the Roman newspaper *La Tribuna* making clear that it had not been his idea to step down from the podium on this occasion. From that moment, relations between these two oversized egos froze into a mutual dislike that never thawed.

The Roman audience's reaction was enthusiastic, but once again the critical reaction was less so. During 1893 and 1894 *I Rantzau* made the rounds of the major opera houses of Italy, Germany, and Austria. Its initial success, attributable to the novelty of the work and to the fascination of the public with its composer, was not long sustained; Sonzogno wrote Menasci that "even in Berlin, where it was so well launched, the box office receipts dropped off from performance to performance, until the management withdrew it." After the Vienna performance, Hanslick wrote a thoughtful essay on the opera, concluding: "We would advise this fortunate composer, about whose future we care so much, to let his great talent rest for at least two years, and allow his talent to ripen. . . . as Goethe said: 'the personal qualities are there, and remain; on his part, he should busy himself cultivating them.'" *I Rantzau* was soon set aside, and it has since remained Mascagni's least-performed opera. Since the 1890s it has been staged only once, in a 1992 Livorno revival.

From its portentous opening bars, throughout its four acts with their preludes, intermezzi, and postludes, *I Rantzau* inhabits a far more serious world than *L'Amico Fritz*. Mascagni saw this opera not only as a leap into modernism but also as more than another love story. In its reconciliation of two brothers he saw a significant moral dimension, paralleling that found in the major works of Verdi and Wagner. The result, unfortunately, is an opera overloaded by the composer's dramatic and musical ambitions, sinking beyond serious hope of redemption.

Although the composer felt strongly about the importance of the opera's subject, that conviction alone was inadequate to unleash his deeper creative impulses. Mascagni was not, at heart, a composer whose muse responded to political and economic themes; as Bastianelli has noted, "if Mascagni can sing of . . . the hatred of carnal jealousy, he will never, because it is too complex and too foreign to his being, sing the hatred born of cupidity . . . between two brothers over money." His librettists gave him little to work with, providing neither a confrontation between the brothers nor individual scenes in which they could express their feelings. The two brothers remain ciphers, with Gianni coming alive only in the powerful second-act scene with Luisa, where the intensity of the conflict between father and daughter briefly unleashes Mascagni's creative passion. Even the final reconciliation scene, despite the composer's efforts, falls flat.

The music of the opera is an uncomfortable mixture of the adventuresome and the conventional. Abounding in harmonic and rhythmic experimentation, *I Rantzau* also offers both an old-fashioned *coro d'introduzione* and an enormous concertato finale in the first act, both throwbacks reflecting the composer's desire to make this opera self-consciously "grand." Neither these grand moments nor many of the composer's experiments fully succeed musically. Apart from the second-act scene between Gianni and Luisa, the opera comes truly to life only in the third-act choral Cicaleccio (Chattering scene), a delightful scherzo in which the composer shows off his contrapuntal skills, and in the fourth-act love duet between Giorgio and Luisa.

Mascagni, who had high hopes for the work, was deeply upset by its failure, which at least at first he saw very differently from his critics. Before the first Roman performance, he wrote Lina:

> *I have no great illusions about my opera being immediately understood. I have tried to do something new, to break away, as much as possible, from the old traditions. The scoring of Rantzau boldly challenges all the scholastic rules, and for this they have not wanted to understand me and have thrown a cross on my back. . . . The public is not ready yet for this musical modernism and does not understand well enough what I have wanted to do. But why, while everything evolves, must music remain immobile, constrained by the old rules?*

Admirable sentiments, arguably, yet strangely at odds with the reality of the opera he had written or its critical reception. Mascagni's bravado, in any event, did not last long. After retreating to Cerignola to lick his wounds, and after receiving a sharp letter from Sonzogno, he wrote the publisher in January, with a mixture of rueful humor and self-pity:

> *From the Campidoglio to the Tarpeian Rock. Luckily, I am the only one to blame for this disaster. Mea culpa, mea maxima culpa! Everything in this world comes to an end. . . . I will go back to being bandmaster in Cerignola. Brunetto is leaving at Easter, and I will replace him. . . . that's how I started, and that's how I'll end. My life was crossed by a splendid dream.*

And a few months later, with resignation, "You don't want to put on *I Rantzau?* What can I tell you? You're the boss. All I can do is bow my head." By now, however, Mascagni was already deeply involved with a new opera, or rather an old opera revisited—*Guglielmo Ratcliff.*

6. *Back to* Ratcliff,

1893—1895

Pietro Mascagni's life quickly began to reflect his sudden prosperity. In 1892 he purchased a carriage, a pair of horses, and a twenty-eight-room mansion next to the Teatro Goldoni, Livorno's principal opera house. He indulged his love of display, from the rings on his fingers to his brightly colored waist-coats, the lavish furnishings he bought for his new mansion, and his mania for collecting. As his daughter Emy described, he collected almost anything:

> *His most unusual collections were his ties and walking sticks, including Rossini's walking stick. . . . The most valuable, the collection of paintings; the most varied, the ceramics; the richest, the watches; the most interesting, the collection of musical in-struments, among which Mozart's spinet . . . stood out. He also collected out-of-use bank notes; medals; ancient scrolls; conductors' batons, including the beautiful one that Queen Victoria of England gave him.*

He loved to show off his possessions to friends and family and complained vigorously if they were moved from their proper place on his desk or bor-rowed without his knowledge.

Mascagni put on a brilliant public display, not only in his appearance, his dazzling clothes, his jewelry, and his resplendent coiffure, but even more in his verbal virtuosity, his puns, and his witticisms. The famous scientist

Guglielmo Marconi enjoyed Mascagni's company, he once said, for "the total pleasure of listening to him." His conversation often had a sharp edge,
however, as the journalist Armando Fraccaroli wrote: "At times his words are
like mosquitoes: not because they are annoying (no, no, never!) but because,
after having fluttered about with an air of innocence, they land on someone
and sting."

Although at first he delighted in the adulation of the crowds that followed him everywhere, the delight soon passed. Already in September 1892,
during his first visit to Vienna, he wrote an old friend from Cerignola: "Yes,
I know, I have immense rewards; few men have been honored as I have; here
everything is Mascagni: on cigarette papers, on hats, on ties, on tie pins,
everyone kisses me; plenty are satisfied to kiss my companions instead. . . .
I constantly think of those few who loved me back then, who would have
me in their homes before May 17, 1890." Beneath the glittering surface were
darker undercurrents, reflected in his rueful comment to De Carlo late in his
life, "The man that the world knows is not the way I really am. Everyone believes that I was made for good spirits and happiness, but it's not that way: I
am instead very much a melancholic and have always made an enormous effort not to show myself the way I really am. I think I've succeeded."

He was given to emotional extremes, as he was described in connection with one of his many lawsuits:

> *He experiences all feelings at an extreme level; average or normal feelings are al-*
> *most unknown to him. For a trifle he feels exalted, for a trifle he collapses into dejec-*
> *tion. . . . It is enough to treat him with common courtesy to become seen as a beneficent*
> *deity, protecting and illuminating his entire existence. The most trivial setback or*
> *opposition is enough to make him feel persecuted by a cruel destiny, by the hatred of*
> *all humanity.*

He would turn on close friends over trivial matters, yet would almost always
quickly restore the friendship with an apology or a thoughtful, caring gesture. He was easily moved. A dead bird, a line in a sentimental poem, or a
child's smile would bring tears to his eyes; a thoughtful gift or a parting from
a friend would make him sob openly.

Mascagni suffered all his life from a manic-depressive or bipolar condition, in which episodes of depression alternated with manic episodes, during which virtually all his creative activity took place. He would regularly
undergo bouts of depression and inactivity that lasted weeks or months, during which he would have difficulty sleeping and eating and would doubt that
he would ever write another note. Yet each depression would eventually lift,

often to be replaced by episodes of intense productive activity. He would socialize all evening, playing cards and regaling his friends with a never-ending flow of jokes and stories; then, around ten, he would sit down at the piano and work without a break until the morning, and then sleep until midafternoon.

Attacks and criticism inevitably followed Mascagni's growing fame. Claques were hired to break up the performances of his operas, including the first Milan performance of *L'Amico Fritz*. His self-confident manner, bordering on arrogance, and his heedless tendency to speak his mind, often tactlessly and thoughtlessly, brought frequent criticism upon him, filling the pages of Italy's newspapers and magazines.

The most widely read attack on Mascagni was a September 1892 article by Gabriele D'Annunzio entitled "Il Capobanda" (The bandmaster). D'Annunzio—poet, novelist, playwright, and controversialist—was already on his way to becoming Italy's most prominent literary figure, and his pronouncements were widely noted. He and Mascagni had never met, but in private he had been a bitter critic of Mascagni's music. D'Annunzio attacked Mascagni's person as much as his music, writing, "Could it be that he is a born bandmaster, the way others are born musicians, poets, painters? . . . Mr. Sonzogno has . . . found the musician he wanted. The firm will get rich off him."

D'Annunzio argued that Mascagni's music exemplified the commercial exploitation, and thus the destruction, of true art: "Why does Mr. Pietro Mascagni want us to believe that he 'is concerned with art'? Why does he dare pronounce that sacred word? [He] is concerned only with business and is incapable of being concerned with anything else." Mascagni was bitterly offended by "Il Capobanda," denouncing its author in equally personal terms. Despite their mutual vilification, the two men were ultimately to become friends for a time and collaborate on Mascagni's most ambitious opera, *Parisina*.

AN OLD OPERA AND A NEW ONE

During 1892 and 1893 the Italian operatic landscape changed decisively. Important new faces appeared, while an older figure finally and dramatically realized his earlier promise. The year 1892 witnessed the premieres of Giordano's *Mala vita* and Leoncavallo's *Pagliacci*, both of which showed the extent to which *Cavalleria rusticana* had come to mold the thinking of Mascagni's contemporaries, who sought to capitalize not only on that opera's innovations but also on its commercial success. Leoncavallo was the only one to succeed, and Mascagni resented his success, seeing in it not just calculation but also plagiarism.

Leoncavallo, Giordano, and Cilea, whose promising *Tilda* also appeared in 1892, were not perceived as serious challengers for the popular title of "Verdi's heir." Puccini was different. His *Manon Lescaut,* which appeared in February 1893, the work of a mature composer with his own rich, distinctive musical vocabulary, was an instant success, propelling Puccini from obscurity to the first rank of Italian composers. The *Gazzetta del Popolo* hailed Puccini as "one of the strongest, if not indeed the strongest, of the younger Italian opera composers," while George Bernard Shaw wrote, after the opera's London premiere, "Puccini looks to me more like the heir of Verdi than any other of his rivals." In the highly competitive world of Italian opera, a race was now on. The principal competitors were Mascagni and Puccini, assiduously promoted by their rival publishers, Sonzogno and Ricordi, with all the means at their disposal.

By 1893 Mascagni found himself juggling three different operas, to which a fourth would soon be added. While working fitfully on *Vistilia,* he had in hand a new libretto by Targioni and Menasci, entitled *Zanetto* and based on *Le Passant* by the French playwright François Coppée, a popular Sarah Bernhardt vehicle depicting a brief encounter in Renaissance Florence between a youthful minstrel and a jaded courtesan. Sonzogno hoped to see both operas emerge in the near future, writing the librettists in June 1892 that "it will not be possible to give *Vistilia* before 1894, after *Zanetto,* which will serve to keep [Mascagni] in practice." While Sonzogno may have seen the one-act *Zanetto* as a potential companion for *Cavalleria rusticana,* it did not appear until 1896, by which time that role had already been filled by *Pagliacci.*

Both *Zanetto* and *Vistilia* receded into the background as Mascagni became more and more deeply engaged in revisiting his early *Guglielmo Ratcliff.* When he returned to Cerignola in mid-March 1893 after a February tour of Germany, he plunged into *Ratcliff* immediately, writing Gianfranceschi at the end of the month that it "is going quickly: . . . I have a very good idea what parts are good and what are bad; I assure you that I will know how to hold on to the former and fix up the latter." By the end of May he had rewritten all of the third and fourth acts, as well as the introduction to the first act.

Ratcliff was put aside as Mascagni left Cerignola early in June for London to conduct his operas, including the English premiere of *I Rantzau* with Nellie Melba at Covent Garden. He was feted by both London's aristocracy and its Italian community, ending with a command performance of *Cavalleria* and the second act of *Fritz* for Queen Victoria at Windsor Castle, after which he was presented with a "splendid photograph of the queen, of massive proportions, in a silver frame, signed 'Victoria, queen and empress.'"

Mascagni remained in London far longer than he had planned. More rehearsal time was needed for *I Rantzau*, and the command performance was delayed, in order not to conflict with the scheduled wedding of Victoria's grandson, the future King George V. The extended visit began to tell on the increasingly jealous Lina, who was convinced that her husband was prolonging his stay in London to carry on an affair with Melba. After receiving a letter full of accusations, he wrote back indignantly:

> *I don't care for Melba one bit. . . . Signora Melba and I meet nowhere but on stage: singer and conductor. . . . And there's another reason that's even stronger—in choosing the singers to go to the queen at Windsor, I rejected Melba . . . and chose Calvé, for both* Cavalleria *and* Fritz. *You see, then, how much feeling Melba is likely to have for me.*

Whether or not Melba and Mascagni had had an affair in London, which is doubtful, it is clear that Lina had become deeply suspicious of her handsome and charming husband's possible extracurricular activities as he made the rounds of Europe's capitals.

By September Mascagni was in Livorno, back at work on *Ratcliff*. By the end of October he had finished the first act and begun the second, the last to be completed. A year after *I Rantzau*, he was under intense pressure from Sonzogno to bring out a new, and more successful, opera. Disappointed with *I Rantzau*'s weak showing and concerned about Mascagni's extravagant ways, he began to press the composer, writing to Menasci on October 20 that "*Cavalleria* is making less, *Fritz* doesn't make that much, and *Rantzau* makes nothing. . . . Mascagni must not have any illusions. He must cut down on his expenses and must finish *Ratcliff* as soon as possible."

Sonzogno, an astute judge of the theater despite his initial lapse with respect to *Cavalleria*, expected *Ratcliff* to be no more than a succès d'estime and commissioned Targioni-Tozzetti to fashion a new libretto to recapture the popular visceral appeal of Mascagni's first success. Targioni began to prepare *Romano*, an adaptation of "Romain d'Etretat," a grim tale set in a Norman fishing village by the French writer Alphonse Karr. After much of the libretto had been written, however, Sonzogno was unable to obtain the rights to the work from Karr's estate. To avoid litigation, Targioni stripped his libretto of any details of plot or character that might raise legal questions, renamed it *Silvano*, and relocated it to southern Italy's Adriatic coast.

The story is a simple one. Silvano, a young fisherman-turned-smuggler engaged to Matilda, has fled the police into the hills. During his absence,

Matilda has been taken over, as it were, by Silvano's rival, Renzo. After an amnesty, Silvano returns. Matilda returns to him, hiding her secret. When Silvano discovers her with Renzo, he shoots his rival and flees, leaving the miserable Matilda behind. The story bears some resemblance to *Cavalleria* and is even closer to Spinelli's *Labilia*, the runner-up in the Sonzogno competition. The libretto showed clearly, however, that Targioni's powers of creative invention, without a strong underlying text, were limited. It is little more than a sketch of an opera, rather than a fully realized work.

Mascagni finished reworking *Ratcliff* early in January 1894 and signed a new contract in May with Sonzogno for both *Ratcliff* and *Silvano*. Although he had known about *Silvano* since July 1893, when it was still called *Romano*, and had now agreed to deliver it before the end of 1894, he was in no hurry to begin work. Remaining in Livorno for the year, he traveled little and produced no new operas. Speculation about his plans abounded, but Mascagni held his peace, working intermittently and socializing with his Livorno friends, surrounded by his family and his growing accumulation of objets d'art and assorted treasures.

Mascagni wrote two of his finest songs that year. "Serenata," to a poem by Lorenzo Stecchetti, a beautiful and evocative piece, was written entirely in one afternoon. It is the most popular of his twenty-odd songs and still appears on the recital programs of Italian opera singers. Another song written that fall, a wedding present for the daughter of Mascagni's early benefactor, the Count de Larderel, which deserves to be far better known, is the exquisite "Sera d'ottobre," to a text by the famous poet Giovanni Pascoli.

Mascagni procrastinated, avoiding serious work on *Silvano* through most of 1894. While he dipped into it from time to time, by the time he left for Milan early in November to conduct *I Rantzau* at the Teatro Lirico, he had barely begun work on an opera scheduled to be performed the following March. Finally, in mid-November, he began to work seriously on *Silvano*, writing virtually the entire opera in two short, intense bursts of effort, and finishing it on New Year's Eve; he wrote Galli late in December that "*Silvano* is like Death: it is slow in coming! But finally even it has arrived."

It had not come easily. The uninspired libretto and, more important, the fact that with *Silvano* he was revisiting for commercial reasons a genre in which he had lost interest, made Mascagni thoroughly indifferent to the entire project. His attitude was reflected in an account that appeared in the *Gazzetta dei Teatri*: when "asked by [a] reporter, on the eve of the first performance, what, in his opinion, was the best moment in his new opera, Mascagni replied 'the pistol shot that ends it.'" After hearing the work, the writer for the *Gazzetta* characterized this as a "severe but fair criticism."

After sending Galli the manuscript of *Silvano*, he followed it to Milan early in January 1895 to prepare the orchestral score and to begin rehearsing the first performance of *Guglielmo Ratcliff*. Both works were to be performed at the jewel of Italy's opera houses, Milan's La Scala theater. In recent years La Scala had been Ricordi's territory and had rarely scheduled Mascagni's operas. *Cavalleria* did not reach La Scala until after it had been done in almost every other Italian operatic center, while in 1895 *L'Amico Fritz* had yet to appear there. Sonzogno had taken control of the theater for the 1895 season, however, and was eager to present the latest works of his most prominent composer. In a typically grandiose gesture, he scheduled the premieres of *Ratcliff* and *Silvano* barely a month apart.

After more than two years without a new opera from Mascagni's pen, *Guglielmo Ratcliff* was eagerly awaited. Andrea Maffei's translation of Heine's play was known, at least by reputation, to the Milanese cultural world, and since the 1892 publication of Mascagni's memoir "Prima di *Cavalleria*," the romantic tale of the valise in which *Ratcliff* accompanied the composer around Italy had become famous. No anticipation was greater, though, than Mascagni's own. A few days before the first performance he wrote Checchi, "I don't live, I have never lived, except for my *Ratcliff*. Oh, how much I hope the public will be able to penetrate the poet's mysterious concepts! Then, only then, will I be certain of success." He also noted: "The style of this work is very unusual; there are hardly any distinct numbers; its overall character is that of a continuous musical representation of the drama. The artists' lungs will be put to a tough test, not only because of the vocal tessitura, but because of the prolonged continuity of the music." The tenor role of Guglielmo, in particular, demands nothing less than a Wagnerian heldentenor. Except for the first act, he is onstage for nearly the entire opera, singing almost constantly in the second and third acts. At the first performance, the role was sung by Gian Battista De Negri, one of the first Italian Wagnerian tenors; as Nappi in *La Perseveranza* noted:

> It will be hard for Mascagni to find another leading singer to equal De Negri, whose fullness and intensity of voice, clear diction, powerful declamation, and richness of superb moments of musical and dramatic expression resulted in general admiration. We were also amazed by the strength of his lungs, something needed in such a truly overwhelming role.

The first performance took place on February 16, 1895, with Mascagni on the podium. Although the young American mezzo Della Rogers stepped in at the last minute to replace the indisposed Renée Vidal in the role of Margherita, she had been unable to prepare her most important section, her extended fourth-act narrative. On the first night, the music was performed by the orchestra, while she stood on stage miming her part.

Despite those unfortunate circumstances, the performance was a triumph for Mascagni and his music. The strength and beauty of the music were widely recognized, as was his achievement in creating a valid musical structure out of such an unwieldy drama. The greatest difficulty with the opera, however, lay in the drama itself. Giulio Ricordi, writing in the pages of his own *Gazzetta Musicale di Milano*, praised the music but dismissed the underlying drama in scathing terms:

> All of the characters are unpleasant. It is hard to imagine a more unusual collection of hysterics, fantasists, lunatics, thieves, and assassins. . . . hardly any of the action takes place in front of the spectators . . . instead, one after another the characters of Ratcliff tell their stories, with narrative after narrative, description piled on description, long, discursive, and often obscure.

Despite his dislike for the play, Ricordi found Mascagni's treatment remarkably successful. He also praised Mascagni's conducting, which he described as showing "outstanding ability, without affectation, without exaggeration."

Other critical reactions were more favorable. "Leporello" (Achille Tedeschi) in *L'Illustrazione Italiana* evoked a number of familiar themes:

> That which has become known as the "Mascagni phenomenon" is not, as some have believed, a meteor, destined to blaze for a moment and go out, but has demonstrated solidity and staying power. . . . let us not analyze too much, but rather admire how much beauty there is [in Ratcliff], delighted that with this opera a new Mascagni begins, a powerful, serious, composer.

The *Gazzetta dei Teatri*, after commenting that *Ratcliff* is "as far from its predecessors, in terms of intrinsic musical worth, as Yokohama from Cerignola," concluded nevertheless, echoing Sonzogno's concerns, that "it will never come close to making the money that *Cavalleria* does."

As Sonzogno had feared, *Guglielmo Ratcliff* was not a popular success. While the opera went on to a more than respectable run of fourteen performances at La Scala, it was perhaps the only one of Mascagni's operas before or since to be received more favorably by the critical establishment than by the general public. Despite the accolades it received, tenors avoided the punishing title role, and it never generated the sustained enthusiasm that would enable it to overcome its difficulties of casting and execution and enter the repertory.

Ratcliff's failure was of a different order than that of *I Rantzau*. While that opera suffers as much from musical as from dramatic inadequacies, much of

Ratcliff is Mascagni at his best, standing high among Mascagni's operas in its sustained intensity and passion, and in the remarkable prodigality of its melodic invention. Verdi, who rarely commented on the works of his younger counterparts, broke his rule far enough to declare that it was "a deeply felt opera, rich and vibrant in inspiration, that must succeed despite the dreariness of the subject."

Since the first performance of *Cavalleria*, Verdi had observed Mascagni's career with reservations. While he had mixed feelings about the music of *Cavalleria*, he was less taken with *L'Amico Fritz*, and still less, perhaps, with Mascagni's brash, aggressive manner, reflected in the *Nerone* episode as reported to him through the newspapers and the comments of his intimates. Reading through *Ratcliff*, the most Verdian of Mascagni's operas, the elderly Verdi felt a kinship with Mascagni for the first time.

Verdi's admiration for *Ratcliff* broke down the reserve he had felt toward the younger composer, and the two met for the first time, at Verdi's invitation, not long after the opera's first performance. During the six years remaining before Verdi's death, a warm relationship, which Mascagni prized deeply, grew up between them, a relationship that contributed to the growing sense of artistic purpose that Mascagni developed during the late 1890s. Verdi offered him a disinterested but affectionate paternal figure whom he could admire without reservation, without the strains that colored his dealings with Sonzogno or with his father. As he wrote, Verdi "was the sweetest, the warmest, man that could be imagined. . . . [My] intimate conversations with him were the most wonderful conversations of my life."

GUGLIELMO RATCLIFF

Guglielmo Ratcliff is a brilliant but problematic opera. As with so many Mascagni operas, the difficulties begin with the libretto—which in this case is not a libretto at all, but a "dramatic ballad" by Heinrich Heine, never intended to be staged or to serve as a text for an opera. For Heine, the dramatic form was no more than a convention, a framework within which to pour out his highly charged poetry.

The story, for all its dubious Scottish trappings, is a powerful story of a blood debt passed on by one generation to the next. Elizabeth, MacGregor's wife, had loved Edward Ratcliff before her marriage and loves him still. Discovering this, MacGregor kills Edward, who leaves a son, William (Guglielmo). Elizabeth wastes away and dies, leaving a daughter, Mary (Maria). William grows up and falls in love with Mary. Although strangely drawn to him, she does not love him. Tormented by two spectral figures whom he alone can see and who seek in vain to embrace one another, he becomes an outlaw. He kills the first two suitors for Mary's hand; the third, Douglas, defeats him but spares his life. Under the specters' influence, Ratcliff goes to MacGregor's castle and pleads with Mary to flee with him. Although she briefly yields, believing for a moment that they are actually Edward and Elizabeth, she refuses. In despair, he kills her, her father, and then himself, as behind him the two specters finally embrace.

Little of this, however, actually takes place onstage. The play, instead, is constructed out of a series of narratives, through which bits and pieces of the story are told by various characters, with the crucial part—the tale of Edward and Elizabeth and their tragic end—not revealed until just before the play's blood-soaked conclusion. Except for the brief duel between William and Douglas in the third act, there is no onstage action until the violent denouement at the end. Rather than the narratives supporting the drama, as in *Trovatore,* they *are* the drama. The difficulties of this scheme are compounded by the absence of characters capable of maintaining the interest, let alone the sympathy, of the audience. Ratcliff himself has long since lost all but the most tenuous relationship to reality or sanity, McGregor and Douglas are little more than truculent brutes, and Mary is an empty shell.

For Mascagni, barely twenty years old, to choose to turn this story into an opera, and to set the Heine/Maffei text, which was written entirely in *endecasillabi,* a formal Italian meter roughly comparable in its effect to iambic pentameter blank verse in English, rather than have it turned by some competent versifier into a more workable libretto, was a wildly ambitious gesture. Under the sway of the Scapigliati in 1884, the composer saw both the melodramatic, "Nordic" subject and the continuous literary flow of the text as making possible an opera that would be worthy of "the Pope of all present and future musicians," as he dubbed Wagner in an 1887 letter. Even more important was his passionate identification with the opera's hero, the quintessential Romantic figure, a child of privilege turned rebel, driven by forces he cannot begin to comprehend.

Ratcliff spoke to and for the young Mascagni, frustrated with poverty and the stifling routine of the conservatory. During his frequent depressions, he felt himself on the abyss; Ratcliff, on the border between sanity and madness, stood there with him. As he wrote Gianfranceschi in May 1886, stranded and penniless in Ascoli Piceno, "I have closed my eyes and believed myself Guglielmo, I have believed I was embracing Maria, speaking words of love to her." For all his intense engagement with each of his operas, nothing he wrote later had quite the emotional significance *Guglielmo Ratcliff* had for him; in 1942 he would tell Salvatore De Carlo, "*Ratcliff* was always my grand passion. . . . *Ratcliff* was truly my first opera, my first child, truly a child of love." It is not surprising that *Guglielmo Ratcliff* is suffused with an emotional intensity and melodic richness almost unparalleled in Mascagni's other works.

Remarkably, the lack of rhythmic variety in Maffei's text liberated rather than constrained the composer. At its frequent best, the music of *Ratcliff* transcends the rhythmic monotony of the text while gaining amplitude and balance from its larger formal structure, balancing its rhapsodic quality with a sense of organization rare in Mascagni's music. Scenes such as MacGregor's narrative in the first act, Ratcliff's second-act monologue, and Margherita's account in the fourth act fuse lyric beauty with an almost symphonic abstraction and scale.

It is that combination, coupled with the traditionally Romantic cast of its melodic line, that gives *Ratcliff* its unique quality. *Ratcliff* is a young man's opera, full of passion and fire. Internal evidence suggests that the greater part of the opera was indeed written between 1884 and 1887, well before *Cavalleria*. In his 1893 revisions, moreover, Mascagni wisely refrained from changing or adding too much to his earlier ideas, retaining a harmonic and melodic language that is far more rooted in late Verdi and early Wagner than the music Mascagni was writing by 1893. Rather than experimenting, Mascagni was working in a vocabulary with which he was fully comfortable, in which he could allow his lyrical gifts to flourish with no need to be "modern." Indeed, as the critic Guido Salvetti has written, "*Ratcliff* may well be the richest opera in lyrical melody, alternatively tense and passionate, that Mascagni ever wrote."

Ratcliff is prodigal not only with fresh musical ideas but also with beautifully realized extended sections, from the orchestral prelude, a precursor of *Cavalleria* with its offstage vocal interpolation, to the moving third-act intermezzo known as "Ratcliff's Dream" and the fourth-act duet between Guglielmo and Maria. Indeed, nearly the entire fourth act, until the murders begin, is a continuous outpouring of superb, passionate melody, as the drama steadily moves forward to its ultimate conclusion. It is ironic that the opera's weakest moments musically are the few moments of dramatic action, in the third and fourth acts, when Mascagni's lyric muse falls silent and he falls back on the melodramatic formulas of the time.

Had the twenty-year-old Mascagni been more experienced, he would undoubtedly have seen Maffei's text as the overblown, archaic work it is, full of cardboard characters, utterly unsuitable for operatic treatment. Reflecting it through his prism of fantasy and ambition, he convinced himself that it could become the basis for a grand romantic opera. Dreaming of glory, he actually composed such an opera, based on a libretto that existed in large part only in his imagination.

It is an impressive achievement. It is also impressive that Mascagni, after six years and three utterly different operas, could put himself so thoroughly back into that exalted state that he could complete *Guglielmo Ratcliff* without undoing its distinctive quality. It was, however, an achievement that contributed nothing to the increasingly difficult quandary facing the composer after *Cavalleria* and *Fritz*: how to find a direction for his talents that would be relevant to the rapidly changing musical and cultural world in which he lived. Indeed, Mascagni's decision to resurrect *Ratcliff*, as well as his subsequent willingness to spend valuable time on *Silvano*, were both efforts to avoid confronting that dilemma, by taking refuge in solving questions to which he already knew, or believed he knew, the answers.

SILVANO

Silvano appeared under the baton of Rodolfo Ferrari on March 25 at La Scala, five weeks after *Ratcliff's* debut. Of the three principal singers, two had just appeared in *Ratcliff*. Matilda was sung by Adelina Stehle, who had sung Maria in the earlier opera; Renzo was sung by Giuseppe Pacini, who had sung Douglas. The tenor lead, Silvano, was sung by Giuseppe De Lucia. The evening was a personal triumph for De Lucia, in his La Scala debut; the critic for *La Gazzetta dei Teatri* wrote that "De Lucia, to tell the truth, is the only hero of the evening. Woe to Mascagni, if he hadn't had such a truly exceptional singer!"

Silvano's debut was much less of an event than the premiere of *Ratcliff*. The famous musicians and foreign journalists who had attended the former event had gone home, and critics noted that the choice of the journeyman Ferrari as conductor reflected the composer's reluctance to attribute too much importance to the event. Nonetheless, the first-night audience reacted warmly. Two of the numbers were repeated, including the famous second-act tenor aria "S'è spento il sol," and Mascagni was called to the stage ten times.

This reception was lukewarm, though, compared to the reaction to *Cavalleria* or *L'Amico Fritz*, and the critical response was cool. The *Gazzetta Musicale di Milano* found the libretto inferior, and the music uneven: "The subject is neither complicated nor new; the three characters are not carved, but barely

sketched, and are of little interest; while the action moves quickly, it is neither clear nor convincing: the tragic ending is too sudden and fails to move
[the viewer]." While the reviewer found many of the choruses, particularly
those for female voices, musically attractive, he pointed out that the same
choruses "have no link to the action, block it, slow it down, and wind up
boring the audience." Many writers were particularly disappointed with *Sil-*
vano, coming on the heels of the impressive *Ratcliff*, including Colombani,
who wrote, "It would be a terrible shame if maestro Mascagni, after having
demonstrated his powerful qualities as a composer with *Ratcliff*, were to fail
to follow further along that road along which the glories of Italian art can be
foretold."

The product of Sonzogno's cupidity and the voracious financial demands of Mascagni's extravagant way of life, *Silvano* lacks conviction. Mascagni prized sincerity above almost all other compositional virtues. If not
driven by the overwhelming pull of creative necessity, he could not write a
convincing opera. *Silvano*, especially in Targioni's slapdash treatment, engaged neither his emotions nor his imagination. Although the story bears a
superficial resemblance to *Cavalleria*, it lacks both the strong characters and
the powerful social context of the earlier opera. The characters are not only
uninteresting but unpleasant, while the seafront setting adds only superficial
local color. The final confrontation lacks the inevitability of *Cavalleria* and
seems more a product of arbitrary stage manipulation than a logical outcome
of the characters' behavior.

It is a tribute to the irresistible fecundity of Mascagni's melodic gift that,
although not deeply engaged with *Silvano*, he was still able to produce, seemingly without effort, one compelling lyrical idea after another. The music,
however, strikes few dramatic sparks. The single most memorable passage,
Silvano's "S'è spento il sol," is a static apostrophe to love and nature, more like
one of Mascagni's songs than part of a dramatic work. While the orchestral
interludes and choral episodes, particularly the female chorus that precedes
Silvano's aria, are lovely and atmospheric, they are equally undramatic.

It was this beautiful music devoid of dramatic impetus in *Silvano* that
prompted an unusual but strangely appropriate suggestion from the Italian
critic Mario Rinaldi, who wrote that, rather than stage the opera, "it would
be better . . . to perform the piano reduction in one's home, preferably along
with a violin, to make the beautiful lines of the melody stand out." As an
opera, though, *Silvano* is charming but listless. Bastianelli, in his 1910 critical
study of Mascagni's works, aptly noted that "if *Silvano* has any value at all, it
is that of having demonstrated fully to Mascagni his duty to renew himself."

CAVALLERIA + FIVE

After conducting *Ratcliff* and *Silvano* in Naples in April, Mascagni returned with his family to Cerignola in May 1895. Five eventful years had passed since the first performance of *Cavalleria rusticana*. He had become a worldwide celebrity. His operas had been produced throughout the world, and he himself had traveled through Italy, Germany, Austria, and England, adulated by elites and masses alike. At thirty-one, he was a prosperous paterfamilias, established with his wife, their three children, and their German governess in the imposing mansion he had bought with the royalties from *Cavalleria*.

Mascagni had not rested on his laurels. After five years, he had created a substantial body of musical achievement. He had composed four operas since *Cavalleria*, more than any other Italian composer during this period. Of these operas, *Fritz* was an unqualified success, while *Guglielmo Ratcliff* had earned the respect of the musical world. *I Rantzau*, although unsuccessful, had been a serious attempt on the composer's part to explore larger and more complex musical forms, and to integrate new harmonic and melodic ideas into his musical language. The Mascagni of 1895 was in many ways a far more sophisticated composer, at home in a wider variety of forms and techniques, than the composer of *Cavalleria rusticana*.

And yet, for all his progress, something important was missing. It is hard to discern any real direction or purpose in all of this effort; indeed, with the important exception of *Ratcliff*, the realization of a passionately preserved youthful dream, the operas of these years exist largely on the surface. They convey little depth or conviction, suggesting a man adrift and rudderless in a musical sea. While Puccini with *Manon Lescaut* had found the themes that would become his life's work, Mascagni had yet to do so. His two 1895 operas epitomize his failure; the first, the exhumation of an earlier work in a Romantic vein already nearly obsolete when Mascagni first began it in 1883, and the second, a listless effort to recreate the quality that had made *Cavalleria* a success five years earlier.

Unlike Puccini, Mascagni would never identify a single theme or subject matter as being uniquely well suited to his muse. Although one can consider this a virtue or a deficiency, it remains one of the most interesting features of his career, and one that sets him apart from all of his contemporaries. Mascagni spent his entire life experimenting with new genres and subject matter. Almost every opera represents a pronounced departure in subject matter and treatment, and often in musical vocabulary, from its predecessors. Every opera was a new challenge, a battle to be fought and won. The metaphor of opera as a battle recurs throughout his letters, all his life; Iovino aptly subtitled his biography of Mascagni "Opera's Adventurer."

As Mascagni's experience and his understanding of his artistic self deepened, he became better able to select subjects that responded to his innermost musical and emotional concerns, and to press his librettists to give him poetry that triggered his strongest musical instincts. That ability, which even at its greatest remained compromised by Mascagni's own emotional instability and unpredictability, was yet largely undeveloped during these early years. The composer was never more victimized by the inadequacies of his librettists, and more susceptible to pressure from his publisher, than during these years. Under the sway of the importunate Sonzogno, who demanded one opera after another in his drive to capitalize on the success of *Cavalleria*, Mascagni took on operatic projects remote from what he had imagined when he had written Targioni-Tozzetti and Menasci in April 1890, "The genre? up to you. Any genre is fine with me, as long as it has truth, passion, and above all, drama, strong drama."

Targioni and Menasci, for all their industry and their devotion to their famous friend, were no more than mediocre writers and librettists. The best that can be said of them is that given a strong starting point, they could organize a workable operatic vehicle along traditional lines, and that they could produce serviceable verse. The libretto for *Cavalleria* is successful in large part because of the strong Verga play underneath. Charged with creating an original libretto in a similar vein for *Silvano*, Targioni proved that his talents ended with the versification of dramatic situations created by others, and that he had no real powers of literary or dramatic invention. Mascagni eventually realized this. After 1895, although he relied on them often to touch up the work of others, he never sought another original libretto from either.

The sudden and remarkable success of *Cavalleria rusticana* had plunged Mascagni overnight into a world of fame and fortune about which he had dreamed, but for which he was painfully unready. He was overwhelmed by his new reality, by its opportunities, its obligations, and its dangers. Lacking anyone disinterested to whom to turn, he looked to Edoardo Sonzogno to be a mentor, even a substitute father, to him, but found that to the publisher he was little more than a particularly valuable commercial property. Unaccustomed to living in a fishbowl, he resented both the adulation and the criticism of the world's media. A complex and emotional young man, given to violent and extreme reactions and mood swings, he was torn by the world in which he found himself. He craved the limelight, and then tried to run from it. Deeply interested in the commercial success of his operas, he was at the same time passionately concerned about his integrity as an artist and bitterly resented those, like D'Annunzio, who portrayed him as nothing more than a product of commercial manipulation. Although it is a commonplace, it is hard to doubt that however gratifying it may have been, the sudden and phenomenal success of *Cavalleria* seriously hindered what might otherwise have been for Mascagni a more gradual, and perhaps in the long run more successful, process of personal and artistic growth. For all their fame and fortune, the first five years of Mascagni's success were difficult ones.

7. *New Directions and Iris,*

1895—1898

Mascagni still owed Ricordi a new opera to replace *Guglielmo Ratcliff.* The composer's 1894 contract with Sonzogno, which had given him rights to *Ratcliff, Silvano,* and two more operas to be written subsequently, specifically excluded from Sonzogno's otherwise exclusive rights "an opera already committed to the House of Ricordi for the 1896–1897 carnival season." That still-unspecified opera took precedence over the two operas that Mascagni was committed to deliver to Sonzogno before the end of 1897 and 1898 respectively.

Giulio Ricordi urgently wanted an opera from Mascagni. Although he owned all of Verdi's important operas and most of the operas of Bellini, Donizetti, and Rossini, Sonzogno's growing presence worried him. Among the younger composers, whose works commanded the highest rental fees, his rival appeared to have a substantial edge. Ricordi had Puccini, but in 1895 that composer's only profitable work was *Manon Lescaut.* By comparison, Sonzogno had two proven draws in Mascagni and Leoncavallo, as well as two emerging talents, Giordano and Cilea.

In February 1895 Ricordi asked Luigi Illica to prepare a libretto for Mascagni. The son of a prosperous notary, Illica had run off to sea in his teens, returning at twenty-one a seasoned sailor, world traveler, and battle-hardened warrior. During the 1880s he built a modest reputation as a playwright, turning to libretto writing at the end of the decade. In 1895 he was already known for his libretti for Franchetti's *Cristoforo Colombo* and Catalani's *La Wally* and was working on two operas that would establish him as the premier librettist of his generation: Giordano's *Andrea Chénier* and, with the playwright Giuseppe Giacosa, Puccini's *La Bohème*. Ricordi brought Illica and Mascagni together in the spring of 1895. The two quickly became friends and for the next twenty years had an intimate and, as could be expected from two such explosive characters, combative relationship.

Since the previous summer Illica had been nurturing an idea for a libretto on an unusual Japanese subject, and he was eager to find a composer who would share his fascination with exotic Japan and his elusive ideas about the opera of the future. Illica's vision, which would be realized in *Iris*, was far removed from the conventionally exotic libretti of his time. Influenced by contemporary writers such as Maurice Maeterlinck and Joris-Karl Huysmans, he was looking for operatic parallels to the literary and artistic experimentation taking place in Europe in the 1890s, leaving behind the trappings of romantic melodrama and capturing the atmospheric, symbolic quality with which these writers imbued their work. In a note to himself at the time, he wrote "idea of a new [type of] opera. New form. Opening up a new horizon, a type of new expression. It is hard for the moment to define what it could be and what is needed to bring this still unspecific idea to life; I am forced, however, to follow it blindly."

Frustrated with the increasing emptiness of both form and content in conventional romantic melodrama, and with the sentimental clichés that, in a variety of guises, still made up the dramatic vocabulary of Italian opera, Illica hoped to replace those clichés with a new operatic vocabulary. While he could imagine that new forms of opera might be possible, creating those forms was to be beyond his creative means. Despite his intentions, the old-fashioned machinery still clanks and wheezes beneath his symbolic and decorative apparatus.

In Mascagni Illica had found the only prominent Italian operatic composer whose frustration with both his own work and the conventions of Italian opera matched his own. In the spring of 1895, however, Mascagni was still unready to commit himself to Illica's project, as yet unaware of the extent to which his own creative renewal demanded a thoroughgoing break with his own past practices. He still owed Sonzogno *Zanetto*, which had been waiting for over three years. The composition of that work took place over the rest of the summer of 1895. In August, however, with *Zanetto* nearly complete, a chain of events began that put the question of his new opera out of his mind until the following spring.

Late that month, Mascagni received a visit from Augusto Guidi-Carnevali, president of the governing board of the Liceo Musicale Rossini in the coastal city of Pesaro. That conservatory, which had been founded in 1882 with a large bequest by the composer Gioacchino Rossini, had been leaderless since the resignation of its first director, Carlo Pedrotti, two years earlier. Mascagni immediately recommended his former professor, Amintore Galli, whom he knew to be actively seeking the post. As Mascagni later wrote Galli, Guidi-Carnevali cut him off, "[saying] it would be desirable, as director, to have an operatic composer in order to comply with the terms of Rossini's will. Then he asked me for a few ideas, by way of advice, finally asking me pointedly what I thought of the conservatories. Then, seeing what an opportunity I had, I laid out all my ideas."

Mascagni thought little more of the meeting. On September 19 he finished *Zanetto*, and early in October he left for an extended tour of Germany and Central Europe. On October 12 he received a letter forwarded to Frankfurt from Livorno, in which the board of the Liceo Rossini offered him the position of director. His reaction was intense and immediate. "Mistreated by the critics," he wrote Galli, "talked down to like a child, humiliated by almost every conservatory professor, even put down by some of my colleagues, I suddenly felt as if my heart would burst and responded with my acceptance."

All his life, but never more than during the first few years after the unprecedented success of *Cavalleria*, Mascagni never felt that he was given his due as a serious musician by the musical world inhabited by people such as Ricordi, Boito, and Toscanini, and he bitterly resented the often condescending criticism of his work from the arbiters of Italian musical taste. To this, the appointment as director of the Liceo Rossini was a powerful rejoinder. At thirty-one, the young man who had left the Milan Conservatory without his diploma was finally invited to enter the musical establishment.

Mascagni's appointment was not only a personal vindication but also an opportunity to pursue the reform of Italian conservatory education. Like all of Mascagni's crusades, it blended legitimate issues with a desire to redress personal injuries, real or imaginary. While the roots of his concern for educational reform can be found in his misery and frustration at the Milan Conservatory, his determination to replace a system grounded in rote memorization with one based on practical experience marks him as an unusually progressive figure in Italian musical education of the time. Not long after taking charge of the Liceo Rossini, Mascagni explained his feelings on the subject:

> [Conservatory education] is vastly inferior to what it must be. It is a serious error, for example, to teach music like a catechism: making one learn it by rote, rule by rule . . . the best way to teach music, above all, is to [enable students] to make practical use of the ideas they are being taught, through a breadth of explanation, and a wide variety of illustrative examples. . . . One discusses, one inquires: that is the only way by which one can learn the inner essence of art, which . . . is the one thing that it is truly necessary to get young people to understand.

At Pesaro, Mascagni set out to right the wrongs he had suffered ten years earlier in Milan on behalf of a new generation of students.

Upon receiving his acceptance, Guidi-Carnevali submitted his name to the Pesaro municipal council, which approved the nomination on November 24. The position paid a substantial twelve thousand lire per year, twice that of the longer-established Parma Conservatory, and included a lavish penthouse apartment in the conservatory building. Mascagni arrived in Pesaro early in December 1895, eager to take up his new duties.

EARLY YEARS IN PESARO

Mascagni and the Pesarese entered their new relationship with high expectations. While the composer saw it as both personal vindication and the opportunity to place his stamp on Italian musical education, the school and the city saw his appointment as a step that would put Pesaro on the map and take the Liceo Rossini to the front rank of Italian conservatories. Despite its illustrious name, the Liceo Rossini was not considered the equal of the great conservatories in Milan, Rome, and Naples, or even smaller but longer-established institutions such as the Parma Conservatory. An upstart institution, it had a small student body and had yet to produce any graduates of particular note. Only seventy-three students were enrolled for the 1894–95 academic year, and only ten diplomas were awarded at the end of the year. Pesaro itself, a small seaside city far from Italy's major centers, offered little of the cultural and intellectual stimulation that drew outstanding students and professionals to Milan, Rome, and Naples.

Within a few years, the relationship between Mascagni and Pesaro would deteriorate, and his removal would spark a nationwide controversy. His first years as director of the Liceo Rossini, however, were dynamic and exciting ones. Shortly after accepting the position, he wrote Galli, "If I have the strength, you will see that before long the Liceo Rossini will be much spoken of." This was, if anything, an understatement.

For the next three years, Mascagni devoted nearly all of his time and energy to the school. Even after beginning work on *Iris*, he remained in Pesaro throughout the academic year, squeezing nearly all of his creative activity into the extended vacation period from the middle of August until late fall. He threw himself into an almost endless series of new projects and reorganization plans. Teaching the advanced composition course himself, he established a student orchestra; established *La Cronaca Musicale*, the first conservatory-based musical journal in Italy; strengthened the curriculum in literary and historical subjects; and redesigned the curriculum in harmony and counterpoint. He added four new faculty members, established the first course of study in sacred music at an Italian conservatory, and required all students to study vocal solfège and choral singing.

Under his direction, the student body and the number of diplomas granted grew dramatically. After four years, enrollment had more than doubled to 151, while the number of diplomas granted kept pace, rising to twenty-four. The increase was most dramatic in the area of composition and theory, which went from being a minor sideline in a school devoted to the training of singers and instrumentalists to the single largest area of study, engaging nearly one-third of the entire student body. Instrumental instruction moved from the performance of largely trivial solo showpieces to ensemble activity. Orchestral training became the heart of the instrumental curriculum, and string students were required to form string quartets.

The centerpiece of the curriculum was the Liceo orchestra, in which both faculty and students participated, the first standing orchestra established by an Italian conservatory. In February 1896, only three months after his arrival in Pesaro, Mascagni presented the orchestra under his baton for the first time, performing works by Beethoven, Rossini, and Wagner at the opening concert of the Rossini birthday celebrations held at the *liceo* every four years. The birthday concerts continued with a performance of Rossini's *Petite messe solennelle* on the twenty-ninth, Rossini's birthday, and the premiere of Mascagni's *Zanetto* on March 2, featuring two *liceo* students, Maria Pizzagalli as Sylvia and Stefania Collamarini in the trouser role of Zanetto.

Mascagni took *Zanetto* to La Scala, where it was performed with the same cast on March 18. Although received with enthusiasm in Pesaro, it did not fare as well in Milan, which Edoardo Pompei attributed to "more than anything else La Scala's not being a setting proportional to the form and the dimensions of *Zanetto*. It would be as if one exhibited a miniature from a fourth-floor window and then expected the public to appreciate it from the street."

Despite its lukewarm reception, *Zanetto* was picked up and performed widely over the next year. Its fresh charm, delicacy, and lyric beauty have kept it alive, and it continues to receive occasional performances today.

Zanetto, initially dubbed a "scena lyrica" rather than a full-fledged opera by its composer, depicts a brief moonlit encounter between two souls who connect momentarily and pass on. Sylvia, a wealthy but unhappy courtesan, is bemoaning her life in her villa overlooking Florence. Touched by the chance visit of the young Zanetto, her heart opens to him; tempted to accept the love he offers, she ultimately rejects it to protect his simplicity and purity, in the process rediscovering her own long-lost innocence. As he leaves, she buries her head in her hands and cries. As she cries, she sings, "Blessed be love, I can cry again!"

Zanetto is a precursor of Mascagni's new style as it was soon to emerge in *Iris*. It is written in an almost continuous arioso texture, from which rich musical ideas emerge, but only one, Sylvia's beautiful "Non andare da Sylvia," the musical and emotional climax of the work, resembles a conventional aria. In place of extended melodies and set pieces, recurrent short themes and motifs, small but distinctive melodic cells, weave in and out of the musical ebb and flow, with the orchestra commenting upon and amplifying the emotional content of the vocal lines, interacting with the singers almost as if it were another character in the opera. The orchestration is delicate and transparent; strings and solo winds predominate, and subtle but effective touches, such as the exquisite opening a capella humming chorus, enhance the moonlit atmosphere of the work.

Zanetto will always remain too slender in its drama, and too modest in its musical means, ever to become widely popular. Lost in grand halls such as La Scala, it is best heard in intimate settings, where the audience can enjoy its tender sentiments and delicate melodic qualities. Well performed, as recent productions have shown, it still works its magic on sympathetic audiences.

The Liceo orchestra gave the students the opportunity to learn the orchestral repertory under professional conditions, offering a preparation for future orchestral careers unequaled in the Italian conservatory system. It permitted student composers to have their works heard, and student conductors to practice their trade with a competent ensemble. It was an effective vehicle for making the school and its achievements known throughout Italy and beyond. Drawn by Mascagni's name and reputation, important musicians and powerful critics came to hear the orchestra and went away praising it.

Finally, it served Mascagni's interests. Through the orchestra he could win public recognition for himself and his achievements at the Liceo Rossini.

Moreover, it provided him with the opportunity to achieve mastery as a conductor in a sympathetic but challenging environment. Before he arrived in Pesaro, his conducting experience had been largely limited to directing his own operas, a practice not unusual at the time for composers without any special conducting skill. In Pesaro, Mascagni began to turn himself into a true conductor, refining his technique and beginning to build his orchestral repertory. By the spring of 1898, when he made his orchestral debut with the La Scala orchestra in Milan, he was well on his way to becoming a polished symphonic conductor.

Mascagni was an inspired teacher to those students who, after completing the basic courses in harmony and counterpoint, were admitted to his advanced composition course. Luigi Ferrari Trecate, who had a distinguished career both as a composer and as director of the Parma Conservatory, wrote: "He was never pedantic. He knew how to instill his own overwhelming musicality in each of us . . . inspiring us under the influence of a magical and stimulating atmosphere. At Pesaro, at that time, the environment was, to use [another student]'s happy expression, saturated with a dreamlike glorious aura." In addition to Ferrari Trecate, Mascagni's students included Riccardo Zandonai, composer of *Francesca da Rimini* and the leading operatic composer of the next generation; Francesco Ballila Pratella, leader of the musical wing of the Italian Futurist movement and composer of the avant-garde opera *L'Aviatore Dro*; the Croatian Josip Hatze, pioneer of Yugoslav national opera in the 1920s; and the conductors Agide Jacchia, Iginio Nini-Belluci, and Roberto Moranzoni. Among the many singers who were produced at the Liceo Rossini under Mascagni were Ernestina Poli, later known as Tina Poli-Randaccio, who created the title role in his 1913 *Parisina*; Maria Farneti, a famous Iris; Umberto Macnez; and Piero Schiavazzi.

The most dramatic effect of Mascagni's activities, however, was on the composer himself. His conducting and teaching, as well as his daily contact with outstanding colleagues, steadily added to his own musical sophistication and technical skill. On the *liceo* orchestra podium and in the pages of the *Cronaca Musicale*, as well as in the informal forums that the school offered him daily, surrounded by admiring students and supportive faculty, he was able to gradually build his skills as a writer, critic, conductor, and lecturer. In Pompei's words, he "fell in love with that which up to then had remained for him a distant, obscure, abstraction—that is, the discipline of inculcating learning into students. Swallowing a good-sized dose of it himself, he became a disciplined man."

Finally, Mascagni briefly found in Pesaro the balance that comes from settling into one place and one occupation, blessed with a clear sense of purpose and direction. In this environment, he was able to concentrate his creative energies more effectively than ever before. The product was the extraordinary opera *Iris*, written during his first years at the Liceo Rossini. Whatever the final judgment on its merits may be, it reveals a new level of creative maturity on the part of the composer; moreover, it remains arguably the one Mascagni opera after *Cavalleria* in which there are no significant lapses of concentration, in which nearly every moment maintains the same high level of intensity and creativity.

Although Mascagni's first years at Pesaro were not without difficulties, his disagreements with the authorities through 1898 were still occasional and insignificant and did not suggest the intensity of the conflicts that were to follow. Through his efforts, the school was growing dramatically, receiving favorable attention throughout Italy. At the same time, though, his indifference to the initial murmurs of discontent with his highly charged pursuit of his personal vision for the school, along with his insensitivity to the concerns of local dignitaries with their own personal stake in the school, was preparing the ground for the controversy that would soon erupt.

IRIS AND THE "COMMEDIA"

Mascagni accepted Illica's Japanese project in March 1896. That same month, Ricordi wrote Illica, "Well then, long live Japan! It is a great victory. I am delighted, thanks to my 'stubbornness' in pulling off something I have been grinding away at for two years. Out with Vulcan, Etna, Fujiyama." Illica began converting his sketches into a libretto, along with his commentary on the opera, long descriptive passages that set the scene for each act, writing Ricordi, "The novelty lies in the commentary, my tic, my neuralgia, my cancer, what you will. . . . You will see what poetry it is!"

Meanwhile, Mascagni spent time studying Japanese music, writing Illica early in June, "I have had typical Japanese music up to here. . . . I am thoroughly Japanesed [*ingiapponesato*]," and again a week later, "The Japanese girl is moving ahead: I have studied that type of music a great deal, and I believe that I've caught its spirit." By this time, Mascagni had already received most of a draft libretto for the first two acts from Illica and was eager to have the writer come to Pesaro, in order to have the direct contact with his librettist that the composer had come to find necessary in preparing the final version of an operatic libretto.

Though before *Iris* Mascagni had accepted libretti casually, from this point onward he became increasingly selective, rejecting proposal after proposal before finding one that fired his creative drives. Once he found a subject, he would then insist on spending weeks, even months, working and living side by side with the author. Having taken a country cottage near Pesaro for his family, he found one nearby for Illica and his female companion, the writer Alma D'Alma, arranging for them to arrive as soon as the final examinations were over.

By August Mascagni had already written a considerable amount of music for *Iris*. Delighted with Mascagni's progress, Illica wrote a long letter to Ricordi from Pesaro, which offers an insightful look at the composer's modus operandi:

> *Yesterday Mascagni had me listen to a good deal of the first and second acts. . . . We go forward and backward at the same time, but are doing well. In any event, Mascagni is truly doing something new and beautiful. . . .*
>
> *Mascagni does not work like Puccini, working simultaneously on the musical idea and its instrumental and vocal development, so that when Puccini says, "I've done the first scene," it's understood that it is written, scored, and orchestrated, ready for the copyist. Mascagni writes nothing but a few notes, goes over the libretto. At the beginning this surprised me, and I suspected a trick. . . . I believed that Mascagni was actually improvising.*
>
> *No, it's not that way. He repeated the same thing note for note many times . . . and, making some changes, played it with the changes.*

Illica concluded, "He is . . . determined to write a serious work. He is a new Mascagni. He is a Mascagni who has benefited not a little from the *liceo*: he is a very different Mascagni."

Blessed with a powerful and retentive musical memory, Mascagni composed in his head. Sitting at the piano, he stored his musical materials in his mind, moving them around and reworking them before writing down anything beyond, at most, a few short notes. When the section on which he was working had taken final form in his mind, he would write it down, in the form of a piano-vocal score, with few indications of the ultimate instrumentation. Once he had written something down, he would hardly ever change a note. If a rare correction involved more than a handful of notes, rather than allow the correction to show, he would cut a clean piece of music paper to fit and paste it over the bars to be corrected, writing them again on the clean paper.

By August 1896 Illica's libretto for the first two acts of *Iris* was in nearly final form. The story is set in the self-contained, timeless Japan before its nineteenth-century opening to the West. Innocent and beautiful, Iris lives with her blind father in a cottage in the shadow of Mount Fuji, where she has been spotted by the wealthy libertine Osaka. Craving her, he arranges for the Edo brothel keeper Kyoto to abduct her and take her to the Yoshiwara, Edo's pleasure quarter. Believing her to have gone there of her free will, her father sets out after her, not to rescue her, but to curse her.

In the second act, Osaka attempts to seduce Iris, plying her with gifts and promises. Unable to penetrate her innocence, he rejects her. Kyoto, eager to recoup his investment, places her on display in the window of his brothel. As crowds gather to admire her beauty, Osaka returns and once again yearns for her. Before he can reach her, her father arrives. Iris cries out in joy, but when her father reaches her, he pelts her with mud, cursing her for having abandoned him. In despair, Iris throws herself from the window into the sewer and is carried away.

A simple, grim story, for both Illica and Mascagni it was a starting point for decoration, symbolism, and even a sort of decadent mysticism. In August 1896, however, the problem was the third act—how to end the opera in a way that resolves Iris's fate in a manner both dramatically and symbolically appropriate. From a dramatic standpoint, nothing more is left to happen after the end of the second act, yet to end the opera at that point would inevitably leave it little more than a crude Grand Guignol show. It would not be until early in 1898, after much trial and error, that a solution to the third act would be found.

Although immersed in *Iris*, Mascagni was still obliged to deliver a new opera to Sonzogno in little more than a year. Fortunately, a second operatic subject was at hand. During Illica's visit, he and Mascagni had come up with an idea for a comedy based on the traditional Italian masked, improvisational theater known as the commedia dell'arte. At this point it was nothing more than an idea, but it was enough for Sonzogno, for whom Illica's association with the project was more important than the specific subject. Early in October, Sonzogno wrote Mascagni and Illica accepting the proposal. Now, by virtue of the imprudent contract he had signed in 1894, Mascagni was committed to write two operas simultaneously for two separate publishers, and to consign both to their respective publishers before the end of 1897.

For the moment, however, all of his attention was still directed to *Iris*, which had come to engage Mascagni more intensely than any opera since his first years with *Ratcliff* in the 1880s. Two weeks after a fall 1896 visit to Cerignola by Illica and Ricordi, he wrote Illica, in an unprecedented state of fear mixed with exaltation:

> At times my imagination carries me beyond the human mind: I don't know if anything of the sort is possible, but it is a fact that I feel like a different person, that I hardly feel mortal, and it seems to me that I am creating beautiful music never heard

before; and I play this music, I hear it clearly, but then I imagine that it is not my music, that it is too beautiful to be my music . . . and I'm afraid.

Iris had become an intensely personal exploration into the heart of his creative impulse, as can be seen even more clearly in a letter to his old friend Gianfranceschi:

I keep coming up against difficulties that seem insurmountable: but it is precisely these difficulties that drive me forward: I feel dizzy: I see the dangers, but I am drawn to them. . . . every day I have a new idea, a formless thought, and bit by bit it grows, it spreads, it expands, it fills my entire mind, and . . . I have no idea what will come forth, but I know that this is the first time that I have been so utterly gripped by a work.

Mascagni's stay in Cerignola from August to October 1896 was the defining moment for his new opera. By the time he returned to Pesaro for the new academic year he had established the musical character of the opera and set down many of its most important musical ideas. At that point, however, with Mascagni caught up in his duties at the conservatory, the opera took second place. He did not resume active work on the score until the spring of 1897.

The year 1896 was also Mascagni's last year in Cerignola. After he had returned to Pesaro, Lina and the children, along with their governess, Anna Dietze, stayed on in Cerignola. Early in 1897 the Protestant Dietze came down fatally with typhoid fever. The devout Lina, seeking religious consolation for a woman who had become virtually a member of the family, found to her horror that the bishop of the diocese would permit neither a visit by a priest nor a religious funeral, unless the dying woman would agree to convert to Catholicism. In the end, the only concession that could be won from the bishop was that she could be buried in the cemetery. With the help of Mascagni's old friend Cannone, still mayor, a suitable funeral procession, led by the town band, was held for the unfortunate woman. The bishop would not allow a priest, however, to officiate at the funeral.

When Mascagni learned this on arriving for the funeral, he flew into a rage. As soon as the funeral was over, he ordered the family's household goods and furnishings packed and the house vacated. It was the end of an intimate ten-year relationship with the town that had welcomed him in 1887, and where he had written *Cavalleria*. Although he briefly visited Cerignola on occasion later, neither he nor any member of the Mascagni family ever lived there again.

By the spring of 1897 Mascagni was again working on his opera. In April, after attending the first performance of Franchetti's latest opera at La Scala, he made his first visit to Illica's home in Castell'Arquato, a picturesque hill town overlooking the Po Valley near Piacenza. In Castell'Arquato, Mascagni and Illica discussed both *Iris* and the new opera, which was still known only as the "Commedia." Illica had been hard at work, and Mascagni was able to take the first act back with him to Pesaro. Excited, he stopped at Bologna to write Illica, "It is a true masterpiece! The more I read it the more I'm convinced. We will do great things!"

The third act of *Iris*, in which she dies and is reunited with the sun, was still unresolved. At first, Illica saw the third act as no more than a brief epilogue, opening with Iris discovered by a band of scavengers in the sewer, as he wrote Ricordi:

> In the epilogue . . . the figure of the father is pointless. The ragpickers are necessary, because otherwise the epilogue would come across as an entirely imaginary ending, while the ragpickers are specifically there to give the touch of human truth that the entire work has. Here in the epilogue we have no more need of either Osaka, or Kyoto, or the father. . . . There must be, however, the presence of the sun, and the apotheosis of the flowers.

This was too austere for Mascagni, who appealed to Illica that summer, somewhat uncertainly, "As to Iris's death, I feel as well that it needs a compounding of feelings, perhaps going from the reminiscences of the second act to those of the first, having her die with the recollection of the sun 'Ma sol tu vieni, etc.' [But] do as you want and as your feelings tell you." Mascagni, as always, was looking for the emotional center of the work, telling Illica, "Don't worry about me . . . if it moves me, I will know how to move the public."

The impasse continued as Illica refused to change his initial version and Mascagni continued to insist on the need to raise the last act's emotional temperature. By February 1898, with the first two acts already complete except for their orchestration, Mascagni wrote Ricordi: "I am not by any means opposed to [Illica's] ideas; all I want is that Iris sing something that means something, that moves, that makes one think back on her innocence, her childhood happiness, and just might make one reflect on the illusions and deceptions of this world."

Illica arrived in Pesaro at the end of the month, and at long last, in the course of a few days, the two revised the third act to their mutual satisfaction. The final version retains Illica's overall scheme, with the addition of an extended vocal scene for Iris, culminating in the reappearance of her phrase "Ma, sol, tu vieni" from the first act, as the composer had earlier proposed. Effective as was Illica's basic idea, Iris's scene adds precisely the measure of feeling that was needed to balance the grotesque quality of the ragpickers and the cold distancing effect of the three Egoisms.

Mascagni's work on *Iris* was once again interrupted by activities that made it impossible for him to devote much time to either *Iris* or the "Commedia" for the next few months. In March 1898, after a series of concerts with the Liceo orchestra, he left Pesaro for his first extended tour since taking charge of the school in 1895. After a week in the Netherlands, he arrived in Milan for his true public debut as a symphonic conductor, five concerts with the La Scala orchestra beginning March 27.

For the first time, Mascagni as a symphonic conductor was facing an audience outside the friendly confines of the Liceo Rossini. The spring concerts at La Scala were a Milanese institution; as the *Corriere della Sera* noted, he was filling a "post left by proven conductors such as Mancinelli, Faccio, Bolzoni, Martucci, Lamoureux, Vanzo, and Toscanini." Mascagni's programs were adventuresome and included a series of Italian premieres of important works by contemporary European composers, including Tchaikovsky's *Pathétique*, the Symphony no. 1 by the Norwegian composer Johann Svendsen, Grieg's Piano Concerto, Humperdinck's *Hänsel and Gretel* overture, and the Good Friday Spell from Wagner's *Parsifal*. One concert was devoted entirely to Italian symphonic works. Making it clear that he wished to be judged as a conductor rather than as a composer, he programmed nothing of his own, only adding the two intermezzi from *Guglielmo Ratcliff* at the last concert.

Mascagni's conducting was well received by the critical Milan audience. After noting that the composer was still, in a sense, learning the conducting trade, Colombani in the *Corriere della Sera* concluded on a positive note:

> *Indeed, Mascagni at his first . . . appearance has disarmed more than one prejudice and encouraged more than a few hopes. He is already self-confident: he knows how to command the orchestra and shows a wonderful ability to grasp the importance of effects and the value of musical ideas. He lacks so far a certain precision, attention to details. But these are precisely the gifts that can be acquired, not with great love, but with extended study. Thus, one can be patient.*

After the last concert, Colombani summed up Mascagni's debut with cautious enthusiasm:

> *Mascagni clearly has enviable natural gifts. He is a born musician; he possesses the sacred fire of art and knows how to pass it on to others. He is a conductor full of dash, audacity, passion. He puts his entire self, his entire artist's soul, into every piece. . . . his improvement during this month has been so considerable that the weight of those doubts that were widely expressed at the beginning is diminished.*

Mascagni soon became a familiar podium figure throughout Europe as both a symphonic and an operatic conductor. Typical of the times, his repertoire was largely drawn from the nineteenth century, dominated by the symphonies of Beethoven and the later European masters such as Tchaikovsky, Dvořák, Brahms, and Goldmark.

At the end of April he returned to Pesaro, working frantically to finish *Iris*. By the end of May he finished orchestrating the first act and began on the second, which he hoped to finish by the end of June. He was driven by his determination to make *Iris* something new and different, not only in his own catalogue, but in Italian opera; as he wrote Ricordi, "I have studied intensely how I can extract every effect possible and imaginable from the instruments. I am creating a true symphonic poem, far removed from the orchestration of all other operas."

At the same time, he was engaged in preparations for the elaborate observances to be held in the nearby town of Recanati in honor of the centenary of the birth of their greatest native, the poet and philosopher Giacomo Leopardi. In addition to preparing programs for four concerts with the Liceo orchestra, he also found time to compose a major new work for the event, a symphonic poem for orchestra with soprano entitled *A Giacomo Leopardi*, also known as the *Poema*.

With his orchestra reinforced by experienced orchestral players brought in for the occasion, Mascagni's Recanati concerts, attended by much of the Italian musical establishment, were a great success. The *Poema* was enthusiastically received, although the reaction of the writer for the *Corriere della Sera* was mixed:

> *Its success was great, unquestionable. Mascagni's work constitutes without a doubt a beautiful page of music. Some sections . . . including the finale are exquisitely worked; just the same, the wave of sensual music that dominates the* Poema *seemed not entirely consistent with the spirit of [Leopardi's] poetry and the reality of the poet's life. Nevertheless, there is no little amount of good in the work.*

Looking at it today, that reaction seems generous. Mascagni's *Poema* is an ambitious work on a large scale, but not a successful one.

Mascagni, who responded to Leopardi in straightforwardly emotional fashion, was unable to find a musical language to capture that dimension of the poet's work that makes him the greatest of Italian poets since Dante: the philosophical depth, the cosmic consciousness, that enables even the simplest of Leopardi's mature works to transcend the commonplace. Instead, he conceived of the *Poema* as a sort of biographical anthology of Leopardi's principal poetic themes, from sadness to the first stirrings of love, through life and love of country to, as he wrote, "death, death desired, invoked, liberating death."

Integrating this many diverse elements into a single coherent and tightly organized framework without a single overarching theme proved impossible for the composer, particularly at a time when *Iris* was engaging his most serious musical concerns. The *Poema*, as a result, is a work of discrete and often poorly integrated sections. Most are attractive, a few are beautiful, but the work never coheres as a satisfactory whole.

Meanwhile, Sonzogno was forcing the issue of the opera promised him in his 1894 contract. Since the previous fall, when it was apparent that Mascagni would not meet the deadlines set forth in that contract, Sonzogno had been repeatedly pressing him to set *Iris* aside and concentrate on the "Commedia." Mascagni, who had yet to receive the complete libretto from Illica, had refused. After an apparently amicable April meeting with Sonzogno, at which time the publisher had extended the time for delivery of the new opera until the fall of 1898, a date which both knew to be unrealistic, the composer continued to concentrate on finishing *Iris.*

In June, however, when Ricordi announced *Iris* for the fall at Rome's Costanzi Theater, Sonzogno changed his mind. Realizing that the "Commedia" was still far from complete, he refused to wait any longer. In order to put pressure on Mascagni to abandon *Iris,* he began once again to withhold the royalty payments due the composer on his operas. Mascagni was stunned, writing Illica, "I seriously believe that Sonzogno wants to put an end to dealing with me; perhaps he lacks faith in my music, perhaps my contracts are too burdensome for him, perhaps there are other reasons; but the fact is that I believe that Sonzogno wants to break with me once and for all." As he would soon learn, his judgment was not far off the mark.

Matters hung fire until the end of 1898, when Mascagni and Sonzogno reached a new agreement, amending the 1894 contract. The composer was relieved of his obligation to provide the publisher with a second opera, and the deadline for the "Commedia" was extended to March 1900. While the new agreement called for "reestablishing between author and publisher an amicable relationship, based on the faithful performance of their respective obligations and a scrupulous respect for their respective rights," it did little more than paper over the underlying conflict between these two strong-willed and increasingly antagonistic individuals.

IRIS MAKES ITS DEBUT

Finally, by the beginning of October, *Iris* was finished. Written in fits and starts, it had taken over two years, far longer than any previous Mascagni opera. On the twenty-first Mascagni left for Rome, taking an apartment for his family a block from the theater. The first performance of the opera was scheduled for November 19.

From the start of rehearsals, the atmosphere in the theater was strained and poisonous. Mascagni was tense and irritable. He had not been happy with Ricordi's choice of Edoardo Mascheroni to conduct *Iris*, having written Ricordi in June, "I won't hide from you that I learned of [Mascheroni's] hiring with some sadness, considering that in Milan I had made it clear to you that Mascheroni was not a saint in my calendar." Although Mascheroni was on the podium, the composer was everywhere else, fighting, criticizing, and making changes. After two weeks of rehearsal, everyone was at one another's throat, prompting Illica, who was trying to keep the peace, to send a letter to Ricordi in Milan: "The moment one incident is over, another one begins, and these incidents are far from the usual cases of nerves, bad tempers, and gossiping. Everything is completely insane here. . . . As far as the overall impression of the opera is concerned, I can't tell you a thing; if I had to give you my judgment, I would say that *Iris* is an opera fit only for the madhouse."

That same day, after one last fight with Mascagni, Mascheroni put down his baton—according to one account, snapped it in pieces and threw them at the composer—and stormed out of the theater. Returning to his hotel, he packed quickly and left Rome, although not before sending off a letter to the *Tribuna*, a major Roman daily newspaper, writing sarcastically, "Dear Maestro, desirous of leaving to you the pleasure of conducting your new opera *Iris*, I am willingly ceding my position." The composer's equally sarcastic response appeared the next day, followed by Mascheroni's. The two did not speak to one another for nearly twenty-two years, until they finally made peace in the summer of 1920.

Although the break with Mascheroni may have been predictable, the composer's increasingly erratic behavior during the rehearsals was less so. By November Mascagni was exhausted from the incessant labor of the previous months, anxious about his still unresolved conflict with Sonzogno, and full of foreboding for the opera on which his future depended. A week before the first performance, now set for November 22, as Giulio Ricordi arrived in Rome to try to take control of matters, Mascagni lapsed into depression. As Adami, Ricordi's biographer, describes the scene:

> [*Ricordi*] *arrived at the theater punctually at the hour set for the rehearsal. . . . But Mascagni wasn't there. He waited for him. Minutes, quarter hours, half hours, and the maestro did not arrive. What could have happened? Ricordi found out when, to resolve matters, he went to Mascagni's apartment and found himself facing this scene:*

the composer immobile, in bed, his head tragically gripped in his hands, with his children around him on their knees, crying out, as instructed by their mother, "Papa, get up; papa, get up."

Finally, the publisher, adopting his most authoritative manner, was able to convince the distraught composer to get out of bed and return to the theater.

Mascagni was never able to assert full control over the musicians assembled for the first performance. While the orchestra, despite some unhappiness over Mascheroni's precipitous departure, responded well to the composer's direction, the singers were another matter. Fernando De Lucia's unhappiness may have carried over into what was a distinctly substandard performance, of which Colombani wrote that he "sang less well than both his vocal resources and his artistic intelligence had led one to expect," while the singers generally, as Mascagni later complained, improvised "pauses, accents, tone colors, and a thousand other things."

Iris's premiere was a gala event in the Roman cultural calendar. Queen Margherita was there, accompanied by the entire Roman aristocracy. The grand old man of Italian poetry, Giosuè Carducci, was there, with a blue rose in his buttonhole, along with Gabriele D'Annunzio, eager to hear the latest work of the "bandmaster" he had reviled in print six years before. The musical world was represented by Puccini, Franchetti, Boito, and a host of others, including Siegfried Wagner, Richard Wagner's son and an important composer in his own right, and by critics from every part of Europe. A telegraphic office had been set up behind the second row of boxes, enabling news of the premiere to reach every corner of the world within seconds.

In the intensely competitive Italian operatic world, Mascagni urgently needed a major success. It had been over three years since he had last presented the public with a major new opera. *Guglielmo Ratcliff,* although well received, had not entered the repertory, and by 1898 performances of the work had become rare. *Silvano* and *I Rantzau* had disappeared entirely, and even the popular *L'Amico Fritz* had begun to lose ground to the exciting new operas that had appeared since. Only *Cavalleria* retained its unbroken hold on the Italian public. The competition was getting stiffer. *La Bohème* had proven that Puccini's *Manon Lescaut* had been no fluke, while *Andrea Chénier* had established Giordano as an important figure to be reckoned with.

The opera that Mascagni was presenting to the public after his long silence was a challenging and difficult work. While Mascagni, Illica, and Ricordi all hoped that the subject would appeal to the growing fin de siècle taste for the exotic, it was nonetheless potentially repellent to those not attuned to the decadent winds blowing from Paris and Vienna. Mascagni had written music for *Iris* that was far removed from the crowd-pleasing vulgarities of *Cavalleria*, as he told Eugenio Checchi just before the first performance:

> *I want* Iris *to be judged as a work of art conceived as a whole, written according to my own criteria, with ideas that emerged from my own imagination. Rather than laying on effects, to make it easy for the tenor, the soprano, or the baritone to show off their virtuosity, I have toned down, have minimized [those effects]: there are moments where the interruption created by applause would violate the aesthetic continuity of the opera.*

Iris was a challenge to the Italian opera audience of the time, particularly in its third act, which was to remain for years a source of controversy.

As the house lights dimmed and the curtain rose, the first growling notes of the double bass were heard. At the end of the rousing prelude, the "Inno del sole" (Hymn of the sun), which was soon to become world famous, the audience roared its approval. After a sustained ovation and cries of "bis," Mascagni performed the prelude again. Although the wild demonstrations that greeted the "Inno del sole" were not equaled the rest of the evening, the audience remained enthusiastic throughout the first two acts. Many of the most dramatic moments, such as Osaka's act 1 serenade and Iris's act 2 "Un dì, ero piccina," were acclaimed and repeated, and at the end of the second act, Mascagni took ten curtain calls. As Alberto Gasco wrote, he "was certain to have succeeded, even triumphed." The third act, however, was a different matter.

While the first two acts, however unusual, were still rooted in familiar language, the third act cast the audience adrift. From the moment the curtain rose on the desolate scene of the scavengers scurrying through Edo's refuse heaps, and they heard the first strange, almost atonal, notes of the prelude, the audience started to squirm. "In the course of a few moments," Gasco wrote, "the thermometer went from the boiling point to freezing." As the act continued, the muttering of the audience was followed by an epidemic of coughing, while those eager to hear the music began calling out for silence and others began shouting out their disapproval of the proceedings. Mascagni kept going, seemingly impervious to the near-riot shaking the theater. Slowly, as Hariclea Darclée began Iris's final aria, the audience began to settle down and listen again; finally, as the majestic chords of the "Inno del sole" returned, the climate began once again to warm. At the end, the applause was strong but hardly universal; Mascagni, joined by Illica, took five curtain calls, generated in part, according to one jaundiced reviewer, by the large numbers of Mascagni's "faithful Livornese" in the audience.

The critical reaction to the work was cool, as summarized by Pompei:

The critics, with a few exceptions, were generally severe on the new work. Sharp spears were launched against the libretto, which was judged empty, vague, and incapable of sustaining the least bit of interest—and Mascagni was reproached, with unusual rigor, for his harmonic practices and his abstruse instrumentation. For the majority of critics, Iris was an absolutely unsuccessful opera.

Pompei may have been thinking of Ippolito Valletta, writing in the important journal *Nuova Antologia*:

We have eccentric harmonies, altered intervals, disagreeable movements, leaps rather than orderly progressions, cadences lined up one after another, sudden bursts of unexpected, unappealing, rhythms. . . . his practice of throwing in everything prohibited up to now by musical syntax and good taste, just to come up with something new, seems particularly deplorable and should be condemned.

Valletta concluded by urging Mascagni "to have the courage to abandon the entire rancid baggage of this new musical *japonisme* . . . [and] return to his senses, return quickly to the serene inspiration, the sincerity of feeling, the fundamentally Latin character of his genius."

Although few writers had anything good to say about Illica's libretto, many found much good to say about the music, although there was little agreement among them. Many critics found the third act weak, strange, or uncomfortable, including the eminent Parisotti, who wrote in *Popolo Romano*, "The prelude to the third act is something monotonous and indecipherable. The art of false relations and of diminished and augmented intervals, without respite, renders it incomprehensible; it is more than bizarre, it is insane." Others, such as the writer for *L'Opinione*, found it the most interesting of the three acts, singling out the chorus of the scavengers as being "wonderfully atmospheric and absolutely original." There were a few outright admirers, not only the predictable Checchi in *Fanfulla* but also Spada in *Don Chisciotte*, who wrote: "Not only has Pietro Mascagni carried out his longest, hardest, and most challenging ascent toward his artistic destination, but he has also composed at least three pieces of which no composer today—leaving aside Verdi, who belongs to the ages—could better combine greater depth of technique with a richer vein of genius." Despite the mixed reviews, audiences flocked to the new opera. Even hostile critics recognized that, whatever their own feelings, the work was a hit with the Roman audience. *Iris* was performed fourteen times to packed, wildly cheering houses.

From Rome *Iris* moved on to Milan, where its production under Toscanini's baton prompted further controversy, as the composer, still seething over his Rome experience, took exception to nearly every aspect of the production, not least Toscanini's conducting. On January 26 he denounced the Milan production—which he had not seen—in a letter to Ricordi, writing, "What, however, has surprised me more than anything, has been the fact that Toscanini has gotten all the tempi wrong. How could that happen? Couldn't you and Tito have straightened him out?"

With Ricordi firmly in control of the Milan production, Mascagni could do no more than snipe from the sidelines, and the production went forward under Toscanini's baton. Despite the conductor's efforts, the Milan critics were even cooler to the opera than their Roman colleagues, and the first performance, at least, was poorly received. As at Rome, though, the public warmed to the new work, and each performance was noticeably more successful than the one before. *Iris* had a respectable run of ten performances in Milan to growing, enthusiastic, audiences. Toscanini himself went on to conduct *Iris*, the sole Mascagni opera for which he felt genuine enthusiasm, often, both in Italy and at the Metropolitan Opera in New York.

Despite its equivocal baptism, *Iris* soon won a substantial following, both in Italy and in Latin America. Although it is no longer part of the Italian repertory, it was close to a standard work during Mascagni's lifetime. As it became better known, it even obtained critical respectability; in 1910 the severe Bastianelli, stating that it was the only Mascagni opera "worthy of being considered a sister to *Cavalleria*," concluded, paraphrasing Osaka's lines, that "despite the theatrical *japonisme*, despite the many defects, of which the worst is its pseudo-symbolism, this opera has a soul."

For Mascagni, *Iris*'s success was of inestimable significance. Precisely at the point when such a demonstration was most needed, he had shown the Italian musical world that he was still a dynamic figure, still actively competing for the laurels offered to Italy's most successful operatic composers. After the success of *Iris*, the premiere of Mascagni's next opera, now eagerly awaited, would be an even more momentous event.

IRIS

Despite Illica's 1894 description of *Iris* as "a Japanese subject taken from the legend 'The Girl in Love with Flowers,'" it is doubtful that the subject of *Iris* is truly of Japanese origin. No story resembling *Iris* appears in any readily available collection of Japanese legends or folk tales, while the distinguished scholar of Japanese literature Donald Keene commented in a note to me, "My guess is that the story does not come from a Japanese source. . . . I have no

idea what Illica's notes might mean, but there were many phony Japanese stories in circulation at the time." For all its trappings, the story itself has nothing particularly Japanese about it; as Cesare Orselli notes, "In *Iris* we find expressed the creed of a belle époque seducer, . . . while [the Yoshiwara] is no
more than an elegant Roman bordello, barely disguised."

It is more likely that Illica found his inspiration in the symbolist and
decadent writers of the time, above all in Joris-Karl Huysmans's 1884 novel
À rebours (Against the grain). *À rebours* was perhaps the most widely read
novel of the period, and its enervated hero, the Baron Des Esseintes, became
a model for a generation of youthful poseurs. Osaka, the opera's jaded libertine, is a simplified Des Esseintes in Japanese garb; the episode in the novel
in which Des Esseintes pursues and then abandons a beautiful acrobat, of
which Huysmans writes, "Although, just at first, the freshness and splendor
of her beauty had surprised Des Esseintes and kept him captivated, it was not
long before he sought to sever the connexion and bring about a speedy rupture, for his premature impotency grew yet more marked when confronted
with the icy woman's caresses and prudish passivity," might well have been
Illica's inspiration for the encounter between Osaka and the childlike, passive
Iris that forms the dramatic center of the opera.

Setting the opera in Japan, however, served many purposes. Japan, to
fin de siècle Europe, was still more an imaginary land than part of the modern world, a mysterious land of kimono-clad maidens and sword-bearing
samurai occupying a picturesque landscape presided over by Mount Fuji.
That exotic setting offered the distance that Illica needed to create an abstract, symbolic world for the opera, in which the story would be free of
realistic associations and in which his fantasies could bloom unhindered.
While Illica did more to create a credible Japanese atmosphere than he is often given credit for, working in generally accurate references to samisens,
kamuros, and Edo's Simonoseki market, he had no interest in recreating an
authentic Japanese environment. His decision to name his leading characters
after the Japanese cities of Osaka and Kyoto, rather than give them credible
Japanese names, was neither an ignorant nor offhand gesture, but a deliberate reminder that *Iris*'s Japan is a symbolic, metaphorical land, not to be confused with the real thing.

The Japanese setting also offered a rich vocabulary of visual and poetic
images for *Iris*, linking it intimately to the art nouveau movement, a movement that drew deeply from Japanese art for its inspiration. The opera's title
itself is significant; the iris, a flower important in the Japanese decorative arts,
was, in its distinctive sinuosity and delicate patterning, almost the emblem-
atic image of art nouveau. Illica's libretto, with its luxuriant floral imagery, its

vampires, and its juxtapositions of light and darkness, blood and tears, lies squarely at the intersection of art nouveau with the symbolist, decadent poetry of Baudelaire, Mallarmé, and Rimbaud. *Iris* is the supreme reflection of art nouveau on the operatic stage, arguably the only Italian art nouveau opera.

Mascagni faced the overwhelming task of finding a musical counterpart to the language and visual imagery of Illica's libretto. In contrast to Puccini's approach to *Madama Butterfly*, Mascagni had no interest in salting his score with authentic Japanese melodies. His interest in Japanese music was limited to the creation of musical color, reflected in the entrance of the puppet show in the first act and the opening of the second, where violin, flute, and harp conjure up a mysterious oriental air, a musical parallel to Illica's use of Japanese words as a decorative element in the libretto.

Mascagni was far more interested in finding ways of creating a musical atmosphere to parallel the particular sinuosity of Illica's art nouveau imagery. *Iris*'s music is far more chromatic than that of any earlier work of the composer; in addition, he uses a recurrent winding motif, moving up and down by a semitone (such as F–E–F, or F♯–G–F♯), in many of the most important moments of the music. This motif appears in Osaka's principal solos, including the famous first-act serenade, "Apri la tua finestra," and in many orchestral passages, including the theme that comes to stand for Iris's beauty in the second act, as well as the third-act prelude. The third-act prelude is Mascagni's finest achievement in tone painting; a work of otherworldly mystery, it blends chromaticism and the whole-tone scale to create a musical counterpart to Illica's overwrought lines: "The three sinister nights: the starless night of the heavens, the night of the stagnant waters reflecting nothing back, the tearless night of nature's indifference."

Mascagni is not Debussy, and the magnitude of *Iris*'s departures from the Italian operatic language of the time should not be overstated. Although the conservative audiences of the day saw *Iris* as new and different, to today's audiences it clearly belongs to its time and place. What is significant is the plasticity of Mascagni's language and the extent to which he was able to mold it to fit Illica's libretto. *Iris* is instantly recognizable as Mascagni, and yet it has a melodic, harmonic, and orchestral *tinta* that distinguishes it instantly from any of his other operas.

Iris contains fewer of the long-limbed melodies and arias that Italian audiences had come to expect from Mascagni. In their place, however, he has strewn his score so liberally with short motives, themes, melodies, and ideas of such variety that much of *Iris* has an almost shimmering quality. Mascagni, a great melodist, was at the peak of his powers in *Iris*, prodigal with fresh, moving musical ideas, from the cellos' opening theme in the "Inno del sole" to the scavenger's song to the moon, piercing through the dark, scurrying noises of the third act.

Iris has its set pieces, few but important. Osaka's serenade, which he sings in his role as the sun god during the first-act puppet show, is the closest *Iris* comes to a conventional aria. While it is an effective showpiece, it is far more than that. It is a cell from which much of the opera springs. Much of the second act, including the central scene between Iris and Osaka, grows out of its distinctive melodic matrix, while Iris's disconsolate singing of the same melody later in that act, as she holds the sun god puppet in her arms, is perhaps the most poignant moment in the opera, one of the few moments in which the human misery of the story breaks through Illica's symbolic trappings. The other set pieces are Iris's two scenes in the second act: the touching "Io pingo" as she wakes up in the pleasure house of the Yoshiwara, and "Un dì, ero piccina," also known as the "Aria della piovra" (Octopus aria).

This justly famous scene is Iris's description of a screen she had seen in a Buddhist temple as a small child, depicting "the shores of a great dead sea . . . and a blood-red sky" on which a monstrous octopus is coiling its tentacles around a young woman, as a priest intones, "That octopus is Pleasure . . . that octopus is Death!" Mascagni has set this scene using a fast, even tempo in which the harmony changes on every beat, so that one feels that it is being sung almost in a single breath, all leading up to the climax on the priest's fateful words. It is breathtaking, a tour de force for the singer, and a moment of overwhelming dramatic impact.

Iris sings for the last time in the third act, over which Illica and Mascagni had so much difficulty. This act encapsulates the opera's symbolic images. It opens in near darkness, as grotesque figures move around with lanterns and hooks, looking for treasures in the swamps at the edge of the city. They discover the battered and unconscious Iris, begin to strip off her finery, but flee when a movement reveals she is still alive. As she lies there whispering "why?" she hears offstage voices, the "egoisms" of Osaka, Kyoto, and her father, expounding a cynical, heartless view of the world. As she once again asks her agonized "why?" the sun begins to rise, and she turns to it for salvation. As she sinks and dies, we hear the strains of the "Inno del sole" once again, and she is transported toward the sun as flowers rise from the fetid swamp, and the stage is brilliantly illuminated with the light of day.

It is musically superb, from its hushed, mysterious opening to the orchestra's and chorus's blazing away at the end, yet it is unclear what it all *means*, from the cynical words of the "egoisms" to Illica's mystical idea of Iris's union with the sun, giver of light, giver of life. Therein, perhaps, lies the central difficulty with *Iris*. The distance that Illica sought in order to create his abstract, symbolic world creates a barrier between the audience and the characters of the opera, undermining the emotional impact of the events depicted onstage, without providing any truly transcendent vision with which to replace it. Iris is less an innocent, beautiful girl than a symbol of innocence and beauty, except for a few isolated moments when the music allows her humanity to break through the wall created by the libretto. For all the terrible things that befall her, the audience is less likely to be moved by her plight than they are by Puccini's Butterfly, even in a mediocre performance.

Iris is still performed today, but not often. The lack of emotional connection with the audience, coupled with the substantial difficulty of successfully casting and producing the opera, means that it is unlikely to be a candidate for the standard repertory in the future. Still, of all of the less-known operas of Mascagni, there is none more worthy of regular revival than *Iris*, for the sheer quality of its music, and, despite its weaknesses, for its strange, compelling power as a work of musical theater.

8. Le Maschere *and the Pesaro Disaster,*

1899—1902

At the end of March 1899, with *Iris* successfully launched, Mascagni returned to Pesaro. He now had a complete draft libretto for his new opera, which had been baptized *Le Maschere* (The Masks), and was nearly ready to begin serious work. The next few months, though, were fully occupied with preparing the student concerts and the year's final examinations. Then, late in May, Mascagni learned that his father, who had been failing for months, was near death. He left Pesaro immediately, only to find on his arrival in Livorno that his father had already slipped into a coma. He died the next day. Soon afterward Mascagni wrote Illica, "He died without recognizing me, without ever knowing that I was there, by his bed, . . . he never recognized his own Pietro; he died without knowing that he was surrounded by my care, by my sacred affection."

His father's death was rendered even more painful by his inability to speak to his father, or hear his father speak, in their final moments. All his life, Mascagni had desperately tried to show himself worthy of his father's love. After leaving Livorno in 1882, he wrote him time and again, trying to convince him that he had indeed chosen an honorable path and that the success he was seeking was not far off. As early as 1884, while still a struggling student, he began to send his father money, writing him just before New Year's

Day 1885, "I will send you ten more lire, so that in these days that I won't be among you, you will think of me more happily."

His efforts to buy his father's approval never ended. Even when living from hand to mouth as a traveling musician, he continued to send his father money, or apologized abjectly if unable to do so. After the success of *Cavalleria* Mascagni lavished money on his father, arranging for him to leave the bakery, paying off his considerable debts, and making sure that he could live his last years in comfort and contentment. Domenico Mascagni came to take an almost belligerent pride in his son's fame, writing his sister-in-law Maria in San Miniato in 1892, "It is well known already that Pietro's bursting in so suddenly and successfully on the modern music scene has hit a lot of people the wrong way, and they'll try any kind of foul play to knock him down."

It was one thing, however, for the taciturn Tuscan to write his sister-in-law, and another to admit to his son that he had misjudged him and his choice of a career. In the years after *Cavalleria's* appearance, there is no evidence that Mascagni, despite the money and the protestations of love and affection that he lavished on his father, ever received the approval he was seeking. His hopeless struggle is mirrored in the uncomprehending or angry paternal figures that appear in so many of his operas, whose indifference or hostility brings on their children's destruction. *Iris's* blind father, who curses her and who can think only of himself as she lies dying, is but one of many such figures.

On Mascagni's return to Pesaro he plunged back into work in the hope that it would relieve his depression, but as he wrote Illica, "I feel like I'm dying. I can't sleep anymore . . . the long, interminable, nights are an utter agony for me. O Gigi, I can't work anymore: my mind is gone, my body is sick." His drive to compose, though, soon asserted itself. Before the end of June he had started work, and by the end of August he would write enthusiastically, albeit overoptimistically, "*Le Maschere* is going magnificently! I'm almost sure to have it done in two months. It will be given in the Carnival season [early 1900]."

Illica's libretto, although not taken from any actual commedia dell'arte scenario, closely followed traditional models. The "masks" from which the opera draws its title are the characters themselves, the stock figures of the tradition: Pantalone, the avaricious father; Florindo and Rosaura (Pantalone's daughter), the lovers; Captain Spavento, the vainglorious military man; Arlecchino, Columbina, and so forth. The story is simplicity itself. Florindo and Rosaura are in love, but Pantalone has promised Rosaura's hand to Captain Spavento. The lovers' allies prevent the signing of the marriage contract by releasing a magical powder that sends everyone into a state of babbling confusion. The next morning, Captain Spavento is revealed as a liar, bigamist, and cheat, and Pantalone reluctantly agrees to allow Rosaura to marry Florindo.

As Mascagni gradually came to realize as he became more deeply immersed in the libretto, it is too simple. The magic powder is thin stuff. As Baldacchi has written, Mascagni "intuitively understood that a dramatic treatment extended through an introduction and three acts could not be based on such an insipid invention." In October 1899, after an extended visit with Illica, Mascagni wrote him that "as to the new powder, I can't be specific yet: on first sight I have the impression that it's too simple, seeing as it is the principal idea of the comedy. I would have liked it heavier, more satirical."

Although the magic powder was not to become the bone of contention that the third act of *Iris* had been, it was a serious problem, in that it was almost the entirety of Illica's modest plot. At this late date he was unwilling to consider any fundamental changes to his scheme, defending it vociferously to Sonzogno: "First of all, I must tell you that the commedia dell'arte, far from being a simple matter, is instead a very complicated one. Whether written or improvised, it was always a 'comedy of intrigue.'" Not only did Illica miss Mascagni's point entirely, but he also lacked feeling for the clockwork complexity of relationships and misunderstandings that were the essence of the commedia.

For once, Mascagni ducked a potential confrontation. For all his objections, he had immense respect and affection for his librettist, as well as his own emotional investment in the work. Unwilling to risk all in defense of his judgment, he abandoned his position, writing Illica on December 22, "So be it, the second act finale stays." Illica appeased the composer with minor changes, and peace was restored. Meanwhile, Mascagni had already written much of the opera, including the overture and large parts of the first and third acts.

By the end of 1899 matters had become far more complicated for the beleaguered director of the Liceo Rossini, already under attack for his extended absences from the conservatory during the year. Although he still retained the confidence of Guidi-Carnevali and the governing board of the conservatory, attacks on him by the Pesaro city council led to an inspection of the Liceo Rossini by a delegation appointed by the minister of public instruction, including such distinguished figures as Arrigo Boito and Filippo Marchetti. Arriving in February 1900, the team, while acknowledging Mascagni's excessive absenteeism, found that the school was properly run and went so far as to suggest that the council was excessively involved in the management of the conservatory. Although the immediate issue was put to rest, the episode added to the bad feeling between Mascagni and a substantial part of the community's more prominent citizens.

Guidi-Carnevali died in February 1900. He had never wavered in his support for the man he had recruited in 1895 and had kept the board solidly behind him, despite pressure from the city council. Under Benedetto Passeri-Modi, the new president, Mascagni could no longer count on the board's unconditional support. Beyond his students and some of the faculty, Mascagni had few friends left in Pesaro.

Mascagni never understood the need for tact and sensitivity in his dealings with politicians and civic leaders, and he could not tolerate the involvement of those he considered musically incompetent in the conservatory's affairs. All that mattered to him about the Liceo was the quality of the music and the musicians that it produced and its reputation in musical circles, not its position in the social and cultural life of the city. In his heedless, insensitive way, he managed to antagonize numerous individuals who might otherwise have become his supporters and defenders.

Despite the battles in Pesaro, Mascagni continued to work on *Le Maschere* through the fall and into the winter. By February 1900 *Le Maschere* was all but complete except for a few sections for which its composer still awaited further revisions from Illica. Meanwhile, Sonzogno, who had already promised the work to Rome's Teatro Adriano for its fall 1900 season, announced that the premiere would also take place in his own theater, Milan's Teatro Lirico.

Mascagni put *Le Maschere* aside again in February, leaving for Venice to deliver a public lecture, "The Evolution of Music in the Twentieth Century," and continuing on for a concert tour of Russia. Mascagni's appearance in Venice, which attracted so much attention that the event had to be moved from a lecture hall to the Goldoni theater, was his debut in yet another role, that of orator. Famous for his verbal agility in a land where oratory was a popular spectator sport, it was inevitable that sooner or later he would add public speaking to his activities. His orations, like those of his contemporaries, were carefully staged performances; lasting well over an hour, they would be admired as much for their elegant turns of phrase, dramatic perorations, and rhetorical set pieces as for the continuity and precision of their analysis.

"The Evolution of Music" was representative of the genre. More than an hour and a half long, it was less a single discourse than a series of discussions, analytical and anecdotal in turn, on different themes whose relationship to one another is not always entirely clear. In the end, however, he tied his themes together, concluding that each nation has its own musical character, and that each nation's musical character is reflected in both a musical vocabulary and specific musical forms.

Mascagni's lecture, which he repeated in Ferrara and in Ancona, received considerable public attention. In March excerpts were published in the

Cronaca Musicale, and it appeared later that year as a pamphlet. Buoyed by his success, he gave two more public lectures that spring, speaking on Verdi in Florence and in Bari on the eighteenth-century composer Niccolò Piccinni. He was soon in much demand as a speaker, both on general topics such as "The Evolution of Music" and at commemorative events honoring famous musical figures. He devoted considerable attention to his lectures, carefully seeking to match his subject to his audience. After being invited to speak at the Università Popolare in Milan in 1903, he wrote Gianfranceschi: "I must find a specialized theme with which I can comfortably present a new side of myself to the Ambrosian public, one in which my public image and my name figure minimally. . . . Furthermore, under no circumstances do I want to present myself to Milan as a library mouse, with notes and citations and opinions pulled out of old books."

The lecture Mascagni eventually gave was entitled "The Opera of the Future."

SIX FIASCOS AND ONE SUCCESS

Although by the spring of 1900 Mascagni was enthusiastically finishing *Le Maschere,* relations between him and its publisher had deteriorated badly. The composer was unhappy with Sonzogno's plan to hold a simultaneous premiere in Milan, which he considered unfair to the Adriano Theater, and he had yet to receive the five thousand lire due him on the delivery of the prologue and first act of *Le Maschere,* which had been in Sonzogno's hands for some months. The publisher had resumed the practice, specifically barred in their current agreement, of subtracting a 5 percent "commission" from gross rentals before calculating the composer's 30 percent royalty, while the sharp-eyed Lina, who routinely reviewed Sonzogno's royalty statements, kept finding discrepancies, invariably to the composer's disadvantage.

Matters were patched up once again, and the opera continued to move forward. By the fall Mascagni was writing Illica, "I don't know when I eat, when I sleep: I am totally absorbed in orchestrating *Le Maschere.* Imagine, I have reached a point of scoring thirty-five pages a day . . . that is, a night. Bear in mind that it has more than a thousand pages." The sheer volume of notes for this fast-paced work was far greater than in any of his earlier operas. "When *Le Maschere* is printed," he added, "it will be fatter than *Tosca* and *Iris* put together."

Meanwhile, the controversy surrounding Mascagni's role as director of the Liceo Rossini raged. During the summer of 1900 the conservatory was

investigated both by Giovanni Tebaldini, director of the Parma Conservatory, hired by the city council, and by Giovanni Sgambati, the distinguished
composer and professor at the Santa Cecilia Conservatory in Rome. Although
the council refused to release Tebaldini's report, Sgambati strongly affirmed
Mascagni's leadership, writing, "Maestro Mascagni's direction has unques-
tionably conferred luster and popularity on the Liceo Rossini. His authority,
creativity, and goodwill and the prestige of his name have yielded all those
benefits possible except where difficulties have been created, often paralyz-
ing his authority." In September, his report still unreleased, the embarrassed
Tebaldini wrote Mascagni directly, stating that in his report he had expressed
his convictions "sincerely, trying above all to put into evidence how much—
under your guidance—the Liceo has accomplished and promises to accomplish." He closed by calling on the composer to remain "steadfast, [showing]
the willpower and the fiber of resistance of which you give proof every day."

By the fall of 1900 the controversy had spread beyond Pesaro's borders
and had started to become fodder for the popular media. Despite the advice
of Italy's senior statesman Giolitti, who urged Mascagni to get out, noting
that "despite all the saints, this world isn't Paradise," the composer dug in his
heels. Short of being fired, he was determined that no one would make him
leave his position at the Liceo Rossini.

Under these inauspicious circumstances, *Le Maschere* approached its January 1901 debut. The unprecedented decision to hold it not in one major theater, as was customary, or even two, but in seven major opera houses across
Italy on the same January night was to add further to the seemingly incessant
stream of controversy swirling around Mascagni's head. While this decision
colored both the public and the critical reactions to the opera and would hang
like a millstone around Mascagni's neck for the rest of his life, any effort to
determine precisely how it came about can be no more than speculation.

Less than a year before, as the opera neared completion, neither Mascagni nor Sonzogno was thinking in grandiose terms about its premiere. Indeed, the original plans for its fall 1900 debut, in which Rome's Adriano,
along with the Teatro Lirico, figured, were unusually modest. Both were secondary houses and rarely the sites of important premieres. The choice may
have been purely pragmatic, since the major houses were generally closed in
the fall, or may have been suggested by the intimate character of the work.

With the opera's debut delayed until January 1901, a premiere at a major house now became possible, but the question of which theater remained.
According to Pompei, the multiple premieres originated in a disagreement
between Mascagni and Sonzogno: "The composer had promised the pre-

miere to the Costanzi [in Rome], and the publisher was instead obligated to give the work to La Scala; neither wanting, or able, to give way to the other, they had recourse to the expedient of giving the opera in both theaters on the same night." This is plausible enough, given the stubborn streak both shared; indeed, something similar would happen with the first Italian performance of Mascagni's *Isabeau* in 1912. But it does not explain how two simultaneous premieres would blossom into seven.

Arranging for a new opera to be simultaneously inserted into the seasons of seven different theaters was a difficult undertaking. Since most Italian opera houses took their season's repertory exclusively from either Sonzogno or Ricordi, it was not easy for a publisher to induce an impresario to add a new opera to a season made up of works provided by the other—as was the case at both La Scala and the Carlo Felice—particularly on short notice. The massive organizational effort necessary to create the multiple premieres of *Le Maschere* was within Sonzogno's reach, but not Mascagni's, and demanded far more of Sonzogno than of Mascagni. This would argue that the scheme was more the publisher's doing than the composer's. Even assuming that to be the case, Mascagni responded warmly to the idea. Not only did it fit his own self-promotional bent, but it also reflected his convictions about the opera that he was about to present to the Italian public.

Le Maschere, for Mascagni, was not just another opera. It was a polemic on behalf of a vanishing Italian tradition, as he commented in an interview:

> To enable the commedia dell'arte to emerge once again . . . seems to me to be a work worthy of an artist of conscience. Did not Rossini, the great optimist of our theater, draw from the pure springs of the commedia dell'arte in The Barber of Seville? And why . . . shouldn't one of us try to open the gloomy atmosphere of the contemporary theater a crack to let in that smile, that joyful and serene satire, and link our own activity to that glorious tradition?

For an opera that he had come to think of almost as a cultural manifesto, he was unlikely to consider any number of simultaneous premieres excessive. Meanwhile, in keeping with the temper of the times, a rumor rapidly spread that Mascagni had dedicated his new score "to myself, as a gesture of esteem and constant affection." Although untrue and easily disproved, it was widely believed, confirming the already strong convictions of the many observers who believed that Mascagni's egomania had burst all reasonable bounds.

The seven theaters assembled for the premiere were the Costanzi in Rome, La Scala in Milan, the Carlo Felice in Genoa, the San Carlo in Naples, the Regio in Turin, La Fenice in Venice, and the Filarmonico in Verona, all but the last generally recognized as Italy's principal opera theaters. Only six theaters actually shared the simultaneous premiere, as the Neapolitan performance was delayed two days because of the tenor Anselmi's indisposition.

An impressive array of singers and conductors was assembled for the event. In Milan, the young Caruso sang with Emma Carelli under Toscanini's baton, while other prominent conductors included Edoardo Vitale in Genoa and Leopoldo Mugnone in Naples. Agide Jacchia, Mascagni's former pupil, with only two years of professional experience behind him, had been retained to conduct in Venice, where another recent Pesaro graduate, Maria Farneti, sang the role of Rosaura. Two other Liceo graduates, Umberto Macnez and Pietro Schiavazzi, sang the role of Arlecchino, in Verona and in Naples. Mascagni himself conducted the Rome performance, assisted by Roberto Moranzoni, another former student.

The rehearsals were largely free of the conflict that characterized the preparation of *Iris*. Mascagni arrived at the Costanzi Theater "smiling, easygoing, utterly calm . . . not with the fury of Brünnhilde's father but with the innocent, noisy gaiety of a student on vacation." Signs of future difficulty, however, if not outright disaster, were visible. Despite the sprinkling of stars, most of the singers retained for the performances were journeymen of modest attainments or promising young singers with scant professional experience; one singer's accomplishments were so limited that the most a promotional booklet could say of him was that he was "a modest artist, but very useful."

It was impossible to ensure the quality of all seven productions. The role of stage director hardly existed in the Italian operatic world. To the extent that the staging of an opera was to be more than the sum of the stock gestures of its singers, it was the duty of the conductor, the composer, or the librettist to provide the necessary direction. Given the modest dramatic values expected by the audiences of the time, this rarely posed a serious problem. Singers soon learned how to move through the better-known operas that made up the heart of the repertory, while most new operas required little more of the conductor or composer than straightforward blocking to create a framework within which the singers could employ their traditional gestures. *Le Maschere* was different. It demands agile, athletic, singing actors, with some roles demanding singers who can dance. Even once a proper cast is assembled, a daunting task in 1901, they must mesh with as much precision of timing and gesture as in a Feydeau farce.

Mascagni was accustomed to taking charge of staging the operas he conducted, but he could not exert control over seven productions spread across the country. Although Illica spent the weeks before opening night rushing between the five northern cities involved in the extravaganza, and Mascagni made one extended tour to all seven theaters, it is likely that none of the productions outside Rome offered more than a pallid impression of the dramatic quality of Mascagni's comedy.

Finally, on the evening of January 17, 1901, after an unusually cold day, *Le Maschere* was ready to face the public. As Mascagni stepped onto the podium a few minutes past nine in Rome, five other conductors did the same in five other theaters. The outcome is well known. Other than the warm reception in Rome, the evening was a disaster for Mascagni and his new opera. In many theaters the opening moments, when the actor who plays Giocadio, the stage manager, breaks into the overture and begins to expound on the point of the work, were a signal for booing and hissing to begin, suggesting that the disaster may have been in part orchestrated by claques hostile to the composer. From that inauspicious start, the work rarely regained its ground. In Genoa, the catcalls and whistles at the opening of the third act made it impossible to finish the performance. Although the Milan performance continued to the end, it too was a disaster; the critic for the *Corriere della Sera* wrote, "Already during the first act, the public seemed truly attacked by an untamable fury." When Columbina began her short "Cuor di macigno" aria, their fury exploded, as "a long mocking cry of amazement burst from a thousand mouths. The public recognized the theme." A parody of the composer's own "Aria della piovra" from *Iris,* it was viciously booed. Mascagni's affectionate parodies, of his own music and of Italian composers since Rossini and Bellini, were lost on the audience. "The theater was agitated and boiling. A furious hunt for borrowings, reminiscences, similarities began. At the height of the love duet a voice cried out, *'La Bohème';* another answered, 'Viva Puccini!'"

Although the second act met with greater approval and even a smattering of applause at the end, the audience was tired. After applauding Caruso for his singing of the Serenata early in the third act, they were ready to leave. As soon as the last chords had been heard, the audience beat a rapid retreat with few boos, few hisses, and less applause. The sheer length of *Le Maschere* was a problem not only in Milan. In Turin, too, the audience was worn out by its length, and at the end left unceremoniously. *Le Maschere* was very long, running well over three hours, nearly twice as long as the Rossini comic operas that were its models.

The Roman reception, although warm, was not an unalloyed triumph. While many individual numbers were greeted with enthusiastic applause and cries of "bis," the work as a whole received a mixed response. Although the audience reaction at the end of the second act had been enthusiastic, at the end of the evening the composer was called back to the stage only twice. As with *Iris*, though, Roman enthusiasm for the work grew steadily. Substantially trimmed after the first evening, the opera ended up receiving a remarkable twenty-two performances.

The critical reaction to *Le Maschere* was often more favorable than that of the opening-night audiences. Many reviewers found merit in the score, with Montefiore in the *Tribuna* remarking that "if in *Iris* we noted a step forward on this path [of progress], *Le Maschere* shows us an even more significant step beyond the composer's other works." After praising many individual numbers, however, Montefiore came to an ambivalent conclusion: "On the other hand, Mascagni seems often to have lost his way with the overall balance of his newest work: not so much in the cut of the separate numbers, but in the overall effect the opera makes, coming across highly diffuse, by virtue of the excesses of its poorly conceived and still more poorly structured libretto." He recommended careful but substantial cuts, so that Mascagni's music "so beautiful throughout, [will] be appreciated for its great value, no less than for the admirable purpose with which it is imbued."

Alberto Cametti, in the *Gazzetta Musicale di Milano*, had a similar reaction; after praising the beauty of many of the individual parts of the score, he turned his attention to Illica's effort: "It is clear that Illica was not cut out to give us jolly comedies. Over and above the puerile simplemindedness of the intrigue, the humor of the masks, not always of good quality, is forced and unspontaneous . . . one has the impression that the author is trying to force us to laugh against our will." While Primo Levi (L'Italico) found the opera worthy of its great predecessors, most of the critics would have agreed with the *Messaggero* that "however great Mascagni's talent may be, the successor to Cimarosa and Rossini has not yet arrived."

Although much of the criticism was well deserved, many of the elements in *Le Maschere* that make it most interesting today—the exploration of what was not yet known as neoclassicism, the extensive use of parody, and the Pirandellian prologue, with its interplay between the actors and their roles—mystified both the audiences and the critics of the time. Secure in their faith in the conventions of late nineteenth-century opera, many critics simply could not understand why Illica and Mascagni—or anyone—should have wanted to revive an obsolete and deservedly dead genre.

Finding the right balance for *Le Maschere* was a recurrent preoccupation of the composer for the next thirty years. A revised version was presented in 1905, in which the prologue was set aside and extensive cuts were made in both the second and third acts. Mascagni was not satisfied with this version, considering it too barren and too far from his and Illica's original intentions. In 1931, with the help of Giovacchino Forzano, he prepared the third and definitive version of the opera for La Scala, restoring most of the prologue and much of the music that had been removed in 1905, while retaining the tighter structure, and many of the cuts, of that edition.

Le Maschere waited over a year and a half for another performance, in Bologna in August 1902. It next appeared, after its first revision, at Rome's Teatro Adriano in the fall of 1905. That revival was an unqualified triumph, of which the French critic Charles de Platen wrote enthusiastically: "The composer has shown himself capable of creating a true *opéra comique*, overflowing with youthful humor, tied to such magnificent lyrical beauty that this work, despite the rather old-fashioned and trivial plot, and even more the banal and stupid verses of Illica, has every chance of becoming popular." Although it was revived periodically during Mascagni's lifetime, particularly during the 1930s, Le Maschere has never achieved sustained popularity. It has been performed only rarely in more recent times.

LE MASCHERE

Mascagni's Le Maschere is an attempt to recreate the world of the seventeenth-century commedia dell'arte. A tribute to what Mascagni considered the wellsprings of the Italian opera tradition, it reflects the same desire to challenge the tired conventions of operatic melodrama as had Iris, although in a radically different direction. The result is a pioneering work that, despite its failure at the time, was both musically distinguished and a precursor of many important tendencies in the music of the next generation of composers.

Illica's libretto shows a thorough acquaintance with the traditional traits of the commedia dell'arte players and their interactions with one another. Despite his careful study, however, he failed to capture the dramatic complexity that made the commedia more than a series of speeches and comic routines. The essence of the commedia lies in its ability to keep the audience on the edge of their seats as intrigues and confusions multiply, until all is resolved at the end. Although Illica understood this, he was unable to recreate it. As so many critics pointed out, the dramatic weakness of the libretto is the opera's Achilles' heel.

After the prologue and the overture, the curtain rises on a Venetian square. Florindo and Rosaura are in love, as are Rosaura's maid, Columbina, and Brighella, a peddler. They discover with horror that Rosaura's father, Pantalone, has promised her to Captain Spavento. The Captain arrives with his servant, Arlecchino, who is carrying a fat valise. As the lovers wonder what to do, Brighella offers them a magic powder, promising that if mixed with the wine to be served at the evening's festivities, the powder will make it impossible for the marriage contract to be signed.

In the second act, after a tender scene between Rosaura and Florindo, and an attempt by Arlecchino to win Columbina's heart, the festivities in Pantalone's house begin with singing and dancing. As the powder takes effect, chaos ensues, and the act ends with the entire cast babbling uncontrollably.

As the third act opens the following morning, though, nothing has changed. Rosaura decides to plead with the Captain, while Florindo decides to challenge him to a duel. Columbina sets out to seduce Arlecchino, who reveals that the valise contains documents compromising the Captain. He agrees to bring her the valise, only to discover that it has disappeared. A moment later, Doctor Graziano and Brighella enter with the valise and reveal that the Captain is a liar and a thief and already married. As the Captain is led away, Pantalone reluctantly gives Rosaura to Florindo, and all rejoice.

Le Maschere has little intrigue worthy of the name. The magic powder, of which so much is made in the first two acts, fizzles, while nothing prepares us for the revelations that seal the Captain's fate. Indeed, we never learn how the suitcase came into the Doctor's hands. While Illica's fertile brain has come up with a variety of entertaining moments during the opera's course, they lack dramatic resonance. Even the competition between Arlecchino and Brighella for Columbina's love, which could have made a promising subplot, goes nowhere.

Just the same, the libretto, or perhaps the ideas that it represented, inspired Mascagni. For the only time in his life, he was moved to compose an opera by the sheer intellectual challenge of a creative experiment. With Rossini as his model, he saw the restoration of opera buffa as the musical path to the recreation of the commedia dell'arte. Rather than write imitation Rossini, however, he sought instead to capture the Rossinian spirit while still remaining true to his own muse and his own time and place.

Except for scattered passages of clearly parodistic intent, he made no attempt to change his distinctive melodic vein, and his effort to remain true to himself while working under a somewhat arbitrary body of stylistic constraints proved remarkably fruitful. Those constraints purified his language, removing much of the excess and bombast that mar many of his works. Recreating his style within "Rossinian" boundaries, Mascagni created what is arguably the most important precursor of the next generation's neoclassical efforts, the most thoroughgoing essay in neoclassicism *avant la lettre* yet seen in the musical world.

From its opening D-major chords, *Le Maschere* is insistently diatonic. *Iris*'s unsettled chromaticism is gone, replaced by old-fashioned triads and progressions, resolved with conventional dominant-tonic cadences. The pace of the opera is much faster, and its rhythmic pulse much more regular, than that of any other Mascagni opera. Slow passages, such as Rosaura's letter aria and the second-act love duet, are rare moments of repose, contrasting sharply with the brisk, bubbly, even hyperactive quality of the work.

Le Maschere is an opera of ensembles. While Mascagni and his generation had rejected the formal ensemble typical of early nineteenth-century opera, here he revels in it, relishing the opportunity to play with earlier operatic conventions, from the delightful first-act buffa quartet with its Gilbert-and-Sullivanesque refrain, "Non si firmerà" (It won't be signed), to the exquisite second-act love duet, not one but two third-act quartets, and the magnificent concertato finale that ends the first act. In homage to his old teacher Ponchielli, Mascagni ends his finale by mirroring, step by step, the famous third-act finale of *La Gioconda*. At the very end, though, as the orchestra cuts through the chorus with the predictable *fortissimo* reprise of the big theme, Mascagni has one more trick up his sleeve. After only three bars, the passionate peroration dissolves into a jolly neo-Rossinian phrase, and with a flourish of dominant and tonic chords, the curtain comes down.

The affectionate parody of Ponchielli in the first-act finale is but one of many parodies in *Le Maschere*. Mascagni was not above making fun of himself. In addition to Columbina's "Cuor di macigno" (Heart of stone) aria, the lovers' theme in the first-act finale recalls Osaka's famous serenade from *Iris*. Mascagni evokes a Bellini cantilena for Columbina to sing, "I dream of a worthless man, of the lowest class, a boor with muddy shoes," and when the stuttering Tartaglia finally finds his voice in the midst of the babbling confusion of the second-act finale, he sings a patter song to the tune of "Pizzica, pizzica" from the last act of Verdi's *Falstaff*. As the first-act finale pays homage to Ponchielli, the second is a tribute to Rossini and *The Barber of Seville*.

The parody element in *Le Maschere* was received poorly. The most serious-minded critics were particularly harsh, with Valetta writing:

> *He ends up trying every path, his own and that of others, penetrating into the alleyways of* L'Amico Fritz *and* La Bohème, *halting in the piazzas of Ponchielli and Bizet, praying to all the saints, major and minor, from Bellini, Wagner, and Verdi . . . and winding up as if he is improvising wildly, ending up with an olla potrida, where everyone can find stuff to his taste in the mess, but which . . . is impossible to swallow.*

The unbridled hostility of their reaction seems impossible to understand today. For all of *Le Maschere*'s gestures, the opera is instilled with a thoroughgoing stylistic unity, very much Mascagni's own. To those imbued with the nineteenth-century Romantic aesthetic, however, parody was simply not acceptable behavior for a serious composer such as Mascagni.

Mascagni's parodies are gentle, affectionate gestures to composers with whom he felt a personal as well as musical affinity. Indeed, the entire work is an homage, an extended expression of filial respect to bygone Italian musical and dramatic traditions. This quality may well explain in part why *Le Maschere*, for all its abundance of delightful music, has never won a place in the repertory. It is too respectful. It lacks hard edges.

Although the commedia dell'arte had a sharp satirical quality, that quality was lost as Illica put his characters on pedestals, less restoring the commedia than commenting on it. The opera's characters are not only the classic figures of the commedia but also, as Illica reminds us far too often, its symbol, carrying the weight of Italian tradition on their shoulders. If there is no bite in the opera, neither is there the sort of sustained characterization or emotional quality that can make up for it. Neither Mascagni nor Illica could become part of Rossini's cold-blooded world of unsentimental frivolity, but by trying, they lost the opportunity to give their work the individuality and feeling characteristic of their own aesthetic.

Mascagni's opera, which the 1901 audiences found so unsettling, was soon seen as the precursor of a growing genre. Ermanno Wolf-Ferrari found in *Le Maschere* the inspiration for his Venetian operas based on Goldoni's plays. As a new sensibility emerged in European music, composers of the 1910s and 1920s, including such figures as Busoni, Prokofiev, and Stravinsky, all discovered a kinship—real or imagined—with the commedia dell'arte and opera buffa traditions, leapfrogging backward over a century of Romantic excess. Gavazzeni's conclusion that "Mascagni and Illica stand behind that world with [their] innovative genius" is at worst a modest exaggeration.

It would be a mistake to suggest that *Le Maschere*'s merit lies only in its historic significance. It stands on its own as an entertaining work capable of delighting audiences, full of music in the composer's most successful vein. From the opening bars of the overture, long recognized as one of his finest achievements, to the last bars of the closing chorus, *Le Maschere* is imbued with a charm and a freshness, and at its best a purity of lyrical expression and sentiment unique among Mascagni's major operas.

LOSING GROUND

In the aftermath of the *Le Maschere* fiasco, Mascagni and Sonzogno, in an atmosphere heavy with charges and countercharges, ended their eleven-year relationship. Mascagni, believing himself cheated by Sonzogno and convinced that his works—other than the ubiquitous *Cavalleria*—were being neglected to his competitors' advantage, had lost all faith in his publisher.

Sonzogno, angered by the unsuccessful outcome of Le Maschere and resenting Mascagni's ties to Ricordi, had lost interest in maintaining a relationship with the composer.

With only two opera publishers in Italy and with Sonzogno now behind him, Mascagni was completely dependent on Ricordi. Fortunately, or so it appeared, Ricordi was eager to have a new opera from Mascagni. Iris was increasingly successful, and Ricordi was convinced that a sustained relationship with Mascagni would be both artistically and commercially productive. Since the spring of 1899 he had been waiting patiently, occasionally sending a note to Illica urging him to remind Mascagni of the publisher's continued interest.

Painfully aware that Illica's libretti had generated the harshest criticism of both Iris and Le Maschere, Ricordi decided to enlist Giuseppe Giacosa to work with Illica on a new libretto for Mascagni. While Illica, even without Giacosa, could produce conventionally effective libretti for other composers, his collaboration with Mascagni seemed to reinforce some of his worst characteristics. Mascagni's readiness to embrace change pushed Illica toward new and untried areas, where he was eager to go but was out of his creative depth. A collaboration between Illica and the more thoughtful Giacosa on a Mascagni opera might well have been productive. Although Illica may have had a greater imaginative reach, Giacosa was a better poetic and dramatic craftsman, whose work was far more graceful and better suited for musical treatment than Illica's often crude and overwrought verse.

Illica was still bitter over the reaction to his first two libretti for Mascagni, writing Ricordi that "as soon as you began talking about a new libretto for Mascagni, it was my strong desire to be left on the sidelines"; still, he acceded to Ricordi's proposal out of loyalty to Sor Giulio, hoping that Giacosa would act as a buffer between himself and Mascagni's more arbitrary demands. In the spring of 1901, therefore, he agreed to prepare a scenario for a new libretto, to be versified by him and Giacosa. Although Mascagni too accepted the collaboration, under pressure from both Ricordi and Illica, he was concerned that Giacosa's involvement would delay the production of a new libretto, as both Giacosa and Illica were already involved with Puccini's new opera, Madama Butterfly.

After Mascagni's return in the summer of 1901 from a trip to Vienna, where he conducted Verdi's Requiem as the centerpiece of that city's Verdi memorial observances, Illica presented the composer with a new proposal based on an episode in Dostoevsky's From the House of the Dead. Although it was seemingly an unlikely subject for operatic treatment, Russian topics were in vogue in Italy at the time, as Morini writes: "Nihilism and the horrors of the

Siberian camps for political prisoners were a subject of common conversation. . . . It was only natural that all of this would reach the operatic stage." Illica, in fact, had already written a libretto for Giordano entitled *Siberia*.

Ricordi accepted the proposal, and Mascagni, eager to resume work, agreed to look at an initial treatment. Word soon appeared in the Italian musical press that Mascagni's new opera, to be written by Illica and Giacosa, would be on a Russian theme. Giordano, whose *Siberia* was to debut in the fall at Sonzogno's Lirico Theater in Milan, was upset, writing Illica in August, "That [opera] of Mascagni's is my nightmare. Move the subject to Calabria, Corsica, Hungary, Spain, and you will be doing God's work for me and for him."

Giordano's concern soon resolved itself, as Mascagni, having read Illica's draft of the first two acts, wrote Ricordi, "The basic subject simply does not convince me. . . . It is a dark, gray drama, without a ray of light." The project was abandoned, but not without adding to the strain between Mascagni, Illica, and Giacosa. While Illica wrote Mascagni in October promising a new subject, Giacosa refused to do any more work for Mascagni until he had finished *Madama Butterfly*. Soon realizing that *Butterfly* would require all of his attention for far longer than anticipated, he withdrew entirely from the project. By November, still waiting for the promised scenario, Mascagni wrote Illica, "I am reduced to huddling miserably at the sumptuous gates of the rich, to stretching out my hand, whimpering, 'A bit of libretto, for the love of God!'" He offered Ricordi *Vistilia* as an alternative, but the publisher had little interest in a work that was clearly of only intermittent interest to its own composer. Ricordi wanted a new opera from Mascagni, but on his own terms.

Illica finally presented Mascagni with a new subject in December, based on the story of the ill-fated Marie Antoinette, which the desperate composer reluctantly agreed to accept. With Giacosa out of the picture, Mascagni hoped soon to have a libretto in his hands and wrote Ricordi early in February, "If we are going with *Maria Antonietta* with Illica's libretto, we must start right away. I don't want to lose any more time." As he read about the period, however, Mascagni began to doubt whether the story of Louis XVI and Marie Antoinette offered the material for an effective opera. At the end of the month, he wrote Illica from Vienna explaining his feelings:

> In all that I've read I've found not a single thing that offers any visual, dramatic, or emotional impact. Marie Antoinette is a very simpleminded, ordinary woman; she never had a lover; she is typical of her race and her family; she is primitive and honest in her habits. She had a beautiful death, but nothing up to that point. Louis is decent, plump, has a good appetite, keeps doing stupid things: a true king!

He concluded, "What can we do with these two characters?—A drama?—I don't think it's possible."

It was now a year since he had first discussed a new opera with Ricordi, and he had yet to receive even the first page of a workable libretto. Thoroughly depressed, he added to Illica that he was "beginning really to believe that [he was] destined to accomplish nothing else in [his] life." His life as an operatic composer, in fact, would remain fixed precisely at this point for more than a year, as once again turmoil elsewhere took precedence.

THE FINAL CONFRONTATION AT PESARO

In 1902 matters finally came to a head between Mascagni and the Liceo Rossini. He was spending little time in Pesaro. After passing much of the winter in Rome, Mascagni left in March for a tour of Vienna and eastern Europe, returning to Pesaro only at the end of April. To the outrage of Passeri-Modi, who had ordered him to obtain written approval for his absences, he left again for Rome after only four days. Having let the board know—in a letter from Budapest—that he had been invited to conduct a performance of *Don Giovanni* in Madrid in honor of the coronation of King Alfonso XIII, he left for Spain on May 11. From Madrid he wrote Passeri-Modi a high-handed letter, concluding, "When the citizens of Pesaro finally recognize the need for serenity and peace in the interest of their fine institution, only then will I return to my position," further infuriating the governing board.

Finally returning to Pesaro on June 10, he appeared before the board on the thirteenth, somewhat contrite, and, according to the minutes, "confessed that this year his absences had been excessive, but that he had done it out of spite, because he felt that the administration was trying to make his position impossible." A brief truce was reached while Mascagni and the school prepared for the appearance of the Liceo orchestra at the unveiling of Rossini's tomb in Florence's historic Santa Croce church.

This appearance was Mascagni's last hurrah at the Liceo. Accompanied by a host of Pesaro dignitaries, Mascagni and the orchestra performed at the dedication ceremonies with the tenor Francesco Marconi and gave two well-received concerts at the Teatro Verdi. On the return to Pesaro, Mascagni issued a message to the faculty and student body of the Liceo Rossini. After thanking them warmly as artists for "having fully lived up to the faith [he] placed in them," he could not resist the opportunity for yet another gratuitous attack: "I am unhappy that I cannot similarly communicate anything from the mayor of Pesaro, who considered it appropriate to express his appreciation through the intermediacy of the president of the Liceo, obviously forgetting that the supreme artistic authority of our school is represented exclusively by the director." The truce was over. The next day Mascagni, citing "private family celebrations," left Pesaro, not returning until early July.

Open conflict on a new issue erupted on his return. An administrative officer in schools such as the Liceo Rossini at the time was the "inspector," an official in charge of maintaining discipline within the institution. Mascagni considered the position unnecessary and, upon the retirement of the incumbent, had urged the board not to replace him. Seeing this as evidence of laxity on the director's part, the board disregarded his request and, while he was in Spain, appointed one Ubaldo Ceccarelli, who was apparently held in low esteem by the composer, to the post. On Mascagni's return he wrote angrily to Passeri-Modi, "Fine behavior to nominate an inspector for the Liceo Rossini without even telling the director! . . . In this case, however, I will do my duty."

His letters and a plea at a board meeting were ignored, and he returned in July to find a newly painted sign with the word "inspector" on an office door. He ripped it down. Later that day, in his absence, it was replaced by order of the president. When Mascagni returned, he pulled the sign down again and locked it in his desk drawer. At the next day's board meeting he once again asked for the abolition of the position. Instead, the board voted to censure him and ordered him to restore the sign and present Ceccarelli to the school's faculty within twenty-four hours. Mascagni refused indignantly, triggering another exchange with Passeri-Modi. Even this matter, however, could conceivably have been resolved—although it is doubtful that either side was even remotely open to a peaceful resolution by this point—had it not been for the emergence of yet another, far more fundamental, bone of contention.

As at every Italian conservatory, the climax of the academic year at the Liceo Rossini was the series of concerts and student "exercises" that took place during July and early August, in which the students demonstrated their achievements as instrumentalists, singers, and composers. Under Mascagni, the scope of these exercises had grown considerably to include performances of student operas and oratorios, as well as symphonic concerts, in which the entire student body participated. Inevitably, their cost had risen as well.

Mascagni was not a careful financial manager. In the past, given discretion by the board, he had run substantial deficits in both the 1897–98 and 1898–99 academic years. Much of the deficit came from the exercises, for which he hired outside performers and commissioned elaborate sets and costumes. In 1902 the board, which had assumed closer control over the school's finances, allocated 2,000 lire for the student exercises. When Mascagni presented his proposal, with a budget of 4,460 lire, it was immediately rejected.

Unlike the other controversies between Mascagni and the board, this could not be treated as a private quarrel. Mascagni's presentation to the board was a matter of common knowledge among the student body, as was his subsequent appearance on July 19 to plead for more money for the exercises. When his plea was rejected, he offered to add to the budget from his own pocket. The board, openly hostile, rejected this proposal as well, as one member "laughed in his face, telling him that if he couldn't put on *I Due Foscari* [Verdi's *The Two Foscaris*], then he could put on only one." Faced with the spread of the conflict to the entire school, the board announced an abrupt end to the academic year, closing the school and putting off final exams to the following November.

While the faculty appears to have largely stood aside from the increasingly vehement controversy, the student body was thoroughly on the composer's side. That same day, caught up in the revolutionary atmosphere that seems to have permeated the school, the student body adopted a resolution stating that "unless by Sunday, July 20, at noon, funds are not increased for the exercises in keeping with the director's proposal, the board should resign immediately, being incapable and unworthy of its own duties."

It is unclear whether Mascagni had anything to do with prompting this daring and foolhardy gesture. Once it had happened, however, even he began to realize that things had gone too far, urging the students to sign a letter ending with the statement that "the students promise to drop their protest against the administration, which may have resulted from excessive youthful spirits." Matters had gone beyond his control, and the students refused. The next day he wrote a conciliatory letter to Passeri-Modi, begging him not to close the school down: "I do not want the good name and the future of the school to be compromised, and the steady flow of students . . . which is its first and foremost reason for existence, to be cut off. I do not want its vigorous upward march to be interrupted even for a day, or that the sacred wishes of its great master be, even in the slightest detail, betrayed." He added that on reflection he now believed that he could carry out his plan of exercises for two thousand lire, along with the box office receipts, and reiterated his earlier verbal offer to guarantee the difference from his own pocket.

It was too late. His offer was rejected, and on July 24, the president wrote Mascagni that "the responsibility for the ongoing student agitation is principally yours, because you were the first to claim that the board was infringing the rights of the students, rights that do not exist. . . . Your behavior . . . has been one of open and continuous opposition to the board, which has encouraged the students to persist in their agitation, which you, as disciplinary authority, had the duty to end." On July 26 the student body held a banquet at which, according to some accounts, the "menu was designed to be a vulgar vilification of the board's authority." The next day, the board ordered the entire student body home.

In a final gesture, Mascagni issued certificates to all of his students who would otherwise have graduated, attesting to their full musical qualifications, adding:

> *The student* _____ *would, without the shadow of a doubt, have received his diploma . . . with great honor for himself and for the school that has given him his artistic education, if the governing board of the Liceo had not arbitrarily ordered the suspension of the examinations, denying in this manner from the young students the satisfaction of reaping the fruits of their labors and their high aspirations, and openly infringing the sacred rights of the students.*

Two weeks later, citing his excessive absences, his insubordination in the matter of the inspector, and his responsibility for the student agitation, the board voted to fire Mascagni. The action was immediately confirmed by the city council. Mascagni appealed his dismissal to Nasi, the Minister of Public Education, who appointed an advisory committee to review the matter.

People throughout Italy took sides for or against Mascagni, prompting a 1902 headline in the popular *L'illustrazione Italiana* reading, "In Italy today we have only three real issues: [legalizing] divorce—the salt tax—and Mascagni." Deputies rose in Parliament to demand an investigation of the matter, pro-Mascagni demonstrations took place in Livorno and elsewhere, and Mascagni received telegrams of support from across the country, including one signed by 350 Pesaro citizens. On December 6 the advisory committee recommended that the minister confirm the board's decision, and on January 20, 1903, Nasi signed a decree confirming the removal of Mascagni as director of the Liceo Rossini. Although Mascagni appealed this decision in turn and managed to keep the matter in the courts for another two years before being finally rebuffed by the highest court of appeals, the matter was effectively over.

Although Mascagni's absences were clearly excessive, even Passeri-Modi acknowledged at the time that they had not led to the deterioration of the educational or artistic program at the conservatory. Similarly, the episode of the inspector seems to have been used by both parties to provoke a confrontation with the other, with little regard to the merits of the matter. Of the three issues, the controversy over the final exercises, with the resulting student agitation, was by far the most important one.

The students' revolt was a direct challenge to the board's authority, an authority that was guarded far more jealously than would be the case today. It could not be tolerated, and it was not unreasonable to place the responsibility for the uprising at Mascagni's feet. Whatever his role in fomenting the students' rebellion, there is little question that his actions, and his vociferous claims that the board was violating the students' rights, created a climate in which a body of usually passive students felt ready to overtly challenge the board's authority. For years he had repeatedly challenged the board's authority over the governance of the Liceo Rossini. He had gone far beyond the expression of legitimate differences, becoming insulting and overtly offensive. For him not to have understood that his behavior would sooner or later trigger an equal and opposite reaction is more than unrealistic—it borders on the delusional.

Mascagni was not capable of deferring to a lay board over artistic matters, nor was he capable of pursuing the subtle strategies through which generations of astute artistic directors have been able to mold boards into their instruments of power, rather than their rivals. To the minister of education's advisory committee, the root of the problem lay in "the supremacy that maestro Mascagni sought to exercise over the Liceo, where the administration of same is entrusted to a board." That was the real basis for affirming the decision of the governing board to remove their director. It was clear to everyone, except perhaps Mascagni himself, that it was no longer possible for him to remain director of the Liceo Rossini.

The following spring, the new president of the board, a soap manufacturer named Tullio Cinotti, addressed the school on the subject of seeking a new director:

> We will not direct our attention toward names of opera composers, even if they have public renown. The opera composer, in addition to being steeped in liberties, has his mind always focused on his own compositions and all of the interests that flow from them. In the double capacity of director of an educational institution and operatic composer, he cannot but betray one or the other.

The Liceo Rossini was fortunate in their new director. Although the position was not filled until 1905, the new director, Amilcare Zanella, was quite successful, remaining at the school until 1940. Zanella was not an operatic composer but a respected pianist and composer of orchestral and chamber music.

Under his direction the Liceo Rossini remained a useful, even distinguished educational institution, although it never recaptured the excitement that it briefly had had under Mascagni. Zanella and Mascagni became friendly over the years; in his 1942 reminiscences, the composer refers to him affectionately, but dismissively, as "a good fellow, but a bit of a simpleton."

9. *Travels, Troubles, and Amica,*
1902—1905

Despite Mascagni's warfare with the Pesaro authorities, his spirit was not broken, as *L'Illustrazione Italiana* commented: "The battles of Pesaro . . . have not worn down Mascagni's nerves or troubled his spirit; indeed, they seem to have injected fresh sulfur into his veins. . . . What other composer would even think of writing operas . . . [while fighting] the guerrilla warfare of hallways and stairwells."

Throughout the summer of 1902, his treatment of the governing board of the Liceo Rossini, spicing defiance with gratuitous insults, and the casual fashion in which he took on new challenges with little regard for his existing obligations, reflected the energy of the manic state. During July alone Mascagni undertook to stage and direct *Le Maschere* in Bologna and *Iris* in Livorno within a month, to recruit an orchestra and a full complement of solo singers by September for an extended tour of the United States, and to write orchestral interludes for a new play nearly ready for its first performance, all the while fighting daily battles at the Pesaro conservatory.

The news that Mascagni was to write incidental music for *The Eternal City*, a new play by the English writer Hall Caine, immediately set off a fresh controversy. Caine's play was about the liberation of a repressive, dictatorial Italy by a Christlike radical leader, set in a contemporary Rome half realistic and half imaginary. Although the story is wildly fanciful, many of the events in the play, which conservative Italians found most offensive, closely paralleled the repressions of 1898, in which more than a hundred Italians, nearly all unarmed workers, were killed and thousands jailed by draconian military tribunals.

Italians eager that the world see Italy as a modern, progressive nation took umbrage at this picture of their country and were furious that Mascagni would contribute his talents to such a work. Mascagni went on writing, asserting in his defense that his music was expressing "the sentiment of love, the passion that knows no fatherland." While hostile pieces continued to appear, the *Eternal City* controversy never overtook the Pesaro affair, which continued to spawn new revelations throughout the summer. Soon both would be supplanted by Mascagni's even more melodramatic misadventures in the United States. By his return in the spring of 1903, the controversy was largely forgotten, and selections from his incidental music were enthusiastically received at a summer concert in Rome.

Mascagni's music is warmly romantic and vividly descriptive, with no overt political content. Each of the interludes depicts a different episode from the play, the most distinctive being the fourth, a delightful carnival scene into which Mascagni ingeniously weaves the love theme from a previous interlude. *The Eternal City* breaks no new ground, although along with charm and lyrical beauty, it offers some interesting contrapuntal effects and harmonic twists. It is far better music than its role as theatrical background music demands.

Caine's play soon disappeared from the stage. Over the next decade, Mascagni occasionally performed selections from his music at his concerts. In the late 1930s, however, when members of a Livorno orchestra approached Mascagni in the hope of performing the work, the score and parts had been lost. Only the piano reduction remains today.

THE PERILS OF PIETRO: MASCAGNI'S AMERICAN TOUR

As the board of the Liceo Rossini was deciding to close the school, the public learned that its director had signed a contract with the American impresario Aubrey Mittenthal for a fifteen-week tour of the United States. The announcement was greeted with particular excitement by the American press and public. Although the United States had the beginnings of a sophisticated musical life, feelings of cultural provincialism were widespread. This was particularly true of opera, which in 1902 was still an imported art, performed by

Europeans or Europeanized Americans singing the works of European composers, and dominated by a system that focused attention on visiting stars
such as Francesco Tamagno or Nellie Melba and often neglected ensemble
and staging. Outside New York and a few other major centers, American
opera devotees relied on the occasional visit by traveling opera companies,
which were often based in more operatically advanced cities such as Havana
and Mexico City.

The United States was not unfamiliar with European musicians. Singers and virtuosi were regular visitors, while Tchaikovsky, Dvořák, and Johann
Strauss had all visited during the 1890s. Mascagni, whose fame preceded him,
was different. Performances of *Cavalleria, Pagliacci,* and *Bohème* had kindled intense public interest in the works of the new Italian composers. Audiences
were eager to hear Mascagni conduct the staple *Cavalleria* and to hear the new
and important *Iris* and *Guglielmo Ratcliff* from the pen of the master of verismo,
while reports of his eccentric dress and behavior appealed to the American
taste for the unusual and the exotic. The expectations for his visit were far too
high to be readily realized.

The *Musical Courier,* quoting the composer as saying that "his operas have
never been given properly outside of Italy," announced that all the singers, the
entire orchestra, and the sets and costumes would be personally selected by
Mascagni in Italy. The article continued: "'This tour will be the most expensive Italian opera engagement . . . ever given in America,' said Mr. Mittenthal
yesterday. 'Mascagni will receive the largest salary ever given a conductor,
$8,000 per week. Before the curtain can go up at the Metropolitan, Mitten-
thal & Kronberg will have expended $125,000.'" Although Mittenthal's fig-
ures were highly exaggerated, Mascagni's contract, providing for $4,000 per
week for the fifteen-week tour, was particularly generous. The total, $60,000,
amounted to 300,000 lire at the then-current rate of exchange, substantially
more than he was likely to earn from his royalties for the entire year.

With barely a month before departure, Mascagni assembled his forces
in slapdash fashion. Perhaps more than a third of the orchestra were recent
graduates of the Liceo Rossini, while others had interrupted their studies to
join the tour. Although enthusiastic and devoted to Mascagni, they were in-
experienced and had never performed as an ensemble. To a cadre of experienced singers such as the soprano Elena Bianchini-Cappelli and the bass
Francesco Navarrini, Mascagni added talented but unseasoned young artists,
including two recent Pesaro graduates, Maria Farneti and Pietro Schiavazzi.
None of these singers, however, were known to the star-minded American
public; the only singer in the company familiar to the American operagoer

was Eugenia Mantelli, a contralto already singing in the United States, who had been engaged by telegram from Italy. If there was a "star" in the company, it was Mascagni himself.

Leaving his difficulties in Pesaro behind, Mascagni and Lina left Livorno on September 24. Arriving in New York, the composer and his wife were engulfed by New York's Italian community, which had turned out by the thousands, and which marched up Broadway with him, bands blaring, to the Savoy Hotel. With some surprise, the reporter from the *New York Times* described the latest celebrity to reach New York: "His appearance was in striking contrast to that of his welcomers. He looks not like an Italian, but a good-looking American business man."

Mascagni's problems began the next day. On his arrival at the Metropolitan Opera House, he found two orchestras waiting for him to begin rehearsals, his own and an American orchestra led by Nahan Franko. As he stood there, a battle raged; according to the *New York Herald:*

> It was decided that Mascagni should bring some Italian musicians for his orchestra to this country. A dozen men were still needed, and Mittenthal Brothers asked Mr. Franko to supply them. The Musical Union would not allow its members to play with the visiting Italians, and so a full orchestra of seventy-eight men was organized in this city by Mr. Franko.

Franko claimed, however, that Mittenthal had hired him to assemble a full orchestra and accused Mascagni of discriminating against American musicians, a charge Mascagni heatedly denied. With the union musicians refusing to join his imported orchestra, Mascagni recruited immigrant Italian musicians to fill the vacant positions. The following day, the Musical Union filed a complaint with the commissioner of immigration demanding that Mascagni's Italian orchestra be deported.

Although the orchestra had traveled together, their music had been sent separately to New York, so that Mascagni had only two days of frantic rehearsal with an unprepared orchestra before opening at the Metropolitan Opera House on October 8 with *Cavalleria rusticana* and *Zanetto*. Under the circumstances, his opening night was more successful than could have been expected. Schiavazzi sang Turridu, while Bianchini-Cappelli sang Sylvia in *Zanetto* and Santuzza in *Cavalleria*. Mantelli also sang two roles, following the trouser role of Zanetto with Lola in *Cavalleria*. The packed house, including many members of the New York Italian community, was wildly enthusiastic, and the composer and singers were repeatedly interrupted by applause. The critical reaction, however, to both the performance and to the evening's novelty, *Zanetto*, was mixed. The *Musical Courier*, for whom Mascagni was a weapon in their battle against the star system, was particularly laudatory, writing that "under Mascagni, without any opportunity to illustrate what is possible with the proper forces under his command, we have heard a better performance, and in fact, the only performance, we have ever heard of *Cavalleria.*"

The *New York Times*, after noting that "the performance, let it be said emphatically, was very good," added that just the same "the orchestral part could have been done certainly as well and apparently cheaper if [Mascagni] had thrown himself upon the mercy of the musical union." The *Herald* was unimpressed with Mascagni's orchestra, finding it "most unsatisfactory, not only in precision and finish, but in both bigness and refinement of tone as well." The same diversity of reaction carried over to *Zanetto.* While the *Musical Courier* praised the opera, the *Herald* dismissed it, concluding that "nothing duller than *Zanetto* has been recently heard at the Metropolitan."

Cavalleria was well known to New York audiences, while *Zanetto* was a minor work. Audiences and critics were eager to hear *Iris* and *Ratcliff.* While giving two more performances of *Cavalleria* and *Zanetto,* Mascagni worked frantically preparing his forces for the first performance of *Iris,* now pushed back to October 11. By the evening of the eleventh, Mascagni decided that *Iris* was not yet ready; as the gala crowd arrived in the middle of a downpour, they learned that the performance had been rescheduled for the sixteenth. While wet and angry operagoers filled the lobby, Mascagni stayed behind locked doors, continuing to rehearse. The first American performance of *Iris* took place in Philadelphia, three days later, with Farneti as Iris and Schiavazzi as Osaka.

The New York critics treated the New York performance two days later as its true American debut. Once again, the critical response was thoroughly mixed, with reviews ranging from passionate enthusiasm to contempt. The *Musical Courier* headed the ranks of the cheerleaders, concluding a full page review:

> *No feeble and inexperienced hand wrote this score. It is a master, a man of deepest and most subtle refinement, and an unconscious metaphysician, unconscious because there is nothing pedantic or dry in all his charming creation. . . . in* Iris *we see the power of authority, the control of forces. . . . one sees clearly how well Mascagni has digested the leitmotif theory without fracturing his skull over Teutonic methods.*

By contrast, the *Tribune* dismissed the work, writing that "what the composer accomplished with tune, characteristic but fluent, eloquent yet sustained, in *Cavalleria,* he tries to achieve in *Iris* with violent, disjointed shifting of keys and splashes of instrumental color."

The American critics recognized something new and different in *Iris* but had difficulty accepting it. The *New York Times* described the work in terms that were to become familiar as further waves of modern music reached American shores: "Mascagni has developed a harmonic vein in this work that is . . . positively uncouth in its crass ugliness and eccentricity, fruitlessly bruising the ear," adding prudishly that "a more uselessly revolting story has not recently been set before this public."

The next night, considering *Ratcliff* still unready, Mascagni substituted a second performance of *Iris*. After a farewell concert on October 19, the company took to the road. Over the next two weeks, Mascagni and his forces passed through Baltimore, Washington, Pittsburgh, Buffalo, Toronto, and Montreal, ending up in Boston on November 3. The composer had still not put *Ratcliff* before the public, alternating performances of *Iris* with a double bill of *Cavalleria* and *Zanetto*.

Despite its difficulties, and the persistent failure of *Ratcliff* to appear, the first month of the tour appeared at least moderately successful. To the largely impoverished immigrant Italian community, Mascagni's presence itself was a triumph, an occasion to glory in their nation's artistic tradition. When Mascagni arrived in Philadelphia, his train delayed until well after midnight, five thousand Italian Americans, bands and all, stood patiently waiting for him at Broad Street station. To Mascagni's amazement, nearly every Italian community in the eastern United States had its Mascagni Society and its Mascagni band.

Although the audiences were enthusiastic, they were not always large. Performances of *Iris* often drew smaller crowds than those of *Cavalleria* and *Zanetto*, as the less sophisticated audiences outside New York seemed to want *Cavalleria* and little else. Still, as the tour reached Boston, it appeared to observers to have settled into a productive routine. The reality was otherwise. Since leaving New York, the musicians, including Mascagni himself, had not been paid. By the time they reached Boston the tour was near collapse.

Boston began well. *Cavalleria* and *Zanetto* were received enthusiastically, with the *Boston Herald* calling *Cavalleria* "a revelation" and *Zanetto* "a gracious and beautiful little work, which might almost be called perfect in its way." The elusive *Ratcliff* was finally ready on the evening of November 5. That day, however, the musicians' patience finally ran out. Learning that they were to miss a third straight payday, they put down their instruments and walked out before the performance could begin. As the disappointed audience left, Mittenthal announced, "I'm glad to be done with it. We abandon the whole thing right here. Mascagni owes us $14,000; I have spent $60,000 on this tour, and I'm done. I won't advance another cent."

Mittenthal's arithmetic is questionable. Mascagni had been paid a total of $24,000 so far, of which $7,000 had been paid him in Italy at the time the contract was signed and another $7,000 as a lump sum credited to his account on his arrival in New York. Subsequently, he had been paid $10,000, or two and a half weekly installments. In a letter to a friend the next day, he wrote "Up to tomorrow I should have taken in $34,000; instead I've received $24,000—I've lost $10,000. From the whole business I've lost $36,000 (180,000 lire)."

While Mittenthal alternately blamed Mascagni and found other excuses, including the implausible one that "he . . . had never had the contract translated, so he could not say exactly how the advance money clauses read," the composer was convinced that Mittenthal had been planning this for some time, writing in the same letter, "I firmly believe that the whole thing was planned in advance: make a little swing as far as Boston, try to keep from paying the bills, and then . . . run for it!" Two days later, the Mittenthals, having convinced a magistrate that Mascagni owed them substantial amounts and was at risk of fleeing the United States, had a warrant executed on him in his suite at the Hotel Touraine. While spared the indignity of appearing at the police station, Mascagni was confined to his suite until his attorney came up with $4,000 bail.

The company disintegrated. Many of the singers made their own arrangements to return to Italy, while the chorus members, hired in New York, drifted back home. Although a few of the orchestra members melted away, most remained in Boston, staying in cheap boardinghouses in the Italian North End, playing in cafés to earn enough to eat and living on Mascagni's promise that, one way or another, he would get them home. With the help of a few prominent Bostonians, he organized a series of benefit concerts with his reduced orchestra, a local chorus, and the handful of singers who had decided to remain with him, including Schiavazzi and Bianchini-Cappelli.

Mascagni's misadventures triggered comment both in Italy and in the United States. The *Musical Courier,* which had praised him without reservation up to this point, turned against him, denouncing him in a sharply worded editorial, asserting that "the people of this country will not endure the disappointments to which they were subjected under the Mascagni conditions" and reminding Americans of "his difficulties with the directors of the Rossini institution at Pesaro."

Nearly every sentient Italian had already taken sides either for or against Mascagni over the Pesaro affair. For many, the latest difficulties of the man Ugo Ojetti called "Italy's Captain Dreyfus" were more of the same in a new setting. While national pride was involved, it cut both ways. To Mascagni's defenders, it was the American treatment of their hero that offended national sentiments; to his detractors, it was his behavior that was the offense to Italy's honor. While most Italians took Mascagni's side, there were dissenting voices. Ojetti, in a much reprinted article in Bologna's *Il Resto di Carlino*, suggested that the entire "caso Mascagni" had become too much:

> *I must confess a sin. When I read that the American sheriff had put Pietro Mascagni behind bars, a sigh of satisfaction escaped me . . . about time! The jails of Boston are roomy and clean . . . the warden would undoubtedly have given our maestro a nice room with a piano, a window overlooking the Charles, and a bunch of flowers on the windowsill . . . And Mascagni, finally far from Pesaro and the four hundred thousand dollars and his terrible Italian friends . . . would have written some music. . . . And the rest of us could have breathed easier. . . . Because, frankly, we can't take any more of this.*

At the end of November Mascagni signed a contract with a new manager, Richard Heard, to resume the tour. Much reduced, with a small orchestra and a handful of soloists, the tour made a series of one-night stands in the American hinterland, performing a single program consisting of instrumental and vocal selections from the operatic repertory followed by a concert performance of *Cavalleria*. Heard was even less reliable than the Mittenthals. Mascagni tried hard to maintain a brave front, but his efforts were more and more desperate, and less and less credible. The way west was strewn with financial disaster, and the tour became a pathetic band of straggling musicians wandering across the American landscape, finally ending in Chicago two days before Christmas. Exhausted and ill, Mascagni canceled the remaining dates and took to his bed. The next day, as he remained in bed, Lina distributed nearly all of the funds he had left to his musicians to enable them to return home. He and Lina spent Christmas barricaded in their hotel room, tended by physicians summoned by the Italian consul.

Despite Lina's pleas, Mascagni decided to remain in the United States until the Massachusetts courts resolved the Mittenthal brothers' suit still hanging over his head. With his musicians heading back to Italy, he decided to continue on his own. A series of successful concerts in January with the Theodore Thomas orchestra (subsequently the Chicago Symphony) helped raise the composer's spirits; more important, they raised enough money for him to be able to leave cold, windy Chicago. At the end of January he and Lina boarded a train for San Francisco.

San Francisco was an inspired choice. The journey across the western states had a tonic effect on the composer, and he arrived in San Francisco reinvigorated. The city took the refugee from storm-tossed shores to its collective heart. For nearly two months, he was feted by every part of San Francisco society, from Italian immigrant workingmen's societies to the exclusive Bohemian Club.

Mascagni had been invited by a local impresario to conduct two symphonic concerts, a sacred Sunday concert featuring Rossini's Stabat Mater, and a popular concert that same evening. The concerts were perhaps the most unqualified success that Mascagni had had since arriving in America more than four months earlier. The first concert, featuring Tchaikovsky's *Pathétique* Symphony, was, in the words of the musical critic of the *San Francisco Examiner*, "a triumph that will remain unforgettable in the musical history of our city." San Francisco, which, as one critic pointed out, "was critical in the extreme and seldom makes a demonstration," was a sophisticated city. It had an active musical life, with opera, orchestral concerts, and recitals, and was a frequent stop on the more extended tours of foreign virtuosi, which at the time of Mascagni's visit included the pianist Ossip Gavrilovitsch and the soprano Zélie de Lussan. The concert series was so successful that Mascagni conducted another round of four performances at the beginning of March, and another four performances after that, to accommodate the demand for tickets.

Between concerts, Mascagni attended an endless round of banquets, including a memorable one at the Italian Chamber of Commerce, where the composer remarked, "From the day I set foot on the American continent, this is the first time that I have been honored so warmly, so thoroughly, so spontaneously, and seen my own compatriots mixing with American citizens." Earlier that week, Mascagni wrote a short piece for piano, a touching lyrical fragment only thirteen bars long, entitled "Un pensiero a San Francisco"; the composer's manuscript was reproduced in the *San Francisco Chronicle* as a present to the people of the city that had welcomed him so warmly.

At the end of February the Massachusetts Supreme Court threw out the Mittenthals' case. Frantic to get back to Italy and see his children again, he was now free to leave. Rejecting proposals for tours in Mexico and Cuba, he left San Francisco on March 27 on the fastest possible train, as he wrote Hirsch, "making like a shot for New York, without even stopping in Chicago." On April 2 he left New York, arriving at Le Havre on the evening of the eighth. By April 11 he was back in Italy and reunited in Florence with his children. The family returned to Rome on the fourteenth, where he was greeted by a throng of admirers at the railroad station. He had been gone more than six months.

Despite his redemption in San Francisco, Mascagni's American tour, characterized by an air of reckless improvisation, was a disaster for him, for his musicians, and for the reputation of his music in the United States. To undertake to perform four operas within a week of his arrival in the United States in an unfamiliar hall, with an orchestra that had never performed as a body, singers who had never sung these works together, and a chorus recruited sight unseen, was at best quixotic, at worst utterly irresponsible. Although he assembled a competent body of singers, his scratch band was an embarrassment in a land with a solid tradition of orchestral musicianship. Mascagni would have fared better—financially and artistically—had Franko indeed assembled an American orchestra for him in New York. Once in America, his insistence on postponing *Iris* until his forces were ready and his refusal to put on an inadequately prepared *Ratcliff* do credit to his integrity, but these decisions had a disastrous effect on the public, as well as on the box office receipts. A tour that was undercapitalized and poorly organized by its managers allowed no room for such errors.

In the final analysis, however, the failure of the Mascagni tour could almost have been predicted; for this we have the uncanny testimony of Frederick Ritter, describing in 1895 "the history of Italian opera in America":

> At the beginning of a season great blowing of trumpets by the manager and his interested friends; the press generally echoes the managerial key-note; the unexpected whim of some jealous singer . . . threatens to spread a cloud over the manager's sanguine hopes; the orchestra and chorus strike for higher wages; or some political crisis occurs. . . . the public, for one cause or the other, becomes indifferent, and stays away from the opera house; the press becomes restless and challenges the manager to reform, or face the consequences of his shortcomings; the manager thinks it advisable to visit, with his company, other cities, in order to replenish his exchequer; he finally goes West and experiences a grand smash-up; the company . . . in small squads succeeds in getting back to New York; general and wholesale abuse of the manager follows.

The difference, however, lies in the expectations raised by Mascagni's visit. He was no ordinary musician but a renowned celebrity. His visit was the operatic event of the season. To many, including the editors of the *Musical Courier*, it was to be a vital blow for the reform of the American operatic world.

The tour was not a total fiasco. Audiences responded warmly to Mascagni and his music. Although Mascagni denounced the United States and its "musical crudities" on his return, one writer's conclusion is appropriate: "His comments could never tarnish the glow Mascagni left behind. Audiences everywhere had experienced the musical event of their lives and would always remember the day the maestro came to town."

STARTING OVER

On his return to Rome, Mascagni's life resumed almost as if the traumas of the past year had never happened. Although echoes of the Pesaro battle would recur periodically as he continued to fight his obsessive battle for vindication through the tortuous Italian legal system, it was in the hands of his attorneys. He himself was ready to begin anew—as conductor, teacher, writer, and even as a composer.

As a composer, Mascagni was just holding his own. The year 1902 had seen two new operas appear that seemed likely to enter the repertory: *Germania*, by Franchetti, and Cilea's *Adriana Lecouvreur*. *Germania*, assiduously promoted by Ricordi to fill the void created by Puccini's delays with *Butterfly*, took off quickly after its March premiere but faded after two or three years. *Adriana*, although perhaps less immediately successful, had more staying power and has remained alive long after *Germania* has been forgotten. Leoncavallo, with both *Zazà* and his version of *La Bohème* successful, was at the peak of his fame.

Iris's movement into the repertory helped Mascagni retain his competitive position. While still viewed equivocally by the critical establishment, it had won popular favor and was receiving frequent productions in both Italy and South America. While *Cavalleria* continued to be a staple, *L'Amico Fritz* also regularly appeared at smaller houses in the major cities or in towns such as Forlì, Siena, and Casalpusterlengo. Even *Guglielmo Ratcliff* was not neglected, appearing in both Venice and Livorno during 1903.

Although the wounds of Pesaro were still far from healed, in October 1903 Mascagni accepted the post of director and professor of composition at the six-year-old National Music School in Rome, a struggling private institution whose name reflected more its aspirations than its reality. Though he served as director until 1910, he minimized the burdens of office by recruiting his Pesaro colleague Tancredo Mantovani to be his deputy and stand in during his frequent absences. Required by school regulations to give forty lessons in composition each year, he met the letter of his obligations, as a former pupil recalled: "In the last month of the year, the maestro was back, and the lessons followed one another daily until the required number was reached."

Lacking government subsidy, the National Music School was an uncertain venture. Mascagni's reputation enabled it to find a wealthy patron in Count Giovanni Angelo Bastogi, whose support enabled the school to move from modest quarters in the Piazza Santa Chiara to more impressive facilities in the Palazzo del Grillo. When Bastogi's financial empire collapsed in 1910, however, the school was cast adrift, and it dissolved little more than a year later.

Meanwhile, Mascagni decided to establish himself permanently in Rome. After a succession of hotel suites and short-term rentals, in mid-1904 he rented a floor of the Palazzo Maggiorani, on the Corso Vittorio Emanuele in old Rome. The Mascagni family lived there until 1910, when they moved into their new home on the Via Po, near the Borghese gardens.

A NEW OPERA AT LONG LAST

Mascagni was still frustrated in his attempts to pursue the only work that really mattered, the composition of another opera. More than a year had gone by since the Pesaro affair and his American tour had put an end to his discussions with Ricordi and Illica, but nothing had changed. After testing the waters on his return, he wrote Illica dejectedly in June, "I had thought for a moment that things were looking up, because Ricordi seemed almost to have decided to provide me with a libretto; but that hope lasted about as long as one of Leoncavallo's successes."

Illica passed Mascagni's letter on to Ricordi, and a few days later a meeting took place in Rome between the composer and the publisher, at which Ricordi reiterated his desire to see Mascagni set Illica's still unwritten *Maria Antonietta*. A few days after the meeting, Mascagni wrote Ricordi confirming his willingness to accept *Maria Antonietta*, but reminding him that "the love interest is still a question mark," and asking the publisher for an outline of the work "so I can study the structure of the drama as a whole, and judge whether . . . the personages are capable of exciting my spirit first, as they must excite the spirit of the public later."

Still without a libretto, Mascagni wrote Illica asking, "Is it then my destiny never again to write another note of music?" He then wrote Ricordi in mid-August: "I find no satisfaction except with *Vistilia*, but that is a platonic, byzantine, academic comfort. . . . If you don't want anything more from me, I will accept your decision with my usual serenity. . . . I am always ready for anything. But this idleness, this sloth that overwhelms me, this silence that surrounds me, this void all around me, I cannot stand."

In the fall of 1903 Illica finally began to work on *Maria Antonietta*, which he had conceived, in Morini's words, as "a series of grand historical tableaux: from Maria's farewell to her mother in Vienna—April 1770—before leaving for Paris . . . up to the tragic epilogue of the infamous trial and the beheading—October 1793." By the start of 1904 Illica had prepared an outline in four acts, each in two scenes, preceded by a "symphonic prologue" that "would form, through the events [it] would summarize and express, a drama in itself, an 'antedrama.'" He finished the first act early in the spring of 1904. By then the frustrated Mascagni had already turned his attention elsewhere.

For years Mascagni had been courted by foreign publishers. Occupied with commissions from Sonzogno and Ricordi, and fiercely protective of what he considered the inherently Italian nature of opera, he spurned their advances. When approached by the Parisian publisher Paul Choudens early in 1904, however, he was less inclined to resist. Choudens was head of the family firm that had published much of the important French music of the nineteenth century, including works by Berlioz, Gounod, and Saint-Saëns. He was also an aspiring librettist, and in soliciting Mascagni to set a play of his own writing, his interests as a publisher were interwoven with—and perhaps in conflict with—his more intimate interests as a writer.

Mascagni had not worked on an opera, except for his "platonic" efforts on *Vistilia*, since finishing *Le Maschere* in 1900. That was frustration enough, as musical ideas came and went without being put to use, but by 1904 the prospect that he might never be able to work on an opera again had become a genuine possibility. This situation arose from the character of the Italian opera industry at the turn of the century, and the unique role that music publishers played in that industry.

By the end of the nineteenth century there were only two important operatic publishers in Italy, Ricordi and Sonzogno. They owned the works of virtually all Italian composers, living and dead, and the Italian rights for all major foreign operas. They controlled not only the publication but also the performance of opera in Italy; as Mascagni wrote in his 1905 polemic against the system, *Per l'opere dell'ingegno* (On behalf of creative works), "In musical matters in Italy, the author without a publisher does not exist and is incapable of existing. The system of operatic performance in our theaters is governed entirely by relationships between publishers and impresarios."

Most Italian theaters contracted to an impresario for a season at a time; the impresario then contracted with either Ricordi or Sonzogno to provide him with a season's operas. Since rental fees were highly negotiable, publishers offered impresarios attractive package deals in return for exclusive rights to the season and the opportunity to promote the latest works by members of their stable, as Ricordi did with Franchetti's *Germania*. There were few exceptions to this rule, limited largely to the most important theaters, or the activities of the most well established impresarios.

If a fledgling composer wanted to see his work performed and could convince an impresario—the composer bearing the entire expense of the production—the impresario then had to obtain the permission of the publisher with whom he had contracted before adding the work to his season's schedule. Only with Ricordi's permission was Wolf-Ferrari able to have his first opera, *Cenerentola*, put on at the Fenice Theater in Venice, and the composer had to pay the impresario Cesari the substantial sum of ten thousand lire for the opportunity.

That this system failed to stifle younger Italian composers' creative drives was attributable to the intense public demand for new operas. That demand enabled the publishers to charge substantially higher rental fees for the new works of Puccini, Mascagni, and Giordano than for the familiar classics of Verdi and Donizetti. Publishers were constantly seeking new talent and were happy to permit impresarios to put on the works of unpublished authors at no cost to them. If the work was successful, the composer was signed by the publisher; if not, no harm had been done.

The system froze Mascagni into immobility. It made no sense to him to devote years of effort and expense to write an opera without a publisher. As an established composer, he could expect one or the other publisher to block any attempt to personally subsidize a production of a new opera, even were he willing to consider it. Sonzogno had no interest in a new opera from him, while Ricordi seemed almost obsessively determined that he set Illica's still unfinished *Maria Antonietta*. Mascagni, after three years, was losing faith that it would ever materialize. Moreover, he was increasingly doubtful that if it were ever completed, it would contain the qualities that he needed in a libretto. It is hard, indeed, to think of any subject less suited to his muse than the pageant of historic tableaux, devoid of a serious love interest or intense emotional— as distinct from political – confrontations, that Illica was constructing.

Choudens's proposal offered Mascagni a way out, along with exceptionally generous terms. The principal source of income for Italian composers was their percentage of the rental fees charged by the publishers to the theaters producing the opera. This was an inclusive fee, which comprised not only the right to perform the work but also the score and parts, and often scenery and costumes as well. The contractual terms offered by each of the two Italian publishers to their composers rarely varied. Sonzogno offered his composers 30 percent of gross rental fees for a period of twenty years from publication. Ricordi offered his most valuable composers, such as Puccini and Mascagni, 40 percent of gross rental fees for the duration of the copyright period, which at that time was eighty years. Choudens, eager to have a work by Mascagni in his catalogue and see his name on the title page of a Mascagni opera, offered him the wildly generous terms of 75 percent of rental fees for productions in Italy and 50 percent elsewhere for the duration of the copyright period. In addition, Mascagni received an advance of twenty thousand lire on signing, with an additional forty thousand lire on delivery of the opera.

Mascagni was troubled but determined, writing Illica, "I have waited too long, I have suffered too much. I have been kept on the shelf up to now. And offers from foreign publishers have rained down unbidden, because elsewhere people believe that I am still capable of something." He closed defiantly, "In any case, I would like to see who dares to say I am wrong. God is watching."

Illica and Ricordi were both outraged by Mascagni's actions. Illica, who had finally begun to produce his libretto, exploded, writing Ricordi, who had urged him to try to convince Mascagni to reconsider, that "neither [your] attorneys nor Mascagni's telegrams can put you in a safe position, dealing with a man of such utter bad faith." Despite his own anger, Ricordi continued to communicate with Mascagni, seeking to meet with him before he executed the Choudens contact. Although they were scheduled to meet in Milan at the end of April, the meeting never came off. Ricordi refused to have anything more to do with Mascagni. In September, when Illica urged him to reconsider, hoping that Mascagni might turn to *Maria Antonietta* after meeting his obligations to Choudens, the publisher testily wrote back, "For God's sake, leave Don Pietro be!"

Although Choudens's libretto is a weak, ill-proportioned effort, the underlying tale of rural passion offered Mascagni precisely the sort of charged emotional conflicts, missing from the ill-fated *Maria Antonietta*, that he needed to spur his creative drives. *Amica* opens in a farm in France's mountainous Haute Savoie. Camoine, a wealthy farmer, has raised his niece Amica as his daughter and taken in two orphan brothers, Rinaldo and Giorgio. Rinaldo, a violent, rebellious youth, is thrown off the farm and becomes a shepherd in the mountains, while the docile Giorgio remains behind. Camoine, to rid himself of responsibility for Amica and appease his mistress Maddalena, decides to marry Amica to Giorgio, who has silently loved her for years. Amica, who loves Rinaldo, protests to no avail. Desperate, she calls on Rinaldo. She tells him that Camoine is forcing her to marry another man—but not whom —and they flee into the mountains.

The second act takes place in a mountain pass by a waterfall. Giorgio overtakes the fleeing couple and confronts Rinaldo. When he tells Rinaldo that it was he whom Amica was to marry, Rinaldo, whose love for his brother surpasses his love for Amica, begs her to return to Giorgio. Rejecting her pleas, Rinaldo heads back to the mountains alone. The desperate Amica races after him and, in front of the helpless brothers, falls fatally into the rushing torrent below. Although the idea of a rivalry between two brothers for the same woman is not rare in literature, Choudens's libretto has no direct literary model.

Mascagni received the libretto in May and set to work early in June.

With the greater part of *Amica* finished by the beginning of October, he enlisted his old collaborator Guido Menasci to rewrite two critical sections of Choudens's libretto for him. Once that was done, at the end of the month, he resumed work. With the final touches to the last bars of the Intermezzo, *Amica* was finished at the end of November.

Choudens arrived in Rome late in November and was delighted with Mascagni's work, signing a second contract on the spot for *Vistilia*. With Choudens's departure, Mascagni set himself to orchestrating *Amica*. Working his customary eight to ten hours every night, by early January he had finished all but the last part of the second act and the Intermezzo. On the fourteenth, with the score in his suitcase, he left Rome for Paris, where he met the cast that had been assembled for the March premiere of *Amica* in Monte Carlo, discussed a libretto with the French playwright Sardou, had tea with the prince of Monte Carlo, and conducted the Lamoureux orchestra in two concerts, prompting a heated controversy among the Paris critics over his merits as a symphonic conductor.

He was also able to find time to continue orchestrating *Amica*, and by the end of January had finished all but the Intermezzo, a lengthy, self-contained symphonic poem. He began scoring the Intermezzo on his return to Rome and completed it on February 14. Releasing his pent-up energies after years of inaction, Mascagni wrote *Amica* at a feverish pace that recalled the composer's early days.

The premiere of *Amica* took place in Monte Carlo on March 16, with a cast that included some of the finest French-language singers available. Rinaldo was sung by the great baritone Maurice Renaud, Giorgio by Charles Rousselière, and Amica by Geraldine Farrar, who had been chosen after Emma Calvé, the composer's first choice for the role, and Amelia Karola, whom he had already selected for the Roman premiere, were both unavailable.

The evening was a triumph for the composer. Audience and critics, French and Italian, responded enthusiastically to his new work. *Le Figaro* wrote that "this opera is certainly the most powerful that Mascagni has composed since *Cavalleria rusticana*. . . . its expressive and dramatic qualities permit it to be considered one of the most powerful operas written in Italy in recent years." The *Gaulois* was even more effusive in its praise: "Mascagni's new score is one of the best efforts of the young Italian maestro. It is a strong, original, and seductive opera, powerful yet full of charm, full of creative inspiration and ardor, of strong and harmonious construction, a symphonic drama of such character as to satisfy all of the modern technical demands." The Italian critics who had traveled to Monte Carlo were equally enthusiastic, including

Giovanni Pozza of the *Corriere della Sera,* who identified the composer's new direction in a long, thoughtful review:

> *Already from the scene between Amica and Rinaldo, the musical structure and form appear new and different; there is not a trace left of his early style. The drama unwinds in its principal scenes through free melodic declamation. Mascagni handles his declamation with superb dramatic vigor; . . . he has given it his own stamp, a passionate accent, an impulsive sincerity thoroughly Italian.*

Over the next two weeks eighteen Italian theaters announced plans to stage *Amica* in their next season, with Rome's Costanzi Theater coming first on May 13.

The Roman premiere of *Amica,* translated into Italian by Menasci, was the climax of a monthlong spring season at the Costanzi Theater devoted entirely to Mascagni's works, including productions of *Fritz, Ratcliff,* and *Zanetto.* After the enthusiastic reports from Monte Carlo, anticipation was high for its premiere. The performance, however, with Karola as Amica, Riccardo Stracciari as Rinaldo, and Pietro Schiavazzi as Giorgio, was plagued with difficulties and failed to match the work's earlier success. The first act was greeted warmly, with the Monferrina and the duet between Amica and Rinaldo particularly well received. The Intermezzo was greeted respectfully but with less enthusiasm. From then on things deteriorated: "The mechanism for the waterfall let out every so often through the hall a loud groan that could not be ignored, and that took all of Mascagni's patience to hold out against. At the end the public's attention seemed to perk up, but [then] the tenor went out of tune so badly that the crowd howled. . . . The tenor was miserable," the *Corriere* concluded, "and Karola, too, was without her full vocal resources."

By the second performance, which played to a substantially smaller house, matters had improved. The stage machinery had been fixed, and both Schiavazzi and Karola were in better voice. The encouraging news spread quickly through the Roman grapevine, and the remaining performances, at which Francisca Solari substituted for the erratic Karola, were sold out. *Amica* ran for a respectable ten performances. At the last performance the composer received tributes from his students at the National Music School, a laurel crown from the Costanzi orchestra, and another from the student body of the Liceo Rossini in Pesaro, inscribed to their "never to be forgotten master."

Amica moved slowly after the Rome premiere. Few of the cities that had announced productions in the wake of the Monte Carlo triumph followed through. Although the mixed reports from Rome may have led some theaters to pass up the opera, to Mascagni, the hand of the publishers was at work;

"[*Amica*] has taken, or perhaps will take, a few small steps in Italy," he wrote, "but always during the so-called 'half seasons,' where the publishers' ferocious claws have little grasp. But in the principal seasons, where their autocracy rules despotically, my poor music can't even raise its head." To buttress his case, Mascagni described how, even after he had signed a contract to revive *Amica* at the Costanzi for the 1906 carnival season, it mysteriously disappeared from the schedule before the season began.

While *Amica* did eventually reach the San Carlo in 1906 and the Fenice in 1907, with its grim subject matter and its extravagant scenic and vocal demands, all compressed into an opera taking little more than an hour to perform, it was not greatly in demand. Only where Mascagni, a solid box office attraction in person, conducted the opera, did it attract interest. Eager to promote the work, the composer even organized a company with which he took *Amica* in 1907 and 1908 to provincial theaters in such modest communities as Cremona, Este, Rimini, and Pistoia.

By the end of 1908, engaged with his next opera, Mascagni stopped promoting *Amica*, and the work lost its tenuous place in the repertory. After a few performances during Mascagni's Latin American tour of 1911, it has all but disappeared from the stage. It has never been performed in the United States.

AMICA

Amica is a challenging and problematic work, a work rich in moving, powerful episodes, and yet uneven and ill balanced. It simultaneously looks backward to the raw intensity of *Cavalleria* and forward to Mascagni's continuous, declamatory later style, to the ever more intimate fusion of words and music that was his ultimate goal as a composer; as he told Edoardo Pompei, "My artistic ideals can be summed up in the principle of a total connection between the words and the music, so that the music becomes word, becomes expression."

Much of the problem lies with the libretto. The bond between the two brothers, the love they share for the same woman—who loves but one—and the powerful figure of the farmer Camoine are potentially strong operatic material. In approaching this story, Choudens, taking his cue from *Cavalleria*, chose to concentrate on the event that precipitates the confrontation—Camoine's decision to marry Amica to Giorgio—and the confrontation itself. While he was able to maneuver his characters into that confrontation, however, the amateurish Choudens was unable to make either the underlying situation or the final outcome truly compelling.

Rinaldo, the independent mountain man, is the only successful character in the opera. Giorgio, the puny man of the plains, who faints after his one moment of strong emotion, and who describes himself as "trembling and miserable," is too pathetic even to be an effective foil to his brother. Amica is a cipher, while Camoine is inconsistent. We never understand why a man who has raised Amica as his daughter, taken in two orphan boys, and is apparently beloved by his workers would turn on his ward, brutally reject her pleas, and threaten to "throw her out the door like a dog" unless she marries a man she loathes. *Amica* would have been far stronger if it had been expanded to create more credible characters, with more coherent relationships and motivations.

Mascagni appears to have been unconcerned about the libretto's deficiencies, accepting largely intact what he was given by Choudens. Not only was he desperately eager to resume work, but the concentrated story, its simplified characters, and their elemental passions were also precisely what he wanted, giving him an opportunity to translate their passions into a universal statement about human existence. As Mascagni's artistic goal had its roots in Wagner, his music for *Amica* reflected the German master. The free, declamatory vocal line, the extensive use of the orchestra to propel the drama, and above all, the use of a complex texture of leitmotifs—the most prominent of which, Rinaldo's motif, has a distinctively Wagnerian cast—all reflect the extent to which *Amica* can be considered an experiment in Wagnerism *all'italiana*.

The first act has many powerful moments, including Amica's confrontation with Camoine and her closing duet with Rinaldo, but is more conventional in character. Mascagni's efforts to forge a new direction come into their own in the Intermezzo that separates the two acts, and in the second-act confrontation in the mountains. More than a conventional interlude, the Intermezzo is a massive symphonic poem, built around two themes of a Wagnerian cast, from which much of the second-act material grows. Although at one level it depicts Giorgio's desperate journey into the mountains, it is really Mascagni's effort to capture in symphonic terms the inner drama of the opera and the tangle of emotions that are about to be resolved in the following scene. In the quality of its musical ideas and the breadth of its conception, the Intermezzo stands high among Mascagni's orchestral works. At the same time, it is all but undone by its constant straining for effect, as it pushes relentlessly from one *fortissimo* climax to the next.

The Intermezzo leads directly into the second-act confrontation between Giorgio, Rinaldo, and Amica. The act reaches its dramatic climax with Rinaldo's scene, "Se tu amasti me" (If you ever loved me). In a series of long-limbed lyrical phrases, of the sort only Mascagni among his contemporaries could create, Rinaldo begs Amica to give Giorgio the happiness that without her he could never have. She pleads with him to stay, but he heads off toward the mountains; as she follows him, the orchestra takes over, pouring forth a welter of leitmotifs. Mascagni has saved his ultimate orchestral blow for this climactic moment. As she falls into the rushing torrent, the entire orchestra lets loose with what may be the most brutal noise yet heard in an Italian opera, a *fortissimo*, outrageously dissonant, descending chromatic scale, finally ending in a toneless rumble of tubas, trombones, and double basses.

This massive orchestral peroration to accompany poor Amica's death reflects the extent to which Mascagni strives to use his music to intensify the emotional weight of the opera, paralleling the symbolic weight with which he tries to invest his characters. He falls into excess, caught up in the thrill of his thematic manipulations and exhilarated by the sheer volume of sound he can generate from his orchestra. In the end, for all the opera's powerful and moving moments, its composer lost sight that the libretto he was setting was no more than a short, unpretentious story about the misfortunes of a group of modest Alpine country folk. These simple souls were unable to bear the weight of his desire to create a work of symbolic meaning and universal significance.

10. *Illica,* Isabeau, *and Anna Lolli,*

1905—1910

In 1906 a chance meeting in Naples with Giulio Ricordi's son Tito led to revived interest from the Ricordi firm. Soon, after five years of silence, Edoardo
Sonzogno, eager to prevent Mascagni from being recaptured by his rival,
made contact with the composer through Walter Mocchi, a young man beginning to build a reputation as an impresario both in his native Italy and in
Latin America.

By the fall of 1906 Mascagni was negotiating with Mocchi and with Lorenzo (Renzo) Sonzogno, Signor Edoardo's astute nephew. Their offer to re-
negotiate the terms of Mascagni's contracts for his earlier operas was a powerful inducement for him to return to his old publisher. By 1906 his contract
for *Cavalleria rusticana* had only four more years to run, *L'Amico Fritz,* only five.
Without the fees from these two operas, his financial future would become
perilous. Sonzogno offered to extend Mascagni's royalties from twenty years
to the maximum copyright period of eighty years. In return, Mascagni agreed
to compose a new opera for Sonzogno, to be completed within two years of
his receipt of an acceptable libretto from the publisher. Another provision,
which later became a bone of contention, gave the publisher the option to
commission a second opera upon completion of the first.

The new contract was signed on November 20. Within a week Mascagni was listening to a young poet, Fausto Salvatori, read aloud a new libretto entitled *La Festa del grano*. Less than three weeks later, Mascagni wrote Sonzogno that he would accept Salvatori's libretto, advising Sonzogno that he had put *Vistilia* aside, and writing that "you can be sure that under any circumstances I will write for your firm before any French publisher." For all his efforts, *Vistilia* continued to elude him. As he told a friend years later, "The atmospheric details took priority over the drama. The characters were lost and overwhelmed by the setting, in its scale and variety. Rather than a rich, impassioned, and organic drama, *Vistilia* turned into a . . . sort of picturesque tableau of Roman folklore."

Despite Mascagni's initial enthusiasm, *La Festa del grano* turned out to be another intractable subject. By August 1907 he was writing Sonzogno that "the conviction that this work is absolutely unsuitable continues to grow in my mind," and by February 1908 he had abandoned it as well. Although he had over thirty-two hundred unsolicited libretti in cartons in his basement, the libretto that would engage his emotions and enable him to begin composing again seemed more remote than ever. For more than three years he had not written an opera.

A proposal from Luigi Illica in May ended the drought. Although his friendship with Mascagni had survived the battle with Ricordi, Illica found the composer, with his unpredictable demands and demonic bursts of energy, a difficult creative partner and had not approached him since *Maria Antonietta's* demise. By 1908, however, Illica needed Mascagni. *Maria Antonietta* had been rejected by Puccini as well and was finally abandoned unfinished by its author. Since *Madama Butterfly*, written with Giacosa, Illica had not had a success. He had not worked with Giordano since *Siberia;* since Giacosa's death in 1906, Puccini had rebuffed Illica's proposals, clearly reluctant to trust his solo efforts.

Illica presented Mascagni with a scenario entitled *Isabeau*, inspired by Lord Tennyson's familiar poem on the Lady Godiva story. It was not a new project. He had drafted it initially in 1904 and offered it to Bossi, Puccini, and Franchetti without success. Mascagni, however, embraced it enthusiastically. In July 1908 he wrote Sonzogno, asking that it be substituted for the *Festa del grano;* he wrote simultaneously to Illica that if Sonzogno should reject the libretto, he would write the music "on [his] own account."

Isabeau is not a retelling of the Lady Godiva story, but rather, as Mascagni stressed, "a new drama, which may have a few points in common with the source of its inspiration." Set in medieval England, it is the story of the beautiful, chaste princess Isabeau and the woodsman Folco. Her father, the king, manipulated by his evil counselor Cornelius, demands that the devout Isabeau marry. To this end, he sponsors a tournament of love, to which knights come to win her love, not by force of arms, but by their pleas and their yearning eyes.

Isabeau rejects them all, observed by Folco, who has come to the city after dreaming of falling in love with her. As her punishment, the king orders her to ride through the city at noon on her white horse, "naked, to every insult of the people's eyes and the sun's rays." In response to the people's outrage, the king decrees that anyone who looks upon the maiden during her ride shall have his eyes put out. Folco ignores the edict and greets her, throwing flowers and singing her praises. She cries out, and Folco is dragged away by the outraged townspeople.

In the last act, Isabeau confronts Folco. Responding to the purity and intensity of his love, love stirs in her heart for the first time. She rushes to tell her father that she will obey him and marry Folco. Determined that the match not take place, Cornelius incites the crowd surrounding the palace. They rush in and drag Folco away. As Isabeau returns, she sees the mob killing her lover and throws herself into the mêlée to die with him.

The exuberant romanticism of the libretto stirred Mascagni deeply. Folco is a kindred spirit to Guglielmo Ratcliff, while Isabeau, in her innocence and her victimization by a harsh father figure, is the archetypal Mascagni heroine. It was, at the same time, something new for him. To capture Folco's otherworldly dimension and Isabeau's psychological transformation in music was precisely the challenge that Mascagni wanted from a new opera. *Isabeau* simultaneously appealed to Mascagni's sense of creative adventure and his deepest emotional drives.

Sonzogno accepted the new libretto in July 1908. By the end of September Mascagni had begun composing, but soon wrote Illica, "I am more and more convinced of the magnificent quality of your powerful work; here and there, however, a few verses will have to be changed." By early December he had set everything he considered to be in suitable form and was impatient for Illica to revise the libretto. Illica went to Rome at the end of January 1909 and worked on *Isabeau* throughout February. When Mascagni resumed work on the opera in June, he was still unsatisfied: "I need you: now that I have the libretto in my grasp, I feel that it is necessary to change a few things here and there. If you will help me, I will send you bit by bit those sections that I want changed, with precise indications of my desiderata. Agreed?" He rejected Sonzogno's suggestion to call in Targioni to fix things up, writing him that "this isn't just a matter of correcting and fixing up some verses." While

Mascagni and Illica would continue to work on the libretto through the summer, his progress soon came to a halt. The next year was consumed by personal and professional turmoil, and he would not resume work on the opera until the spring of 1910.

ROME AND THE COSTANZI THEATER

By 1905 Mascagni and his family were established in Rome. He visited Livorno to conduct his operas and to maintain his ties with the city of his youth, but as a visitor rather than as a resident. He no longer used his mansion but stayed instead in the luxurious Hotel Giappone, an establishment that offered both a "garage pour automobiles" and a modern "ascenseur lift." In 1909, learning that his rent at the Palazzo Maggiorani was to be tripled, Mascagni decided to become a Roman homeowner. In the spring he bought a lot for ninety thousand lire on the Via Po, in an elegant residential area being developed near the Borghese gardens. By fall a palatial new home designed to his specifications, containing two rental apartments as well as spacious quarters for himself and his family, was under construction.

From 1909 he regularly conducted the symphonic concerts at the Augusteo (Corea) Theater, expanding his repertory to include a wide variety of new works, including Brahms's Symphony no. 2 and Richard Strauss's Serenade for Wind Instruments, op. 7. After his January 1909 concerts, the prominent critic Raffaelo de Rensis wrote that "last year's memorable concerts at the Corea were those conducted by Mengelberg; this year, so far, the memorable ones have been those conducted by Mascagni." He served on boards and commissions, selected candidates for the government's musical scholarships, and chaired the observances in honor of the centenary of Pergolesi's death, where he delivered one of his first jeremiads against the course of modern music, issuing "a severe warning against the disoriented direction down which the art [of music] of our time, in such turmoil, is heading." In the midst of these activities, in the summer of 1909 Mascagni took on the direction of the Costanzi Theater, Rome's principal opera house.

Early in the century, the Italian opera industry was in crisis. Rising costs, and the growing reluctance of municipal taxpayers to subsidize their opera houses, led to economic turmoil. Some theaters, including La Scala, closed their doors for entire seasons, while all groped for alternatives to the traditional impresario system. One of the more radical products of this climate was an early operatic consortium, the Società Teatrale Internazionale, or

STIN. STIN aimed to control enough theaters in Italy and Latin America to create economies of scale and end the competition for star singers afflicting the opera houses of both continents. STIN was also an uneasy alliance between strong and potentially incompatible personalities, particularly Walter Mocchi, its general manager as well as its largest single stockholder, Renzo Sonzogno, and Enrico di San Martino, president of the Santa Cecilia Conservatory, the dominant lay figure in the Roman musical world.

In 1908 STIN purchased the Costanzi Theater, making it the flagship of their Italian operations. Their first season, under the leadership of the composer Giacomo Orefice, was a disaster. The house closed little more than a month after the season opened, and after a stormy meeting with the STIN board, Orefice resigned. To salvage some financial return, STIN rented the Costanzi Theater for the rest of the spring to an operetta company, which used the opera house to perform *The Merry Widow* along with a slapdash number called *Pirlimpinpin's Magic Powder.*

Looking for a dramatic gesture to reverse the 1908–9 debacle, Mocchi convinced his reluctant board to entrust the next season to Pietro Mascagni. For Mascagni, the opportunity to run the Costanzi was a gift from heaven. For years he had been an unsparing critic of everyone associated with the production of opera, making no secret of his firm conviction that, given the opportunity, he could do better than any of them. He set *Isabeau* aside to devote his full energy to the Costanzi, and by fall his success in putting his stamp on the theater was recognized by the magazine *Ars et Labor*, which heralded him as "The Czar of the Costanzi Theater":

> *Here Mascagni stands in his newest roles as administrator, conductor, stage director, etc., etc. at the Costanzi Theater in Rome; here [he] stands onstage, superintending the renovation of the theater; he is also architect, electrician, stagehand . . . and, we hope, central heating installer as well, recalling some polar temperatures . . . that forced us to huddle in our seats, wrapped up in furs.*

He had the theater completely rebuilt. The orchestra pit was lowered, clearing sight lines to the stage and improving the acoustics. A new lighting system was installed, frameworks were constructed to support the banks of stage lights, and runners to move sets on and off stage were laid. The lights were now centrally controlled from a room under the proscenium, from which the operator could communicate directly by telephone with the prompter, the stage electrician, and the conductor on the podium. The stage was rebuilt and two substage levels added for circulation and storage.

Mascagni's season balanced masterworks of the past with modern operas, including a few new to the Rome audience. Wagner was represented by *Lohengrin* and *Tristan und Isolde.* The other classic operas were Italian: *The Barber of Seville,* Bellini's *Norma,* Boito's *Mefistofele,* and Verdi's *Don Carlos.* From among established newer operas he chose Puccini's *La Bohème* and his own *Iris* and *Cavalleria rusticana,* paired with Giordano's latest work, *Mese Mariano.* Other novelties included the first Rome performances of *La Festa del grano* by the Piedmontese composer Giocondo Fino, to the Salvatori libretto that Mascagni had rejected in 1906, and the debut of Leoncavallo's latest opera, *Maia.* Mascagni had hoped to present Richard Strauss's *Elektra* but had been dissuaded by the publisher's fee demands.

By the end of September, after auditioning hundreds of singers and instrumentalists, he had rebuilt the orchestra around a new body of experienced musicians and assembled a full company of singers, including his former Pesaro pupils Maria Farneti and Umberto Macnez; the baritone Titta Ruffo; the tenors Amadeo Bassi and Charles Rousselière; and the sopranos Emma Carelli, Giannina Russ, and the Polish Felicia Kaschovska, a Wagner specialist. His efforts to recruit Chaliapin to sing Mefistofele and Boris Godunov, however, were unsuccessful.

The season opened on December 16 with *Tristan und Isolde* with the king and queen in attendance, although they left midway through the second act. The public reaction was warm but not enthusiastic; Wagner's later works were still a rarity in Rome, and, as Barini noted, "this score is not one that reveals all its virtues on first hearing." Despite the lukewarm public reaction, Mascagni's conducting and staging of the opera were acclaimed, as Adriano Belli wrote in the *Corriere d'Italia:* "Mascagni has mastered every detail of this score with great thoroughness and true artistic sensitivity; he has thus obtained a performance that was bright and balanced, and at the same time warm and nuanced."

A week later, the public greeted *La Bohème* more enthusiastically. Puccini, unable to attend, sent Mascagni a telegram that began, "The success of your *Bohème* delights me and makes me remember the bohemian days we lived together, sadly so long ago." *Mefistofele,* which followed on New Year's Day, was also successful, but Leoncavallo's *Maia,* two weeks later, was not. The *Messaggero* wrote that "perhaps no opera has ever before been the object of such fraternal care and attention as Mascagni has expended in his hope that Victory would smile on the composer. But his efforts did not yield the anticipated return." None of the season's novelties attracted much response, and all soon vanished from the stage.

Don Carlos, which followed on January 29, was perhaps the high point of the season, as a superb performance enabled many listeners to appreciate for the first time this remarkable score, which had never before been staged at the Costanzi. As Mario Incagliati wrote:

> It was [at the end of the third act] that the public sprung up, overwhelmed by their great enthusiasm, and standing, gave a long ovation to Pietro Mascagni, who achieved an interpretation and execution with his baton so clear, so precise, so unique, so powerful, and so nuanced, fully to deserve the honor of making this old opera live again with all the glory and all the breath of a new existence.

After *Lohengrin* in February, the season was interrupted by another conflict between Mascagni and the STIN board. Since the preceding summer, the committee planning the Roman commemoration of the fiftieth anniversary of the unification of Italy, or the "1911 celebrations," had been busily at work. Opera was to play a major role in the celebrations, and in the fall of 1909 Mascagni had submitted a proposal for a historical retrospective of Italian opera, from the works of Monteverdi, Peri, and Cavalli, all but unknown at the time, up to "the newest works of the young [composers] for whom the theater must be their proving ground." He fully expected, after his successful 1909–10 season, to be entrusted with the 1911 celebrations.

STIN had no such intentions. Despite his achievements, Mascagni was not popular with the board. His lack of deference to their concerns, his meddling in board affairs, his insistence on complete control of the theater, and the readiness with which he threatened to resign when crossed—knowing that his resignation would bring immediate pressure on the board from his adoring Roman public—made him a difficult person to have around.

The board had split into "Italian" and "Argentine" factions, led by San Martino and Mocchi respectively, a split that would soon lead to the dissolution of the trust. San Martino, head of the 1911 committee, had reason to distrust Mascagni, who was involved in an intrigue to replace him as president of the STIN board with La Scala's Visconti di Modrone. Mocchi was Mascagni's friend, but the composer could not count on him. While supporting Mascagni for the moment, he had other, long-term plans. Soon after Mascagni was out of the way, Mocchi placed his wife, the singer Emma Carelli, as general manager of the Costanzi, where she remained until the mid-1920s.

The news that STIN planned to lease the Costanzi to San Martino and the 1911 committee outraged Mascagni, who immediately submitted his resignation. The public besieged the theater, demanding their money back for the rest of the season. With the season hanging in the balance, the board issued a public apology and an announcement that plans for the 1911 season would be reconsidered. Mascagni withdrew his resignation, and the season continued. A week later it was announced that Mascagni would remain as director through the end of the 1912 season.

Peace temporarily restored, the season continued. *Iris* with Maria Farneti was followed by an outstanding *Norma* with Giannina Russ. The theater was then devoted to *La Festa del grano* for a week, during which the conductor Tullio Serafin, together with the singers from the Turin premiere a month earlier, took over the hall. On April 4 Mascagni returned to the podium for *The Barber of Seville*, with Titta Ruffo as Figaro. The final production of the season opened on the twelfth, a double bill of Giordano's *Mese Mariano*, in its first Roman appearance, and *Cavalleria rusticana*. The season ended on April 17; as described by Rinaldi, "the closing night was a paean to Mascagni, acclaimed as 'the savior of the Costanzi,' and the cries and waving handkerchiefs from every part of the hall moved—according to one newspaper—'even those accustomed to triumphs.'" At a time when operatic deficits were considered almost a law of nature, the season ended with a profit of 100,000 lire.

Whatever the meaning of the earlier announcement, as soon as the season was over, the STIN board resumed its negotiations with the 1911 committee as if the earlier unpleasantness had never happened and soon concluded a lease for a symbolic rent of two hundred lire. When the committee announced its 1911 season, Mascagni was not involved. Although billed as a historic survey of Italian opera, the season contained no works preceding the nineteenth century, no premieres, and no works by young, emerging composers. Mascagni was represented by *L'Amico Fritz*.

MASCAGNI IN LOVE

By the spring of 1910 Pietro Mascagni was forty-six years old. For all his volcanic temperament and impassioned music, romantic passion had played little part in his personal life. His most intimate attachment, his youthful romance with Giuseppina Acconci in Livorno, lay far in the past. Although his relationship with Lina, begun as one of companionship and convenience, had blossomed in Cerignola, over time it had come to resemble a business partnership more than an emotional one. Lina, whose unsophisticated manner hid a sharp intelligence, kept a close eye on his business affairs, tenaciously pursuing those who owed her husband money; with a resigned air, Mascagni wrote Gianfranceschi, "You know how money questions are her only continuous, permanent preoccupation."

Mascagni may have had affairs during the first two decades of his marriage. Liaisons were common in his world; life in the theater, then as now, threw men and women together in settings that seemed almost designed for the rapid making and unmaking of emotional ties. At different times, rumors linked Mascagni to a number of singers, including Nellie Melba—during his London sojourn of 1893—and Maria Farneti. Whatever the extent of those adventures, they were most probably few and insignificant. An adventurer in his music, he was conventional in his personal life. Molded by his religious upbringing, he believed intensely in the traditional virtues of home and family and was passionately devoted to his three charming but improvident children, on whom he lavished both affection and expensive presents.

Lina, moreover, was intensely jealous. It is doubtful that Mascagni actually had an affair with Melba in London, but Lina certainly believed he had. Adriano Lualdi, who assisted Mascagni as a young musician, remembered a 1907 episode in Venice:

> I was sitting at a small writing table [in the Mascagnis' hotel room] and the maestro, standing nearby, had just finished dictating a telegram. . . . Signora Lina was across the room, on the other side of the bed. . . . Suddenly Signora Lina attacked her husband: "Well, are you ready to stop carrying on with that slut (name and surname)?" Then . . . the maestro lost his temper and snapped back at her, with the immediate effect that a hairbrush was thrown hard, quick as lightning, by Lina in the direction of her husband's head.

The hairbrush missed the composer entirely and, narrowly missing Lualdi, flew out the window into the Grand Canal.

This unromantic status quo came to a sudden end in 1910, when Mascagni fell in love with Anna Lolli, a twenty-one-year-old chorus member at the Costanzi when Mascagni arrived in the summer of 1909, beginning a passionate relationship that would last until his death thirty-five years later. He had first noticed her in Livorno in 1908, where she had also been in the chorus. As he later wrote her sister, he had wanted to approach her: "I suddenly realized that she was my dream, my ideal; but I lacked the courage to express my feelings." Then, in the spring of 1910, after a rehearsal of *Iris*,

> I came upon her here in Rome, sorrowful, afflicted, wearing mourning. I was overcome by a strange feeling and without saying a word, just with my eyes, I told her everything: I told her of my dream, of my ideal. . . . With my eyes alone I opened my entire soul to her. And Annuccia [little Anna] understood me: with her beautiful eyes she told me that she understood. [emphasis in original]

Lolli's mother had died, and Mascagni's heart went out to her. Soon afterward, when they momentarily found themselves alone, they fell into each other's arms and cried long and hard. "And between our tears," Mascagni went on, "we told each other our entire lives, our terrible sorrows. I too lost my mama, and I was small, smaller than you, dear Rosina! And thus," he continued, "Annuccia and I united our souls, our *destinies.*" That first encounter took place on April 4.

Although Mascagni managed to finish the season, he spent the last weeks at the Costanzi overwhelmed by the sudden rush of passionate feeling that threatened to overturn the foundations of his once orderly life. A few days after the season ended he wrote Illica, "I am going through a terrible crisis, and I'm suffering horribly. . . . And nothing like this has ever happened to me!" Adding to the excitement and the difficulty of the moment, his passion had reawakened his drive to compose. He was frantic to resume work on *Isabeau,* which he now saw as a token of his love, writing Illica, "I must, you understand, I must overcome this crisis. I must finish *Isabeau!*" In this state of barely controlled desperation, he left Rome on April 27 to conduct a series of concerts in Naples, leaving Lolli behind.

Lolli was equally frantic and even more frightened. A young girl from a small village in the Po valley, deeply religious, traditional in her values and her beliefs, she was frightened not only by the intensity of her own feelings but also by the enormity of the sin that she was on the verge of committing. As soon as Mascagni reached Naples, she began writing him letters full of guilt and the conviction that he would soon tire of her and leave her. On April 29 he responded: "How can you think that of your Pietro? How can I ever have a thought for the rest of my life that is not of you? Oh, never forget that you are above everything else in my heart, *above everything else,* do you understand? Our love is not a sacrilege, not a crime. . . . It is the love that God himself ordained, that destiny has chosen."

Although it had been only a few weeks, Mascagni had already committed himself totally. The fear of losing her, after only a few weeks, sent him to his bed, where he remained, assailed by fevers and horrible nightmares, dragging himself out of bed only for rehearsals. On May 1, the day of the first concert, he received an affectionate letter from her; that night, after the concert, he wrote her, "Imagine how I conducted the concert! I cried and cried before starting. . . . I conducted for you, just for you." The next day, he sat down to express his feelings in more orderly fashion: "You have not yet understood me: you thought my love to be a passing caprice, a vanity, a trifle. . . . Perhaps you believed that I wanted you for the brutal pleasure of possessing a young, beautiful woman. I don't want to believe those things, *and I don't even want to think them.* Only death can divide us. Understand me, Annuccia! *Only death!"* Mascagni was histrionic and sentimental, but there is no doubt that he was also sincere.

On his return to Rome, Lolli, more fearful than ever, avoided him. Spotting her at the Costanzi, he pulled her into his office. "When we were alone," he wrote her the next day, "you had not a single good word for me; coldly, you told me to work up my courage and not even think of seeing you again." He spent the rest of the day locked in his office, sobbing and holding his head in his hands. Once home, he could stand it no longer: "I tried to kill myself; they took the revolver away from me. They called the doctors, who announced that I had had a nervous breakdown; they wanted to prohibit me from working. . . . God will have to give me the strength to survive this week." Lolli was adamant, and after a tense meeting they agreed not to see each other again. Mascagni left for Illica's home in Castell'Arquato on June 1. He had written Anna before leaving, "I am leaving Rome without even finishing my obligations: I have completely abandoned *Isabeau*," but he was far too caught up in the opera to abandon it. Whatever the outcome of their encounter, his explosion of passionate feeling was finding its outlet in his music.

Although Mascagni had begun *Isabeau* in 1908, he had spent far more time worrying over the libretto than writing music. Despite Illica's early 1909 revisions, the subsequent version was still far from satisfactory to the composer, who wanted nearly the entire text rewritten. By the time Illica's newest revisions had begun to arrive in mid-1909, Mascagni's energies were directed elsewhere, and he had put aside thoughts of composing. In April 1910, driven by his feelings for Anna, he had picked up the opera again. In emotional turmoil and pressed by incessant demands on his time, though, he had written little.

Mascagni was also under external pressure to complete *Isabeau*. In the fall of 1909 he had been approached by the New York impresarios H. Liebler and Company with a proposal for a five-month tour of the United States, opening in New York with *Isabeau's* premiere, with the young American soprano Bessie Abott in the title role. The terms were attractive, and Mascagni signed a contract calling for the opera's debut to take place in November 1910. By May the deadline was pressing; as he wrote Illica, "The Americans are afraid that I won't finish the opera. . . . But what can I do? I can't manufacture music."

As June 1 approached, Lolli began to reconsider. Finally, she reached a decision. The day of his departure, Mascagni received a letter from her pledging her love and enclosing a lock of her hair. As his train moved north, he wrote her a long, passionate, letter ending, "Annuccia, Annuccia, saintly and good, darling and blessed, my own soul, thank you, thank you, thank you!" The next day, he asked her to join him there in Castell'Arquato.

She was again uncertain. A week later he wrote her, "You write me that I want you to be my slave, that I want you to do everything I want, while I make no sacrifices for you. But, my Annuccia, when have I ever given you reason to speak to me like this?" He was again lying awake shaking and sweating, scaring his hosts. Finally, a resigned letter from Mascagni, accepting that their love was not to be, crystallized her own feelings and ended the emotional seesaw. By midmonth she agreed to join him in Castell'Arquato. She arrived on June 20, and on the night of the twenty-first, Mascagni and Lolli made love for the first time.

Anna Lolli was a virgin, and as a traditional young woman in a sentimental age, this was her ultimate commitment. The occasion had equal significance for the older Mascagni; as he wrote her a few days later, after she had returned to Rome, "I am writing in the throes of an ineffable ecstasy, of passion made of love and idolatry. 'Pietro, never forget!' you said to me. Oh, my love, my beautiful love, my saintly love! *Forget?*" For the rest of their lives, they observed June 21 as the sentimental anniversary of their love. When he could not be with her on that day, he sent her flowers and wrote her long letters revisiting that day in 1910.

Lolli returned to Castell'Arquato early in July and stayed until mid-August, when she left for her parents' house in Lugo and Mascagni returned to Rome. During those months he worked at white heat. By August 27 he had completed everything in short score except for the second-act intermezzo, which he finished on September 2. A week later, on her twenty-second birthday, he presented her with a copy of the sketch of the intermezzo, inscribed to "Annuccia, divine inspiration of my music." Almost all of the most ambitious and complex opera Mascagni had ever written was composed in only three months.

On his arrival in Rome, Mascagni pressed Anna to return to Rome. Constant prey to jealous fantasies, he wrote her, "You go out constantly, who knows with whom, who knows whom you have dates with; everyone courts you." Lolli never accepted such accusations passively but responded indignantly, invariably prompting immediate apologies from Mascagni. However ashamed he might momentarily be of his jealousy, it would soon reappear, and the cycle would repeat itself over and over. The intensity of his feelings had no limits. He had already placed Anna on a pedestal, seeing her as the pure, saintly creature who would inspire him to greater creative heights and rejecting anything that failed to correspond to his vision.

Relations with Lina, who had begun to receive anonymous letters about the affair, were becoming strained. "Lina has serious suspicions but so far knows nothing specific," he wrote, "but she made a terrible scene, accusing Peppino [Hirsch] and Rossetti of giving me the keys of their apartments so I could take women there." From the beginning, Mascagni was remarkably indiscreet. In his excitement, he took pleasure in telling not only intimate friends such as Hirsch and Illica but even casual acquaintances about the joy that had entered his life. Rumors began to circulate in Rome's cafés. Rossetti, a young man who helped Mascagni with business matters, was accosted by the writer Luigi Lodi, who demanded "if it was true that [Mascagni] had found a singer from Lugo . . . and was planning to make her a star."

Pressures mounted. Ralph Edmunds, Liebler's representative, was pressing to conclude arrangements for the American tour, which by now had begun to receive massive publicity in the American press. Although complete in short score, *Isabeau* remained to be orchestrated, an effort requiring many months. Meanwhile, the family's new home was finally complete, and arrangements for the move to the Via Po needed to be made.

Leaving the move in Lina's hands, Mascagni decided to take a room in Milan and orchestrate his opera there. After sending detailed travel instructions to Anna, who was to meet him there along with her sister Rosina, he set off for Milan on September 11. Before leaving, he had found an apartment in Rome for the two sisters and charged Hirsch with arranging the repairs and furnishings needed so that they would be able to move in by winter.

In Milan they settled into a suite with a piano in the luxurious Hotel Regina, on the Via Santa Margherita one block from the Galleria. Mascagni and Lolli were discreet and rarely went out together, eating meals sent up by the hotel's restaurant. He went to meetings and conferences, leaving Anna and Rosina to entertain themselves, or they went out while he remained in his room, in pajamas, working on the orchestral score of *Isabeau*. On one of their few excursions together, Mascagni took Anna to meet his ailing brother Francesco, who had been in a Milan nursing home since 1905.

Milan was the scene of an emotional reunion with Puccini, who sought out his old friend on the eve of his own departure for New York for the first performance of *La Fanciulla del West*. The strain of their careers, and the constant public attention given their inherently competitive activities, had taken its toll on their friendship. In Milan they shared a rare moment revisiting their youth, as Mascagni described the scene later: "Our embrace carried us in one bound twenty years back, when we spent the day at the keyboard and in the halls of the conservatory, sharing a few cubic meters in the plainest little rooms. . . . a crowd of memories, of figures and images of that long-gone world, flooded in." They spent an hour and a half together. Mascagni played some passages of his new opera for Puccini, and they promised to meet again in New York City.

It was too late for them to fully recapture their intimacy. Their lives had gone in different directions. Much as they might imagine otherwise, they were, inevitably and forever, rivals not only in the public eye but to one another as well. Mascagni, for all his affection toward his old classmate, resented his greater success. In the midst of *Isabeau*'s 1911 Buenos Aires triumph, he could take pleasure in writing Lolli that *La Fanciulla del West* had "had only a fake success in Rome." Trapped in his conflicted feelings of affection and resentment, he was strangely diffident in his dealings with Puccini, rarely initiating their meetings and occasionally even avoiding an encounter. Puccini, not Mascagni, initiated the Milan visit.

Puccini, though, could be just as petty as his rival. After reading a 1921 article in the *Giornale d'Italia* hailing Mascagni's new *Il Piccolo Marat* and describing him as "the noblest creator of Italian music," Puccini tore out the article and sent it to Renato Simoni and Giuseppe Adami. "They've discovered the creator (the most noble!) of Italian music!" he scrawled. "Verdi will be at least first trumpet! And all this after that little bit of a Revolution . . . of the stomach."

Lolli left Milan on November 8. Lina arrived a few days later, having completed the move to the Via Po. The orchestration of the new opera was still far from complete. He had already pushed back the date of the American tour and was becoming increasingly reluctant to leave at all. Finally, on November 27, the same day he completed orchestrating *Isabeau*, he confronted Lina and Edmunds: "Yesterday Lina, Edmunds, and I had a terrible scene. I announced that I was not budging from Rome! No one could untangle me from my idea, which has turned into an obsession. . . . I feel that if I go to America, I will die: I cannot live far away from you." The tour never took place. Although Mascagni never formally broke the contract, his delays had led Liebler to begin the tour without him. With Abott's singing poorly received, and with Mascagni's arrival still uncertain, the promoter decided to abandon the tour early in January 1911.

On December 8 Mascagni moved into his new home. Later the same day, he met Lolli and her sister and took them to their new apartment, on Via Vicenza near the Termini railway station and the Costanzi Theater. A little more than a week later, Mascagni gave the first rendition of *Isabeau* at the piano in his new house, singing the parts in his high-pitched voice to a small group of friends, musicians, and critics. He had no idea what he would do next, or where and when his new opera would finally be performed, but as 1910 ended his life appeared to be more under his control than it had been for a long time.

ISABEAU

Wagner's *Tristan und Isolde* was in the Italian air at the end of the first decade of the new century. The transcendent love-death of that ill-fated couple echoed not only in Mascagni's *Isabeau* and *Parisina* but also in other important operas of the time, including Montemezzi's *L'Amore di tre re*, Zandonai's *Francesca da Rimini*, and Pizzetti's *Fedra*. All of these composers, but none more than Mascagni, looked to Wagner's inspiration to free themselves from the conventions of operatic melodrama. *Isabeau* was the first major Italian opera to attempt, albeit with mixed success, this emancipation.

The appearance of Wagner's famous "*Tristan* chord" in *Isabeau* is no coincidence. *Isabeau* is Mascagni's most Wagnerian opera, set in that same legendary Middle Ages of which Wagner was so fond. Folco, with his innocence and radiant spirituality, could be a brother to Parsifal, while Isabeau herself bears more than a slight resemblance to *Tannhäuser's* heroine, as does her name, a variant of the name Elizabeth. Like *Tristan*, *Isabeau* is not just medievalism tinged with violence but a story of spiritual transformation through love.

The essence of the story is in the inner life of its two central characters, Folco and Isabeau. Illica's Folco is no simple woodsman but a mystical being who through his dreams has perceived the essence of things. To him, as Stivender writes, "it is possible to surrender one's eyes, since the world of the mind is no longer dependent on sensation. He is able to live in his mind, and it is into this world that he seeks to draw Isabeau." The three acts of the opera chart Isabeau's transformation under Folco's influence and her surrender to his world of pure love and inner perception. As they discover their love in the third act they all but fuse in a Wagnerian ecstasy, only to learn in the end that there is no place for them in a world ruled by the deceit of kings and the brutality of the mob.

Two figures frame the interior drama of Folco and Isabeau. One is the king, seemingly kind and loving, who, with his evil doppelgänger, Cornelius, sets the tragedy of the two lovers in motion, and the other—even more important—is the omnipresent populace, who first appear hailing their beloved princess but who turn into a murderous mob, killing both her and Folco in the end. Unlike the chorus in *Cavalleria*, who frame and define the action but do not engage in it directly, the townspeople in *Isabeau* are as much a character in the opera as any individual, not commenting on the action but driving it forward. No Italian opera had ever made the people such a central figure; indeed, not even in *Boris Godunov* does the chorus play such a significant role throughout the entire opera.

Mascagni writes music of great richness and variety for the chorus, capturing their many shifting moods, from the sweetness of the women's voices that greet Isabeau in the first act, and the richly harmonized choral march that opens the tournament, to the cries of "Morte!" as the mob drags Folco from his prison cell and the final horrified screams, set against wrenching major seventh chords in the orchestra, as the people realize that in their frenzy they have killed their beloved princess.

The world of the people exists side by side with the private world of Isabeau and Folco in mutual incomprehension, vividly reflected in their sharply contrasting musical vocabularies. While the people's music—and that of the royal court—is rhythmically regular and organized around recognizable tonal centers, the lovers' music comes from a passionate world of exfoliating chromatic harmony, of lyrically intense and complex melody, where sustained rhapsodic passages grow organically from short melodic cells, and where the orchestra weaves a rich texture of leitmotifs around the vocal line. Much of the couple's music can be counted among Mascagni's finest efforts, culminating in the opera's emotional climax, the love duet "I tuoi occhi" (Your eyes), in which the first-act motif of the cloak becomes a symbol of Isabeau's discovery of the world of love.

In *Isabeau*, over a decade later, Mascagni has resumed the struggle begun with *Iris* to transcend conventional melodrama and write operas that seek to plumb the depths of emotional experience. Unlike *Iris*, though, which is ultimately undone by its emotional distance and its absence of human relationships, the intensity of Folco's love and Isabeau's ultimate surrender provide *Isabeau* with the emotional center that *Iris* lacks. It is, moreover, dramatically effective. Starting from his initial inspiration in Tennyson's nude cavalcade, Illica constructed a strong story that moves steadily and plausibly toward its end, providing Mascagni with precisely the sort of material that challenged and rewarded his musical gifts while holding them within a manageable framework. Unlike its successor, the magnificent but excessive *Parisina*, *Isabeau* does not overstay its welcome.

Mascagni's musical language had come far since the days of *Cavalleria*. In *Isabeau* what has been called his "declamatory" style, in which recitative and arioso freely move back and forth, reinforced by and interwoven with a complex orchestral texture, emerges fully. It is more difficult music to follow than that in his earlier operas, with fewer familiar harmonic and rhythmic reference points; it reflects a second powerful transalpine influence, that of the Richard Strauss of *Salome* and *Elektra.* He was not yet fully comfortable, though, with this language; for all its power and beauty, the music of *Isabeau* is uneven, often carrying with it an odor of willed modernity at odds with the dictates of the composer's heart.

If there is a central flaw to *Isabeau,* it is that it is the work of a composer straining for a musical and dramatic vision beyond his reach. Mascagni was not Wagner, and the mystical dimension in art was fundamentally alien to him. He tries valiantly in *Isabeau,* painting with thick layers of orchestral sound and complex harmonies, yet in the end it is not entirely convincing. Although at an intellectual level he welcomed the challenge of finding a musical counterpart to Illica's mystical imagery, he was not able to find the music within him that would make it come fully to life. At the same time, the tension between Mascagni's aspirations and his achievement adds strangely to *Isabeau's* undeniable power. Its awkwardness and its overreaching, which parallel the strange mystical fantasy life of its hero, Folco, along with the almost painful beauty of its finest moments, give the work a poignancy and intensity of a rare order.

In his next opera, *Parisina,* Mascagni came as close as he would ever come to a synthesis of mind and heart, finding in the more carnal love between Ugo and Parisina the inspiration he needed to tap a richer emotional vein, while finding in Gabriele D'Annunzio's complex verse—far richer and more musical than Illica's efforts—the spur to construct his most ambitious musical edifice. Without *Isabeau,* however, Mascagni could not have composed *Parisina.* Together, they represent the high point in Mascagni's career, both as a composer of operas and as a pioneering figure of early twentieth-century Italian opera.

Pietro Mascagni's father, Domenico Mascagni. (Museo mascagnano, Livorno)

Pietro Mascagni's mother, Emilia Rebua. (Museo mascagnano, Livorno)

Mascagni's birthplace, in the Piazza delle Erbe, Livorno. The building was demolished in the early 1970s. (Museo mascagnano, Livorno)

Mascagni during his years at the Milan Conservatory. This is the only known photograph of Mascagni showing facial hair. (Garzanti Editore)

Mascagni and his two younger brothers, Paolo and Carlo. (Museo mascagnano, Livorno).

Edoardo Sonzogno, during the period
of *Cavalleria*. (Museo mascagnano,
Livorno)

Mascagni with the cast of the first performance of *Cavalleria*, 1890. (Museo mascagnano, Livorno)

Mascagni and the librettists of *Cavalleria Rusticana*, Giovanni Targioni-Tozzetti (left) and Guido Menasci (right). (Garzanti Editore)

Mascagni's wife, Lina Carbognani Mascagni. (Museo mascagnano, Livorno)

A caricature of Mascagni conducting,
1893. (Museo mascagnano, Livorno)

Mascagni with his fellow composers Franchetti (center) and Puccini (right) in 1896.
(Museo mascagnano, Livorno)

alla mia buona Anna, per due celebrazioni cinquantenarie: la "Cavalleria" e questa fotografia. Dicono che la "Cavalleria", dopo cinquant'anni, è fresca come il primo giorno di sua vita: peccato che non si possa dire altrettanto di me, dopo cinquant'anni di vita di questa fotografia!

26 anni e 5 mesi

76 anni e 5 mesi

Roma, 5 giugno 1940, XVIII.

con l'anima sempre giovanile e col cuore sempre tuo, Anna cara, ti dice tutto il suo amore il tuo

P. Mascagni

Mascagni in 1890, with a dedication to Anna Lolli written in 1940. The dedication reads, in part, "they say that Cavalleria, after fifty years, is as fresh as on the first day of its life; it's a pity that one can't say the same for me, after fifty years." (Museo mascagnano, Bagnara di Romagna)

Luigi Illica, the librettist of *Iris*, *Le Maschere*, and *Isabeau*. (Museo mascagnano, Livorno).

The Mascagni family in 1907. From left to right, Edoardo, Pietro, Emy, Domenico, and Lina. (Museo mascagnano, Livorno)

Peter Mascagnoff

A caricature prompted by Mascagni's leading a concert in honor of a visit by the Russian czar in 1909. The caricature appeared in *Avanti,* the Socialist newspaper. (Garzanti Editore)

Mascagni, in a photograph taken in Illica's home in Castell'Arquato, while working on *Isabeau* in 1910. (Mascagni family collection).

Sketch from the Postlude to act 2 of *Parisina*, composed at Bellevue, France, in 1912. (Museo mascagnano, Bagnara di Romagna)

Anna Lolli, in a photograph taken in Alberto Franchetti's villa near Florence in 1912. (Museo mascagnano, Bagnara di Romagna)

REALE ACCADEMIA D'ITALIA

21 Giugno 1910 - 21 Giugno 1935.

(Annuccia mia, ti scrivo in preda alla più viva Commozione!)

Per i venticinque anni di fede, di dolore, di sacrifizio, di martirio, Tu, creatura divina, martire Santa, Tu, Annuccia adorata, hai acquistato il diritto ad un avvenire di pace, di serenità.

Se io non ho potuto darti quella felicità che ho sognato sempre, non è stato per mia colpa: il Destino non mi ha Concesso la fortuna. Ma la Provvidenza Divina riconoscerà tutto il tuo

A letter to Anna Lolli, written on June 21, 1935, the twenty-fifth anniversary of the night they first made love. The heading reads, "My Annuccia, I am writing you in the grip of the most intense feeling!" (Museo mascagnano, Bagnara di Romagna)

Mascagni in Paris with (from left to right) Gabriele D'Annunzio, the publisher Lorenzo (Renzo) Sonzogno, Sonzogno's attorney Barducci, and D'Annunzio's secretary and biographer Tom Antongini, in 1912. (Museo mascagnano, Bagnara di Romagna)

Caricature by Autori of Mascagni and Puccini fighting over the rights to Ouida's *Two Little Wooden Shoes*, 1914. (Museo mascagnano, Livorno)

Mascagni with stagehands at the Arena in Verona, during rehearsals for *Il Piccolo Marat*, in 1921. (Museo mascagnano, Livorno)

Mascagni in his uniform as a member of the Italian Royal Academy, around 1930. (Museo mascagnano, Livorno)

Mascagni in black shirt, "standing guard" at the Exposition of the Fascist Revolution in Rome, in 1934. (Museo mascagnano, Bagnara di Romagna)

Mascagni and his grandson Pietrino. (Museo mascagnano, Bagnara di Romagna)

The Hotel Plaza on the Via del Corso in Rome, Mascagni's last residence, and the scene of his death in 1945. (Photograph by the author)

The last picture of Pietro Mascagni, taken by Luigi Ricci on July 27, 1945, five days before the composer's death. (Edizioni Curci)

11. Isabeau, *Gabriele D'Annunzio, and* Parisina, *1911—1914*

For twenty years the music of Puccini, Mascagni, and their contemporaries had defined the course of modern Italian music. As the new century entered its second decade, however, the Italian musical scene was changing dramatically. New figures, and new doctrines such as Modernism and Futurism, began to appear. Meanwhile, much of the dynamism of a generation of Italian composers had vanished. Of all those who had risen to fame in the 1890s, making their operas, in Gatti's worlds, "the beacon to which all young composers turned," Mascagni and Puccini alone were still creative forces.

The new generation was epitomized by two critics—Giannotto Bastianelli and Fausto Torrefranca—whose work began to appear around 1910. Despite their differences, both saw the nineteenth-century Italian operatic tradition as outmoded and corrupt, a parallel to the nation's corrupt political system. Bastianelli, while respecting the operatic tradition, in which he saw a distinctive "Italian spirit," considered it doomed by its "nineteenth-century chromaticism" and its bourgeois sentimentality. Torrefranca went further, seeing its popularity as proof of its debasement of the Italian spirit; to him, late Romantic opera was the music of the social status quo, reflecting in its sentimentality and lack of moral strength the corruption of bourgeois politics. Its practitioners, Puccini in particular, were the enemy. In his bilious book-length attack on that composer, he denounced Puccini's vulgarity, the cheapness of his success, and his "well-stocked junk shop internationalism."

While Torrefranca wanted to return to pre-Romantic traditions, others embraced modernity. Led by F. T. Marinetti, the Futurists dreamed of an art that fused nationalism and technology, glorifying speed, noise, and the dynamism of the machine. As he wrote in 1909, in his famous *Futurist Manifesto*, "We hold that the magnificence of the world has been enriched by a new beauty: the beauty of speed. A racing car with its bonnet adorned with big tubes like serpents with fiery breath . . . a roaring automobile, that seems to be running on a machine gun, is more beautiful that the Victory of Samothrace." Futurism's musical stance emerged in two manifestos that appeared in 1910 and 1911, written by Mascagni's former student Francesco Balilla Pratella. The first, which was largely devoted to denouncing the operatic world dominated by the "base, stunted, and vulgar operas of Puccini and Giordano," was followed by the *Technical Manifesto of Futurist Music*, which suggested the form that the new music would take, offering such grandiose but hazy edicts as "through the fusion of harmony and counterpoint, create polyphony in the absolute sense, never before dared," and calling on composers to "give musical expression to the mob, to the great factories, trains, ocean liners, battleships, automobiles, and aeroplanes."

While Pratella and the Futurists had little influence beyond their coterie, three composers who emerged during this period laid the groundwork for musical modernism in Italy. Ildebrando Pizzetti, Alfredo Casella, and Gian Francesco Malipiero, all born in the 1880s, came to be known as the "generazione dell'Ottanta." Pizzetti and, above all, Casella had a significant effect on the course of Italian musical life.

Largely sharing Bastianelli's views, Pizzetti sought to create music that would express "profound feelings . . . and profound aspirations to a purer and more selfless existence" inspired by the ancient Greeks and by medieval ecclesiastic modes. To Pizzetti, opera, albeit as a morally elevated genre purified of Romantic sentimentality, still remained the highest calling of an Italian composer. Casella, who had associated with Ravel and Stravinsky in Paris, saw opera itself as the problem. As he wrote in his memoirs, "To understand the gravity of the most essential problem our generation had to face . . . at all costs we had to get out of the atmosphere in which we had been born and reared, that of the opera." To Casella, Italian opera, with its unself-conscious appeal to an untutored public and its resistance to the avant-garde currents sweeping more advanced centers, symbolized all that was provincial and retrograde about Italian musical culture. Casella set himself the mission, which he pursued with determination for three decades, to "deprovincialize" Italian music, bringing it into the European mainstream represented by his Parisian friends.

In the end, these musicians and critics accomplished little beyond undermining the intimate bond between composer and audience that had sustained the Italian operatic tradition for nearly a hundred years. The extent to which nineteenth-century Italy had offered a mass audience for high art in the form of opera, and the importance that opera had held in its life, was unique in Western cultural history. Whether that bond could have been indefinitely sustained is doubtful, but there is no question that the new generation, with its disdain not only for the mass audience but for any music that appealed directly to that audience, hastened its end. The second decade of the twentieth century marked the beginning of the long march of Italian music toward cultural irrelevance. Pietro Mascagni was the last composer whose music mattered deeply for the Italian people, and whose premieres were events not only of musical interest but also of public significance.

Mascagni himself emerged remarkably well from the new generation's scrutiny. To Bastianelli, he towered over his contemporaries. In his 1910 book on Mascagni, the first serious critical study of the composer to appear, he characterized him as the only composer of his generation true to the tradition of Rossini and Verdi, whose intrinsically Italian spirit renders his music honest and pure; as he wrote, "In the presence of the terrible crisis that has the great musical world of Europe in agony, Italy has in Mascagni a pure representative of its ancient popular [tradition of] opera."

Pratella also found Mascagni the only one of his generation worthy of respect, praising him for his challenge to the publishers' monopolies and his spirit of adventure, writing that "Pietro Mascagni has truly sought to innovate in the harmonic and lyrical dimensions of opera, although he has yet to liberate himself from traditional forms." Many younger composers saw Mascagni as a better role model than Puccini, who, for all his great talent and success—or perhaps because of that great success—was seen as far more compromised and manipulative in his music, catering to the basest desires of his audiences rather than pursuing a personal vision. Even Casella, with whom Mascagni crossed swords more than once, respected him, writing years later that Mascagni "was an impetuous genius who had the noble virtues of faith and sincerity, and who loved art . . . with that intense love of which only a handful of the elect are capable."

Despite this grudging recognition from the partisans of the new music, Mascagni had little sympathy for their ideas or their music. Although he had considered himself a Modernist when his models were early Strauss and Debussy, by the 1910s he had parted company with Modernism. To him, art was the expression of feeling, as he said in a 1924 interview: "A work of art that does not convey well-delineated human feelings can never speak to the heart of its audience. In music, as in painting, as in poetry, art is not, cannot, be cerebral." The most important means by which music was capable of conveying human feelings was melody; as he said in 1910, in a phrase that expresses his deepest beliefs, "Art . . . must have a fundamental essence: in music, that fundamental essence is melody." Harmony, counterpoint, orchestration were means by which melody could be more effectively and powerfully expressed.

Mascagni saw the music of Stravinsky, Schoenberg, and their Italian disciples as the denial of true music. From the late 1910s onward, he lost few opportunities to denounce them and their pernicious influence on Italian musical life. Still, he retained some hope, as he expressed in the same 1924 interview: "This wave of collective madness too will pass. . . . in the end the sound concept of art as heart, feeling, creativity will triumph."

THE MANY PREMIERES OF *ISABEAU*

As 1911 dawned, Mascagni faced two immediate concerns: first, to launch his new opera, and then to secure a new source of income to replace that lost with the collapse of his American tour. Now supporting Anna Lolli and her sister, and with his new house to be paid for, Mascagni had substantial financial obligations. The directorship of Rome's Costanzi Theater also gone, his prospects appeared bleak.

In mid-January Walter Mocchi stepped into the breach, inviting Mascagni to lead an Italian opera company on a tour of Latin America, including *Isabeau*'s debut in Buenos Aires. Although the major Italian theaters were eager to present his new opera, the financial rewards of a La Scala premiere were insignificant by comparison to the proposed tour. Although reluctant to leave Lolli, Mascagni did not hesitate long. Within a week he signed a contract with Mocchi and began to prepare to leave in the spring.

For decades Italian musicians had divided their time between Europe and South America, taking advantage of the reversal of the seasons between the two continents. Leaving Italy at the end of the carnival season in time for the Argentine winter season, they would return to rejoin the Italian musical world in the fall. In contrast to that of the United States, dominated by German musical culture, the musical life of South American, particularly Argentina with its large and prosperous Italian community, was Italian in spirit. Operatic life even in the smaller cities of Argentina and Brazil was far more sophisticated than that Mascagni had encountered in the United States. A Latin American tour run by the experienced Mocchi offered few of the uncertainties that had bedeviled Mascagni's ill-fated 1902 North American tour.

Mascagni left Rome early in April for Genoa, where he met his musicians and began rehearsing *Isabeau.* Although delighted with his orchestra, he was less pleased with the two principal singers, Maria Farneti and Antonio Saludas; he wrote Lolli, "They lack the spirit to sing my opera. They are two cold fish." On the fifteenth they sailed for Buenos Aires on the S.S. *Tommaso di Savoia.* After stopping briefly in Barcelona and Rio de Janeiro, the ship arrived in Buenos Aires on May 2.

Mascagni's arrival was awaited with intense excitement. Although many Italian musicians had visited or settled in Argentina, no composer of Mascagni's stature had ever toured Latin America, let alone given the continent the opportunity to stage the world premiere of his new opera. Mascagni's music was at least as popular in Argentina as it was in Italy; *Iris* was nearly as well known in Buenos Aires as *Cavalleria,* having been regularly performed there for nearly a decade. Of Buenos Aires' population of 1.25 million in 1911, nearly 300,000 had been born in Italy.

By the time the *Tommaso di Savoia* came into sight, the waiting crowd had grown to immense proportions, with fifty thousand people jamming the docks and the square and spilling over into the nearby streets and sidewalks. As the ship docked, the crowd burst into cheers, and the municipal band broke into the "Inno del sole" from *Iris.* As Mascagni stepped onto land, the cheering crowd swept him toward the square, surrounding him so that only with the help of the police was he able to get into the waiting limousine. The crowd pressed so tightly around the car that it could not move, until Mascagni mounted the roof of the car and spoke to the crowd. Only then, with the police beating a path, did they reluctantly give way. Thousands more lined the route from the the docks to the Hotel Cecil and surrounded the hotel. Once there, Mascagni had to appear on the balcony and speak to the crowd, which slowly dispersed, cries of "Evviva Mascagni!" and "Evviva l'Italia!" echoing for hours through the city's streets.

After six days of rehearsal, Mascagni opened the season with Verdi's *Aida* in the Coliseo Theater. It was a great success, with twenty curtain calls at the end. During the first week they performed *Aida, Lohengrin, La Bohème,* and *Il Trovatore,* adding *Iris* and *Mefistofele* the following week, all to sold-out houses. Meanwhile, Mascagni had begun to rehearse *Isabeau,* set to appear on June 2. He was still not satisfied with his artists, as he wrote Lolli on May 31: "Last night's dress rehearsal didn't go well at all: Farneti is listless, Saludas sang like a dog, fouling up the entire third act, so much so that toward the end I slammed the score shut and sent everybody home before we got to the end." Despite its difficulties, *Isabeau* went on as planned, turning into a triumph for its composer and conductor.

Mocchi had allowed a month to go by after Mascagni's arrival in Buenos Aires to allow public anticipation to build before unveiling the new opera. The theater, despite the highest prices ever charged there for tickets, had been sold out for weeks. At the end of the first act, which was interrupted four times by extended applause, Mascagni was called forward fourteen times. There were fifteen curtain calls for him at the end of the second. At the end of the opera, following closely on the heels of a long sustained ovation for the third-act duet between Isabeau and Folco, one reporter wrote:

> *Mascagni had to present himself onstage another twenty times amid the roaring applause of the audience, which was no longer capable of holding back its enthusiasm. The spectators were all on their feet. . . . the ovations went on, one after the other, for over half an hour. Enthusiasm of this sort has never been seen before in Buenos Aires.*

Late that night, the exhausted but radiant Mascagni telegraphed Lolli, "Thunderous success, total triumph, affection, gratitude, devotion."

Most of the Argentine critics greeted the new opera with equal warmth. The writer for *El Diario* praised the work as fusing the "lively and nuanced art of the admirable Debussy with the dramatic potency of the author of *Salome*." Many of the reviews touched on Mascagni's modernity and his new "advanced" style; Luigi Romaniello, the respected critic of the Italian-language *Giornale d'Italia*, wrote:

> *The harmonic and orchestral proceedings—always richly polyphonic—have an intensely modern character, while the melodic essence is always personal, alive, endless, inspiring. It is never confined by the limits of bar lines: it is continuous, infinite; often a "harmonic melody," that is, where all or almost all the notes have their distinct harmonic significance.*

Eight more performances of *Isabeau*, all sold out, were given, along with a short all-Mascagni season, including *Cavalleria*, *Ratcliff*, *L'Amico Fritz*, and *Amica*. The pace was grueling; as the composer wrote Lolli, "I am working constantly: I rehearse from noon to six; then I go have a bite and take a nap in an armchair; at 8:30 I'm back in the theater for the performance and leave at one in the morning. That's my life, without a single day off."

On June 21, seven weeks after arriving in Buenos Aires, the company left for Rosario, Argentina's second city. That night, the anniversary of his first night with Lolli in Castell'Arquato, Mascagni sat up alone in his room with a glass of champagne, thinking of her, and praying, as he wrote her, that he "had not destroyed your life, your future, the dreams of your youth." From

Rosario they returned to Buenos Aires to make a cold, rough crossing to Rio de Janeiro. Within a few days the cold weather had disappeared, replaced by an asphyxiating heat wave. *Isabeau* triumphed again; after an ovation in which the audience threw their hats onto the stage, "the students invaded the stage and came into my dressing room, where they found me in my underwear, and, just as I was, picked me up on their shoulders and carried me in triumph all through the theater."

From Rio the company went on to São Paolo, where forty thousand people welcomed Mascagni at the train station, and from there to Montevideo. After two weeks in Montevideo they returned to Buenos Aires, turning around after a single performance of *Iris* and boarding a train for Chile. The tour was making money, and Mocchi was filling every moment. After months on the road, Mascagni was tired, writing Lolli in mid-September, "I find my nerves are easily irritated: this separation from my children, and from you, my soul, makes me every day more sensitive to the smallest things." The tour finally ended on October 31, with two farewell orchestral concerts at the Colón Theater in Buenos Aires. After the second concert, bags packed, the company went down to the harbor and boarded the *Tommaso di Savoia* to return to Genoa.

It had been a lucrative venture but a fatiguing one. During a total of 182 days from arrival to departure—many spent on boats and trains—Mascagni conducted 163 operatic performances and 11 concerts. The only days not entirely devoted to rehearsals and performances were spent in transit across the vast South American landscape. The ocean voyage back to Italy was a welcome respite for the composer and his exhausted musicians.

Back in Italy, setting the time and place for the Italian premiere of *Isabeau*, which both Mascagni and the Italian musical world considered the true premiere, became a complicated matter. Before leaving for South America, when he still expected to resume control of the Costanzi, he had signed a contract calling for the new opera to be given by him in Rome. By midsummer it was clear that he would not return to the Costanzi, and he had written Riccardo Sonzogno to suggest that the publisher negotiate with La Scala, adding, strangely, that he had no desire to conduct the premiere himself. In the fall Sonzogno signed a contract to have *Isabeau* performed under Tullio Serafin's baton during the La Scala 1911–12 carnival season, tentatively set for January 10, 1912.

The contract gave La Scala the right to present the opera but not the absolute right to its Italian premiere. In language retained from the first contract, Mascagni reserved the right to give the first Italian performance of *Isabeau* under his direction, at a theater of his choosing, up to January 31, 1912. Riccardo Sonzogno gave little heed to this provision, which he may have believed had been rendered moot by the end of Mascagni's relationship with the Costanzi. That was indeed the case, until December.

Early in 1911 Venice's La Fenice Theater, succumbing to financial difficulties, had canceled its 1912 season. In the fall a group of Venetian notables, unhappy at the thought of a carnival season without opera, decided to organize a season. They concluded, moreover, that an opening night in which Mascagni would conduct the first Italian performance of his *Isabeau* would be a superb coup for themselves and for La Fenice.

Mascagni was first approached by the Venetians early in December 1911 but did not take their offer seriously, long since used to bootless offers from aspiring impresarios. He was already uneasy with the La Scala production, however, and increasingly reluctant to remain on the sidelines. When the Venetians returned on the twenty-second with firm financial guarantees, he soon reached agreement with them. The date for the first Italian performance of *Isabeau*, at La Fenice, was soon set for January 18, 1912.

With Mascagni exercising his priority clause, La Scala reluctantly agreed to move their opening back to the twentieth. The composer began rehearsals in Venice on January 7 but soon realized that his *Isabeau* would not be ready for the eighteenth. On the fourteenth he telegraphed Sonzogno in Milan, demanding that La Scala again push their opening night back. Visconti immediately and indignantly refused. Meanwhile, Mascagni had rescheduled his opening night for January 20. On the afternoon of the twentieth, Sonzogno sought a police order banning the night's performance at La Scala. After a hastily called hearing, in which Visconti was able to convince the officer that La Scala had acted in good faith, the request was rejected. The show went on. On the night of January 20, 1912, *Isabeau* had its Italian premiere simultaneously in Milan and Venice.

Expectations were high for *Isabeau*. The opera's success in Buenos Aires had been widely reported in Italy, as had been the controversy over its Italian premiere. In both Milan and Venice the public reaction was as enthusiastic as in Buenos Aires. Scene after scene prompted wild applause, and each act ended with numerous curtain calls for the artists and, in Venice, for the composer. For Bernardo De Muro, the young tenor who created Folco in Milan, it was the start of a major career. For the rest of his career he was identified with the part, which he sang more than three hundred times; when he wrote his memoirs, he entitled them *Quando ero Folco* (When I was Folco).

Critical reaction, while mixed, was generally positive. Many Buenos Aires critics had commented on *Isabeau*'s "modernity," but some Italian critics stressed precisely the opposite, as did Giovanni Pozza in a generally positive review in the *Corriere della Sera*:

[Pietro Mascagni] writes as he has [always] written. . . . An unbreakable faith in himself makes him able to work quickly and easily, an acute sense of stage effect governs his conceptions; a natural eloquence gives his discourse warmth and point. He still knows how to give value to the sung word, still knows how to write an expressive and truly vocal melody.

At the same time, Pozza pointed out that the times were changing, and audiences with them: "[We] feel the absence of that which modern music boasts, the variety and the intensity of expression, the elegance and delicacy of the forms."

Even the most hostile writers found points to praise, while others found the overall effect of the work, despite its weaknesses, compelling. The authoritative Giorgio Barini, writing in *Nuova Antologia*, while expressing some reservations, concluded that "overall, *Isabeau* is a score worthy of a powerful composer and one that may have a long, happy life, above all if the first act is tightened."

The public loved *Isabeau*. It was given eighteen performances both at La Fenice and at La Scala, and as the *Corriere della Sera* reported, "Its financial success exceeded the most optimistic predictions." It was taken up quickly by other Italian theaters and within a few years arrived in Vienna, Chicago, and New York, where it was done at the Lexington Theater in 1918, with Rosa Raisa as Isabeau. Although it never entered the American repertory, *Isabeau* remained popular in Italy up to the eve of World War II.

THE SONZOGNOS AND GABRIELE D'ANNUNZIO

With *Isabeau* launched, Mascagni was eager to begin work on a new opera. An opera, however, was as much a business as an artistic proposition, and the composer's efforts soon became interwoven with the crisis engulfing the Casa Musicale Sonzogno. By 1912 the firm was near collapse. Edoardo Sonzogno, who had founded the firm and made it a competitor of the ancient House of Ricordi, had retired from active management in 1907, turning the firm over to the two rivals for his estate, his son Riccardo and his nephew Renzo. Their mutual dislike was exacerbated by their shared conviction that sooner or later only one could remain in charge and that the other would have to be forced out. By 1910 matters had reached the point at which Mascagni addressed a desperate letter to Renzo Sonzogno:

I know that the business is falling apart, and I see my interests, totally in the hands of the House of Sonzogno, totally in jeopardy. . . . Because, dear Renzo, the battle between you and Riccardo is going on with such pigheadedness, such backbiting, so many personal quarrels, that the interests of your poor composers have been completely abandoned.

Soon matters came to a head, although not as the composer might have preferred. Finding financial irregularities in Renzo's books, Riccardo forced him from the firm, taking total control into his own hands.

Renzo, however, had inherited Sor Edoardo's abilities. His cousin Riccardo was at best a well-intentioned dabbler; as Mascagni wrote Illica in 1911, "He's full of good ideas, but has neither the temperament nor the inclination for work, at least for this sort of work." While he dithered, his cousin, going into competition with the family firm as the Casa Lorenzo Sonzogno, showed himself brilliantly adept at recruiting both younger Italian composers and major European operatic figures; he introduced a dazzling series of new operas to Italy, including the first major works of Wolf-Ferrari and Respighi, Richard Strauss's *Rosenkavalier,* and a host of other important works including Humperdinck's *Königskinder,* Dukas's *Ariane et Barbe-Bleu,* and Rimsky-Korsakov's *Maid of Pskov.* The last three operas were all on the 1911–12 roster at La Scala. Riccardo had only *Isabeau,* his purely by virtue of Renzo's 1906 manipulations.

While Renzo built up his firm, the Casa Sonzogno continued to deteriorate, selling off valuable assets accumulated over decades. Mascagni had completely lost faith in Riccardo and his father, concluding that unless Renzo was brought back into the firm, he would have to associate himself in the future with Renzo's firm. Mascagni lobbied Sor Edoardo unsuccessfully on Renzo's behalf, as Edoardo Sonzogno, who had never accepted that the deferential youth of twenty years earlier was no more, wrote Illica in March 1912: "Mascagni has tried to poison my stay in Pau with a tedious polemical correspondence on behalf of Renzo and against Riccardo. . . . Finally, the last one I received was personally offensive, to which I felt obligated to respond in no uncertain terms, putting him in his place, and breaking off definitively with him." Mascagni had already begun to explore a new operatic project with Renzo. Sor Edoardo's contemptuous rejection was the last straw, driving him unequivocally into Renzo's camp.

In May 1911 Renzo had gone to Paris to attend the first performance of *Le Martyre de Saint Sebastien,* a dramatic work by Gabriele D'Annunzio with music by Claude Debussy. Hoping that Debussy might set a D'Annunzio libretto for his firm, Renzo Sonzogno signed a contract with the poet on May 22 for a libretto on the story of Ugo and Parisina, a subject that had attracted D'Annunzio for many years. Although Sonzogno explored the project with Debussy and his publisher Durand, he and the poet came to feel that it would be more suitable for an Italian composer. In February 1912 Renzo proposed the subject to an enthusiastic Mascagni. D'Annunzio finished the libretto on March 25 and sent it to the publisher, who forwarded it immediately to Mascagni. A contract was quickly drafted and was signed by Mascagni on April 20.

Since the 1890s D'Annunzio had been Italy's most widely known literary figure. Born the same year as Mascagni, the two men were the two stars of Italian cultural life, the two figures that the country had produced since unification who were known throughout the land, admired as much for their flamboyant personalities as for their art. The writer Eugenio Checchi, in an essay entitled "Mascagni e D'Annunzio," offered a profile of the poet:

> *In everything he does, he writes, he publishes, Gabriele D'Annunzio is an exquisite calculator: surrounded by the learned indiscretions of neophytes, the expected hosannas of his admirers, the proud apotheoses of his disciples, and the elegant, slightly vacuous chirping of ladies. Hermit and voluptuary, he seals himself in the fertile solitude of a country house among his fantasies: thus he chisels, sculpts, illuminates, polishes, and turns those phrases that always capture, in prose or poetry, a unique musical sweetness.*

To Checchi, as to the Italian public, D'Annunzio and Mascagni were polar opposites.

Few appreciated Mascagni's eagerness to extend himself into the poet's domain. Mascagni in 1912 felt himself to be at the height of his creative powers and saw D'Annunzio's poetry as the parallel of what he hoped to achieve with his own music. He believed that D'Annunzio might give him the opportunity to achieve the creative synthesis, the masterwork, even, of which he felt himself capable. D'Annunzio's own feelings about Mascagni were far different from those he had expressed in his 1892 diatribe. Since 1898, when the two met shortly after the first performance of *Iris* in Rome, they had discovered, to their mutual surprise, that they enjoyed one another's company. While nothing had come of their conversations then about collaborating on an opera, they had formed a real, although tenuous, bond.

While making plans for his new opera and trying to safeguard his interests in the face of the imminent fall of the House of Sonzogno, Mascagni's family situation was increasingly tense. With Lina now fully aware of her husband's intimacy with Anna Lolli, the marital relationship had become increasingly embattled. By late January 1912 Mascagni had started to explore the idea of a separation between him and Lina. With divorce unavailable, he and Lolli would be unable to marry, but they would be free to be together.

In mid-February he wrote Lolli that "with my friends I am exploring a way to find a solution to this state of affairs. I want to avoid any scandal, and above all, to see that your name, your immaculate person, never comes into the picture!" A few days later he left for London, accompanied by Lina and Emy, with matters still unresolved. From London, where he conducted two performances a day of *Cavalleria* at the Hippodrome for a month, earning a reported fee of fifty thousand lire per week, he wrote Lolli, "I carry on my usual life, I sleep alone, I go to the theater with Lina and Emy, I see no one."

Early in May Mascagni went to Paris to meet with D'Annunzio. For three days the two men talked and read the libretto aloud to one another, feeling, as D'Annunzio's secretary Tom Antongini wrote, "the most complete and empathetic fusion of souls and intentions." Mascagni wrote Lina that after having played the first pages he had composed, "D'Annunzio said to me, 'Don't touch that music. You've expressed everything I was feeling. Even more, I tell you that in the music there is something more than my verses.' I am truly encouraged to keep on going." Mascagni had not yet put any music down on paper. As was his practice, the music he played for the impressionable poet was still entirely in his head.

Matters with Lina were approaching a crisis; in mid-June the composer received a frantic note from Guido Farinelli, a young conductor who would soon become Mascagni's son-in-law: "I'm desperate: I've received news from Rome that the Signora Lina knows all, everything. . . . For God's sake, maestro, watch out for her, be careful—otherwise the most terrible tragedy might happen." Lying in wait by Lolli's building early in July after discovering her address, Lina waylaid her husband as he was arriving for a visit. Even Mascagni was coming to realize that his precarious double life of the previous two years was coming to an end.

Finding it impossible to compose in the tense emotional climate in Rome, Mascagni was intrigued by D'Annunzio's suggestion that Mascagni join him in Arcachon, the poet's refuge on the French Atlantic coast. Although Arcachon was too primitive for the composer's tastes, he needed to get away from Rome with Lolli; ever since having written *Isabeau* at fever pitch with her by his side in Castell'Arquato, he felt her presence to be essential for his creative work. On July 6 he fled Rome precipitously, reaching Paris on the eighth, and checking into the Grand Hotel as "Armando Basevi, engineer." The next day, Lolli left Rome for Lugo. Mascagni returned to Italy, met Lolli, and took her back to France with him after picking up his daughter, Emy, who by now had become good friends with her father's mistress, in Milan.

Precisely what may have taken place between Mascagni and Lina dur-

ing those few days is not known, but on July 12 news of Mascagni's "elopement with a chorus girl," and Lina's desperate pursuit—in some versions
armed with a knife—of the guilty couple, appeared in nearly every newspaper in Europe, as well as on the front page of the *New York Times*. Whatever the
facts of the matter, by the thirteenth, Emy, Lolli, and the composer—still under his alias of Basevi—were safely in Paris. He soon found Castel Fleury, a
furnished villa surrounded by gardens in nearby Bellevue, and moved in with
his entourage, which included Emy's maid and her Pomeranian dog, Tomina.
He was now ready to begin writing *Parisina*.

COMPOSING *PARISINA*

Parisina is the fifteenth-century story of the fatal love of Ugo, bastard son of
Nicolò d'Este, Duke of Ferrara, for his father's young wife, Parisina. Discovered by her husband—his father—they were put to death, perhaps as D'Annunzio imagined it:

> They shall have the same block,
> under the same ax,
> Two heads, and two bloods,
> making a single pool.

A famous tale of medieval cruelty and passion, it was the subject of a poem
by Byron, which Romani adapted into a libretto for Donizetti's *Parisina*, popular in its day but barely a memory in 1912.

Settled in by late July, Mascagni began working immediately. With
D'Annunzio coming almost daily to hear the music written the night before
and to discuss changes to the libretto, life at Castel Fleury took on an unusual
but regular routine, as Emy described it:

> *We had breakfast at 3:30 [P.M.] and, after breakfast, went down to the tennis court
> and played tamburello. D'Annunzio arrived every evening about six . . . after tea,
> he went into the living room with my father. He sat near the piano, and Daddy
> sat down to play. At ten we had lunch. After lunch, we played Ping-Pong or bil-
> liards. . . . At midnight we walked with D'Annunzio to the town square, where he
> took a taxi; when we came back, Daddy went into his study to work, while I stayed
> in the living room reading or embroidering; sometimes I fell asleep in a huge armchair,
> together with Tomina. At dawn Daddy came calling for me. . . . before going to to
> bed, we wrapped ourselves up like two brigands and went to get a breath of fresh
> air. . . . Toward six, sometimes seven in the morning, we went to bed.*

Mascagni and D'Annunzio, both susceptible souls, felt an almost mystical rapport with one another. From Arcachon, D'Annunzio wrote Mascagni on August 12, "Toward evening, when the tide goes out and the winds are calm, it seems to me that I hear passing through the bay some waves of your distant song." A week later, Mascagni wrote back, "At the same time as you were writing me, I was conceiving and writing down 'The Song of the Oars and the Sails,' setting down the first strokes of the atmosphere of the harmonious sea of the Marches." Soon D'Annunzio moved back to Paris from Arcachon, to be near Mascagni, and to pursue a new romantic adventure with the American dancer Isadora Duncan.

Despite his own fame, Mascagni did not feel himself the poet's equal and was strangely deferential in D'Annunzio's presence. He delighted in D'Annunzio's visits, expressing his gratitude for the poet's friendship in obsequious terms, writing, "I can't tell you what a void your departure has left in my heart; I truly suffer, also because it seems to me that I have never been able to express to you my deep gratitude for the fraternal affection that you have chosen to show me." The intensity of feeling was largely one-sided. While D'Annunzio's feelings about Mascagni were not without affection, the cynical poet maintained his emotional distance, seeing Mascagni more as an entertaining companion or a fascinating specimen of humanity rather than a truly intimate friend.

By early September Mascagni had set parts of each of the four acts, concentrating on those episodes in each act that most revealed the essential character of the two central figures, Ugo and Parisina. During these months his life took on dreamlike contours, which he was always to remember with intense longing. Sheltered in a beautiful setting remote from the many woes that assailed him at home, in the company of his adoring daughter and mistress, he worked steadily and productively, in a manic state that he described in a letter to his old friend Vittorio Gianfranceschi: "It is as if I am in ecstasy: I constantly move forward, I work, I compose, I conceive, I write. . . . At times it seems impossible to me that I have done so much. I am in a strange state of hypersensitivity, and I feel as if I am writing automatically without the slightest pressure on my brain and my will!" By the first week of October he had already set over half of *Parisina*.

Mascagni's idyllic existence was soon interrupted. Through Renzo Sonzogno he received messages from Lina seeking a meeting, offering to reach an understanding that would accommodate the composer's by now well-established relationship with Lolli. D'Annunzio, far more experienced in matters of the heart than Mascagni, and to whom the composer had turned for counsel, advised him against the meeting in unequivocal terms: "There isn't the slightest need—not even sentimental—for this trip. I've just received a letter from your wife in Genoa. It is full of weirdness . . . but—deep down—it is calm. . . . with the deepest sincerity I tell you that by going you are committing the gravest of errors: an irreparable sacrilege against . . . your spirit. . . . A 'modus vivendi' is nothing but a trap. Believe me."

Despite D'Annunzio's warning, Mascagni went to Genoa to meet with Lina. It seemed to go well, and he wrote Lolli afterward: "Lina is keeping her word: no reproaches, and few set speeches. . . . In essence, she was upset that everyone would believe her to be totally abandoned, and she was looking for a sign that I had not abandoned the family. That's all. Moreover, she said that in Rome I will have my freedom." It is impossible to tell whether Mascagni read more into Lina's temporary submission than was there, or whether the desperate Lina made promises that later she was unwilling or unable to maintain. As coming years were repeatedly to show, D'Annunzio's words, however cynical, were painfully prescient.

Mascagni returned to Castel Fleury at the end of October. Early in November he wrote D'Annunzio that he had set 1,030 lines, with only 400 left. His work, however, was becoming more difficult. The second act, with its intricate tapestry of Latin litanies, hymns, sailor's chants, and battle cries framing Ugo and Parisina's unfolding passion, was coming slowly. His letters testify to numerous false starts, unusual for him, in his efforts to resolve the problems created by the act. More serious were his fears about *Parisina's* inordinate length, as he wrote the poet: "I am very worried when I calculate that *Parisina* will be more than four hours of music: will it be unperformable, or will it at a minimum lack that practicality [of execution] that is essential for any opera's real success?" His growing awareness of the fatal flaw at the heart of the work that he had set out to make his masterpiece continued to eat away at his self-confidence; after another few weeks of work, he returned to the same theme, writing D'Annunzio, "You understand that an opera must be made for the theater, and the performance cannot go beyond the limits set by custom and by human endurance."

The idyll was over. Demoralized by the near-certainty that the work on which he had lavished so much effort would not be theatrically viable, and with his return to Italy set for mid-December, Mascagni's mental state deteriorated during November. By the first days of December 1912, as he started to "close shop" without having finished *Parisina,* he was in despair, writing that "all of my dear hopes have flown away; my four and a half months of work are lost; all the sacrifices made, all the worries, all the tortures, all fallen into oblivion."

Back in Rome, Mascagni sank into depression, unable to compose, thinking back on the days in Bellevue and writing D'Annunzio, "Now, instead, here I am sealed in my sumptous tomb struggling with my anguish and misery, counting the hours, the days, the weeks that pass slowly and uselessly." Finally, toward the end of January he began to work again, although, as he wrote D'Annunzio, it was "without life, without warmth." Before leaving for Genoa and Udine early in February 1913 to conduct *Isabeau,* Mascagni finished the second-act battle scene and the pivotal third-act scene where Parisina muses on Tristan and Isolde to the song of the nightingale. The last notes of *Parisina* were finally written on March 28.

After opening the spring concert season at La Scala, Mascagni returned to Rome to begin orchestrating *Parisina,* which would take until mid-November. In August he moved to Milan, to remain there through the premiere of his new opera, set for December 15. That fall he bought a house in Milan, on the Via Faruffini in the then-elegant San Siro section of the city, adding it to those he already owned in Rome and Livorno. Although his work took him often to Milan, he had few ties there and no particular affection for the city. Lina, however, enjoyed Milan. The house was part of his persistent fantasy of a life in which Lina would leave him free to be with his beloved Anna; as he wrote her, the house would give him a means "to send Lina to Milan, and I can be in Rome, alone, always with you." As with all such fantasies he nurtured, he was to be bitterly disappointed.

That same fall in Milan Emy married Mascagni's former student Guido Farinelli. The two witnesses, or sponsors, were Vittorio Gianfranceschi and Renzo Sonzogno. Emy, twenty-one and the youngest of his three children, was the first to marry. Mimi, twenty-four, nominally enrolled at the University of Genoa, was living a wild life, often embroiled with women and gambling debts from which his father was periodically forced to extricate him. Dino, twenty-two, a student at the Turin Polytechnic, had already come to love cars and motorcycles, the one constant in his short and unhappy life.

The rehearsals of *Parisina* went smoothly. La Scala had mounted an elaborate production with sets by Rovescalli and costumes by Caramba based on frescos from the Palace of Schifanoia. Two rising young singers, chosen to meet the physical as well as the vocal demands of their roles, were cast in the principal roles: Ugo was Hipólito Lázaro, a young Spanish tenor on his way to stardom, and Parisina was Tina Poli-Randaccio, a graduate of the Liceo Rossini from Mascagni's time. Carlo Galeffi, a famous baritone, sang the role of Nicolò.

Expectations for Mascagni's new opera were intense, and on the night of the premiere, almost every Italian musician of importance was there, including Puccini, Giordano, Boito, Franchetti, Zandonai, and Alfano. Even Riccardo Sonzogno was there, eager to hear for himself what the composer—with whom he was now in litigation—and D'Annunzio had accomplished.

At 8:30, half an hour before the usual curtain time, Mascagni strode to the podium and began the opera. At the end of the first act, slightly over an hour later, an excited audience called Mascagni onstage five times. The second act, which lasted nearly an hour and a half, began at 10 P.M. At the end, the applause was strong, but mixed with less enthusiastic reactions; during the interval, as one observer commented, "The length of the act was the principal theme of most conversations. . . . 'Beautiful, but long,' said those favorably inclined; 'long, but not so beautiful,' said others." The curtain rose on the third act shortly before midnight. Despite the lateness of the hour, the audience "remained silent, and listened . . . with complete attention." At the end of the act, the applause was enthusiastic. It was nearly one, however, when the fourth act began. At the final curtain, while the applause was warm, all but the most passionate enthusiasts were eager to leave, and cries for a second curtain call for the composer were greeted by hooting and whistling. It was 1:35 A.M..

The critical reaction the next day, as with nearly all of Mascagni's operas, was mixed, although the critics were unanimous in their praise of the performance and the production. Pozza in the *Corriere della Sera,* one of the most positive critics, saw *Parisina* as a major step forward for its composer:

> *The music is able to trace the finest sinuosities of the poetry; each character lives and moves in their own musical atmosphere, which is charged by a thousand emotional shivers without falling into excess. To the successive revelations of the text it responds with a play of precisely measured shadings, in a context of carefully planned colors . . . the separation from traditional opera is complete.*

Another favorable review came from Alberto Gasco in the *Tribuna,* who wrote that "*Parisina* represents Mascagni's most successful effort to reconcile the demands of cantabile melody with those of the drama in its modern sense." In both of these reviews, however, one feels less passion than what Guido, in *L'Illustrazione Italiana,* characterized as the predominant opinion, which he shared, of "respectful enthusiasm."

Other critics showed less respect or enthusiasm. Nappi in *La Perseveranza* concluded that Mascagni "had written an opera of noble intentions, but not the opera of such excellence that it could stand as the principal document of his career." Even favorable critics were concerned about the opera's length; Pozza concluded that "its excessive length, if not addressed, cannot but weigh heavily on the future of *Parisina* . . . even the most unbridled admirer of the maestro must hope that the surest and simplest remedy is applied: cut, cut, cut." Gasco flatly suggested that he delete the fourth act.

For the second performance, the entire fourth act was cut, along with the second-act postlude, the third-act prelude, and smaller cuts elsewhere. The truncated opera, reduced in duration by nearly an hour, was warmly received, and ten days later the *Corriere della Sera* noted that "this way, in three acts, the public has greeted it with greater favor, and each succeeding performance forms part of a crescendo of success." The opera had a successful run of twelve performances.

Parisina, although Mascagni's grandest and most ambitious conception, an opera that contains much of his finest music, has subsequently had the most limited performance history of any Mascagni opera since his ill-fated *I Rantzau*. After a handful of productions between 1914 and 1916, it all but vanished, never again seeing the stage during the rest of Mascagni's lifetime. It has been revived rarely since World War II, most recently in Montpellier during the summer of 1999, and before that in Rome in 1979, in a version cut far more drastically than anything the composer contemplated or in all probability would have tolerated.

PARISINA

The conjunction of love and death was a recurrent theme in D'Annunzio's work, as it was to an entire generation under the spell of Wagner's *Tristan*. The doomed figures of Tristan and Isolde, Paolo and Francesca, and Ugo and Parisina inhabited a realm of pure passion that few could emulate but which many looked on with yearning, as D'Annunzio wrote in "La Contemplazione della morte":

> With my own soul I molded two beings full of dark blood,
> and I lived in them, to understand sin . . .
> With Ugo and Parisina I explored the shadows.

Parisina opens in the Este villa on an island in the Po River. Ugo is restless and unhappy. His mother, Stella dell'Assassino, who has been discarded by Nicolò d'Este for his new bride Parisina, urges Ugo to poison her. As Parisina enters, Stella curses her vehemently and leaves. Nicolò returns from the hunt, and Parisina denounces Stella to him. Ugo interrupts Parisina, and Nicolò turns angrily on his son. Ugo rushes off, crying that he will seek his death in battle and that they will never see him again.

The second act is set at the shrine of the Virgin at Loreto, on Italy's Adriatic coast. Parisina, accompanied by Ugo, has come to find peace for her troubled soul. The shrine is attacked by pirates, who are beaten off by Ugo and his men. As Parisina greets the victorious Ugo, they feel an intense passion for one another. Although she at first resists his pleas, she soon yields, and they fall into each other's arms at the foot of the statue of the Virgin.

The third act takes place a year later in the villa of Belfiore. As Parisina waits for Ugo, she reads the story of Tristan. Ugo finally arrives, and she comforts him. Nicolò suddenly appears, and Ugo hides. As the Duke moves toward the curtains, drawing his sword, Parisina screams, "It is Ugo, your son!" Nicolò confronts the lovers and orders them taken away for execution. In the last act, in the dungeons of the Este Castle, Ugo and Parisina are alone, lost in a transfigured dream of love and death. Stella bursts in, demanding that Parisina release her son. Although Parisina urges him to embrace his mother, Ugo, already far away in another world, does not move. As the executioner appears, Stella screams in agony, but the couple go calmly forward to the block.

This story, and the libretto D'Annunzio made of it, fit Mascagni's aspirations perfectly. *Isabeau* had been a watershed for the composer. After nearly a decade of frustration, he had written his most ambitious work and had been rewarded by public and critical acclaim. He had dared greatly and had prevailed. Reinvigorated by his love for Anna Lolli, fortified in his artistic convictions by *Isabeau's* success, he felt himself ready to create the work in which he would fuse words and music into a transcendent whole, even—although he would never be so presumptuous to say so in public—create an Italian *Tristan*.

Although D'Annunzio's libretto has its faults, it is hard to imagine a libretto better able to stimulate the composer's muse. With his sensitivity to the word, he could not but appreciate that D'Annunzio's poetry was far finer than anything he had set before, either from Illica or his old friend Targioni-Tozzetti. For all his precious neologisms, D'Annunzio was a true poet. More important, he had given Mascagni a drama in which the characters' powerful emotions exist in pure, concentrated form. The desperate love of Ugo and Parisina, Stella's blazing hatred, and Nicolò's anger and grief are intensely felt and richly depicted in striking verse. These emotions, and the highly charged encounters that they provoke, are the very stuff of the drama. Indeed, the only moment in the opera's entire four hours that can be considered conventional dramatic action is Nicolò's sudden irruption into the lovers' bedchamber. Everything else is emotion, from the conflicts of the first act, through the unfolding of Ugo and Parisina's love in the second, to Stella's final confrontation with the doomed lovers at the end. These relationships echo the psychological themes so important to the composer. Ugo and Parisina are among the desperate, doomed souls with whom Mascagni had identified ever since his youthful identification with the mad Guglielmo Ratcliff. From the ferocity of Stella's maternal love Mascagni was able to create his strongest mother-son relationship, while there can be few fathers more destructive than one who sends his own son to the executioner's block. Finally, Parisina, as Isabeau before her and Lodoletta after, was Anna Lolli.

Parisina, who inspired Mascagni's finest portrayal of a woman's transformation through love, is the heart of the opera. During the course of the opera, the childish, guilt-ridden woman of act 1 grows in stature, and in the end her entire being is transfigured by her contemplation and acceptance of death. Ugo and Parisina follow opposite paths; as she grows stronger, he grows weaker. His intensity overwhelms her at Loreto, but in the third act it is she who comforts him in his misery, and at the end her transcendent spirit sustains them both.

All of this met Mascagni's need to pursue his idiosyncratic vision of opera not as theater of action and events but as expression of emotion and revelation of psychology, a vision that places the mature Mascagni closer to the Debussy of *Pelléas* or the German Expressionists—although he might not acknowledge the kinship—than to most of his Italian contemporaries. Puccini's reaction to *Parisina* that "in the theater one doesn't want words, one wants actions" reflects the radical difference between their respective visions. For Mascagni, dramatic action in the conventional sense was never an end in itself, but the means of bringing about the emotional confrontations that would illuminate the characters' psychology and that his music would render dramatic. For that, he wanted words; as he told Fraccaroli, "My constant thought is to recreate the words in [my] music. Not to comment on them, but to create a fusion of words and music."

Mascagni came closer to this in *Parisina* than ever before or after, creating a work that can well be considered his masterpiece. Although *Parisina* builds on *Isabeau*, it is a radically different work. While the tension in the earlier work flows from the conflict between the inner world of Isabeau and Folco and the outer world of the court and the people, in *Parisina* only the inner world of the characters' emotions exists, a world stripped of everything but feeling. The opera itself is a series of extended scenes, usually for one or two characters, built on emotional states and confrontations, interwoven with orchestral and choral passages that heighten the drama by creating an atmospheric frame for the characters' soliloquies and dialogues.

To recreate this drama in music, Mascagni vastly expanded the musical language that he had used in Isabeau. His technique had become far more subtle and refined, capable of expressing a far wider range of emotions and mental states than he had ever attempted, capturing not only the emotions but also the essence of the characters and their relationships. While Mascagni had always been able to write music for lovers, in the first-act encounter between Ugo and his mother he depicts not only her blazing hatred for Parisina but also her smothering maternal feeling and her son's mixture of love, fear, and bravado. In the third act he shows not only Nicolò's anger but also his faltering effort to retain his dignity in the face of his discovery, and his final collapse into the agony of his personal Calvary as he realizes that the two people—perhaps the only two people—in the world that he truly loves have betrayed him, their eyes and hearts only for each other.

Parisina blends declamation and arioso with a flexibility and subtlety hitherto beyond the composer's grasp. No longer are there points of demarcation, as still exist in Isabeau, where the one begins and the other ends. Scenes flow with a continuous flux of music, constantly shifting in pace and character, with new ideas emerging from the orchestra and being woven into the vocal texture. Although leitmotifs in the literal Wagnerian sense are few, the texture of recurrent motifs and musical images is richer than in any other Mascagni opera. While the harmonic language is as complex and chromatic as in Isabeau, it has been purged of that opera's eccentricities; the composer has assimilated it and no longer feels the need to wear his modernism on his sleeve. The music moves smoothly between sections that are clearly tonal in character and those in which tonality is at most evanescent, at times vanishing entirely. With his newfound control of his complex harmonic language, Mascagni has reached the point where his melodic gifts can flow freely, far more freely than in Isabeau. For sheer poignancy and lyrical beauty, moments such as Parisina's prayer to the Virgin in the second act and the two scenes between her and Ugo in the third and fourth acts are hardly equaled elsewhere in Mascagni's music.

In place of the chorus as protagonist, the chorus in Parisina becomes almost a second orchestra, singing or chanting from offstage, a vehicle by which the composer establishes the mysterious, almost dreamlike world of his protagonists. He succeeds brilliantly, particularly in the second act, where he mixes the chanting of the monks, distant fishermen's cries, and orchestral interjections to create a magical atmosphere for the revelation of Ugo and Parisina's love for one another. A second magical moment occurs at the end of the first act, after Ugo's wild outburst; as Parisina stares after him, the offstage chorus whispers a melancholy refrain, followed by a solo viola, intoning an insidious winding theme. The same theme will reappear in the second act, where it accompanies the first stirrings of love for Ugo in Parisina's heart.

No other Mascagni opera contains the musical and dramatic riches of *Parisina*; indeed, of all of the composer's works, only *Iris* even approaches it in its quality and power. And yet *Parisina* appears nonetheless to be nearly unperformable. The most obvious culprit is the work's length. Few composers have dared to write such long operas, and none but Wagner has been able to create works that hold the stage for so long. However noble Mascagni's aspirations, he does not command the musical resources to hold any but the most sympathetic audience for more than four hours. Moreover, during those four hours, *Parisina* offers that audience little overt drama, focusing instead on realizing the emotional states of D'Annunzio's characters and capturing the subtle intentions of D'Annunzio's poetry. Even in *Tristan*, hardly a conventional melodrama, far more action takes place than in Mascagni's work. It may be possible to create a successful opera that is little more than a musical reflection of the characters' emotional states—Debussy's *Pelléas and Mélisande* could almost be described in those terms—but it is doubtful whether Mascagni could ever have crafted such an opera.

While for Mascagni every opera was, in a sense, a new adventure, he had never before so consciously and deliberately set out to compose a work that would be the *summa* not only of his musical gifts but also of his vision of the ideal opera. What is notable is not that he failed to create the Italian *Tristan* but how close to success he came, and what a remarkable work he was able to create. He would never again even attempt a work of such ambition, let alone realize such an achievement.

12. *World War I and* Lodoletta,
1914—1917

Parisina's debut led to another important encounter for Mascagni: between performances Renzo Sonzogno introduced him to the young playwright Giovacchino Forzano. Before leaving Milan, Mascagni agreed to have Forzano write two libretti for him, the first of which was to be *Lodoletta* (The little lark), based on the sentimental Victorian novel *Two Little Wooden Shoes* by Ouida, pen name of the popular English writer Marie Louise de la Ramée. As soon as Mascagni had left Milan, Forzano gave an interview to the *Corriere d'Italia*, letting the world know of his plans. While the composer was upset by the premature announcement, Puccini was even more startled, since he had been planning an opera based on Ouida's novel since 1911. Although he wrote a friend, "Well, it will be like the two *Bohème*s. That means good luck for me," he did not take the news lightly and immediately set out to secure the rights to the novel. After a strange chain of events, culminating in a public auction of the rights to the work in Viareggio in March 1915, he was successful. Although Forzano had already drafted the first two acts of his libretto, he set it aside. Meanwhile, Mascagni had begun to write a score for Rome's Cines film studio.

MASCAGNI AND THE CINEMA

The Italian silent film came of age in the early 1910s, as the first motion picture palaces opened in Italy's cities and the cinema began to attract a respectable bourgeois audience. Led by the dynamic Baron Alberto Fassini, Cines led the way in making films for that audience, coming out with two of Italy's first cinematic blockbusters, *Quo Vadis* in 1912 and *Marcantonio e Cleopatra* in 1913.

Fassini's competitor, Ambrosio, however, first brought outside artistic figures into the cinema, including Italy's most noted literary lion, Gabriele D'Annunzio. After releasing movie versions of a number of his plays, in 1914 Ambrosio released the spectacular *Cabiria*, which was based on an original D'Annunzio scenario. While the poet contributed little to the film beyond a sketch of the plot and the names of the characters, he allowed his name to be associated with the work in return for a substantial fee. D'Annunzio also recruited his disciple, the young Pizzetti, to compose a "Symphony of Fire" for the human sacrifice scene. *Cabiria*'s April 1914 debut was a major event, receiving almost as much attention as an operatic premiere.

Cultural fusion became the norm in the Italian cinema; as one writer has noted, "in an intermarriage of the arts that was unique to Italy, writers, poets, painters, illustrators, architects and scenographers . . . were very much a creative part of the film industry." The adventuresome Mascagni was drawn to this world, and the industry was eager to enlist both his talent and his fame. In May 1914 he signed a contract with Cines to compose two scores. The first would be for a film already completed entitled *Rapsodia satanica*, while the second would be for a film on the life of Garibaldi.

Produced on the eve of a war that would render it a period piece, *Rapsodia satanica* epitomized Italian cinema's moment of fin de siècle estheticism. The movie, in a prologue and two parts, is a variation on the Faust legend, in which the elderly Alba D'Oltrevita—roughly, "dawn of another life," a name rich with facile symbolism—renounces love to induce Mephisto to grant her back her lost youth. Once again young and beautiful, she meets two brothers, Sergio and Tristan, both of whom fall in love with her. She chooses Tristan, and Sergio kills himself in despair. Tristan abandons Alba, who feels "love's poison slip into her heart." Months later, Tristan returns. As she rushes to meet him, Mephisto steps between them and takes her for his own.

The movie was directed by Nino Oxilia, a young director who was to die in the trenches in 1917. Oxilia, who has been described as "not so much a . . . director as a poet who applied his poetry to the stage and the cinema," gave the movie a brooding, almost Bergmanesque quality. Alba was played by Lyda Borelli, the most prominent Italian film star of the period, slender, refined and sensual, and given to sinuous, flowing gestures that were carefully imitated by a generation of young Italian women.

Mascagni plunged into his new project energetically, unaware of how difficult it would be. No Italian composer before Mascagni had attempted to create an original work designed to follow the twists and turns of screen action in music. Even Pizzetti's "Symphony of Fire," for all its brief notoriety, had been no more than a self-contained piece of music written to provide background to a single cinematic episode. During May Mascagni watched *Rapsodia satanica* over and over, taking down the timing of each scene, each gesture, and each encounter with a stopwatch. Meanwhile, he began sketching out the major parts of his score, as well as the important motifs associated with the characters or their feelings. By the time he left Rome in August for Livorno, he had composed a considerable amount of material. None of it, however, had yet been put into a form in which it would ultimately correspond second by second to the events and gestures taking place on the screen.

Money and family, meanwhile, were much on Mascagni's mind. In April he had taken possession of his new house in Milan. He had also for some time been looking for a waterfront villa in Livorno, something more suitable for summers and holidays than the downtown mansion he still owned but had not occupied for years. In May he found a villa in Ardenza, just south of Livorno. With the help of his friend Leonino Nunes, who found a buyer for the mansion, he closed simultaneously on both properties in June, coming out ahead by ten thousand lire.

Having devoted nearly all of 1912 and 1913 to *Parisina,* and with Riccardo Sonzogno withholding his royalties, the substantial nest egg that he had accumulated as a result of his Latin American tour and his London engagement was shrinking. Meanwhile, the financial demands from the many needy or improvident members of his family were mounting. Since Emy's wedding to Farinelli, who was struggling to build a career as a conductor, Mascagni had been their principal source of support, buying their furniture, paying the rent on their Milan apartment, and sending them a monthly expense check. After less than a year, the young couple were constantly at one another's throats. At one point, Guido abused her and rushed out of the house, disappearing for nearly a week. While Emy took him back after a series of pleading telegrams, their marriage was already faltering badly.

Mascagni was also supporting his two surviving siblings: his youngest brother, Paolo, whose tuberculosis had diminished his ability to support his family, and his older brother, Francesco, in a nursing home for nearly a decade. With few other immediate sources of income at hand, the forty-five thousand lire from Cines for *Rapsodia satanica,* as well as the fifty thousand promised for a second film score, were much on his mind.

Meanwhile, Europe was gradually moving toward war. From the beginning, Mascagni was passionately opposed to Italy's involvement, convinced that only if Italy stayed out of the war could his homeland come through without material or moral disaster. At home, too, he found little solace. His relationship with Lina had become cold and distant; as he wrote, "Yesterday I had lunch with Lina. . . . I ate reading, as usual, my newspaper, without speaking a word." Spending the summer in the Livorno villa, they barely spoke to each other, except for her tirades over his relationship with Lolli. Fights between Mimi and his mother, between Emy and her husband, or between Emy and her brother Dino had become part of the daily household routine.

Except for stolen moments with Lolli, who was in Livorno until mid-September, he lavished his energy on the *Rapsodia satanica* soundtrack. He was working with a manually operated movie projector sent by Cines, and the process went slowly, with excruciating difficulty, as hours of work were needed for every few seconds of music. Fortunately, as he wrote Lolli, "the manual work is provided by Dino, who is bored out of his mind in Livorno and has no better recreation than turning the crank of the machine."

By mid-October Mascagni had finished the prologue and the second part, the shorter of the two principal sections of the film. Although he had already written the main themes for the complicated first part, it took him over a month to complete. Finally, by mid-November he was able to write Lolli, "I have no idea how many hundreds of times I've repeated the same little phrases, the same few seconds; always with stopwatch in hand. But I'm moving forward: now it's a question of two or three days." Mascagni finally finished his score for *Rapsodia satanica* on November 21.

Mascagni's *Rapsodia satanica* is not only a pioneering work of cinematic music but also Mascagni's most important nonoperatic composition, a work that both parallels the events on screen and yet stands by itself as a coherent symphonic work. By using recurrent musical ideas throughout the score, ranging from short and distinctive motifs to expansive lyrical themes, and by balancing the more intensely emotional passages with lighter, dancelike music, Mascagni gave his forty-five-minute score an overarching unity and forward motion that enables it to transcend many of the compromises made necessary by the cinematic medium.

Echoes of *Parisina* are frequent in *Rapsodia satanica,* beginning with the chromatic opening, into which, as a subtle but pointed comment on the film's many references to Tristan, Mascagni has embedded a brief quotation from Wagner's famous prelude. The chromatic intensity of such moments is set off by the many dances and genre pieces that appear throughout the score, beginning with a stately yet unsettling gavotte that accompanies the opening scenes of the film, a polacca for the boisterous party in part 1, a pastorale and minuet in the neoclassical vein of the composer's *Le Maschere,* and above all, the scherzo that accompanies the fête champêtre that takes up much of the first part of the film.

Although Mascagni finished the work in February 1915 and after some effort received his fee, the work itself fell into a mysterious limbo. Cines announced the film's spring 1915 release, but it failed to appear. Stranger still, in April 1916, when Emma Carelli sought to have the film shown at the Costanzi Theater in Rome, Cines set such difficult conditions that she abandoned the idea. The work was finally performed for the first time over two years later, on July 2, 1917, at a concert conducted by the composer in Rome to benefit war victims.

Despite the concert's august setting and noble purpose, some members of the audience were openly hostile, either to Mascagni or to his having demeaned himself and the good name of Italian music by composing music for the cinema. As the performance began, in one observer's words, "The lights were lowered . . . and—the fun began! The first cry one heard, from the gallery of course, was 'Enough of this—basta, basta!' Others immediately took up the cry of 'Evviva Mascagni!'" Mascagni stopped the music and the projectionist stopped the film, as the house lights came back on and the ushers evicted the offenders. After some twenty minutes, the performance of *Rapsodia satanica* was begun again and went on to the end without interruption. The ovation was long and enthusiastic.

Although the performance was not reviewed extensively, the critic of *Musica* was sensitive to Mascagni's achievement:

> [The score], while obedient to the technical requirements of cinematographic action
> . . . has preserved its own compact, integrated line. The composer has made a great
> effort to maintain throughout the different episodes and many adventures of the film a
> single spinal cord, retaining as much as possible the essence of a self-sustained sym-
> phonic poem. At the same time, the composer has not neglected a single exterior or in-
> terior event of the screen action.

A second review, in the *London Musical Times,* was even more enthusiastic, writing that "in all the opportunities for musical expression which offer themselves in this story, Mascagni has succeeded even, perhaps, beyond his wildest expectations."

Mascagni tried to save *Rapsodia satanica* from the oblivion that seemed otherwise to be its destiny. He gave it again in Florence in December, and twice daily for a month at a movie theater in Turin early in 1918. Cines col-lapsed soon after the end of the war, and not long thereafter the orchestral score itself disappeared. In 1961 the score was reconstructed from the or-chestral parts, and Mascagni's work, both as a symphonic work and in con-junction with the film, has been performed often in Italy and elsewhere in Europe.

ITALY ENTERS THE WAR

Intervention dominated Italian political life through the fall of 1914 and early 1915. With Italy rejecting entering the war on the side of her nominal allies, Austria-Hungary and Germany, the issue became one of neutrality or inter-vention on the side of the Entente—England, France, and Russia. Although Italy's masses, with memories of the bloody 1912 Libyan war still fresh, were unenthusiastic, the nationalist camp, dreaming of regaining Trent and Trieste, pressed for intervention. By the end of 1914, after unsuccessfully attempting to convince Austria to cede those lands in return for Italian neutrality, the Italian government had already decided secretly to intervene. Long having considered public opinion something to manipulate rather than respect, the government, while seeking the best deal with the Entente, began to prepare the Italian people for war. On April 26 Italy signed the secret Treaty of Lon-don, agreeing to intervene on the side of the Entente. Before the end of May, Italy was at war.

During early 1915 Mascagni was largely unaware, like most of his com-patriots, of the political maneuvering taking place. After finishing *Rapsodia satanica* in February, he returned to Rome, where he had been engaged to conduct a short opera season dedicating the newly rebuilt Quirino The-ater, which had been transformed by the architect Marcello Piacentini into the most modern theater in Rome. Mascagni opened his season with *L'Amico Fritz* on February 26, continuing with Thomas's *Mignon* and Meyerbeer's *Di-norah*, with a cast headed by Elvira da Hidalgo, Giuseppe De Luca, and Mat-tia Battistini.

These operas were a prelude to Mascagni's major effort of the season, a revival of Rossini's long-unheard biblical opera *Mosè*. For all that his name was a household word, few of Rossini's operas were performed in early twentieth-century Italy. Only the ubiquitous *Barbiere* was truly part of the repertory, while one or two other comic operas such as *Cenerentola* received sporadic re-vivals. Mascagni's production of *Mosè* with the basso Nazzareno De Angelis and soprano Giannina Russ was as a result treated much like a premiere of a major new work and was awaited with great anticipation.

Mosè was wildly successful, with the audience calling Mascagni back repeatedly for solo curtain calls, as if it were the first night of one of his own operas. The critical reaction was ecstatic; as Savarino wrote in *La Tribuna*, "We cannot separate from Rossini's triumph the triumph of Mascagni, who felt able to call *Mosè* back to life, and who set about the task with that youthful enthusiasm that is the essence of his being and the sustenance of his spirit," concluding that "rarely is it given to one to attend a performance like that of last night." For Mascagni, a passionate devotee of Rossini's music, the production of *Mosè* was a personal gesture to its composer, the man he once called "my eternal deity."

With the end of the short Quirino season, a tour was formed to present the opera with the same cast under Mascagni's direction around Italy, opening in Florence on April 29. At the fourth performance in Florence, Mascagni collapsed in his dressing room after the first act, with a high fever and acute rectal pains. After a visit from a local doctor, he managed to finish the opera. The next day, as the tour moved to Livorno, the pain was so severe that he was able to go on and conduct the night's performance only after he had been given a morphine injection. His condition was soon diagnosed as a rectal fissure, known as a rhagades. A week later, in Bologna, he was in desperate pain: "What I am suffering is unbelievable: one continuous spasm, day and night; a misery that's driving me crazy. Last night I couldn't close my eyes at all, for a second. And the night before I was in the train, mentally destroyed by this unbearable misery." He had gone from morphine to heroin injections to dull the pain, but even so, he found it difficult merely to stand on the podium. For a man whose health since childhood—except for episodes more emotional than physical—had been nearly perfect, this condition, which would torment him for the next few years, was painfully demoralizing.

By May preparations for intervention were clearly visible. Arriving in Milan, Mascagni was shocked to see signs of mobilization—troops, long lines of trucks and automobiles—everywhere. Frightened and outraged, he tried hard to convince himself that Italy was not about to enter the war, writing Lolli: "The war will not be! It would be Italy's ruin, total, irreversible, eternal ruin! It is not possible that our land lacks one man, just one, capable of opening the eyes of our rulers. . . . And if [there is war] I will weep forever over my country, destroyed by . . . a band of madmen and criminals." War fever had pushed everything else aside, and the tour was disbanded. The entire city, lying in the shadow of the Austrian lines in the Alps, was preparing for war; as he wrote Lolli, Milan "was in a state of total lunatic delirium."

In nearly constant pain, he withdrew to his Milan villa, taking frequent short hot baths, applying gauze soaked in cocaine rectally, and going back to bed, determined to avoid the operation his doctors were pressing on him. He no longer had any illusions about the course of the war, writing Lolli, "I see with the greatest misery that our leaders are lunatics: to push this country into war is a true crime!"

Italy's musical world shared the nation's ambivalence. Toscanini and Leoncavallo were passionate interventionists. Leoncavallo, who was "determined," in Weaver's words, "to become the bard of the holy war, in conscious imitation of Verdi," quickly composed a patriotic opera, *Goffredo Mameli.* Luigi Illica, too, was an interventionist. Although fifty-eight years old, he set aside his work and left Castell'Arquato, enlisting as a corporal in the artillery.

Although Mascagni had little fondness for the French, who he felt had manipulated Italy into war, and considerable personal affection for Vienna and the Viennese, these feelings paled in comparison to his horror of Italian intervention. Puccini shared Mascagni's sentiments. Although his emotional sympathies may have been with the Central Powers, his opposition to the war itself went far deeper, as he wrote Tito Ricordi early in 1915: "Much as I may be a Germanophile, I have never wanted to show myself publicly for either side, so much do I deplore the way war spreads its torments in the world."

Once Italy had entered the war, Mascagni dutifully supported his country and his two patriotic sons, both eager to take part in the war. Dino planned to sign up immediately, while Mimi wanted to join as soon as he finished his exams at the University of Urbino, to which his father had sent him in the hopes that in that isolated spot he might finally settle down and earn his law degree. Mascagni, as always the doting father, set about smoothing his sons' path into the war. Although still in intense pain, he left Milan immediately for Turin, where Dino, who had opened a motorcycle workshop, sought his help to obtain a coveted spot in an aviation battalion. A week later, after Mimi had finished his exams, he joined them in Turin, seeking to be accepted in an equally competitive automotive battalion. Mascagni went to work lobbying for his sons' appointments, offering the army the use of the family sedan and even trying to arrange for Teresio, the Mascagni family chauffeur, to be assigned to the same unit as Mimi.

Mascagni threw himself into the war effort, spending much of his energy organizing and conducting benefit concerts, even putting aside his feelings to share the podium at La Scala in 1916 with the French composer André Messager in a benefit for the Franco-Italian League. For all his willingness to devote his time to benefit concerts, Mascagni steadfastly refused to compose patriotic music, prompting criticism both from colleagues and the public. Mascagni's refusal led the nationalist deputy Innocenzo Cappa to denounce him and Puccini in an article in the spring of 1918, closing with the vituperous accusation that "the Italian people, when the hour of victory arrives, will finally be able to ask of you whether the sad reproof of your hearts, your shared silence, did not have this meaning: perhaps you did not dare hope for an Italian victory and fell silent because of your lack of faith." Mascagni did contribute a short work, however, to an album assembled by the Italian Red Cross to benefit the victims of the war. His contribution was a romance entitled "Bimba bionda" (Little blond girl), a setting of a poem by Anna Lolli. In the interest of decorum, the published song bears the heading "words by Nino Pareto," an anagram of Anna and Pietro.

Although Mascagni was ready to do his duty as an Italian, he never wavered in his conviction that the war was a tragedy, for humanity in general and for Italy in particular. He voiced his position with unusual clarity in an article entitled "To the Sources of Melody," which he wrote for the weekly *Il Mondo* in November 1915, explaining his feelings about patriotic music, and the war itself, in thoughtful, even prescient words:

> *Those who set about writing operas on patriotic subjects are making a mistake. . . . when the war is over, our disgust over this terrible slaughter will be so overwhelming that no one will want in the least either to hear or speak about those works. . . . The war is dragging us back centuries. It is making us walk backward on the path of civilization. . . . Where will the most daring social ideas, the achievements of internationalism and socialism, end up? All is drowned, lost.*

He then set forth what was to be his artistic credo for the war years, his definition of the music demanded by such terrible times. "The war must carry us back to the music of feeling, to the sources of melody," he wrote. "We have all seen the evolution that has taken place in music during the last years of universal peace. Let us hope that [the war] will lead us back to the simplicity and purity of melody." This credo stands behind *Lodoletta*, the one opera Mascagni composed during the war years.

THE COMPOSITION OF *LODOLETTA*

During the first half of 1915, Mascagni's work at the Quirino in Rome, his chronic pain, and the gathering war clouds had occupied his mind and prevented him from thinking about operatic projects. By August yet another matter had arisen to engage his energy.

After Mascagni's decision early in 1912 to compose *Parisina* for Renzo Sonzogno, his relationship with the remaining husk of the once-glorious Casa Sonzogno had continued to deteriorate. Finally, in April 1913 Mascagni had lost patience with his former publisher and brought suit not only to recover royalties unpaid since April 1912 but also to obtain compensation for other losses, including the unauthorized sale of the English and French rights to *Cavalleria rusticana*. Citing Sonzogno's repeated contract violations over the years, he asked the court to restore to him the rights to his operas. In the spring of 1915 his attorneys had obtained an order attaching the assets of the Sonzogno firm, which by this time included little beyond Milan's Teatro Lirico, and the firm's bank accounts. By July *Mascagni* v. *Sonzogno* was ready to come to trial.

On the eve of trial, Riccardo Sonzogno, not yet forty years old, suddenly died. With Riccardo's cousin Renzo, who had financed Mascagni's lawsuit, moving to gain control of the rudderless firm, Mascagni was approached by the firm's attorneys with settlement proposals. Despite his own lawyer's reservations, he was eager to seek a settlement; as he explained to Lolli, "I must admit . . . that I'm afraid of this lawsuit, especially because, even if I win again and again, I don't know if I'll ever get any money." Negotiations dragged on into the fall. Finally, early in November, Walter Mocchi intervened. Mascagni's febrile mental state by this time shows clearly in his first encounter with Mocchi: "While I was telling Walter about my life full of sacrifices, he asked me, 'And how's Annuccia?' I felt a lump grow in my throat; I had barely time to answer, 'Oh, Walter, it's been more than six months since I saw her last!' and I broke down crying so violently that it seemed I would suffocate." With Mocchi involved, a settlement was reached in mid-November. The firm, now controlled by Renzo, retained the rights to Mascagni's operas in return for a substantial payment. In addition, Sonzogno and Mascagni entered into a contract for a new opera, to be delivered no later than November 16, 1918.

Although Puccini had worked on Ouida's novel during 1915, by the end of the year his attention had turned to a new project, a one-act opera based on Didier Gold's play *La Houppelande*, which became *Il Tabarro*. He abandoned the Dutch girl and her wooden shoes, later using her music in *Suor Angelica*. Forzano had not been idle. Observing Puccini's lack of progress, he had resumed work on his own libretto late in 1915, finishing the third act early in 1916. Aware that Puccini had set Adami's treatment aside, Forzano approached him—despite his contract with Mascagni—hoping that his approach to the story might rekindle Puccini's appetite. Puccini, however, had already lost interest in the subject, and Ricordi had already sold his rights to Sonzogno. Forzano, mildly embarrassed but undaunted, presented Mascagni with his libretto in April 1916. The composer was soon working his way into the project, as he wrote Lolli from Turin in mid-May: "I find a bit of relief with Forzano, with whom I discuss and mull over the libretto of *Lodoletta*, as together we are forming the basis for setting decisively to work."

At the end of September Forzano arrived in Livorno, and he and Mascagni set down to work. From the beginning their relationship was a difficult one. Mascagni mistrusted Forzano, seeing him as an unprincipled intriguer who would use him, Puccini, or anyone else for his own advantage. Moreover, Forzano was unwilling to devote himself totally to the composer's needs, as Mascagni, spoiled by Targioni-Tozzetti and Illica, expected. To the busy writer, Mascagni was but one of many competing interests. Instead of staying by his side in Livorno, as the composer expected, Forzano rushed back and forth to Milan, to Zurich, feeding Mascagni's suspicions; as he wrote Lolli at one point, "Forzano is in Milan working for Puccini, against me!"

In contrast to his affection and respect for Illica and the awe he felt for D'Annunzio, Mascagni considered Forzano little more than a hack. Forzano was given to a peculiarly Italian brand of sentimentality, known as *mammismo e bambinismo*, but had little poetry in his soul. His craftsmanship, however, was considerable. Both *Lodoletta* and *Il Piccolo Marat*, his two libretti for Mascagni, are conventional but effective theater, more so than any of the composer's libretti since *Cavalleria*.

Ouida's novel, from which Forzano took the heart of the story, is the sentimental tale of Bebée, a beautiful and innocent Flemish flower girl, and her hopeless love for Flammen, a famous Parisian painter in exile in Belgium. Although Mascagni might have been drawn in any event to this story of an orphaned girl and her doomed love, with its echoes of *Iris* and *L'Amico Fritz*, his relationship with Anna Lolli gave it a deeper meaning for him. He saw almost mystical parallels between the unfolding of the love between Lodoletta (as Forzano had renamed her) and Flammen, and his love for Anna, from the moment he found her—as Flammen finds Lodoletta—alone and crying over the loss of a parent. Although both *Isabeau* and *Parisina* have something of Lolli in them, Lodoletta was to be a portrait of Anna herself; as he wrote her, "I want [the libretto] to show our romance. . . . I want it to be the story of our lives, the story of our great love! . . . I want to show the public the perfect creature of my dreams and my art."

During the month of October, with Forzano available only sporadically, Mascagni tried to mold the libretto to his liking. By the end of the month he had enough acceptable material for the first two acts to begin writing. Although Forzano arrived at the end of the month, to stay through early December, Mascagni found himself increasingly frustrated with his collaborator. His vision of Lodoletta remained a stumbling block for Forzano, as Mascagni wrote Lolli in mid-November: "He repeatedly contaminates this divine character with words that don't fit her elevation of feeling. Lodoletta is an elevated creature, capable of feeling a love beyond mortal love. Forzano does not understand this." Despite the scenes and shouting bouts, however,

Lodoletta made progress. By December 9, when the exhausted Forzano left Livorno for a much-needed respite, the composer had largely completed the first two acts.

As thoughts of *Lodoletta*'s first performance began to arise, Mascagni's yearning for Anna began to influence his thinking. He had hoped to compose *Lodoletta* in Rome, but, under intense pressure from Lina, he found himself instead in Livorno writing under his wife's watchful eye, far from the woman whom he considered his muse as well as lover. Although, despite his protestations, he was able to compose in her absence, he was miserable, pouring out his yearning in letter after letter.

In order to return to Rome, Mascagni decided that the opera, which he would conduct himself, should make its debut at the Costanzi Theater. Although at first his scheme appeared to meet no difficulty, complications soon developed. Sonzogno and Walter Mocchi, for reasons of their own, wanted *Lodoletta* to be given first at La Scala. Soon the Costanzi's Emma Carelli, under pressure from her husband, decided that she did not really want *Lodoletta* after all. All winter long the wrangle continued through letters and telegrams, as Mascagni insisted that the opera be premiered in Rome.

By February 1917 the composer's always volatile temper had begun to surface. On the twenty-fourth he lost what was left of his patience. He sent telegrams to the Costanzi and to La Scala withdrawing the opera, and another to Renzo informing him that the opera would be his on November 16, 1918, the contract deadline, and not a day sooner. After receiving the predictably threatening response, he calmly restated his point. "I have no obligation to send you anything," he wrote. "I will send you *Lodoletta* on November 16, 1918, as my contract requires. And meanwhile, I might just set fire to what I've written, because I'll have plenty of time to write the whole opera all over again."

Whether Mascagni's fit of anger was a bluff will never be known, since it was successful. Sonzogno immediately backed down. Rushing to Rome, he convinced Carelli to reverse herself, and on March 11 he was on Mascagni's doorstep with the news that *Lodoletta* would make its debut at the Costanzi in April. Four days later, Mascagni went to Rome and signed a contract with Carelli. Exhilarated by his success, he wrote Lolli, "Never has a work of art been more written for [love of] a woman! . . . Imagine, I undertook to write *Lodoletta* just to be able to come to Rome!"

While this struggle was taking place, Mascagni had not yet actually completed the opera. Although he had finished the first two acts early in December, the third act proved elusive, with the gap between his demands and Forzano's efforts growing steadily wider. Neither the structure of Forzano's third act nor its language, particularly Lodoletta's extended soliloquy, was acceptable. As he wrote Lolli on New Year's Eve, his frustration was mounting:

> *Forzano can't pull it off: he lacks the feeling to do it: he can't find the tone to move one! Last night I sat down to work with him; I suggested words to him, I gave him all of the impassioned phrases that a soul in agony would find, I spoke to him of the tears of a heart that loves without hope. Nothing! Nothing! Forzano doesn't feel, and can't do it.*

In January he took matters into his own hands. Rejecting Forzano's finale, in which Lodoletta faints, awakening for a closing duet with Flammen as she dies in his arms, the composer crafted the closing scenes of the opera himself with Targioni-Tozzetti's help, from Lodoletta's final vision of Flammen holding her as she dies to Flammen's cry of "Morire con te!" that ends the opera. Within a few days the opera was finished. Despite his complaints, *Lodoletta* was the most quickly written and scored of all his major operas, having been written in little more than three months, and orchestrated in only two months more.

Through February and March Mascagni worked frantically to orchestrate *Lodoletta* and prepare for the first performance. Although Mascagni was able to obtain his first choice, Rosina Storchio, for Lodoletta, a suitable tenor seemed impossible to find. In the end, Flammen was sung by the young Sicilian tenor Giuseppe Campioni, who stepped into the role little more than a week before opening night. Mascagni arrived in Rome on April 1 and began rehearsals immediately while continuing to orchestrate the third act of the opera, for which parts were not available until little more than a week before the performance.

In an interview late in April the composer explained that he "wanted . . . [his] music to convey a gentle feeling of comfort, a quality restorative of humanity's emotional life, as it passes through the great drama of the war." At its debut on April 30 *Lodoletta*, with its simplicity and gentle melodic quality, was well received by the Roman audience. At the end Mascagni was called forward for eight curtain calls; a warm but not overwhelming welcome for his new work.

The critical reaction was cordial but less than enthusiastic—more appreciative, perhaps, of Mascagni and of his efforts on behalf of Italy's operatic traditions than of the work itself. Barini, in *La Perseveranza*, wrote more eloquently of the composer's music, "in which we hear the heart of our people beating," than of *Lodoletta* itself. The widely respected Bastianelli, writing in *La Nazione*, was sharply critical: "The passions, the contrasts, the cut of the scenes, even the children and the Dutch neighbors, are all conventional.

Above all, the music is conventional, if one makes an exception for the funeral march, the milkmaids' chorus, and a bit of the carnival music in the third act. Too little . . . for over three hours of music." Adriano Lualdi, in *Musica*, praised many individual passages, but found that although Mascagni "was able to reproduce the drama with power of line and harmony, he was not able to grip firmly the collective soul of the audience and move them irresistably to emotion." Lualdi concluded that "what was missing, in our opinion, was total sincerity of expression." Mascagni's return to his earlier, simpler style he found "willed, not felt."

Rosina Storchio won praise in the title role, but Campioni, as Lualdi wrote, "came close to provoking a disaster. Not only was his voice inappropriate for the role, but onstage he was stiff, icy, and incoherent." Both composer and opera were far better served in the opera's next production, in Livorno, where Lodoletta was sung by Bianca Stagno Bellincioni, whose mother had been the first Santuzza, and Flammen by Beniamino Gigli. While Mascagni saw Flammen as much older than the twenty-seven-year-old Gigli, writing that Flammen should be at least forty-five—not by chance Mascagni's age when he first met Anna Lolli—he acknowledged afterward that Gigli had been magnificent. The production was a great success, and the Livorno audience called Mascagni back more than thirty times. At the third performance, a telegram was read from the stage reporting the simultaneous triumph of *Lodoletta* in Buenos Aires, where it was sung by Gilda Dalla Rizza and Enrico Caruso.

Lodoletta was off to a good start, and Mascagni could write Lolli that fall that "*Lodoletta* is off and flying by herself, using her own wings, without needing my help." In January 1918 the opera reached the Metropolitan Opera in New York, with Geraldine Farrar as Lodoletta and Caruso again as Flammen. It was warmly received by the New York audience; as the critic for the *New York Herald* noted, "Judging from the reception by the audience, *Lodoletta* will have a wide appeal." Although revived for Caruso the following year, it subsequently disappeared from the repertory, and its next American performance was not until 1989.

Lodoletta was staged frequently in Italy during the 1920s and 1930s, where the singers who sang the title role, aside from Storchio, Bellincioni, and Dalla Rizza, form something of an honor roll of Italian sopranos of the time, including Toti dal Monte, Iris Adami Corradetti, Maria Carbone, Juanita Caracciolo, and Mafalda Favero. It never attained the popularity of *Iris* or *Isabeau*, however, and has been performed only rarely since World War II.

Along with the launching of *Lodoletta*, the summer of 1917 saw the arrival of Mascagni's first grandchild, who was born to Emy and Guido Farinelli on August 30. Mascagni rushed up to Milan the next day, and immediately wrote Lolli: "The baby is a beauty: a big fat boy . . . and hungry. His mind works like mine: when I came into the room, I found the baby attached to Emy's breast. You alone can imagine how moved I was! I cried and cried, and for the longest time I had a lump in my throat that made it impossible for me to speak." Two weeks later, with Mascagni holding him in his arms, the baby was baptised Piermarcello. Despite the new arrival, the Farinelli marriage existed in little more than name. Soon Emy, along with little Piermarcello, would permanently leave her husband and return to her parents' home.

LODOLETTA

Ouida's novel, highly popular in its day, tells the sad story of the orphan Bebée and the painter Flammen. They meet by chance; he is charmed by her, but she falls in love with him. After he returns to Paris, he assumes that she will eventually marry Jeannot, the village woodcutter who loves her, and she becomes little more than a tender memory. Bebée yearns for him, uninterested in the crude, jealous Jeannot. Reading in an old newspaper that Flammen is ill, she sets off on a grueling trip to Paris to nurse him back to health, only, as she finally enters his apartment, to find him lying on a bed playing cards, a painted hussy's arm around his neck. Although at the last second he sees her, shaking off "his beautiful brown harlot . . . with an oath," it is too late. Bebée rushes away. She throws herself in the Seine, only to be rescued by Jeannot, who has followed her to Paris. He takes her back to the village, where she drowns herself in the river.

Forzano changed much of the story, making Flammen a sentimental lover rather than the aloof figure of the novel. In his libretto, a novel of gradually unfolding feeling has become an effective stage work, built around a series of dramatic events, but still true, however, to the underlying sentiment of Ouida's work. Bebée, now Lodoletta, has been moved from Belgium to Holland. Her sixteenth birthday celebration, on a beautiful spring day, is tragically interrupted by the sudden death of her father, Antonio. Flammen, who has just arrived in the village, finds her alone and sobbing and takes her in his arms to comfort her. In the second act he has moved to the village and is painting her portrait. It is now fall, and a deep but chaste, and as yet unacknowledged, love has grown up between them. Learning that their relationship has made the village shun her, Lodoletta sadly drives him away.

In the last act, it is New Year's Eve in Paris and snow is falling. Lodoletta arrives, having come to nurse Flammen back to health, only to find his house brilliantly lit and to see him dancing in the arms of a beautiful woman. She does not realize that Flammen has been pining for her, and that his friends are holding a ball at his house in hopes of distracting him. Exhausted from her long journey, she tries to flee but sinks into the snow and dies, leaving behind the bright red wooden shoes that her father gave her for her birthday. As the bells ring in the new year, Flammen's friends go off to Montmartre, but he remains behind, nursing his sorrow. Suddenly, he sees the red shoes, and discovers Lodoletta's lifeless body. He cries out, begging to die with her, as the curtain falls.

Mascagni was moved by this pathetic tale and inspired by the thought of making its heroine into a musical portrait of Anna Lolli. Working at fever pitch, and drawing on a pastoral vein reminiscent of *L'Amico Fritz*, he created a work of charm and beauty. At the same time, in the context of its composer's remarkably consistent creative growth over fifteen years, from *Iris* through *Parisina*, it is a disappointing step backward, not only in its modest aspirations but also in the quality of its achievement.

The first act is a case in point. The funeral march that follows Antonio's death is superb, a moving cantilena above a slow-moving bass that captures the stoic quality of the villagers as well as their sorrow. It is followed by Flammen's equally fine lullaby to the grieving Lodoletta, "Bimba, non piangere," which leads to the act's close, an orchestral coda that Stivender aptly describes as "perfectly depict[ing] the serenity and quietude of a spring night." If the entire act were at the level of its last fifteen minutes, it would be a masterpiece. Unfortunately, that is not the case. Mascagni's evocations of rural life, the children's birthday song, the village fiddler, and Lodoletta's own bubbly spirit are pretty but undistinguished and lack the dramatic impetus needed to engage the audience in this modest tale.

It is this lack of dramatic urgency that, in the final analysis, is the weakest point of *Lodoletta*. Mascagni, who was able to give powerful dramatic momentum to a literary libretto of an untheatrical cast such as *Parisina*, appears ill at ease in the conventional, Pucciniesque world of *Lodoletta*. There is far too much going on in the way of dramatic action, much of it trivial, for Mascagni to find the room to turn the few highly charged emotional moments into an equally charged opera. The outcome is an opera that moves dramatically by fits and starts. The ubiquitous children of the first two acts, however charming their music, are dramatically static; the lovely milkmaids' chorus in the second act, which even Bastianelli found praiseworthy, serves only to impede what little dramatic flow exists. The New Year's Eve music, which opens the last act, is delightful but goes on far too long for an act that ultimately contains nothing but Flammen's misery and Lodoletta's pathetic death in the snow.

The opera's difficulties are compounded by the painful faux-naïf quality of Forzano's libretto. Lodoletta's death, however deeply Mascagni may have felt it, is too much a sentimental cliché, already tired in 1917, to be taken entirely seriously. While it can be touching for Lodoletta, a pretty sixteen-year-old, to tell Flammen, "They always told me that I was born from a flower and a fairy," the audience soon wearies of the repeated imagery of flowers, fairies, and birds. While Mascagni may sincerely have felt that he was writing a work that would serve as a corrective to the horrors of the war, he was unable to graft his sincerity onto a libretto in which true feeling and passion—as he accurately divined—were so largely lacking.

Moreover, although Mascagni's emotional sincerity in writing *Lodoletta* is not in doubt, the creative integrity of the work remains questionable. Lualdi's criticism is apt. There is a quality of recycled goods about *Lodoletta*, of a willed attempt to capture the faraway spirit of *L'Amico Fritz*, or even of *Iris*, another story of an innocent girl lost in the big city. Both *L'Amico Fritz* and *Iris* succeed, whatever the weaknesses of their libretti, because they reflected Mascagni's strongest creative drives at the time he was writing them. *Silvano*, an attempt to look backward and recreate the atmosphere of *Cavalleria*, was a failure, however, even more as a dramatic work than a musical one. *Lodoletta* is a more serious effort than *Silvano*, but it too is an attempt to capture a quality no longer intrinsic to the composer's creative spirit. For all its charm and beauty, it remains stillborn.

Although he undoubtedly did not recognize it at the time, the composition of *Lodoletta* represented a watershed in Mascagni's creative life. The course that he had pursued, with great consistency of purpose, of expanding his dramatic horizons while building and refining an original musical language, which took him from *Ratcliff* to *Iris*, and from *Amica* and *Isabeau* to *Parisina*, was now over. While he would compose two more substantial operas, the dynamic of creative growth that was so important to his life as a composer up to this point was no more. Still, he remained willing to confront new dramatic and musical challenges, which he would find in considerable measure in his next opera, *Il Piccolo Marat*.

13. *War, Social Strife, and* Il Piccolo Marat, *1917—1921*

On October 24, 1917, disaster struck Italy. Reinforced by German troops, the Austrians attacked in force, breaking through the Italian lines above Caporetto. The weary Italian troops abandoned their positions, threw away their arms, and fled. By the time the Austrians were stopped on the banks of the Piave, they were deep in Italian territory, 11,000 Italian soldiers were dead, and another 280,000 were Austrian prisoners.

With both of his sons at the front, Mascagni lived for weeks in a state of anxiety, not knowing if they were alive or dead. On November 16 he learned that Mimi was alive but still had no word from Dino, who had been in the heart of the fighting. Finally, on November 29 he learned that Dino was a prisoner of war, in a camp in western Hungary. His son's telegram, in which he begged for clothes and money, sent Mascagni into a frenzy of activity, appealing to the Vatican and sending packets of money everywhere in the hope that one might reach the camp.

Mascagni's concern for his son's fate made his financial worries even more urgent. Offered a lucrative opportunity in Turin, he took it despite the shame he felt. "It's at a movie theater," he wrote Lolli; "it is a beautiful one, grand and elegant, and I know that they are organizing everything very nicely, but it is a movie theater just the same. You see how far I have sunk?" For one thousand lire a day, Mascagni conducted *Rapsodia satanica* twice daily, the film playing above his head. After the month's performances he remained in Turin, bedridden with bronchitis and an attack of gout in his left leg. As he lay in bed, confined by his ailments and the raw Turin winter, as he wrote Lolli, Lina hovered in the background, screaming, "what big horns I'm wearing, because little Anna has a younger man for a lover."

In mid-April he was well enough to return to Milan, where his next project came about through an unexpected visit from Carlo Lombardo, a prominent operetta composer, writer, and promoter. Lombardo was known as a confectioner of theatrical pastiches, writing libretti to the less familiar music of prominent composers. As Mascagni wrote Lolli, Lombardo "came to . . . let me know that he had written a new operetta with *my music* (??); he explained that he had taken *Silvano* and made a delightful operetta out of it." For no more than his signature on a consent form, Mascagni was offered a guarantee of twenty-four thousand lire per year. He vehemently rejected the proposal, but a seed had been planted. After some discussion, he agreed instead to write an original score to Lombardo's libretto, a frivolous concoction entitled *Sì*, or "yes."

Writing operettas had long been considered an unsuitable occupation for a serious composer, and Mascagni had never before contemplated such a step. Still, the operetta world was not what it had been thirty years earlier. Standards had risen, and the better companies had reached a level of professionalism unheard of in Mascagni's operetta days. Leoncavallo had broken the ice in the 1910s with a series of operettas, of which *La Reginetta delle rose* had been particularly successful. Without wanting to emulate Leoncavallo, for whom he had little respect, Mascagni was drawn to the idea of writing a simple and sentimental work, as he wrote Giovanni Orsini, a young poet who had become a fanatical admirer of the composer, later in July. "I fear that my mind, preoccupied with serious and sorrowful thoughts, cannot bear the strain of the serious effort of an opera with a far-reaching concept." The experiment appealed to his restless spirit; not without a touch of defensiveness, though, he felt he had to justify his choice, adding to Orsini, "Wouldn't it be a fine affirmation of *italianità* in this artistic field as well," and, as he wrote Lolli, "I want to teach Italians how one makes an Italian operetta."

If Mascagni had seriously intended to reform Italian operetta he could hardly have found a less effective vehicle than the tired libretto that Lombardo and his coauthor, Arturo Franchi, gave him. Like so many works of its genre, it was set in the lighthearted, imaginary Paris of boulevardiers and showgirls, named *Si* after its heroine, a Folies-Bèrgère dancer of casual morality, who is known as Si because she is unable to say no to anyone.

The story, beneath its frivolity, is unpleasantly cold-blooded. Luciano, the Duke of Chablis, a rake who frequents the Folies-Bergère, must marry if he is to inherit a fortune from an uncle. Although his cousin Vera loves him, he does not want to give up his easygoing bachelor life. He decides instead to marry Si, expecting her to continue in her dissolute ways, which will permit him to act similarly. Having done so, however, he falls in love with Vera. Meanwhile, Si has fallen in love with her husband and become a faithful and devoted wife. In the end, Luciano and Vera browbeat her into divorcing Luciano. As she returns sadder but wiser to the Folies-Bergère, the lovers embrace passionately.

Not only was this story unpleasant, it was not even original. Lombardo, in fact, had recycled much of it from an operetta he had written a few years earlier entitled *La Duchesse du Bal Tabarin*, in turn an adaptation of an earlier work by the Viennese Bruno Granichstädten. Still, as a clothesline on which to string the numbers that made the show, *Si* was not a bad libretto, with everything from comic turns to sentimental love duets, and attractive production numbers set at the Folies-Bergère.

Mascagni expressed no reservations about the libretto but set to work on August 1 as soon as he had its first sections in his hands, hoping to finish by the end of August. Early that month he wrote Lolli, "This music goes easily: there is no profound concept involved, no synthesis; all it takes is a bit of inspiration. . . . And that your Pietro still has, thank God. The operetta is made up of twelve or fourteen numbers: one a day, and the job will be done." He soon set all of the material Lombardo had given him, and had his librettists done their work on time, might well have finished *Si* by his self-imposed deadline. By the end of August he had written over half of the operetta. The rest, though, would be written in bits and pieces and not finished until nearly a year later.

BETWEEN OPERAS

The end of August found Mascagni in Milan, directing the fall season at the Teatro Lirico, where he remained through October. Rain fell constantly, and the influenza epidemic swept through Milan. Emy fell ill, and at one point ten of the fourteen sopranos in his chorus were out with the disease. To amuse himself, he set Anna Lolli's poem "Bimba bionda" to music, sitting down at

the piano at 3 A.M. on the night of September 19, after his return from the
Lirico and a late dinner, writing the song in one sitting, finishing at precisely
7:15 A.M.

Meanwhile, after months of stalemate, the momentum at the front had
finally turned in favor of the Italian army. In an offensive that began on October 24, 1918, the army swept the now disorganized Austrian troops before
them, crossing the Piave, taking Vittorio Veneto on the thirtieth, and entering Trent and Trieste on November 3. The next day the Austrians and Italians signed an armistice. For Mascagni, Italy's victory meant that Dino would
soon be back. Between performances, he rushed to Turin to prepare Dino's
apartment for his return, buying him a new Gillette safety razor and putting
a score of *Lodoletta* on his son's piano.

Two weeks later, the bedridden Dino reached Trieste, from which he
was taken to a military hospital in Teramo, in the foothills of the Abruzzi
mountains. As soon as he had lowered his baton on the last performance of
the season, Mascagni rushed to his son's bedside, where Dino threw himself
into his father's arms, kissing him and sobbing. After a week with his son,
Mascagni was back in Milan, responding to an urgent summons from Renzo
Sonzogno.

After a week in Milan, where between stockholders' meetings and sessions with attorneys Mascagni managed to write two more numbers for *Sì*, he
rushed back south, this time to Naples, to take charge of the San Carlo opera
company for the 1919 carnival season. Opening with *Aida* on December 26,
during the course of the following three months Mascagni presented *Un Ballo
in maschera*, *Il Barbiere di Siviglia*, and Bellini's *Il Puritani*, as well as three of his own
operas, *Lodoletta*, *Isabeau*, and *L'Amico Fritz*. The novelty was *I Puritani*, which was
rarely heard in Italian theaters of the time.

Mascagni's affection and respect for the generation of Rossini and Bellini, as well as the still earlier Cimarosa and Pergolesi, were rare among his
contemporaries. Reviving *I Puritani* was a way of showing that the operatic
tradition that originated with those composers was still alive and still mattered to the musicians and audiences of the twentieth century. Ironically, the
younger generation of composers, upon whom he looked with so much dis-
favor, were also rediscovering the past, as Casella would find Scarlatti and
Malipiero explore Monteverdi. Each was looking for something very different from the same past, however, and had little understanding or sympathy
for the other's position.

In Naples news reached him of the death of his aunt Maria. Maria Tafi,
the widow of his uncle Luigi in San Miniato, was the one surviving relative
to whom he was truly close, the one to whom he had turned when he needed

the money to rent a piano to compose *Cavalleria rusticana*. Her two sons, Luigi and Mario, had grown up to become musicians, both studying with their cousin Pietro at the Liceo Rossini in Pesaro.

Maria Tafi's death was the first of a series of deaths over the next few years that would remove one by one most of the figures from Mascagni's early years. Next came Ruggero Leoncavallo, the first among the band of compos- ers who had emerged along with Mascagni in the 1890s. While for years he had resented what he felt was Leoncavallo's opportunism in writing *Pagliacci*, using him as the butt of some of his sharpest thrusts, that was now forgotten. He wrote Lolli, "Poor Leoncavallo is dead, and his death has truly distressed me: he was a good man: he was far better than his reputation." Mascagni went to his funeral, and afterward he and Puccini had a long intimate talk. They were both beginning to feel like survivors of an earlier age.

A REVOLUTIONARY OPERA FOR REVOLUTIONARY TIMES

The end of the war unleashed the tensions that had been bottled up for years. With unemployment and inflation soaring, embittered nationalists and de- mobilized officers complained about Italy's "mutilated victory," while the resurgent Socialists dreamed of a Bolshevik revolution. With revolutions un- der way across Europe, as one scholar has written, in 1919 "the myth of the Bolshevik revolution radiated throughout the peninsula . . . the organized working masses were charged with revolutionary emotion, and the socialist revolution was heralded as on the immediate agenda." Few believed that the impotent and rudderless governments of the time would be able to resist this seemingly inevitable tide.

Mascagni observed the scene with dismay, recalling his 1915 com- ments, "The situation all over the country is terrible. Sad days are coming. Oh, Annuccia, my prophecies unfortunately are coming true!" Although no more a political man than ever, he had been deeply touched first by the war and now by Italy's social and economic crisis. For the first time in his life he began to contemplate writing an opera with a more explicitly political di- mension, an opera through which he could—in his personal and often con- fused manner—make a statement about revolution and about such funda- mental human values as justice and freedom.

The opportunity to write such an opera was provided by Forzano, who approached him in the fall of 1918 with a proposal for an opera on the life of Robespierre, which failed to interest the composer. Mascagni found Robes- pierre a revolting figure; furthermore, he observed, "I don't know how to blend politics and music. . . . If I sat down at the piano thinking of Robespierre, the only melody that would come out would be the Marseillaise. Do you think that a century from now it will be possible to make Lenin sing?"

The setting, though, intrigued him. He had contemplated subjects drawn from the French Revolution in the past, but none had materialized, perhaps for the same reasons that he spurned Robespierre; now, he told an interviewer, he was "looking for a libretto which, within a revolutionary setting, left out the famous historical figures of the time." Forzano soon came up with a scenario that suited the composer, drawn from two nineteenth-century works on the French Revolution, *Les Noyades de Nantes* (The drownings of Nantes) by Louis Gosselin, and *Sous la terreur* (Under the terror) by Victor Martin. Forzano's craftsmanship is evident in the tight, effective melodrama he created from a series of seemingly unrelated events and situations, finding his framework in the long-neglected tradition of the rescue opera, a genre made prominent, if not actually invented, during the French Revolution.

The opera is set in Nantes, where, under the rule of the Ogre—modeled on Carrier, governor of Nantes in 1793 and 1794—hunger and fear stalk the city. Into this world comes the young Prince Charles de Fleury, who feigns revolutionary ardor to join the Marats, the Ogre's Pretorian Guard, in order to find his imprisoned mother. In the end, with the help of the Carpenter, he escapes with his mother and with the Ogre's niece Mariella, with whom he has fallen in love. An important subplot concerns the Soldier, who arrives from the front to investigate charges that the Ogre has been murdering prisoners without trial; he is ultimately killed, another victim of the Ogre's treachery.

Forzano worked on the libretto during the first months of 1919, while Mascagni was in Naples. By the end of April, when Mascagni returned to Rome, he had enough material to begin work, writing the first bars of *Il Piccolo Marat* on May 1. For the next month and a half he was consumed with his new opera, thinking of little else, writing pieces of different scenes from the first and second acts. He was forced to put the opera aside before the end of June to resume his conducting activities, but, as he wrote his friend Tanzini in Livorno, "These boring travels of mine will force *Il Piccolo Marat* to undergo a period of interruption; in reality, the interruption has already begun, because the good (?) Forzano is up to his Lodolettian tricks; he has sneaked away leaving me at a standstill: I can't do another thing. . . . I haven't a word left to set."

Back in Livorno by the end of July, he resumed work on *Si*, now scheduled for a fall debut at Rome's Quirino Theater, while pressing Forzano, who was now staying with him, to give him the material he needed for *Marat*. At the villa, Forzano was in one room and Arturo Franchi, working on *Si*, in another, as Mascagni wrote Lolli:

> *I have put them both up in my house, keeping them in two separate rooms, where I am making them work hard. My own situation is thoroughly ridiculous, because I have to dictate my ideas to two poets about two totally opposite subjects. I swear that I totally confuse myself. I see my librettists only in the evening, because I sleep during the day and they go to bed early. Then, with my piano and violin, I disturb their rest with a vengeance.*

Meanwhile, his cousin Mario arrived to help him finish orchestrating *Si*. With Forzano, Franchi, and Mario working away, Mascagni was able to finish the operetta during August. Although much orchestration remained, the last number of *Si* was completed on August 31.

With the operetta finished, Mascagni resumed work on *Marat*, picking up the second-act scene between the Soldier and the Ogre where he had put it down in June. He had barely begun when he received a devastating letter from Lolli. "Give me my freedom!" she wrote. "At least I am still young enough to have a family, if, God willing, I can still find a good man."

The nine-year relationship between Mascagni and Lolli had gone through many strains, but this was to be the worst. For more than a year, except for fleeting reconciliations, they would be estranged; Lolli wrote him only rarely, and Mascagni wrote letters full of resentment and self-pity. For all her love for Mascagni, their relationship was profoundly distressing to the devout Lolli. She had long dreamed of marriage and family, finding herself instead in an illicit relationship, without hope of a conventional family life. Although Mascagni had once talked of leaving Lina, it was by now clear that no amicable separation was possible, and neither he nor Lolli could stomach the scandal that would come from a public break. By 1919, after her thirtieth birthday, Lolli had begun to face the painful reality that, if their relationship continued, she would have to renounce forever her dreams of a husband and children.

Having Pietro Mascagni for a lover was not easy. Intensely possessive, he poured out his feelings to her in letter after letter, demanding that she do the same. Rumors that she had been seen with another man would send him into an agony of reproaches against her, against himself for doubting her, against her yet again for creating the circumstances under which he came — if unjustly — to doubt her. Although letters went back and forth almost daily, months could pass between one visit and the next. Between visits, Lolli remained at home with her sister Rosina, limited to the few activities acceptable to the straitlaced Mascagni.

Although the relationship would survive, in 1919 it seemed doomed. Mascagni, whose entire emotional life was centered on his relationship with Lolli, was in despair; as he wrote her in May 1920, "I go on writing you, I go on loving you, I go on desiring you, calling your name, sending you kisses . . . but I know very well that it's all pointless: I know that I have lost you and that my love is without hope." In the end, though, Lolli was far too committed to their relationship to sustain her resolve in the face of his emotional pressure. They would reconcile in the spring of 1921, when Mascagni returned to Rome for the premiere of *Il Piccolo Marat*. Even then, their relationship would remain on edge for years, punctuated by quarrels and reproaches, estrangements and reconciliations.

Mascagni wrote hardly anything for the rest of September 1919 and well into October. His depression over his relationship with Lolli was one factor, but another was his continuing difficulty with Forzano, as a September letter indicates: "*Il Piccolo Marat* has stayed as it was: there's nothing but that which I wrote in Rome . . . my state of mind does not allow me to write any more; Forzano too has contributed a lot to this: he has been here more than a month, in my home, without the decency to write me a single new scene. . . . A pity," he added, "because *Marat*, musically speaking, was turning into a masterpiece."

Mascagni was increasingly frustrated with Forzano, writing in November that "I'm working on *Marat*, without having the words, because that pig Forzano still hasn't shown his face." Finally, through the hasty intervention of Renzo Sonzogno, who was still hoping that the opera would be ready in time for the 1920 carnival season, a sort of truce was made between composer and librettist. By midmonth Forzano was back at work and Mascagni had begun to compose the violent mob scene that dominates the first act of the opera. Under the sway of his excitement as he composed this scene, he wrote Lolli:

> *You have no idea what kind of work* Marat *is: it is ferocity, it is carnage, it is death: there is no music in my new opera: I am not writing it with notes, I'm writing it with fists, with blows, with bites: everything musical that comes to me, I wildly tear to pieces: I am writing the misery of the oppressed, the violence of assassins: I am bringing into art the unhuman cry of revenge and death!*

Mascagni, working intermittently on *Marat*, did not even attend the premiere of *Si*, which appeared on December 13, 1919. The operetta was received with some disappointment, as the expectations that had been raised by Mascagni's pronouncements went largely unrealized. While the music pleased the audience, and many numbers were applauded and even repeated, the tired story and setting seemed to mock the composer's ambitions. The first act was greeted enthusiastically and the second warmly, but disappointment was palpable at the end of the short, unsatisfactory third act, as the public filed out to a mixture of scattered whistles and desultory applause. Savarino, the critic for *La Tribuna*, wrote: "If there were such a thing as a court-martial in the world of art, Carlo Lombardo should be forthwith charged and convicted of high treason. . . . [He] has provided this sort of libretto, squeezed out from a cliché of which the public has long grown tired, for our most Italian musician, who should be writing an Italian operetta." Despite its initially lukewarm reception, *Si* had a long run at the Quirino and soon made the rounds of the Italian operetta circuit. In 1925 it was translated into German and, as *Ja*, had a long successful run in Vienna at the Bürgertheater, traveling from there to a number of German and Austrian cities. Along with the rest of the Italian operetta repertory from the period, *Si* has been neglected in recent decades, but a successful 1987 revival showed that Mascagni's music still entertained and moved the audience, despite the libretto's inadequacies.

The hackneyed quality of the libretto is particularly unfortunate, because the score abounds in delightful melodies and entrancing moments. Although it may lack a single great hit tune, it has many that come close, from the bouncy "Si, paradiso di promesse" to the slow waltz tune, "M'avevan detto, è ver," reminiscent of Lehár. Many of the dances and production numbers are delightful, from the delicate bridal procession scored for solo strings to an amusing ragtime parody entitled "Duetto americano grottesco."

Mascagni's work was again interrupted by death, this time that of his old friend and collaborator Luigi Illica. The old soldier's health had been broken by a winter in the trenches, and he had never resumed active life, lingering on until his death in 1919 at the age of sixty-two. They had not been close since 1912, when they had taken opposing sides in the Sonzogno family struggle, and Illica's contempt, during the dark days of the war, for anyone who failed to share his extreme form of patriotism had further widened the breach. Just the same, the sentimental Mascagni was deeply stricken, remembering the days of their intimacy, when they shared one another's homes as they tested the boundaries of Italian opera. At the writer's grave he was the last to speak, as a local journalist wrote: "As he spoke, the tears streaked his noble cheeks, and he brusquely shook his fine leonine head to try to hold back the tears that kept bursting forth. He gave the last salute to the friend who had been by his side in all his artistic battles . . . [he] ended with a cry that touched the hearts of everyone present, 'Farewell, Gigi, farewell!'" He was angry that other composers had not been there. Puccini had sent a telegram; as Mascagni wrote Lolli, "Giordano condescended to send a wreath. The libretto of *Chénier* deserved something more."

Mascagni and Forzano continued to work on *Marat*, yoked together in an atmosphere of intense strain. Despite, or perhaps because of, the tension, the next month was an exceptionally productive one for the composer. By the middle of January 1920 he had completed the first and third acts and was well into the second. With the end in sight, Forzano received a letter from Puccini

> *begging me to come immediately to Turin to take charge of the staging of* Il Trittico, *that he desperately needed me. . . . Since there was nothing left to do on* Marat *but a handful of minor changes (to the love duet), and a few other insignificant word changes, and given that the first performance of* Trittico *in Turin was not unimportant, I asked Mascagni to let me have a few days off.*

"As I expected," Forzano added, "[Mascagni] took my departure badly."

That was an understatement. To Mascagni, who already disliked and distrusted Forzano, his departure confirmed that Forzano's first loyalty was to Puccini, not to him. Within days of his arrival in Turin, Mascagni sent him a telegram demanding that he return immediately. Forzano refused, and the outraged Mascagni turned to his old collaborator, Targioni-Tozzetti, to finish the opera. During February and March, working with Targioni, who rewrote the second-act love scene and wrote the words for the chorus that opens the third act, Mascagni finished the opera, writing the last bars on March 10, 1920. At Forzano's insistence, when the libretto was published, Targioni's lines were enclosed in brackets to distinguish them from Forzano's text.

Forzano returned to Livorno late in February with Sonzogno and Mocchi, both of whom were determined to pin Mascagni down about *Marat*. The composer, in a foul temper, told them that the opera was never going to be performed. Then, turning on Forzano and castigating him as a traitor and a scoundrel, he threw the poor librettist bodily out of his house. Forzano never returned to Livorno.

Mascagni had barely finished *Il Piccolo Marat* when he was off to another funeral, this time for Edoardo Sonzogno in Milan. Sonzogno, who was eighty-four, had been ailing for many years, and it had been decades since Mascagni had thought of him with affection. Still, as he wrote Lolli, "the memory of *Cavalleria* ties my name to Edoardo Sonzogno's for eternity." While the elderly Sonzogno's death was no surprise, only two weeks later his nephew Renzo, who had held the firm together precariously for the previous five years, died unexpectedly in his American mistress's Milan apartment. Mascagni, whose relationship with Renzo had been close although tempestuous, was shocked by his death. He was even more concerned about the effect Renzo's death would have on his own future; a few days after returning to Milan, he wrote Lolli that "we are surrounded by speculators and bloodsuckers who wouldn't hesitate to sacrifice Renzo's family and all the firm's composers for their . . . own advantage." He left Milan feeling that the world was collapsing around him. "For too long," he wrote Lolli, "I've had death going round and round me: Leoncavallo, Illica, Edoardo Sonzogno, now Renzo."

MASCAGNI THE BOLSHEVIK

The years 1919 and 1920 are still known in Italy as the *biennio rosso*, the "two Red years" of strikes, demonstrations, and revolutionary violence. The agitation reached its climax in September 1920, as "over 400,000 workers took over their factories or shipyards, expelled their managers, ran up the Red (or Black) Flag, and carried on working. . . . It looked remarkably like a revolution." The occupation soon spread to Livorno, a hotbed of working-class radicalism. The city's two principal industries, the Orlando shipyards and the metal works, were taken over, the Italian tricolor pulled down, and the red flag of socialism flown from the factory flagpoles.

Proud of his bond with Livorno's working people, Mascagni readily accepted an invitation to visit from the workers occupying the shipyards. On September 6, accompanied by Lina, Emy, and Dino, and with an entourage of Socialist and trade union dignitaries, he arrived to a thunderous welcome. After touring the plant, he was asked to write a few words as a memento of the day's events. After some thought, he wrote:

> *As a free man, in the most absolute and unequivocal sense of the word, I express my sincere hopes for the workers of the Orlando shipyards, steadfast individuals who have my full admiration and respect. Your victory will signal the end of a disgraceful [history of] exploitation and the collapse of the big corporations, Italy's curse. You seek to be productive and creative. That is a sacred goal. May victory smile upon you!*

The crowd cheered, and the strikers' leader embraced Mascagni, crying out, "You are a true comrade!" Gratified by the warmth of his reception, Mascagni paid a similar visit to the metal works the next day, returning to the shipyards for a second visit two days later.

Mascagni's visits to the factories were news throughout Italy. In the political climate of the time, they were interpreted to mean only one thing: that Italy's preeminent musical figure had joined the cause of Socialist revolution. Mussolini's newspaper, *Il Popolo d'Italia*, referring to "Mascagnian Bolshevism," denounced the composer in a scornful column. "It will come as no surprise," the paper sneered, "that Pietro Mascagni—already completely washed up as a composer, as his latest musical abortions prove—has turned to Bolshevism." Similar although less barbed comments appeared in much of the nation's press, while Puccini, whose right-wing sympathies were well known, wrote a sarcastic letter to their mutual friend Carlo Paladini about "this madness of the workers coming to power, with Mascagni as their godfather."

The composer's actual sentiments are best suggested by his own words, in a letter to the Futurist Balilla Pratella later that month:

> *From an economic standpoint, the position of composers toward publishers is not that different from that of workers toward industrialists. My enthusiasm, therefore, for the rebellion of the workers is more than justified. I believe that this collective movement (if it does not degenerate through political excesses) could signal the beginning of a new era.*

Unlike Puccini, who yearned for a government with "an iron fist," Mascagni identified with the working class and their struggle. While it may seem implausible that a man whose wealth was beyond the dreams of the average Italian would identify with the workers because of his difficulties with his publishers, there is no doubt of his sincerity or, in equal measure, his ultimate naïveté. His identification was emotional, oblivious to the radical intentions behind the occupation of the factories. He saw the workers through a romantic haze, calling on them to be "productive and creative" and naively demanding of the nationalist Prezzolini, "How can you claim that I occupy myself with politics?"

The occupation of the factories soon ended. It was to be the last gasp of the revolution that never happened. The tide was already turning, and in 1921 Fascism would emerge as a powerful movement, growing as the Socialist tide receded. Mascagni gave his visit to the shipyards little further thought. Others, for whom the political struggle was real and often in bloody earnest, remembered more. As Mascagni would learn, many Fascist activists considered him their enemy. After the Fascists had come to power, he was kept at arm's length for years by the regime, until his much publicized rapprochement with Mussolini at the end of 1925. When Mussolini nominated Puccini to Italy's prestigious but symbolic Senate in 1924, Mascagni was pointedly passed over, a gesture widely attributed to the aura of Bolshevism that still hung about him.

ROMAN TRIUMPH: THE PREMIERE OF *IL PICCOLO MARAT*

With the occupation of the factories over, life in Italy briefly assumed a veneer of normality. Mascagni resumed his travels, ending the year in Naples at the San Carlo Theater. Early in January 1921 Walter Mocchi arrived in Naples determined to pry *Il Piccolo Marat* loose from Mascagni's hands. As usual, the persuasive Mocchi had his way, and the composer agreed to present *Marat* at the end of the Costanzi Theater's spring season.

With only three months to go, this was a risky undertaking. Much of the opera had yet to be orchestrated, and nothing had been done either to prepare the orchestral parts or the piano reduction. While Mocchi and Carelli began to assemble the cast for the first performance, Mascagni returned to Rome to complete the opera in time for its debut. He had barely begun when his work was interrupted by the death of his brother Paolo on February 2, who was finally carried away by the tuberculosis that had plagued him for decades. Mascagni rushed to Saluzzo, arriving just after his brother's death. After making arrangements for the funeral, and after assuring Paolo's widow that she and her three children would be adequately supported, he rushed back to Rome. With Paolo's death, his only surviving sibling was his older brother, Cecco, still languishing in a Milan nursing home.

Back in Rome, Sonzogno's copyists were set up in a salon in the Costanzi Theater; as Luigi Ricci, Mascagni's assistant, described the scene, "Whatever the copyists had prepared during the night, [Mascagni] rehearsed with the orchestra the next day. Once the rehearsals were over, he went home and spent all night working on finishing the opera. The next morning he would give the copyists the pages he'd finished." Meanwhile, Mascagni summoned Guido Farinelli from Milan to work alongside the copyists, preparing the piano reduction page by page as they made up the orchestral parts.

The premiere was set for May 2. It had been a difficult opera to cast. Not only does it have a typically taxing Mascagni tenor role as well as highly demanding roles for soprano and bass, but it also calls for two first-rate baritones for the short but important roles of the Soldier and the Carpenter. Carelli had worked wonders. Hipólito Lázaro, the Spanish tenor who had created Ugo in *Parisina*, was the Prince, and the superb young soprano Gilda Dalla Rizza was Mariella. Luigi Ferroni was the Ogre, while Benvenuto Franci and Ernesto Badini were the Soldier and the Carpenter—all singers accustomed to singing principal roles.

Few knew what to expect from the new opera. It was known to be on a revolutionary theme, but its politics were a mystery. Both Socialists and Fascists, unsure of where its sympathies would lie, came prepared to demonstrate for or against the work. Whatever qualms people may have felt about Mascagni's own politics, they were dispelled as the first notes of his new opera were heard. As the chorus rushed onstage and the opening scene unfolded, the audience was electrified; at the end of the first scene a wave of enthusiastic applause brought the opera to a halt for several minutes. From that point on, as the next day's *Giornale d'Italia* described it, "The success grew and grew, assuming unbelievable proportions after the second act, as two thousand people jumped to their feet in the overflowing boxes, in the packed house, in the filled galleries, in a splendid, delirious, manifestation of enthusiasm." A cry of "Viva l'Italia," picked up by the audience, in Morini's words, "resounded in the hall like a spontaneous appeal of the heart . . . and brought everyone together in common feeling as one." At the end of the opera, as Fascists and Socialists alike cheered and screamed "Viva Mascagni," and as thousands of handkerchiefs were waved, Mascagni and his company, and then the composer by himself, were called back on stage fifty times, until finally Carelli came onstage and begged the audience to go home. Those present could think of only one other evening with which to compare that night— the night, almost exactly thirty-one years earlier, when *Cavalleria rusticana* had received its baptism in the same theater.

The critical reaction was highly favorable, with the most thoughtful and independent critics caught up in enthusiasm for the new work. Alberto Gasco, the authoritative critic for *La Tribuna*, while finding some excess and rhetoric, stated that

> this music, even if grim and strenuous, heavy or overstated, becomes profoundly moving, with an unquenchable inner flame. . . . Redundancies, prolixities, heavy-handed moments, but just the same a piercing psychological inquiry, an erotic tinge, a continuous generous impetus, and often an acute sense of the theater. You will look in vain for other modern Italian operas that share such precious qualities.

Bastianelli, who was not at Rome, wrote his review after the Bologna premiere. Although not impressed by much of the first act, he wondered if his "pen dare describe the joy he felt" while listening to the second-act love duet. After the third act he "left the hall in that ecstatic state that the great successes give one." Domenico Alaeona, a modernist writing in *Musica d'oggi*, reacted much as Bastianelli. Less convinced by the "scenes of cruelty, of power and revolt," he too found the opera's strengths in its love music, which he found written "with the intense fervor of sincerity and inspiration." He concluded that it would be those scenes to which Mascagni would owe "the possibility of success and vitality of his opera."

Il Piccolo Marat's Roman triumph was soon repeated throughout Italy and Latin America, where it made its successful Buenos Aires debut in October with Gigli in the title role. It soon became one of Mascagni's most popular operas in Italy, receiving seven productions, for a total of forty-eight performances, in Bari alone. Although rarely performed today, it is still occasionally revived, most recently in Livorno in 1989 and Utrecht in 1992. It has never been performed in the United States.

Although *Il Piccolo Marat* has considerable merit, it is clearly not the incontestable masterwork that the Roman public first took it to be. Admonitory voices were soon heard, including "Petronio" in *L'Illustrazione Italiana*, who wrote, "Those who . . . press its success, and exaggerate it to a level of delirium that the opera would have difficulty finding otherwise by virtue of its merits alone, do the composer a disservice."

In the intensely charged Italian atmosphere of 1921, Mascagni's opera became a rallying point for a seemingly infinite range of beliefs and aspirations. Although ideologically confused, it was fervent and intense in its confusion. Socialists and Fascists could both read their visions into it, while for others it stood as an affirmation of Italian art in an age of artistic as well as political uncertainty. The latter was much on Gasco's mind when he wrote: "It is worth listening to *Il Piccolo Marat* to be able to judge the foolishness of the gloomy prediction that opera is dying. Opera . . . can bloom again, if only composers sweep away theorems, intellectualism, and sophistry and make the effort to give vocal melody back the expressive vigor that it has largely lost." In retrospect, the prophets of gloom may have been more accurate. *Il Piccolo Marat*, for all the raptures that greeted its debut, was, in Petronio's words, "an opera like many others" and was not destined to turn the musical tide.

IL PICCOLO MARAT

Marat is a portrait of life under a precursor of totalitarian rule. The impersonality of the Ogre, the Spy, the Soldier, the Carpenter, and above all, the ever present mob, fosters a sense of being in a world dominated by the pervasive fear and suspicion of an all-powerful state, such as the century would soon experience. The sole note of humanity is provided by the Prince and Mariella, who, along with the Prince's mother, are the only ones to have names, thus becoming individuals rather than shadows. Even they are not entirely real, however, as their ability to remain untouched by the totalitarian world that surrounds them is clearly unreal, self-consciously reflected by the Prince, who describes his own actions by alluding to a fairy tale, "Look! Little Red Riding Hood [*cappuccetto rosso*] is here! And he will save you!"

The politics of all this, however, remains unclear. With only one exception, the characters are driven by personal dreams and desires. The Prince acts from love of his mother, and Mariella from love of the Prince. Even the Ogre, the revolutionary fanatic, is driven less by ideology than by his lust for revenge on a regime that oppressed him and his fellows. Only the Soldier is motivated by values. He is the voice of the composer, who wrote Orsini that

Marat was "the hymn of my conscience." Speaking for what may well be Mascagni's own dream of a truly liberating revolution, he cries out to the cynical Ogre:

> Liberty exists to heal the suffering of the ages,
> Without use of murder or terror!
> The world is yearning for the kingdom of Love!
> In the name of holy Liberty, do not close your heart
> To the throbbing of love and mercy!

For the threat his vision poses to the Ogre's rule, he is dragged away by the mob and drowned in the Loire.

Although the Soldier is brutally murdered, the Prince, Mariella, his mother, and the Carpenter escape, suggesting that liberty can be found only through personal, not political, action. Mascagni had little faith in the utility of political action. One may be able to escape oppression, he believed, but not reform it. His lifelong hostility to power and to those who wielded it was based on a deeply rooted fatalism. Far more of his characters, including Guglielmo Ratcliff, Iris, and Isabeau, are destroyed by power than, as in *Marat*, escape it.

If the opera has an overarching theme, it is one of love triumphant over tyranny. The Prince's love for his mother and for Mariella brings the Soldier's words to life. *Marat* is a profoundly antipolitical work, as only one so thoroughly grounded in an ideologically charged setting can be. Rather than a political statement, it is a plea to abandon political discourse and find meaning in simpler emotional realities, as on a musical level it is a thinly veiled plea to Italy's Modernists to abandon their experiments and return to the roots of their operatic tradition.

Mascagni's music reflects his passionate engagement with Forzano's story and his determination to create an opera that would mirror the intensity of his feelings. Whatever its weaknesses, it is a work of immense power, in which the decorative quality and lack of urgency that marred *Lodoletta* are nowhere to be found. With no prelude other than a few harmonically ambiguous woodwind noises followed by a whispered hymn sung offstage, the work erupts with the most violent crowd scene in Italian opera, as a starving mob rushes onstage in pursuit of the food in Mariella's basket. The chorus shouts as much as it sings, as Mascagni weaves crudely harmonized revolutionary songs into the music, and the opening notes of the "Marseillaise" are heard over and over in the orchestra, underscoring the roots of the mob's violence.

Mascagni sought to give musical form to the conflicts between the individual and the state, and between love and power, by juxtaposing elements of a twentieth-century musical language against an overall framework firmly grounded in nineteenth-century operatic practice. The scenes in which the Ogre and his minions take center stage, often scored with unusual combinations of brass and low woodwinds, flirt with atonality. They contrast with more conventionally romantic passages, in which the strings become prominent, for the intimate scenes between the Prince and Mariella or his mother. These contrasts are often sharp and effective, as when the Princess's lushly romantic theme emerges from the midst of the act 1 prison scene, and when the diatonic "deliverance" theme rises from the tortured chromaticism of the Ogre's troubled dreams as the third act opens, both powerful musical representations of the opera's dramatic tensions and underlying meaning.

Ironically, for all of Mascagni's intention to contrast the purity and beauty of romantic melody against the harshness of his "modern" sounds, it is the latter that, to this listener, sustain the opera, and the former that are less compelling. The musical representations of the Ogre's totalitarian rule, in particular the second-act confrontation between him and the Soldier, crackle with dramatic intensity. The more sentimental scenes, particularly the climactic love duet between the Prince and Mariella that ends the second act, feel forced and uneasy by comparison, as if the composer is no longer sure how to mine a vein of sentiment that in his heart he knows to be not entirely fresh. Self-consciously trying to contrast the romantic and the modern, he rarely displays the sure touch with which he found a vibrant new vocabulary for romantic passion in *Parisina*.

Mascagni was not helped by Forzano, who drapes both the Prince and Mariella in the worst of sentimental clichés. Forzano had neither D'Annunzio's poetic gift nor Illica's ability to create distinctive, memorable characters and situations. Both the Prince and Mariella are stock melodramatic figures whose only dramatic credibility is that reflected from the stark, powerful setting in which they exist. However real Mascagni's sympathy may have been for their plight, these cardboard characters were incapable of inspiring his best music.

The most serious weakness in *Marat*, its third act, also stems from Forzano's limitations. The first two acts, in which the plot—the Prince's rescue of his mother and Mariella—is clearly subordinated to the backdrop of the Revolution and the mob, are powerful, even overwhelming, musical theater. In the third act, however, the Revolution fades into the background. What emerges in its place is the dénouement of a contrived melodrama, complete with villains tied up, guns brandished, sudden plot twists, and finally a spectacular stage tableau as the curtain opens to show our heroes sailing down the

Loire to the rising sun. Effective in its way, but for all of Mascagni's musical efforts, no more than effective kitsch.

Il Piccolo Marat was the last opera that Mascagni was to compose entirely from new material; both *Pinotta* and *Nerone* relied heavily on music written in his younger years. For all its weaknesses, it is a stirring, gripping work, the work of a composer still in full command of his gifts. Largely neglected in recent decades, it is well worth more frequent hearing.

14. Mascagni and Fascism,
1921—1932

Fascism burst onto the Italian political scene in the aftermath of the occupation of the factories, leading an increasingly powerful and violent reaction against the Socialists and their revolutionary ambitions. As the Socialists continued to disintegrate, the new movement became the dominant political force in province after province, drawing small farmers, shopkeepers, and disaffected union members to its banner. By 1921 the government appeared barely capable of maintaining a facade of rule, as many of its nominal followers threw in their lot with Benito Mussolini and his growing movement. By the time Mussolini began his last and greatest bluff in October 1922, the March on Rome, it was uncertain whether the military would even defend the government against an armed insurrection. Rather than test the army, the king summoned Mussolini to Rome and invited him to form a government. The former Socialist gadfly was now Italy's prime minister.

As Italy's political climate shifted, Mascagni tried delicately to counteract his Bolshevik reputation. Conducting in Naples in January 1921, he performed the Marcia Reale as the duke and duchess of Aosta entered the royal box. A modest gesture, but it was noticed. The next day, asked whether his politics had changed since the past September, he stressed that he had never engaged in politics: "I told [the workers]," he said, "that the battle they were fighting was just only as long as any political element was kept strictly out of their thinking."

Many Fascists still considered Mascagni their enemy. In Verona in July he was confronted by *squadristi* and verbally assailed for his lack of true Italian feeling. In Turin in December, hostile demonstrations erupted outside a banquet in his honor and in front of the theater where he was conducting *Marat.* Given a police guard, Mascagni was indignant, writing, "Naturally I objected, stating that I had no need to be protected by anyone, and that if anything happened I knew how to defend myself."

Apart from these episodes, Mascagni gave politics little attention. The impending marriage of his son Mimi, and the prospect of a new libretto by Gabriele D'Annunzio, mattered far more. Despite a series of friendly meetings during the late summer and fall of 1921 between Mascagni and D'Annunzio, though, the libretto never materialized. Their relationship, barely rekindled, soon ruptured when Mascagni learned in December that the poet was planning to stage *Parisina* without his music. To Mascagni, D'Annunzio had broken faith with him; in his eyes the libretto, the foundation of his most ambitious attempt to create a masterpiece, was as much his as it was D'Annunzio's. Swallowing his pride, he wrote the poet seeking to "prevent any doubts and misunderstandings from being formed between us." He was rebuffed in "sharp, even offensive" language, and the disputed production went forward.

Mascagni never forgave D'Annunzio. In 1938, when the poet died, Lolli urged him to attend D'Annunzio's funeral. He testily replied:

> It wasn't you who felt on your back the mortal blows given me by someone who came to be called my brother. . . . Facing death, everything is forgotten. And I have forgotten, and I have sent two condolence telegrams: one to the president of the [Royal] Academy, and one to D'Annunzio's son. Therefore, I have done my duty as an Italian. And that's enough!

Mascagni would regularly rage at his friends and regularly calm down, accept their apologies or beg their forgiveness, and restore the friendship. This was different. He had bared his soul to D'Annunzio, offering him a deference he had granted no one since the death of Verdi. His betrayal could never be forgiven.

In September 1921 Mascagni received a letter from Mimi in Naples, where he had been working for Sonzogno for the past two years. Mimi had not adjusted well to civilian life and was considering rejoining the army. That, however, was before he met Gemma Risgalla, a seventeen-year-old Egyptian girl. It was love at first sight for the thirty-two-year-old Mimi. Within days of meeting her he had already written his father asking for his approval of the match.

Despite the whirlwind romance, the age difference of the couple, and his lack of confidence in his older son, Mascagni hoped for the best. He gave the young couple his blessing and invited Gemma and her father to come immediately to Livorno. He was delighted with Gemma, "a darling young woman, very young, well educated, [who] plays the piano very well." The couple were married the following February; a week before the wedding, Mascagni wrote Lolli that "my life these days is very troubled: I have to sort out all of Mimi's affairs, and I swear I haven't the heart for it: I would never have imagined that Mimi could have created such a mess." The marriage, though, was successful. Gemma and Domenico Mascagni remained together for fifty-five years until his death in 1976, and years afterward his widow would continue to speak of him with warmth and affection.

By the spring of 1922 Mascagni was restless and in need of money. His dealings with the managers of the Casa Sonzogno were increasingly difficult, and threats of lawsuits were again in the air. His relationship with Lolli, despite the previous spring's reconciliation, was still strained and uneasy. With little to hold him in Italy, Mascagni gladly accepted Walter Mocchi's offer to lead another Latin American tour. But 1922 was not 1911. Although Mascagni was once again greeted enthusiastically by the people of Buenos Aires, in other respects conditions were very different. Mocchi had imported a German opera company, presenting it in Buenos Aires and elsewhere simultaneously with the Italian company headed by Mascagni. With the Argentine critical and musical establishment now thoroughly Wagnerite, Mascagni found himself embattled rather than acclaimed. As he wrote his Roman friend Giuseppe Maria Viti, "I was shocked dizzy when I read the first articles about me when I arrived: 'a man who is no longer what he used to be; a failing old man; a disastrous step in the decrepit art of Italy; a shadow without substance . . .' and so on: that was my welcome to Buenos Aires."

The Italian company opened with *Il Piccolo Marat* on May 23, two days after the German company had begun its season. Mascagni saw himself the victim of a conspiracy:

> Marat *prompted unbelievable enthusiasm from the public: the press attacked the opera, attacked me personally, all the singers, and ranted on against Italian art; while it gave unbelievable praise to* Parsifal, *praising Weingartner to the heavens. . . .* Marat *filled the theater . . . but after three performances* Marat *was taken down, and hasn't been spoken of since.*

Within a month of their arrival in Buenos Aires, Mascagni and Mocchi were locked in a struggle that would last for the rest of the trip. As ever the jealous guardian of the dignity of Italian art, the composer made it no secret that he found Mocchi's behavior intolerable, denouncing Mocchi and the Germans at a banquet held by the musicians of the Colón Theater. Stung by Mascagni's outbursts, Mocchi avoided the composer, and—at least in Mascagni's eyes—blocked productions of his operas, forcing him into a tedious routine of *"Rigoletto, Barbiere, and Favorita."*

Matters improved after they left Buenos Aires. Mascagni found enthusiastic crowds waiting for him in the provincial cities of Rosario and Cordoba and a warm greeting in Rio di Janeiro, where his rivals in the German company were poorly received by both public and press. Despite the momentary pleasure of seeing his adversaries discomfited, though, as the tour neared its end Mascagni was sick at heart: "Only God knows how much I've suffered in America: it's been an inhuman agony: far from home, from my children, from you, my beloved; the miseries heaped upon me by Mocchi, the mortifications I've experienced for myself, my music, Italian music . . . the terrible, ferocious, controversies; the threats of lawsuits, of duels." He was not, however, looking forward to his return. As he wrote Viti early in November, in a probable reference to the March on Rome, "[This is] a moment in which my disgust and nausea would suggest I not even come back to Italy." Still, he dismissed the idea of exile: "Love for one's homeland is like love for one's mother. And nothing can ever separate one from the trunk that's given you life."

RETURN TO ITALY

When Mascagni returned to Italy, Mussolini had been prime minister for over a month. One of the few Italian musicians who took immediate notice of his rise to power was Puccini, the most prominent of the musicians who sent congratulatory messages to Mussolini after the March on Rome. Puccini had high hopes for the new regime; as his friend Guido Marotti remembered him saying, "Mussolini had saved Italy from disaster." Over the next few years, however, nearly every prominent Italian musician would declare his support for Mussolini and Fascism.

Little of this interested Mascagni, determined to have his revenge for the humiliations he had suffered in South America. Identifying himself as always with the cause of *italianità*, he considered the South American debacle an insult to Italian art and by extension to the Italian nation. Conducting in Bologna and Piacenza, he gained a respectful hearing from the local Fascist chiefs, including Arpinati, the notorious *ras* of Bologna. Arpinati went so far as to rebuke some of his *squadristi*, who had insulted and threatened the composer, unaware that such behavior was to be discouraged now that the Fascists were in power.

Mascagni was granted an audience with Mussolini in January 1923, hoping to enlist Mussolini's support in his battle with Mocchi, as he explained to two journalists whom he had summoned to his Via Po mansion immediately after the audience: "I did not engage the head of government on abstract artistic problems but on practical matters, arising from my unhappy experiences during the Latin American tour. . . . This is a matter of saving Italian art abroad, and I spoke firmly, citing fully documented facts." Although Mussolini flattered Mascagni, telling him, as he was being ushered out, "You can always count on me," it is doubtful that Mussolini intended to do more than pacify the overwrought composer. He took no action to address Mascagni's demands.

Five months later, Mascagni was still on the attack. Taking the floor at a conference in Rome, he launched into a harangue on the state of Italian opera in Latin America. Finally, he came to the point: "My specific accusation is this: Signor Mocchi is denigrating Italian art abroad in order to use German art to his advantage. He has created companies full of foreign artists, to the damage of our own artists." The accusation set off a tumult in the hall. As the chairman of the conference desperately tried to restore calm, Mocchi stalked across the hall and, in front of hundreds of stunned delegates, punched Mascagni in the face.

Despite these excitements, Mascagni found time at the end of 1922 to write a short symphonic poem entitled *Visione lirica*, subtitled "Guardando la Santa Teresa di Bernini" (Looking at Bernini's *Saint Teresa*), which he completed in January 1923. As he finished the piece he wrote Anna Lolli: "In these days of discomfort and dejection I have held on to . . . the vision of Saint Teresa, that famous and wonderful statue in Santa Maria della Vittoria. . . . Bernini's chisel created not a saint but a mystical ideal, sacred and profane together, a creature of sweetness whose expression is at the same time ascetic and sensual." When Mascagni gave Lolli his original manuscript of the work in Rome that January, he began his dedication, "To my Saint Teresa." It was not difficult for him to see the same conflation of the sacred and profane in his relationship with the deeply devout Lolli. Years later, Anna added her own note to the same manuscript, writing, "I truly was his Saint Teresa."

Visione lirica is a beautiful work, only four minutes long, reminiscent of *Parisina* in its intense but controlled lyricism. It was given its first performance under the composer's direction in Rome on January 14, 1923; "the work," a reviewer wrote, "pleased greatly with its characteristically Mascagnian intense feeling, and a repetition was demanded." Mascagni recorded the work in Berlin in 1927.

Early in August he left Rome to spend the rest of the summer in Livorno. By this time his daughter, Emy, had left Farinelli and was living with her parents. Dino was also in Livorno, having started a motorcycle business in nearly Antignano. He had been living with his parents but left early in 1923, moving with a woman into a small cottage near his factory. While his father was upset about the relationship, he carefully avoided any rupture with his son, who continued to appear regularly—without his companion—at dinner at Ardenza.

In Livorno Mascagni sank into an unusually intense depression; as he wrote Lolli, "I spend day and night in an armchair; at times I doze off (a kind of weighted-down sleep that drains me physically), then I get up, walk about a bit, sit down again, try to force down some food . . . and this is my life." Managers and agents called with projects, but he dismissed them with indifference. As the month went on, his lassitude deepened:

> *I haven't touched the piano or the violin; I feel an overwhelming aversion to any thoughts of work. I don't find (and am not even looking for) any distractions of any sort; . . . I count the hours and the minutes of these interminable days and these interminable nights, and I am overwhelmed by such a melancholy, so uncomfortable, so full of loss, that I feel fully the tragedy of my life, of my solitude, and it seems that it pushes me toward death.*

As his depression slowly lifted, he took another look at *Vistilia*, writing Lolli that "the music in *Vistilia* is the most beautiful music that has ever been written in the whole world." He had already decided, though, to shelve the opera once and for all, convinced that there was no saving the libretto from its inadequacies.

By fall, thoughts of operas were set aside by the need to earn money. Summoning his agent Emilio Ferone to Livorno, he began accepting the first of a series of conducting engagements that would keep him on the road in a stressful peripatetic existence for more than two years. The fall took him first to Treviso, Bologna, and Rome, where he found time to have an affectionate lunch with Puccini; he wrote Lolli that night, "We talked three hours straight about our different things: he is happy, and I envy him his happiness." It was the last time the two longtime friends would see one another. A year later Puccini would be dead in a Brussels clinic, and Mascagni would mourn him from his Viennese exile.

Back in Bologna, Mascagni learned that his brother Cecco's condition had deteriorated. Arriving in Milan at dawn, he found that his brother had died during the night. The next day he led the modest procession to his brother's grave and, as he wrote Lolli, "threw the earth into the grave myself, with my own hands." Having no time to mourn at length, he rushed back to Bologna that evening, to conduct the last performance of *Marat* before leaving the next day for Venice. He was now the only surviving child of Emilia Reboa and Domenico Mascagni.

After leading *Marat* in Venice, by mid-December he was back in Livorno, where he spent a cheerless Christmas; "just the three of us," he wrote, "me, Lina, and Dino: three mutes, three hermits." He left Livorno for Rome just before the New Year, giving three concerts at the Augusteo early in January. The last concert included instrumental selections from *Parisina*, as well as the work that had become the composer's favorite in the symphonic repertory, Tchaikovsky's *Pathétique*. Mascagni saw this work as a reflection of his own life; as he conducted it, he "felt that [he] was singing out his entire life . . . of portraying in [himself] everything the symphony depicted musically." Three days after the last Roman concert he was on a train for Bari for nine performances of *Marat*, making a brief trip to nearby Cerignola, where he was greeted with wild enthusiasm.

It had been nearly twenty years since he had last been in the town where *Cavalleria* was born. Nearly all of his old friends were dead, and at a luncheon given in his honor he found himself surrounded by their sons and grandsons. After lunch he went out into the town square, where thousands had gathered to embrace him and kiss his hand; he wrote Lolli, "the new generation, who never knew me when I lived here, think of me almost as a saint; a legend has grown up that makes me out to be a sort of superman . . . everyone here has a picture of me at the head of their beds!" From the square Mascagni led a procession to the street on which he had lived, which had been renamed the Via Pietro Mascagni in his honor.

Soon he was on his way to Trieste and Fiume, from Fiume to Venice for a second production of *Marat*, to Ferrara, back to Venice, and finally to Milan, where Piero Ostali, a Lombard cotton manufacturer, had offered to buy the Casa Sonzogno and wanted to reach an amicable settlement with Mascagni, the firm's principal asset. Cautiously hopeful, Mascagni returned to Livorno to replace his winter clothes for others more appropriate to a warmer climate, boarding a train the next day for Rome. In Rome he picked up Emy and her young son, Buby, and took the next train for Sicily. Once again, he had no time to see Lolli. They had not seen one another since the previous August.

In eight months from November to the end of June, he gave nearly ninety performances of thirteen separate operatic productions in twelve dif-

ferent cities. In most cases he was responsible for the entire production, su-
pervising the staging and preparing the orchestra and chorus, while coaching singers who were often new to their roles. Although he did not have to
fear jet lag, train trips from Catania to Florence, or from Rome to Trieste, took
far longer than a modern musician's transcontinental journeys.

A RELUCTANT EXILE

Mascagni's peripatetic existence reflected the press of financial necessity. At
sixty he was supporting his three adult children and their families, as he
would for the rest of his active life. He was also supporting Anna Lolli and
wanted to buy her an apartment, another step in ensuring her future. He was
painfully aware of how many people depended on him, and that, as he grew
older, his life "could be cut short at any moment."

The cost of maintaining Lolli and his children was now well over
200,000 lire a year. He maintained large houses in Rome, Livorno, and Milan, while the cost of his travels, including the luxurious hotel suites that he
took wherever he conducted, was over 100,000 lire per year. All in all, by the
1920s Mascagni had to earn over 700,000 lire annually to meet his obligations. By 1923 he found it increasingly difficult to earn enough money in Italy.
Although work was available, it was at small, provincial houses that lacked
the prestige of a San Carlo or a La Scala and paid far less.

Realizing that he could earn substantially more outside Italy, Mascagni
decided to return to the international scene. He had always been popular in
Central Europe. Throughout the 1890s *Cavalleria rusticana* was the most frequently performed opera in Germany's theaters, while from 1892 to 1907 Mascagni appeared regularly in Central Europe's concert halls and opera houses,
drawing enormous crowds, and receiving both popular and critical acclaim.
Arriving in Vienna on July 19 to conduct *Aida*, he was welcomed enthusiastically by a crowd led by the president of Austria. He was delighted to discover that the Viennese still remembered him after seventeen years, writing
that "I am known everywhere in Vienna: everyone greets me on the street: if I
walk into a café or a restaurant, everyone jumps to their feet shouting 'Viva!'"

Aida was performed in a specially constructed amphitheater seating
twenty-five thousand spectators, with a cast of one thousand, along with two
camels and six horses onstage for the second-act finale. Despite intermittent
rain, the production was enthusiastically received. Offers from other cities
poured in, and arrangements were made for the entire production to go to
the Sportpalast in Berlin on completion of its Vienna run.

Mascagni's arrival in Berlin resembled a state visit more than that of a conductor. After a hero's welcome at the train station, where it took him over an hour to pass through the station square packed with photographers, newsreel cameras, and thousands of cheering spectators, he paid a courtesy call on the Italian ambassador, followed by a call on President Ebert the next day. The situation deteriorated, however, after its grand beginning. After a series of disputes between the German promoters and the Italian organizers of the tour, the Germans pulled out, leaving hundreds of Italian musicians, singers, and dancers high and dry. After putting on a series of performances of *Cavalleria* and *Pagliacci* in order to raise funds to send the musicians back to Italy, Mascagni returned to Vienna at the end of October.

Back in Vienna, his plans suddenly changed. When he had left Italy in July, he had done so with every intention of returning by fall and had already accepted a number of Italian engagements for the winter. Now he abruptly canceled his engagements, informing everyone that he would remain in Vienna for the indefinite future.

Money does not explain this decision, unthinkable for a man so deeply rooted in Italy and *italianità*. Although financial considerations played some part after his losses from the Berlin fiasco, more compelling was his estrangement from the Italian political scene, which led him to write Lolli early in November, "My own country's government has seen fit to give me, publically and solemnly, the greatest possible humiliation, with the intent of ruining me economically, putting me in a position of inferiority toward the public, both at home and throughout the world." Although it is unclear precisely what actions prompted this outburst, it was followed by others. In February 1925 he wrote Lolli indignantly from Prague that "the Italian ambassadors abroad have been advised from Italy that I am an *anti-Italian!*"

Soon after taking this painful step, he suffered another blow with Puccini's death. His shock comes through in his letter to his friend Adriano Belli: "Puccini is dead! My God! I don't believe it! I can't think about it! I don't know what to say! Puccini is dead! My mind is in tumult, full of memories . . . and my soul is full of sadness . . . I'm crying . . . I'm crying for my friend, my colleague, my brother, the great composer, the good man." Despite Mascagni's intermittent jealousy toward his more successful rival, their relationship had survived years of competition. Although he had cordial relationships with other musicians of his generation, there was no one with whom he had the bond that he had with Puccini, the only contemporary he considered his equal. With the friend of his conservatory days gone, he felt even more alone in his battle for the soul of Italian opera.

He did not lack for work, leading Italian operas at Vienna's Staatsoper, beginning with *La Traviata* on November 27, commuting to engagements in Budapest, Prague, and Bratislava, and traveling as far as Warsaw, Belgrade, and Ostend, where at the close of *Cavalleria* the orchestra played the Italian Marcia Reale in his honor.

Despite his success, Mascagni was lonely and unhappy away from Italy. Few people were less suited for an exile's life. He was Italian to the core. His ties to the familiar sights and sounds of his native Livorno and his adopted Rome, to his growing family, and to his intimate relationships with his friends were his life. Whatever events may have prompted his self-imposed exile, he had no political ideology or principles to sustain him away from his homeland. As early as April he was writing Lolli, "I must think about establishing the best conditions possible for my return to Italy."

By midsummer Mascagni was desperately eager to return to Italy. Although he had begun to reduce his commitments in Vienna, in August he wrote Lolli, "I have been advised not to return now, because they would take away my passport." His return was complicated by an episode from his June appearances in Prague, about which the playwright Sem Benelli later wrote:

> At the dawn of Mussolini's rule, [Mascagni], finding himself abroad, in Prague, I believe, had spoken to a few journalists and had amused himself tossing off some jokes about the new regime; when he returned to Italy, it happened that blackmail was ready for him too: either surrender to Fascism, or be treated worse than a village bandmaster.

That is precisely what happened on his return to Italy in the fall.

His friends' efforts to resolve matters eventually achieved results. By fall he had received more positive signals from Italy and began to make plans to return. On October 29 he made a farewell appearance at the Volksoper; after a brief engagement in Belgrade, he was on his way home, as he wrote Lolli on the thirtieth, "and thus, my long, eternal, separation from Italy has ended! I won't say how much I suffered in the depths of my soul . . . I have eaten bitter bread, because I was never able to forget that my homeland had refused me even that." Having received assurances that he would be welcome, Mascagni arrived in Milan on November 11. He was surprised and alarmed when on his arrival in Milan he found a telegram from his son Dino, insisting that he wait there—and not continue on to Livorno—until Dino arrived in Milan.

While Mascagni was making his preparations, other preparations were being made in Italy. The powerful Fascist hierarch Costanzo Ciano, a Livorno native who took an interest in Mascagni's welfare, summoned the Livorno politician Aleardo Campana to Rome. "It seems," he told Campana, "that from

Austria . . . some misunderstandings have come out, which have given the Maestro a very bad press," referring to the Prague episode. Ciano would not have been involved if the matter had not been taken seriously by the Fascist inner circle. A decision had been made, probably by Mussolini himself, that Mascagni would not be allowed to resume life in Italy until he had made an explicit gesture of support for the regime.

Ciano told Campana to intercept the composer in Milan and have him send a suitable telegram to Mussolini immediately on his arrival in Italy. Campana, with Dino and Mascagni's old friend Armando Tanzini, left immediately for Milan. The composer, whom they found waiting at the station, balked. Finally, after many hours of argument, he broke down and sent off a studiously neutral telegram to the Duce. It was six hours before the response arrived, during which time Mascagni steadily berated his wife and friends. Finally, a telegram came from Mussolini thanking the composer for his good wishes and inviting him to an audience in Rome.

The meeting took place on November 23, 1925, in the presence of Interior Minister Luigi Federzoni, head of the Fascist police. As Mascagni described it in an interview later that day, the meeting included questions about the composer's anti-Fascist sentiments and reputed anti-Fascist activities abroad; as he indignantly told his interviewer, "I've been accused of having denigrated my country, in the most unjust and uncouth fashion, I who over a thirty-five-year career, at the price of the gravest sacrifices, have carried out efforts on Italy's behalf. Can that be believed?"

Although Mascagni apparently satisfied Mussolini and Federzoni that he was a loyal Italian, it is doubtful that they were much interested in the substance of the accusations. True or not, they could be used to keep the unhappy composer, desperate to remain in his country and win the approval of its new rulers, in line. For Mascagni, poking fun at the idols of the moment was as natural an act as eating or breathing. Whatever he may have said in Prague, Mascagni was no anti-Fascist; even after years of submission to Fascism, he would continue to make jokes, often barbed ones, about the regime. His irreverence would periodically infuriate Mussolini but had no deeper political significance.

Mascagni's act of submission in November 1925 began a process of accommodation on the one hand and seduction on the other that led to the composer's becoming an artistic ornament of the Fascist regime. Although Mascagni was driven by nothing more than a desire to be able to live and work in his own country in peace and comfort, and although other musicians were far more deeply engaged in the machinery of Fascist musical life, his prominence as Italy's most popular musician soon led to his being identified with the regime to a greater extent than any other musician. Meanwhile, less than a week after their meeting, on the eve of his departure for a three-month tour of Egypt, Mascagni sent a telegram to the Duce: "At the moment of taking up once again my work of carrying Italian art to foreign lands, my thoughts turn to Your Excellency, sending you a greeting full of gratitude." He sent another telegram to Anna Lolli, with whom he had spent three precious days in Rome. They were the first moments they had spent together in over two years.

IN THE MUSICAL ESTABLISHMENT

By 1926, its power consolidated, the regime had turned to building the Fascist consensus, as it has come to be known, that dominated Italian political life from the late 1920s until the invasion of Ethiopia in 1936. In contrast to previous Italian governments, which had been fluctuating coalitions of political elites, Fascism saw itself as an ideological mass movement, intensely concerned with its base of support and its public image. It would not be unreasonable to call Italian Fascism the first media-minded political regime, a pioneer of styles and techniques later adopted both by liberal democracies and dictatorships. To that end, the Fascist regime actively cultivated the visible support of the nation's intellectual and cultural leadership.

Mascagni's efforts to be useful to the regime were reciprocated by Mussolini; on the eve of the composer's departure for Vienna to represent the Italian government at the festivities commemorating the one hundredth anniversary of Beethoven's death, in 1927, he was received by the Duce, who turned the full measure of his charm on the composer:

> *Mussolini was very affectionate with me. He wanted to read the speech I am giving in Vienna and congratulated me warmly, begging me to give him the original manuscript as a present. Our conversation (just the two of us) was extremely warm and intimately friendly. At one point Mussolini told me that he wanted to have a photo of the two of us made; he had the photographer come in, and two beautiful pictures of us were made.*

Mussolini's flattery was bearing fruit. Although Mascagni had begun his relationship with the Duce from necessity, his stance toward him was turning into one of devotion. A few years later he could look back and write, "I, not a Fascist, have served the regime enthusiastically for the love I had for its leader." Mussolini was the last of the figures to whom Mascagni pledged his love and devotion, and whose smallest reciprocal gesture was received with almost pathetic gratitude.

The end of 1927 saw Mascagni return to composing after nearly five years, accepting a commission from the Fascist trade union movement to compose a choral hymn to labor. The bombastic text was written by Edmondo Rossoni, a former socialist who was then head of the union movement and a prominent Fascist ideologue, along with the unknown versifier Libero Bovio. During 1928 Mascagni conducted his new "Canto del lavoro" often, including a performance in Milan with a 900-member chorus and 140-member band, and an outdoor concert in the Piazza San Marco in Venice, in front of more than eighty thousand people, who filled every foot of the historic square and overflowed beyond the square onto the quays and the alleys of the city. No more than a pièce d'occasion, it is nonetheless vigorous, foot-tapping music. Sung by a mass of energetic voices backed by a lively brass band, its performances were rousing events.

Mascagni's efforts to ingratiate himself with the regime were rewarded in 1929, when he became one of sixty Italian intellectual and cultural figures appointed to Mussolini's most ambitious cultural enterprise, the Royal Italian Academy. As with many of Mussolini's initiatives, his motives for creating the academy, modeled on the Académie Française, were many. The existence of the academy, which gathered together Italy's most prominent intellectual figures, gave credibility to the regime's claims of having raised the level of Italian cultural and intellectual life. Moreover, it linked people with distinguished reputations with the regime, and in the process, in the words of one writer, "compromise[d] their intellectual independence and neutralize[d] their aversion to Fascism."

Few refused appointment. Whether prompted by the stipend or simply grateful for the honor, the initial sixty members represented the cream of Italy's intellectual elite, including the playwright Pirandello, the inventor Marconi, the architect Piacentini, the Futurist Marinetti, and the composers Giordano and Perosi as well as Mascagni. The academy was established in the elegant Villa Farnesina in Trastevere, which had been thoroughly refurbished for its new tenants. Members were issued elaborate uniforms decked with gold braid, sword, and cocked hat, which they were required to wear to formal sessions. They were addressed as "Your Excellency" and were allowed free first-class passage on all Italian trains and ships.

The academicians took their work as guardians of Italian high culture seriously, organizing conferences, publications, and awards to honor achievement and encourage young talent. Although Mascagni took some pleasure in being called Your Excellency, he soon found the duties of an academician more tiresome than rewarding. A practical musician rather than a scholar, he was not greatly interested in the subject matter of the academy. Academy activities, especially during its first years, often required him to attend three or four meetings a month; that, added to his many other duties, prompted Lina to write his friend Gianfranceschi, "[Pietro] is kept so busy by the different meetings of every sort. . . . it is a real bore, and a waste of time that turns him into a nervous wreck."

The stipend of an academy member, however, was nearly thirty-three thousand lire a year, and the first-class railroad pass in itself was an attractive inducement. Still, near the end of his life, Mascagni summed up the Royal Italian Academy in pungent terms:

> Oh, yes, the academy! The sword, the cocked hat, the plumes. . . . Fine stuff! But what braying, my little ones. Are they donkeys? Well, not all of them, of course, but better not even to compare some of them to donkeys, useful, humble animals that don't offend anyone. . . . I'm [only] a musician, true, but sometimes I'm open-mouthed in amazement.

APPROACHING SEVENTY

Since 1910 Mascagni's principal residence had been the mansion he had had built for himself and his family on Rome's Via Po. The house, a massive neo-classical structure a short walk from the Borghese gardens, was as much a monument to his success as it was a home. Every detail of decor had been carefully planned by the composer, reflecting his grandiose self-image at the time of its construction, including "faithful copies of the Napoleonic furniture of Versailles; only, instead of an 'N' they had an 'M' on their backs." The house had both a public studio, with a grand piano, where Mascagni received his musical friends and performed his latest works, and a small private one, off his bedroom, with an old upright piano, for work.

In September 1927, on his return from Livorno, Mascagni moved out of his house and into a suite with a large sitting room, a small bedroom, and a bath on the mezzanine floor of the Hotel Plaza, where he would live for the rest of his life. The sitting room contained a number of tables and chairs, two pianos, one of which was the old upright piano on which he had written *Cavalleria*, and a massive radio given him by EIAR, the national broadcasting agency. Here he ate his meals, welcomed his friends, played long games of scopone and tresette, and, at increasingly rare intervals, wrote music. Although the Plaza was one of the city's finest hotels, and the suite met Mascagni's needs, one visitor wrote, "It had a certain dreariness that made visitors think regretfully of the villas in the Via Po and in Livorno." Mascagni soon moved out of the Livorno villa as well, taking a suite in the Hotel Corallo, a spa-like establishment on the edge of the city. The villa, to which Mascagni had shipped most of his treasures from Rome, was opened only in the summertime, for the composer's children and their families.

With the children grown and in homes of their own, and with Lina often bedridden, he did not need large houses. He found it convenient to return to a well-run hotel, with a concierge, porters, and assistant managers ready to do his bidding. His moves, though, were more than a matter of convenience. His housing choices had always carried symbolic weight, whether it was the purchase of a grand palazzo in the center of Livorno or the construction of an even grander one on the Via Po. For him to leave his villas and palazzi and move into a modest hotel suite was a true passage, a renunciation of the grandiose style that had characterized his existence until now. As he approached seventy, he was, consciously or not, simplifying his life.

The simple tastes that had survived beneath his love of display were now more visible. He spent long hours at cards, playing almost every night with a regular band of partners, a convivial group of writers, poets, and lawyers, but few musicians. As he played cards, and as he did nearly everything but eat and sleep, he smoked the same strong Tuscan cigars that he had taken up in his teens. He became abstemious and precise in his food and drink. His staple was a plate of spaghetti, brought to the table unsauced. He ate little meat, and then only chicken or veal. He ate no bread, commenting that "I don't want bricks in my stomach," and drank no wine, except for an occasional glass of vermouth, a drink to which Giulio Ricordi had introduced him in the days of *Cavalleria*.

One friend wrote, "He seasoned his meals not only with pepper but with witticisms." He ate slowly, preferably in the company of friends, where he could indulge his love of conversation. His conversation was nearly a monologue, an opportunity for him to take center stage, holding forth on the subjects of the day, dazzling his audience with puns, jokes, and double entendres. His wit was often savage, particularly in his later years, directed impartially at critics, composers, politicians, and publishers, but most often at singers, into whose often tender sensibilities his malicious fancy struck home with great effect.

With Lina resigned to the permanent nature of his ties to Anna Lolli, he would now see Lolli nearly every day when in Rome, often spending the entire day with her in the apartment he had bought for her on the Via Principe Amadeo. After the tempests of earlier years, their relationship had taken on a new stability, nearly twenty years after they had first met and become lovers. They remained lovers; in 1932 the still-passionate Mascagni, nearly seventy, would write her after one visit, "I am still overwhelmed by your beauty. I can't sleep: I am excited, and a great yearning for you makes me breathless. And when I think that I can hold you, kiss you, that I can admire your glorious body . . ."

Family matters were much improved. Emy and Piermarcello, a growing, athletic boy, had moved into their own apartment in Rome, bought for her by her father. Supported by his monthly checks, she had begun to write and see her first efforts appear on the literary pages of Italian newspapers. In 1936 she would publish her most ambitious effort, her wildly unreliable but entertaining memoir of her days with her father and Gabriele D'Annunzio in France in 1912.

Mimi and Gemma had also settled in Rome, where their first child, a boy named Pietro, after his grandfather, was born in 1927. Mascagni was given another grandchild a few years later, when their second child, a daughter named Maria Teresa and known as Miti, was born. Dino had married his companion, Gisella, and had a daughter, named after her grandmother and known as Linina.

Mimi himself had changed, remade both by his new duties as a husband and father and by his intense commitment to the Fascist party. Although nominally practicing law, more of his time was taken up with his Fascist duties, first as a leader of the youth movement, the Avanguardisti, and later as an official of the Fascist militia. Although Mimi's carousing was behind him, his financial demands were still a source of strain to his father. In addition to buying a Roman apartment for his family and providing Mimi with an ample monthly check, Mascagni paid for his life insurance, his office expenses, and his telephone. Much to his father's annoyance, Mimi continued to send Peppino Hirsch, Mascagni's business manager, demands for payment of every conceivable expense, from birthday presents for little Pietrino to tailor's bills and garage bills for his car.

Mascagni grumbled but paid willingly, gratified by his son's new sobriety and by his willingness to help out with his father's always complicated legal affairs. Dino was a far greater worry. After the war Mascagni had paid for his new motorcycle factory outside Livorno. Dino, while a skilled craftsman, was no businessman; by 1927 the business was in serious trouble, and the unhappy Mascagni was spending thousands of lire to keep the plant open. Finally, in the fall of 1931 Dino's improvisations and his father's assistance were no longer enough; as he wrote Lolli: "Dino's situation has reached tragic dimensions. . . . Dino is overloaded with debts, with notes due: the banks have lost all faith in him. And to save him, and save my name, I will have to deal with everything. But I understand that his business is finished forever." For the next two years and more, Mascagni would spend long hours fighting to keep the firm from bankruptcy.

Dino himself was no help. While his father was struggling to keep the business from going under, Dino had taken up with another woman and refused to cooperate with his father's efforts. In the summer of 1934, after the plant had been shut down, he abruptly left Gisella and Linina, fleeing to Switzerland in the company of his mistress. Tracked down in Nice by Mascagni's attorney Renzo Rossi in October, he returned alone and chastened to Italy. A few months later, unwilling to return to Livorno and face his family, the disheartened forty-year-old Dino enlisted in the army. Commissioned a lieutenant in the Engineering Corps, he left Italy for East Africa early in 1935. He would die in the deserts of Somalia only a year later.

Mascagni still retained the vast popularity that had been his since 1890. After nearly forty years on the public scene, his appearances were still occasions for crowds, for demonstrations of affection, and for parades. As Labroca wrote, he "was truly popular and beloved, because his popularity was nourished by the people, who saw in him the closest and most sensitive interpreter of their impulses, their exuberance, their miseries." The gap between Mascagni's adoration by the general public and the indifference, even hostility, with which he was seen by much of the musical world, though, had never been greater, as the leading figures of the new music treated him and his music as artifacts of a bygone era.

By the late 1920s Mascagni had become an isolated figure, largely irrelevant to the new generation of composers. The younger musicians who gathered around the banners of Casella and Malipiero's Corporation for New Music (CDNM) and the International Society for Contemporary Music (ISCM) dismissed him outright, as Casella wrote in a 1926 article:

> 1890 and 1926 are two dates sufficiently distant for a man to have had time to pass from the advance guard to the rear of the troops that lead the intellectual movement. And today, whatever be the respect in which one holds the name of Mascagni, it would certainly be difficult to maintain that he represents the musical thought of new Italy.

Reacting to his isolation, Mascagni adopted an aggressive public posture rejecting, as he called them, the "modernists," "futurists," or "twentieth-centuryists" (*novecentisti*). Although in private he would still comment favorably on some individual works, his public rhetoric became increasingly shrill and condemnatory. On occasion he might treat the subject with humor, but more typical was a widely publicized 1929 speech in which he said, "Yes, the *novecentisti* have won. But their victory is nothing but the imposition of the ugly, the grotesque, the absurd, and the immoral."

For Mascagni, the artist's life had always been one of combat. With en-

emies always present, every opera he wrote, every performance he conducted, was a battle fought and won for himself and for Italian art, in his mind
the two being largely one and the same. In this alien musical climate both his
fears and his fantasies took on ever wilder dimensions. While he dreamed
of being named head of the Costanzi Theater or taking Toscanini's place at
La Scala, he became increasingly certain that his isolation was the product of
a systematic conspiracy of "occult forces" arrayed against him, as he complained to one sympathetic ear. As he wrote Orsini in 1929, "The boycott of
my works and of my person is in full swing. . . . The battle is so uneven, the
noose gets tighter and tighter." He would return regularly to this theme, writing Mussolini in 1935 to denounce the "merciless boycott of my works by the
managements of all the theaters of Italy."

If such a boycott ever existed, it was over by the 1930s. From 1928 at
the Teatro Reale, as the Costanzi was renamed that year, and from 1930 at La
Scala, until the outbreak of the war, his works were performed regularly, often under his baton. After 1935 he was the most frequently performed living
composer in Italy's major opera houses, coming behind only Verdi, Puccini,
and Wagner among all composers.

Despite his publicized rapprochment with Mussolini, Mascagni continued to be viewed with ambivalence by the regime. He remained, despite their
favors, fundamentally uncontrollable. His irrepressible sarcastic vein found
easy targets among the Fascist hierarchs, and he had lost none of his quixotic
and unpredictable determination to see justice done. In 1930 and 1931 he sent
a series of missives to Mussolini denouncing mismanagement and corruption
in the regime's artistic and cultural vehicles, most particularly the Society of
Authors and Publishers (SIAE), implicating a variety of prominent Fascists.
These denunciations, for all their extensive documentation, were politely received and totally ignored; as Nicolodi sums it up: "The episode, as far as it
is known, ended with Mascagni's being the only one resigning, in sharp contrast to the 'new men' brought in to restructure, or 'fascistize,' culture. Between
such men and the composer, for whom art was still a word to be capitalized
. . . any understanding was effectively impossible." As Mascagni failed to appreciate, corruption, within certain bounds, was as much a tool of Fascist rule
as the propaganda with which it blanketed Italy.

Although Mascagni's remarkable physical activity and health in his seventies was a subject of admiration throughout Italy, he was becoming old just
the same, withdrawing gradually into what Casella had called his "disdainful
isolation." Trapped in an endless round of conducting appearances in provincial cities, bedeviled by fears and fantasies, encircled by real or imaginary

enemies, his life was not an easy one. Still, as the 1930s dawned, he began to prepare to fight one more battle in the only arena that mattered, by composing one more opera, his last, *Nerone*. A long period of preparation, however, was necessary before he could actually compose that opera.

RETURNING TO THE FRAY: *LE MASCHERE* AND *PINOTTA*

As the 1920s came to an end, it seemed increasingly likely that Mascagni had finally given up composing, devoting himself to conducting and to long, convivial card-playing sessions. While rumors regularly appeared in the press, as the years passed no new Mascagni opera came forward. Mascagni, however, had never actually renounced writing more operas, as had Rossini. Although his composing drive had slowed, it was still present. After the sorry outcome of a 1926 opera competition, in which no prize was awarded, he wrote Lolli wistfully, "Who knows? If God did me the favor of allowing me to live close to you I swear that I would be able to create an immortal opera."

Near the end of 1927, through Lolli's intervention, Mascagni and Forzano ended their estrangement and began to discuss collaborating on an opera based on Manzoni's historical tapestry *I Promessi sposi*, the central work of modern Italian literature. Mascagni was excited but wary, and the project was not pursued for long. He resumed his itinerant life, traveling steadily throughout 1928, while Forzano, a busy playwright and stage director, went back to his many other activities.

Mascagni and Forzano met again late in 1930, after the composer had accepted La Scala's invitation to stage a new production of *Le Maschere* in 1931. Mascagni's comic opera had hardly been performed for decades and was virtually unknown to an entire generation of operagoers. Mascagni, who had always been unhappy with the drastic cuts made in 1907, saw the La Scala production as an opportunity to present a new and definitive version of the opera to the Italian public. With Forzano's help, Mascagni crafted a new version that effectively blends the best of the 1901 and 1907 versions, restoring the original spoken prologue, along with a chosen few of the 1907 cuts. Forzano's contribution was modest but important, adding two short but significant passages to the second act, for the first time making fully clear the effect of Illica's magic powder. Mascagni was delighted to be once again working on an opera, even in such modest fashion.

The La Scala production of the revised *Le Maschere* opened on March 8, with Mafalda Favero as Columbina and the young Maria Caniglia, a last-

minute substitution who was soon to become a Mascagni favorite, as Rosaura. It was an overwhelming success, as one reviewer noted:

> *If the public's judgment must count when it is unanimous, it must be said that . . .*
> *such unanimity was present: and that it was present with an intensity of enthusiasm*
> *that allows no equivocation: the twenty or more curtain calls at the end of each act,*
> *the heated applause after the overture, not to mention the ovations with which the*
> *public paid clamorous tribute to the Maestro himself, were the undeniable and un-*
> *questionable symbols of success.*

Le Maschere was briefly restored to a modest place in the Italian repertory, with
at least six more productions during the 1930s, as well as two broadcasts. After the war, however, it has suffered the neglect shared by most of Mascagni's
operas.

Mascagni's experience with *Le Maschere* had unleashed his full desire
to compose once again. Early in 1931 an unexpected event would propel him
one more step closer to his ultimate goal. Nearly fifty years earlier, toward the
end of his stay at the Milan Conservatory, Mascagni had lodged in a modest
pensione in Milan's bohemian Brera quarter. Owing his landlord 120 lire, before taking to the road he had left behind a suitcase of his music and other
personal effects as surety. The landlord had long since died, and the composer had long since given up hope of ever seeing his youthful manuscripts
again.

Relaxing with friends in his hotel suite after a rehearsal of *Le Maschere*,
Mascagni recalled the episode, wondering what might have come of the suitcase after all these years. With little to go on, a young admirer of the composer decided to play detective and track down the missing suitcase. A few
evenings later he returned, a mysterious package under his arm:

> *Inside were sheets of music, which Mascagni looked at hesitantly. Suddenly he jumped*
> *up. This was his stuff! And surrounded by total silence, he ran through the pages,*
> *pointed with his hand, hummed something or other, stopped, stared stupefied at his*
> *friends, laughed and laughed, and then threw his head down on the table cluttered*
> *with glasses and cried, cried like a baby.*

It was the miscellany of the young student's life. Harmony and counterpoint
textbooks, letters from friends and teachers, and of course, music—songs,
the first orchestral score of the intermezzo from *Guglielmo Ratcliff*, and the
manuscript of his youthful cantata *In filanda.*

That score, written at seventeen, brought to mind the modest opera
Pinotta, which he had made from it at the Milan Conservatory early in 1883.
Ever since Mascagni had finished it too late to compete in the conservatory's

competition, it had languished. Sent on consignment along with a handful of songs to the Milan publisher Pigna, it lay there until 1890, when Pigna had sought to capitalize on Mascagni's sudden fame by issuing it. Mascagni, however, unwilling to be represented by a student work at that stage in his career, had withdrawn it, putting it in a drawer, where it had gathered dust for forty years.

Back in Livorno, he called Dino, who brought the score of *Pinotta* over on his motorcycle from the villa to his father's suite at the Corallo. By December Mascagni was deeply engaged in reworking the modest opera, enlisting Targioni-Tozzetti to revise Soffredini's pedestrian libretto. He wrote Lolli, his words reflecting his obsession with the modernists: "It is a little nothing, but in the second act there are a few glimmerings of a sincere and truly felt art. But it is tiny stuff, as my youthful mind was then (fifty years ago). Just the same, it is still a weapon against modernism. And my art has always been a battle without quarter." Mascagni remained largely faithful to his 1883 score, reorchestrating the work with the help of his cousin Mario, adding only a few harmonic elaborations and thematic cross-references to enliven his youthful self's charming but unpretentious music.

The premiere of *Pinotta* was hosted by San Remo, near the French border, then the finest winter resort on the Italian Riviera. Its crown jewel was the elegant casino, within which was a small but beautifully appointed opera house. The 1932 season there included three Mascagni operas: *Lodoletta* and a double bill of *Pinotta* and *Cavalleria*. Mafalda Favero, a popular Lodoletta and Suzel, sang the title role in Mascagni's new opera, with Alessandro Ziliani, whose work in La Scala's *Le Maschere* had pleased the composer, singing Baldo, the young millhand who woos the orphan Pinotta.

The audience was wildly enthusiastic. Nearly every number was applauded at length, and at the end of the first act the artists were called out nine times, with Mascagni receiving five more curtain calls. The second act was even more enthusiastically received. The entire love duet was repeated, and at the end the applause went on and on. After the performance the composer was ushered to the balcony of the casino. Outside, the square was filled with the townspeople of San Remo, who had organized a torchlight parade in his honor.

The reviews the next day were appreciative and friendly, as befit the sentimental nature of the occasion, but reserved. After acknowledging the work's success and attributing it to the warm melodic element of "Mascagnian song," Cenzato in the *Corriere della Sera* concluded that "its success should not lead anyone to conclude that *Pinotta* is a theatrical work of any dramatic character beyond that which would be found in a lyrical cantata."

Pinotta is an endearing work, full of lovely melody; the concluding love duet, in which the nineteen-year-old Mascagni recycled his song "La tua stella" to great effect, is particularly appealing. At the same time, it is a period piece, a work of a highly talented youth of the 1880s, with only brief flashes of the distinctive qualities of the mature Mascagni. There is something more than a little pathetic about the spectacle of Mascagni, after a long career of impressive achievement, bringing forth this retouched work of his teens as a gauntlet thrown down at the feet of the Modernist composers he so bitterly resented. Although the applause at its premiere was sincerely meant, it was prompted as much by the audience's feeling for the grand old man of Italian music, and their admiration for his gesture, as by the music. *Pinotta* did not travel far or long. Mascagni had it published at his own expense and over the next two years performed it frequently, paired with *Cavalleria*. By 1934, however, he was fully engaged with his new opera, *Nerone*, and had less interest in promoting his youthful effort. Since his death it has rarely been heard.

15. Nerone *and the Last Years,*

1933—1945

Intoxicated by the warm welcome given *Pinotta* in San Remo, Mascagni returned to Livorno more determined than ever to write another opera. After
three days in July with the poet Arturo Rossato, he had his subject. It was
Pietro Cossa's play *Nerone,* a project Mascagni had first contemplated but reluctantly set aside more than forty years before, in order to avoid appearing
to compete with Arrigo Boito's unfinished, and long delayed, *Nerone.* Mascagni, a lifelong devotee of the theater, was strongly drawn to Cossa's version
of the Roman emperor. Nero, as Mascagni described him, "was never either
a politician or an emperor. His life was that of an artist, a failure if you will,
but an artist. Indeed, in this failure, his aspiration for things beyond his reach,
lies the interesting drama of his existence." Cossa's Nero is an actor playing a
role as emperor, a role that, in the end, becomes his biggest flop.

Late in October Rossato, having turned Cossa's sprawling work into a
compact, effective drama, delivered his libretto. *Nerone* opens in a Roman tavern. As its denizens grumble, a beautiful young woman rushes in, fleeing from
two slaves, who are revealed as the emperor Nero and his crony Menecrate.
Nero sends the girl, a Greek slave named Egloge, to the palace and abandons himself to drink. As he is upbraided by his mistress, Atte, he falls to the

ground in a stupor. He is lifted onto a litter by the Pretorian Guard, as bystanders shout his praises over his senseless figure.

Entranced by Egloge's beauty and spirit, Nero installs her in the palace. Atte demands that she leave; when Egloge refuses, Atte attempts to stab her but is stopped by Nero. A delegation from the Senate arrives, warning Nero that the Pretorian Guard are restless and that the Spanish legions have acclaimed Galba as emperor. After a flash of anger, Nero turns back to Egloge; murmuring "Galba is still far away," he leads her into the palace gardens.

The third act opens with a banquet. As Nero sings, Atte poisons Egloge. As he mourns her, his freedman Faonte warns him that the Roman people have risen against him. With Atte and his two freedmen he flees the palace, taking refuge in Faonte's hovel. As an intermezzo depicts his flight, the scene changes to the hovel, where Nero is lost in theatrical fantasies. Hoping to inspire him to kill himself nobly, Atte kills herself with a dagger. Nero tries to do the same but can stab himself only with Faonte's help, as the legions arrive. A centurion tries to stanch the emperor's wound, but with a final cry of "Too late, soldier . . . and is this your faith?" Nero dies.

Mascagni began *Nerone* in December 1932, transcribing passages from *Vistilia* into his new opera. Musical ideas no longer flowed as freely as they once had, and he might never have undertaken the project without the music already written for the earlier opera. To ease Mascagni's task, Rossato reworked large parts of *Vistilia's* text, for which Mascagni had already written the music, into his libretto for *Nerone*. These include many of the opera's most dramatic scenes and most passionate lyrical passages.

After using most of his *Vistilia* music, Mascagni set the opera aside until April. He was still working with Rossato, but their relationship was becoming increasingly strained. At the end of May Mascagni fired Rossato summarily and replaced him with Targioni-Tozzetti. Rossato was livid, writing in early June to Mascagni's cousin Mario, whom he hoped would intervene with the composer, "If *Nerone* ever comes out, he will have a brand on his forehead and a court order . . . attached to his toga. I have written sixty libretti and never has anyone told me he wouldn't use one." Mascagni brushed off his cousin's inquiries disdainfully and refused to reconsider.

By this time Targioni, who had moved into the Hotel Plaza to be by Mascagni's side, had already set to work. Targioni finished the libretto, changing some of Rossato's verses and adding a substantial amount of new material. Mascagni never referred to Rossato again, and Targioni was given sole credit as the author of *Nerone's* libretto. In a 1934 interview, a few months after Targioni's death, when asked about Rossato's role, Mascagni truculently replied, "Rossato has nothing to do with it. Its sole creator was poor Nanni [Targioni]."

The evidence proves otherwise. Not only did Rossato give the libretto its shape by adapting Cossa's play, but the dating of Mascagni's passages makes clear that much of the opera was composed before Targioni became involved, suggesting that half or more of *Nerone* is Rossato's work. How Rossato was persuaded to withdraw his objections to both his own dismissal and the appropriation of his work by others remains a mystery.

With Targioni at hand, Mascagni worked steadily through the summer. It was like the old days, he wrote Lolli: "[The night before last] I worked eleven consecutive hours, without a break, and last night I worked ten hours. . . . sleep didn't come quickly, because this work keeps my mind so excited." On August 26 he wrote the final bars of the opera, which was now complete except for the third-act intermezzo. On September 16 he sat down to begin the intermezzo. As he wrote, his handwriting, generally so precise and careful, took on an almost feverish haste, as if he realized that this would be his last creative effort. He finished the work on September 26 after writing forty-eight measures that night. After dating and signing the work as always, he added—as he had never done before—the words "Dio sia benedetto," may God be praised.

MASCAGNI'S LAST HURRAH: THE FIRST PERFORMANCE OF *NERONE*

By the 1930s, as Philip Cannistraro writes, *romanità*, or the glorification of ancient Rome, had become "something of an obsession in the [Mussolini] regime's cultural rhetoric." From the "Roman salute" to the excavations in the Roman Forum, the martial spirit of the Roman Empire was presented as a model for the new Fascist society.

Mascagni's opera was Roman, but not necessarily the tribute to ancient Roman virtues that the regime was seeking. Although Rossato had eliminated the more outrageous of Cossa's satirical sallies, the center of the play was still Nero, a poor role model, while recent impersonations of Nero by the famous clown Petrolini, widely seen as having been aimed at Mussolini himself, made it easy to find parallels between the two. The Duce's sensitivity on the subject is suggested in a widely reported and possibly true story, in which he was said to have approached Mascagni and disdainfully told him, "I am not at all happy with you—did you have to pick Nero in particular for a subject?"

Mascagni was not unaware of the sensitive nature of his subject. Chafing, as usual, at the pressures and impositions of the regime, his choice was a psychological rather than a political statement, his way of reminding the powerful that he answered to the higher authority of art; as he wrote a friend in the fall of 1933, "I realize more and more that today any man of character must look like a total idiot."

The political ambiguity of his subject meant that Mascagni's dream of a Rome premiere for *Nerone* became a matter for deliberation at the highest political levels; he wrote Lolli, "I wait for the supreme word, but I don't believe that the word will be a favorable one." He was not surprised when a Rome premiere, with its air of official sanction, was vetoed by the regime. Although the regime did not seek to suppress the opera entirely, the only offer came from Bologna, a secondary theater. Mascagni sent his cousin Mario to make the rounds of other theaters, hoping in vain to find something better.

As *Nerone* neared completion early in 1934, Targioni-Tozzetti's health deteriorated. He completed the last revisions to the libretto from his sickbed, finishing on May 8, little more than three weeks before his death. Mascagni's eulogy appeared in Livorno's newspapers the next day. "Your name," he wrote, "will remain tied to mine from my first to my last opera. No one will ever be able to separate our names in art, as no one ever dared break our friendship, always faithful and affectionate, for over sixty years."

Targioni was not a great poet. Even at his best, his verses carry a conventional, often sentimental stamp; he was, however, a competent versifier and above all, a faithful friend. A man of parts, he was a distinguished professor at the Naval Academy and served Livorno both as an elected mayor in the 1910s and as an appointed mayor under the Fascist regime. Still, as their mutual friend Adolfo Taddei wrote, "He had only one concern, that of satisfying his Pietro." With his death, Mascagni lost the one person who had never failed him over sixty years of unqualified devotion.

Finally, in June 1934 Mascagni received an unexpected offer to host *Nerone*'s debut from La Scala. The eight-month delay suggests that the regime had reversed course and decided to treat the work as a triumph of Fascist culture—in Milan, if not in Rome. Nine days later, Mascagni signed a contract for the first performance, to take place in January 1935. With Mascagni's financial assistance, La Scala spared no expense on sets and costumes, assembling a stellar cast. Aureliano Pertile, who had sung Nero in Boito's opera, was cast in the title role, Margherita Carosio was Egloge, and Lina Bruna Rasa was Atte. Even smaller roles were cast with important singers, such as Tancredi Pasero as Babilio the astrologer and Apollo Granforte as Nero's crony, the actor Menecrate.

Mascagni's preparations for *Nerone*'s debut were interrupted at the end of October by a summons from Rome, instructing the members of the Royal Academy to mount guard at the exhibition of the Fascist revolution. As he wrote Lolli, "I just couldn't refuse; so this evening . . . I leave for Rome, where tomorrow, dressed up like a Fascist, with a rifle on my shoulder, I will play sentinel on the steps of the Via Nazionale." Much as he resented the interruption and the embarrassment, as well as the physical discomfort, of standing for hours "like an overgrown Balilla," he felt that he had no choice. Although to the world he might appear to be a pillar of the regime, he spent his days in a constant state of uncertainty, writing Lolli only a month earlier, "You know that I am not looked on favorably by high personages in the government." With January approaching, he was careful to avoid doing anything that might antagonize those who had given and could easily take away.

On the night of the premiere the facade of La Scala was brilliantly lit by carefully placed spotlights. Although Mussolini and his cabinet were absent, except for Galeazzo Ciano, the undersecretary of press and propaganda and the Duce's son-in-law, the hall nevertheless glittered with Fascist dignitaries, members of the royal family, and the leading lights of Italy's musical and intellectual establishment. Not since the premiere of *Turandot,* wrote the *Corriere della Sera,* "had La Scala seen such an impressive and wonderful audience."

After the obligatory Marcia Reale and the Fascist "Giovinezza," the opera began. Propelled by a visually spectacular production and superb execution, *Nerone*'s debut was a great success. There were six curtain calls for the cast after the first act, nine after the second, and ten after the third; Mascagni himself was called out a total of nineteen times. After the last curtain call, the composer withdrew to his dressing room, where in the company of his family he opened thousands of telegrams, including hundreds from musicians in Italy and abroad, from Franchetti, Cilea, Alfano, Montemezzi, and Perosi, and not least from Jean Sibelius, who wrote, "To the old master Pietro Mascagni, heartfelt wishes from his admirer." After a short rest he went back onstage, where La Scala's managing director presented him with an enormous gold medal and the assembled dignitaries came onstage to pay their respects. Finally, Ciano took the composer aside and told him that Mussolini had telephoned after each of the first two acts, specifically asking "the number of curtain calls and the frequency of applause during each scene."

The reviews the following day were generally warm, singling out many things to praise, but often guarded in their overall assessment of the opera. Egloge's aria "Danzo notte e di," which Gasco heralded as "a Mascagnian page destined never to die," was hailed, as were the second-act love duet and the confrontation between Egloge and Atte. The banquet scene and Egloge's death were also generally praised, but the drier, more declamatory sections in the first and third acts prompted sharply mixed reactions. The stark closing scene, dismissed by some, was seen as the high point of the opera by Inter

(Franco Abbiati) in the *Corriere della Sera:* "It is entirely from this scene that the fearful and inevitable tragedy of the Emperor . . . emerges in its full and desolate depth. . . . A passage truly masterfully depicted by Mascagni, with intimate and moving sobriety, achieving a powerful and expressive concision." Gasco in *La Tribuna* was not impressed with the closing scene but felt that "the second act and the first part of the third act of *Nerone* are superb, and it is to them that the future of the entire opera is entrusted."

A few reviewers took Mascagni to task for his failure to embellish the regime's myth of ancient Rome, particularly *La Regime Fascista*, controlled by Cremona's Farinacci:

> *Mascagni has said over and over that in* Nerone *he intended to express* romanità. *An excellent intention. . . . But . . . there is no* romanità *here. In fact, there is one scene, the finale of the first act, that seems a fierce caricature of* romanità. *. . . Perhaps next time . . . it will not occur to him to set the Hymn to Imperial Rome to the beat of the grunts of a drunkard.*

Such voices were few. Mascagni was able to bask in a nearly unanimous chorus of praise.

After the eight scheduled performances, two more were added by La Scala to meet the demand, and the opera was broadcast throughout Europe. Despite the acclaim *Nerone* received in Milan, though, few new productions were forthcoming. After lengthy negotiations, a summer production in Rome fell through. Other proposals came and went; as Mascagni bitterly wrote Tanzini in June, "All the plans for *Nerone* have fallen through, for secret reasons that I'm never able to learn . . . there's no doubt that there's an order out against me and my music."

Although many of the embittered Mascagni's claims must be taken with some skepticism, the lack of interest in *Nerone,* after its successful debut, is highly suspicious. Theaters seemed reluctant to present this potentially controversial work. During the rest of 1935 its only productions were in Mascagni's home town of Livorno and in Bologna, which had earlier sought the work's premiere. After a La Scala revival in the spring of 1937, the opera vanished. The sole performance outside Italy in Mascagni's lifetime took place in June 1937 in Zurich. After the curtain fell on the last of three Zurich performances, *Nerone* slept, not to be heard again for fifty years.

Mascagni's success did not reconcile him to life under an authoritarian regime. Indeed, emboldened by the success of *Nerone,* he showed his feelings even more readily; in March Farinacci received a report, which he passed on to Mussolini, that Mascagni, "puffed up by his recent success, and by his reception by the Duce . . . came out with an irreverent phrase toward [Mussolini], asserting that he had been able to have *Nerone* performed in spite of him." According to a second source, what he actually said was that he had "stuck *Nerone* up Mussolini's ass!"

Despite Farinacci's efforts, Mascagni was largely immune from pressure. At seventy-one the "obstinate chatterbox," as he called himself, was unlikely to change. Despite his grumbling, his adherence, however superficial, was useful to the Fascist regime, and his sarcasm was in any event devoid of serious political meaning. A harmless nuisance, for his remaining years he was granted a "fool's freedom," in Goetz's words, by Mussolini.

NERONE

Nerone is two operas in an awkward embrace, one based on the *Vistilia* music, written largely between 1903 and 1908, and the other original to *Nerone*, written in 1933. The *Vistilia* music, lush and lyrical, dominates the second act and the first part of the third act. At its best, as in the love duet between Nero and Egloge or the third-act banquet scene, it makes the listener regret that Mascagni did not complete that opera when his inspiration flowed freely.

The music that Mascagni wrote in 1933, with few exceptions, is dry and sparsely orchestrated. In place of his elaborate orchestral commentary, only scattered triads and short orchestral fragments interrupt the declamatory recitative. The most notable exception, Egloge's "Danza notte e dì," which she sings to Nero in the second act, is the gem of the score, capturing perfectly the bittersweet innocence of the Greek slave girl. Although the opera as a whole may not be the masterpiece of Mascagni's old age, this aria deserves that title. The music takes on an understated power in the last scene, where the slow, halting pace of the music, as Nero awaits his death, is broken only by Atte's poignant lament. Sadly, the grandiose intermezzo, while effective enough, lacks the magic of these other moments.

For all its unevenness, *Nerone* is dramatically powerful, particularly after the longueurs of the weak first act, as the libretto weaves the private drama of Nero, Egloge, and Atte into the story of the unraveling of his hapless rule. While Nero, although not without charm, is more pathetic than appealing, Atte is a powerful figure, effectively characterized by her music, which ranges from the blazing intensity of her confrontation with Egloge to the tenderness of her love for Nero, which leads her to sacrifice herself to offer him a model of a good death. It is the dancing girl Egloge, though, who gives the opera its emotional center. In her innocence and the purity of her love, as well as her ultimate tragic end, she is reminiscent of Liu in *Turandot*, yet she radiates a unique quality of simple joy. We know, as Atte warns her, that her adventure will end badly, but as she turns to Atte and, in a limpid, lyrical phrase, responds, "Oh, let me enjoy my youth," she captures the audience's heart.

Mascagni may well have composed *Nerone* more out of a combative desire to prove that neither he nor the traditions of Italian opera were quite ready to be relegated to the dustbin of history than out of a deep creative impulse. He had written little of moment in the decade before *Nerone* and was to write hardly a note during the decade he had left. Mascagni spent all his life fighting battles, often seeking them out if they did not appear on their own. *Nerone* was his last, and in some respects his greatest, creative battle. That it was not fully successful is not, given the circumstances, surprising; that it was as successful as it is, is occasion for gladness.

GOING ON

In 1935 Mussolini invaded Ethiopia, and the uneasy peace that had prevailed since 1918 came to an end. The League of Nations imposed economic sanctions on Italy, but they were more symbolic than real; the Duce turned the sanctions to his advantage, proclaiming the doctrine of autarchy, Italy's ability to stand alone against the rest of the world. In November an article under Mascagni's byline appeared in the Bologna newspaper *Il Resto del Carlino*, urging Italians to see the sanctions as an opportunity rather than a threat. True to his way of reducing every issue to his own preoccupations, he argued that musical autarchy was actually a blessing, since, by removing foreign works from the stage, it would open up "a path for Italy's young composers." Caught up in his fantasies, he saw in this revival of Italian opera the ultimate defeat of the hated Modernists, "who, forgetting the pure and immense glory of our national tradition, have fallen into a dejected impotence; abandoned and desperate, [they] have brutishly asserted that opera is dead." For all his bluster, however, Mascagni had no stomach for Italy's latest military adventure, writing Lolli at the end of 1935, "And here we are ending a miserable year, which closes as the entire world feels terror and has no idea what is happening. Let us turn to God to save us from ruin and give us peace, if not happiness. It seems to me that only Divine Providence offers us any hope."

In 1936 the war touched Mascagni. On May 27, two weeks after Mussolini's announcement that "Ethiopia is Italian," Dino, who had led a road-building battalion in nearby Somalia, died of complications from an infectious disease. The composer had passionately loved his handsome yet wayward son and mourned him bitterly. He sat in his hotel suite, surrounded by his friends and family, ignoring the telegrams and messages that poured in. All that mattered was that his son was dead; at the end of a long letter to Lolli, he wrote, underscoring each word with a thick slash of his pen, "But I will never see him again!" Mascagni wore mourning for a year, but Dino's death remained a source of pain far longer, rarely far from his thoughts; early in 1938 he wrote Lolli, "Today is a sad day for your Pietro: twenty months since poor unlucky Dino died. . . . My soul is as much in agony today as on the day when I had the sad news."

For all his misery, Mascagni could not remain idle. At seventy-three he was still driven by the constant pressure to earn enough to support the many people dependent on him, which now included Lina's brother Paolino, caretaker of the Livorno villa and its treasures, and Paolino's capable son, Antonio (Tonino), Mascagni's private secretary. To cover his expenses he needed to maintain an active conducting schedule. His royalties, most of which came from the perennially popular *Cavalleria rusticana*, typically ran between 200,000 and 300,000 lire per year. In addition, he earned some 100,000 lire annually in rent from his Roman properties, and 30,000 to 40,000 as a member of the Royal Italian Academy. He needed to make an additional 200,000 to 300,000 lire per year from conducting engagements.

During the 1930s he generally received 10,000 lire per performance for operas and 7,000 to 8,000 lire for orchestral concerts or broadcasts. This placed him well above nearly all musicians except for Gigli and a handful of others who could earn as much as 15,000 lire per performance. Earning 200,000 to 300,000 lire per year, which required twenty-five to forty performances in fifteen to twenty-five separate appearances, was not easy. Each appearance, including travel and rehearsal time, with idle days between performances, required ten days to two weeks of the composer's time. Thirty to forty weeks of the year on the road was highly taxing for a man in his seventies.

The high number of separate appearances reflected both change in the Italian opera world and Mascagni's own increasingly marginal place in that world. Since the turn of the century the number of opera houses presenting full seasons had declined sharply, while those that still did, principally in the major cities, presented more operas but fewer performances of each. By the 1930s Mascagni himself was no longer the conductor he had been in the 1910s, when he had led major seasons at the Costanzi and San Carlo and was renowned for his interpretations of Verdi, Rossini, and Wagner. He rarely conducted operas by other composers, and for his last twelve years on the operatic podium, he conducted only his own works. His symphonic repertory also became narrower. While he still presented new works in Rome, else-where he relied heavily on Dvořák's *New World* Symphony and Tchaikovsky's *Pathétique,* along with orchestral selections from his own works. His tempi, always expansive, had become slower and slower. He had become a star turn, booked as much for his drawing power as for his musical gifts, often appear-ing in special events outside the regular opera or concert season. His arrival in small cities such as Noto or Udine was invariably an occasion for a show of public affection but was neither artistically challenging nor lucrative.

Mascagni no longer wanted to travel outside Italy. His delays and ob-jections killed an American tour with the La Scala orchestra, even after it had been announced in the American press. His objections also forced the can-celation of a 1940 German tour actively sought by both regimes. Reluctant to offend the government by rejecting the contract outright, he temporized through most of 1940, but by November, after every objection he had raised had been resolved, he had no choice but flatly to refuse. His refusal triggered an angry telephone call from the German Propaganda Ministry to their em-bassy in Rome, instructing them that they "must make [Mascagni] under-stand that we are angry about this episode. We cannot make such efforts to set the entire apparatus of the ministry in motion and involve the Reich chan-cellery in order to be treated in this fashion."

Lolli still wanted him to attempt another opera and regularly intro-duced him to the young poets and writers she cultivated. It was too late, how-ever, and the composer gently deflected her efforts. Although as late as 1941 Mascagni could write Lolli that "in my soul there are so many songs," his drive to compose was gone. He had lasted longer than any of his contemporaries, but he too had finally burned out. But for six musically unimportant bars writ-ten in 1943 as a gift for Pope Pius XII, Mascagni did not write a note of mu-sic for the last twelve years of his life.

He continued to tour, but despite his amazing energy, he was begin-ning to yield to the ravages of time. In 1937 D'Ambra had noticed that he was unsteady on his feet at the end of a Roman concert, and after a May 1938 gala Emy wrote, "Urged by the public to return for a solo bow, he was over-come by faintness and fell down behind the curtain, [and was] immediately caught and helped to sit down by Gigli." Back in Livorno, he wrote the wor-ried Lolli after a physical examination, "Those symptoms about which you've worried, the tendency to fall forward or backward, are nothing more than ex-haustion . . . it is nothing to worry about." From then on, however, he con-ducted sitting rather than standing.

Whether the doctor was misleading his patient or Mascagni was keep-ing the truth from Lolli is unclear. His difficulties, however, were real; they were the first signs of a progressive deterioration, the onset of the arterio-sclerosis that reduced him to an invalid for the last few years of his life. In the meantime, he could still move about; in June 1939, after Costanzo Ciano's funeral, he wrote Lolli proudly that he "took part in the procession and remained on foot for two hours without feeling any distress."

1940: THE LAST GLORIOUS YEAR

In July 1939 Mascagni had his last audience with Mussolini, at which he pled the cause of the composer Alberto Franchetti, a victim of the Fascist anti-Semitic laws of 1938, "emphasiz[ing] the worthiness of the Franchetti family . . . the worthiness and talent of the composer himself." His pleas to permit a revival of his friend's *Cristoforo Colombo* fell on deaf ears; "Mussolini listened carefully to his words, examining fully the memorandum that Mascagni had given him, and then, closing the folder, wrote on top a large 'no,' followed by his 'M.'"

Mascagni had no sympathy for the 1938 racial laws, enacted not least from a perverse desire to imitate Hitler and Nazi Germany. As a product of polyglot Livorno, he had counted numerous Jews among his closest friends from childhood and throughout his life; he mourned Franchetti's ostracism and the pressures that forced his Roman banker friend Lello Soria into eventual death in exile. Still, although he was pained by the laws' consequences and may have sought to temper their effect on those close to him, his tenacious devotion to Mussolini remained intact.

As 1939 continued, that devotion was tested, but not broken, by Mussolini's belligerent stance. As Hitler invaded Poland in September, millions of Italians waited fearfully to find out whether they would become part of that war. Mascagni continued to trust his hero, writing Lolli in September, "Be calm: our homeland is well cared for: there will be no war. Soon a word and deed, bringing peace back to the world, will come from the Duce. The Duce is silent . . . but he is working. We must trust him."

As 1940 approached, the regime decided that a major celebration of the fiftieth anniversary of Mascagni's first great success was in order; in July 1939 Mascagni wrote Lolli, "Alfieri [minister of popular culture] has sent an order requiring every opera house in Italy to present *Cavalleria* in 1940, whether or not it is included in their repertory." Over the next months, plans for a triumphal tour of the Italian peninsula of Mascagni's most popular opera began to unfold.

The Mascagni year began in Venice in February, with Lina Bruna Rasa as Santuzza. Rasa, who had spent most of the time since her performance in *Nerone* in a mental institution, followed Mascagni around for the year, performing *Cavalleria* with different Turridus and Alfios. She then returned to the institution, where she spent much of the rest of her life. From Venice they went to Rome, where the gala anniversary performance, with the Livornese Galliano Masini as Turridu and Gino Bechi as Alfio, took place on March 5.

The Roman performance, in a theater brilliantly illuminated and decked with flowers, in one writer's words, "assumed the significance of a national celebration." At the intermission the composer, flanked by the singers and chorus, came onstage to be joined by "a small mob of dignitaries." Tears in his eyes, Mascagni asked the audience for a moment of silence in memory of Spinelli and Ferroni, the two long-forgotten composers who had shared the awards in the Sonzogno competition in 1890. At the end of the opera, as the house rang with applause, Mascagni was joined onstage by Gemma Bellincioni, the first Santuzza, now seventy-five.

From Rome the *Cavalleria* tour went to Trieste, San Remo, and Genoa before reaching La Scala early in April. In Milan Rasa was joined by Bechi again and by Beniamino Gigli as Turridu, and a recording of the opera was made under the composer's baton. Then the cavalcade went to Naples, to Palermo, and back to Rome, where the opera was broadcast by EIAR on the actual anniversary date, May 17. Two weeks later, Italy was at war.

Mascagni reacted with resignation, along with continued devotion to the Duce, writing Lolli that "now we must live in the faith that Mussolini inspires in us, and we must pray for our soldiers." The *Cavalleria* tour was halted, and the unhappy composer withdrew to Livorno, spending the summer grumbling about his lost income and making plans for the following fall and winter.

By early fall war fears briefly receded, and early in October the *Cavalleria* tour resumed in Bergamo, followed by two performances in Florence. On October 28 Mussolini, on the anniversary of the March on Rome, sent the Italian Army into Greece. From now on, no Italian could expect normal life soon to resume. Although the seeds of the disaster that was about to overtake Italy had been sown years before, the true magnitude of the nation's tragedy was only now about to emerge.

In November the fifty-one-year-old Mimi, true to his Fascist convictions, left for the front as a volunteer. Mascagni's year, though, still offered one last memorable moment. In December he finally returned to his hometown, presenting *Cavalleria*, preceded by a long program of Mascagni's orchestral works, in Livorno's Goldoni Theater, packed with the city's dignitaries and the composer's surviving contemporaries. "The enthusiasm of the Livornese people," wrote one observer, "expressed itself in such clamorous ovations that Mascagni could not hide his feelings."

For all his worldwide fame, the people of Livorno still saw him as one of them, in the intimate way that Italians still see their fellow townspeople as being part of one large extended family. Although Mascagni would return privately to Livorno a few more times, the anniversary performance of *Cavalleria* was his last public appearance in his native city, the last opportunity for his fellow Livornese to see him conduct, and the last chance they would have in his lifetime to celebrate their kinship with him. One by one, his old ties were becoming undone.

APPROACHING THE END

The regime worked hard to sustain Italy's operatic life during the war years, considering it important for morale on the home front; nevertheless, financial pressures, the growing difficulty of travel, particularly after the Allied bombings began in 1942, and the gradual loss of both musicians and audiences to the war made it harder and harder to keep up the pretense of normality. The year 1940 was the last in which Mascagni maintained a full conducting schedule. From then on his efforts were increasingly curtailed by his infirmities and by the growing effect of the war on Italian society.

He was determined to remain a part of the world of standing ovations and cheers of "Viva Mascagni." Facing an orchestra, he no longer felt like the tired old man he knew himself to be when he sat in his armchair in his hotel suite. Although until nearly the end of his life Mascagni insisted that he was perfectly well, "except for these legs," as he told Belli, "which refuse to work for me the way I want them to," others saw his deterioration more clearly. By 1941 he could walk only with difficulty and was suffering from incontinence and an increasingly painful prostate condition. By 1942 those who remembered his exuberant vitality found it difficult to watch him on the podium. Emilio Gragnani, who had known Mascagni in Livorno, attended a 1942 summer concert in Rome:

> *They carried him to the podium in a wheelchair. . . . Seated heavily on a high seat filled with cushions, he attacked the first movement of the Brahms symphony with amazing vigor, but midway through the work his arm dropped, staying rested on the armrest, as his right hand continued flaccidly to wave the baton. It seemed as if the notes were leading him, rather than he directing the notes.*

Unable to bear watching the man who had been his hero since childhood, Gragnani and his wife slipped out of their seats and quietly left the hall.

Mascagni appeared as a conductor for the last time in February 1944, leading a single performance of *Cavalleria* in the same theater in which it had seen its 1890 debut. Perhaps sensing that this might be his last appearance, an intensely emotional audience filled the hall to overflowing, loudly applauding every moment; "after the intermezzo," a reporter wrote, "these demonstrations were transformed into an overwhelming ovation on the part of the public, orchestra and boxes alike jumping to their feet to cheer."

Between his increasingly rare appearances Mascagni spent his days and nights in his hotel suite; as he wrote Lolli, "I have taken up again my usual life, immersed in my usual thoughts. . . . In the evenings I play scopone with the usual friends who come to comfort me with their company." With fewer activities filling his days, and with visits from friends rarer as the war went on, he was often alone and lonely, perhaps for the first time in his long life. Solitude did not agree with him, as he spent hours dwelling on his diminished physical state or revisiting insults from the distant past.

Finally recognizing that he had no more need for them, he sold his Milan house and rented out the family quarters in the Via Po house. These transactions helped improve his financial condition, as did the ten thousand lire he received monthly from the regime. As he felt death coming closer, an occasional valedictory note entered his thoughts, as he began to look back on a life lived at a breakneck pace that allowed little reflection, writing Lolli, "I alone know how much you've suffered: . . . you sacrified for me all of your youth; and I know that I have been able to do far too little in return for what you've done for me."

In the spring of 1942 Mascagni sought a private audience with the pope on behalf of his granddaughter Linina, who was suffering from tuberculosis in an Alpine sanatorium north of Milan. Pius XII granted the audience readily, as pleased to meet Mascagni as the composer was awed to find himself in the presence of the pontiff; as Mascagni described the visit afterwards, "He spoke to me with great simplicity of my art, remembering in particular the birth of *Cavalleria rusticana*, when His Holiness was a youth . . . he said that he'd never forgotten those days." After making his plea for his granddaughter, the composer got up to leave: "The pope, who was still seated, immediately got up, came toward me with outstretched arms, put his hands on my shoulders, brought his face close to mine, and kissed me on both cheeks." The pope gave Mascagni his blessing and a rosary to send to Linina.

That audience was the first of several, the beginning of a strange and touching friendship between the two men. For Mascagni, who had become increasingly devout in his isolation and physical weakness, his relationship with the pope was a rare bright spot in an increasingly dismal existence. In July 1943, at another audience, he presented His Holiness with a short piece that he had written, a setting for voice and organ of a fragment of a Latin hymn in praise of Saints Peter and Paul. On the manuscript the composer wrote, "To the Supreme Pontiff Pius XII, with a devout and grateful spirit. Humbly, Pietro Mascagni." That December the pontiff presented him with a photograph of himself, on which he had inscribed a long and affectionate dedication, which ended: "May [your] days, which from Our heart we wish to be long and serene, be full of gladness, [as you] seek in the peace of your family, in the mysterious art of sounds, the supreme celestial harmonies."

During the darkest days of 1943 a priest came every Sunday from the Vatican to Mascagni's suite to hear his confession. Those visits enabled Mascagni, for whom the sins of the flesh were now past, to put himself at peace with his God; in July he wrote the woman he had loved for more than thirty years:

> I confessed and took the sacred consecrated Host. . . . I told that monsignor every-
> thing, my entire life: I spoke of you with intense feeling: the monsignor was moved,
> and . . . and he promised me that you would be forgiven by the Lord. . . . I feel that I
> have carried out the most sacred of all my duties to you, my adored Annuccia, and
> I am happy.

Less than a week later, on July 25, the Fascist Grand Council, in its final desperate act, repudiated Mussolini. By the end of the day, the Duce was under arrest and the king had named Marshal Badoglio in his place. That night, Rome burst with "an explosion of emotion that none could ever forget." Along with the rest of the Italian people who had given their Duce so much unquestioning devotion, Mascagni had long since lost his dogged faith in Mussolini. Now his joy was as great as any other Roman. "*Fascism is finished!,*" he wrote Lolli. "The sun of liberty is coming back to shine over us! Let us thank Divine Providence and kiss our sacred soil! In my last years, I can still have one moment of pure joy!"

A month later, Mascagni conducted his last Roman concerts. The centerpiece of his last concert was Beethoven's *Eroica* Symphony, a piece he had rarely conducted before, chosen for a city still rejoicing in the fall of its hated dictator. The Roman dawn, however, was a false one. After forty-five days the Wehrmacht entered Rome and placed the city under German occupation. Soon the city was in a state of terror, as German troops, SS, and Gestapo thugs roamed the streets, hunting down Jews and antifascists for the concentration camps, and rounding up civilians at random for forced labor in Germany.

In his hotel room the elderly Mascagni, his hearing and eyesight failing, was more and more isolated. Now, more than ever, as the darkness began to close in around him, he desperately wanted attention and the sound of friendly voices, but they were not there. Few of his friends dared venture into the streets to visit him. His children were far away. Emy was in Florence, unable to return to Rome, while Mimi, Fascist to the end, had gone north to join Mussolini in his last stand in the Italian Social Republic. While Mimi was fighting for the Fascists, his nephew Piermarcello, who had been interned by the Germans, had escaped and joined the Allies as they moved slowly northward up the peninsula.

One visitor, the composer Franco Casavola, described Mascagni as he found him during a 1943 visit: "Although he needed help from others to raise himself from his armchair, once on his feet he could, dragging his feet and staggering from side to side, cross the room by himself. But the sad state of his health was affecting his character—which was never all that gentle—making him steadily more and more embittered." To Casavola, and to other visitors, he would complain bitterly from the depths of his armchair, "What a miserable old age mine is." After the fall of 1943, except for a handful of occasions when he was wrapped in blankets and carried or pushed in a wheelchair, he never left his suite, sitting day after day in his chair, reading or listening to his radio, waited on by the devoted Tonino.

Casavola saw him again late in March 1944, when the younger man, fleeing a Gestapo dragnet, took refuge in Mascagni's suite. The composer was delighted by the unexpected visit: "When Mascagni realized that I was inclined to stay with him all night, he seemed to grow twenty years younger out of sheer joy. He had invented a two-hand version of scopone, and we played till dawn." Later Casavola realized that as they had been playing cards, only a few doors away, in the suite of Rome's Fascist police chief Caruso, the massacre at the Ardeatine Caves was being planned.

FINALLY AT PEACE

The Allies arrived in June 1944. The Hotel Plaza was taken over by the Free French; only Mascagni and his wife were allowed to remain in their suite, surrounded by French officers. Every day he was helped into his armchair by Tonino and would sit there motionless for hours, as Lina, now far gone in senility, would stare out the window from her bedroom, "listening to mass" at the church across the street. French officers dropped by bearing gifts, but he missed many of his earlier visitors. A number of them were scattered around the country, unable to return to Rome, while others now avoided him for his erstwhile Fascist connections.

Anna Lolli had waited patiently to hear from him since he had ceased to visit in 1943, not daring to venture on her own into the Hotel Plaza. Finally, in December 1944, Emy sent Tonino to ask her to come keep her father company in his last days. From then on, Lolli walked across the devastated city almost every day to the hotel to sit quietly by his side, indifferent to Lina's presence in the next room. Every night when she returned home, she would break down and cry for hours.

More diverting company was provided on occasion by a group of young musicians, led by the composer Franco Mannino and the conductor Franco Ferrara, who took it upon themselves to come evenings to cheer up the forlorn Mascagni. They would gather around Mascagni and Lolli, as the couple held hands, and listen to his tales of bygone triumphs and tragedies. Although his mind was still lucid, it had begun to wander. "At the climax of a story, he would suddenly doze off," Casavola wrote, "or else he would come out by mistake with an account of something distant and insignificant, during which . . . he would break down and burst out in a shower of tears."

He had not completely lost his acerbic touch. One evening the young pianist Tito Aprea played him some Cimarosa pieces arranged by Malipiero, a Modernist composer long disliked by Mascagni. The elderly composer listened attentively, with obvious pleasure. After Aprea had finished, he waited a moment, then remarked, "That's the only way Malipiero will ever get his name associated with real music."

Early in July 1945, as normal life began to return to the battered city, Mascagni paid his last call on the pope. He was carried from his room down the hotel stairs and into a waiting car; at the Vatican he was greeted by an attendant who wheeled him into the pope's study, where Pius XII rose and greeted his visitor with a warm embrace. They talked for half an hour, and then the composer was taken back through the Vatican corridors and across Rome. After the exertions of that trip he had little strength left, even to respond to his visitors. On July 27 the conductor Luigi Ricci, who had assisted Mascagni for more than thirty years and had finally returned to Rome, came to pay a call. He found Mascagni in a sad mood. "Even you, dear Ricci," he said, "have abandoned me." They reminisced for a while, until Ricci saw that Mascagni had fallen asleep. As silently as he could, he kissed the composer's hand and left.

On August 1 a bronchiopulmonary infection attacked his weakened constitution, and by that afternoon he was running a high fever. As his condition deteriorated, the parish priest from the nearby church of San Lorenzo in Lucina rushed over to administer the last sacraments to the dying man. The priest was soon joined by the pope's emissary, Monsignor Pucci, at his bedside, as Mascagni slipped into a coma. He died at 7:15 on the morning of August 2, as Lina, Emy, Gisella and Linina, Tonino, his doctor Vittorio Vanni, and his old friend Adriano Belli sat by his side. Anna Lolli, who had seen him for the last time on July 31, was not there, nor was his son Mimi, imprisoned for his Fascist activities.

From the moment the radio broadcast the news, people began to converge on the Corso in front of the hotel, staring up at its windows and at the French flag, flying at half mast above the door. The critic Raffaello de Rensis remembered finding Mascagni's onetime nemesis Alfredo Casella in the crowd and silently clasping his hand. Inside, the salon where the composer had spent his days had been prepared for his lying in state; behind the bed where he lay with a crucifix in his hands, a black cloth with a golden stripe had been hung on the wall. Beside the bed, on his old worktable, his medals and decorations had been carefully set out. As Renzo Rossellini entered, he felt an air of desolation and mystery in the room. "A few friends," he noted, "were softly crying." When Ricci came in to say his last farewells, he saw Lina, clearly unaware of what was happening, staring down at her husband in his white tie and tails. When she saw Ricci, she looked up. "Is Piero conducting today?" she asked him.

On the morning of the third, as thousands of people filled the street, the public was admitted to his room. From the moment the doors were opened, every part of the hotel was filled with people seeking to make their last farewells, so much so that the French officers were eventually forced to close the hotel doors to the pressing crowd. While the crowd included many musicians, and even a handful of officials who slipped in quietly, reluctant to call attention to their presence, it was above all made up of the ordinary people of Rome, workers, housewives, pensioners, come to pay homage to the man whom they had considered their own.

By the fourth, with the funeral set to take place that morning at the church of San Lorenzo in Lucina, the Piazza in Lucina was a solid, unbroken mass of people from one end to the other, and the Corso was filled its entire length from Piazza Venezia to the Piazza del Popolo with more than two hundred thousand people. At ten o'clock a horse-drawn funeral carriage pulled up beside the hotel, and in total silence Mascagni's coffin was carried down the steps and placed in the carriage. As the carriage moved slowly through the crowd, the policemen's band, much reduced from its prewar numbers, played Chopin's Funeral March. Emy and Lina, along with an array of old friends and musicians, followed behind. Except for a delegation from

Livorno, sent after some controversy, no officials were in evidence. Ferruccio Parri's provisional government, a delicate balance of Resistance factions, had decided to ignore the funeral of the man who had been Italy's greatest living musician.

At 10:30 the funeral procession reached the church. As the carriage stopped in front of the church, the band played the Intermezzo from *Cavalleria rusticana.* The coffin was placed on the altar, under the Guido Reni crucifix. As the crowd packed into the church and the larger crowd beyond listened in silence, Monsignor Pucci celebrated the requiem mass, with music by Palestrina and by the elderly priest-composer Lorenzo Perosi, who sat by, mourning his friend.

After the service, the coffin was placed once again in the carriage, which made its way slowly out to the Verano Cemetery, followed through the streets of Rome by a large, tightly packed crowd. Mascagni's remains were there until 1951, when, as he had so devoutly desired, they were removed, with those of Lina, who died only a few months later, to the Misericordia Cemetery in Livorno, where they were placed in a marble monument built in his honor, to lie in his native earth along with his father, his mother, and his brothers forever.

First Performances of
Mascagni's Operas

CAVALLERIA RUSTICANA

Libretto by Giovanni Targioni-Tozzetti and Guido Menasci, based on the play Cavalleria rustica-
cana *by Giovanni Verga.*

First performance Teatro Costanzi, Rome, May 17, 1890
Leopoldo Mugnone, conductor

Santuzza	Gemma Bellincioni
Turridu	Roberto Stagno
Alfio	Guadenzio Salassa
Lola	Annetta Guli
Lucia	Federica Casali

L'AMICO FRITZ

*Libretto by P. Suardon (Nicola Daspuro), with modifications and additions by Targioni-Tozzetti and
Menasci, based on the novel and play* L'ami Fritz *by Emile Erckmann and Alexandre Chatrian.*

First performance Teatro Costanzi, Rome, October 31, 1891
Rodolfo Ferrari, conductor

Suzel	Emma Calvé
Fritz	Fernando De Lucia

Rabbi David	Paul Lhérie
Caterina	Lina Parpagnoli
Beppe	Ortensia Synnerberg
Federico	Guglielmo Bessi
Hanezò	Giuseppe Cremona

I RANTZAU

Libretto by Targioni-Tozzetti and Menasci, based on the novel and play Les deux frères *by Erck-mann and Chatrian*

First performance Teatro della Pergola, Florence, November 10, 1892
Rodolfo Ferrari, conductor

Luisa	Hariclea Darclée
Giorgio	Fernando De Lucia
Gianni	Mattia Battistini
Giacomo	Luigi Broglio
Fiorenzo	Edoardo Sottolana
Giulia	Anna Cecchini
Lebel	Giovanni Paroli

GUGLIELMO RATCLIFF

Setting of the "dramatic ballad" William Ratcliff *by Heinrich Heine, translated into Italian by Andrea Maffei, with some cuts by the composer.*

First performance Teatro alla Scala, February 16, 1895
Pietro Mascagni, conductor

Maria	Adelina Stehle
Margherita	Della Rogers
Guglielmo Ratcliff	Giovanni Battista De Negri
Douglas	Giuseppe Pacini
MacGregor	Giuseppe De Grazia

SILVANO

Original libretto by Giovanni Targioni-Tozzetti

First performance Teatro alla Scala, March 25, 1895
Rodolfo Ferrari, conductor

Matilde	Adelina Stehle
Silvano	Fernando De Lucia
Renzo	Giuseppe Pacini
Rosa	Nilde Ponzano

ZANETTO

Libretto by Targioni-Tozzetti and Menasci, based on the play Le passant *by François Coppée*
First performance Liceo Musicale G. Rossini, Pesaro, March 2, 1896
Pietro Mascagni, conductor

Silvia	Maria Pizzigalli
Zanetto	Stefania Collamarini

IRIS

Original libretto by Luigi Illica
First performance Teatro Costanzi, Rome, November 22, 1898
Pietro Mascagni, conductor

Iris	Hericlea Darclée
Osaka	Fernando De Lucia
Kyoto	Guglielmo Caruson
Il Cieco	Giuseppe Tisci-Rubini
Dhia	Fausta Labia
Il Cenciaiuolo	Piero Schiavazzi

LE MASCHERE

Original libretto by Luigi Illica, using traditional characters from the commedia dell'arte
First performances Teatro alla Scala, Milan (M); Teatro Carlo Felice, Genoa (G);
Teatro Regio, Turin (T); Teatro Costanzi, Rome (R); Teatro la Fenice, Venice (Vn);
and Teatro Filarmonico, Verona (Vr), January 17, 1901

Conductor	Arturo Toscanini (M), Edoardo Vitale (G), Rodolfo Ferrari (T), Pietro Mascagni (R), Agide Jacchia (Vn), Oscar Anselmi (Vr)
Rosaura	Linda Brambilla (M), Cesira Ferrani (G), Fanny Torresella (T), Celestina Boninsegna (R), Maria Farneti (Vn), Anita Italiano (Vr)
Columbina	Emma Carelli (M), Maria Corti (G), Bianca Barbieri-Grandi (T), Bice Adami (R), Maria Fiori (Vn), Bice Formen (Vr)
Florindo	Enrico Caruso (M), Pietro Zeni (G), Oreste Mieli (T), Amadeo Bassi (R), Elvino Ventura (Vn), Luigi Ceccarelli (Vr)
Arlecchino	Oreste Gennari (M), Augusto Nannetti (G), Angelo Tumisani (T), Francesco Daddi (R), Enrico Giordani (Vn), Umberto Macnez (Vr)

Capitano Spavento	Alessandro Arcangeli (M), Vincenzo Ardito (G), Rodolfo Angelini-Fornari (T), Arturo Pessina (R), Nestore Della Torre (Vn), Pietro Giacomello (Vr)
Tartaglia	Virgilio Bellati (M), Fernando Galletti-Gianoli (G), Ettore Castellini (T), Ferruccio Corradetti (R), Giovanni Bellucci (Vn), Aurelio Viale (Vr)
Brighella	Carlo Ragni (M), Umberto Pitarello (G), Emilio Venturini (T), Luigi Poggi (R), Augusto Balboni (Vn), Federico Coraluppi (Vr)
Pantalone	Oreste Luppi (M), Luigi Rossato (G), Silvio Becucci (T), Costantino Nicolay (R), Ruggero Galli (Vn), Alessandro Nicolini (Vr)
Dottore Graziano	Michele Wigley (M), Attilio Pulcini (G), Vincenzo Reschiglian (T), Giuseppe Cremona (R), Felice Foglia (Vn), Giuseppe Zonzini (Vr)
Giocadio	Claudio Leigheb (M), Giuseppe Pietroboni (G), Enrico Belli-Blanes (T), Luigi Rasi (R), Carlo Duse (Vn), Osvaldo Benassai (Vr)

AMICA

Original libretto by Paul Bérel (Paul Choudens) with modifications and additions by Guido Menasci (Italian translation by Guido Menasci).

First performance Opera de Monte Carlo, Monaco, March 16, 1905
Pietro Mascagni, conductor

Amica	Geraldine Farrar
Giorgio	Charles Rousselière
Renaldo	Maurice Renard
Magdelone	Paola Rainaldi
Camoine	Henri-Alexandre Lequien

ISABEAU

Original libretto by Luigi Illica, inspired by the poem "Lady Godiva" by Alfred, Lord Tennyson

First performance Teatro Coliseo, Buenos Aires, June 2, 1911
Pietro Mascagni, conductor

Isabeau	Maria Farneti
Folco	Antonio Saludas

Re Raimondo	Carlo Galeffi
Cornelius	Giuseppe La Puma
Giglietta	Maria Pozzi
Ermyntrude	Olga Simzis
Ermyngarde	Amelia Colombo
Faidit	Teofilo Dentale

PARISINA

Original libretto by Gabriele D'Annunzio

First performance Teatro alla Scala, Milan, December 15, 1913
Pietro Mascagni, conductor

Parisina	Tina Poli-Randaccio
Ugo	Hipólito Lázaro
Nicolò	Carlo Galeffi
Stella	Luisa Garibaldi
Aldobrandino	Italo Picchi
La Verde	Giuseppina Bertazzoli-Gibellini

LODOLETTA

Libretto by Giovacchino Forzano, loosely adapted from the novel Two Little Wooden Shoes *by*
Ouida (Marie Louise de la Ramée), with modifications and additions by Targioni-Tozzetti

First performance Teatro Costanzi, Rome, April 30, 1917
Pietro Mascagni, conductor

Lodoletta	Rosina Storchio
Flammen	Giuseppe Campioni
Giannotto	Enrico Molinari
Franz	Leone Paci
Antonio	Armando Dadò
La Vanard	Ida De Filippis
La Pazza	Cleofe Braghini

SI

Libretto by Carlo Lombardo and Arturo Franchi, adapted from Lombardo's La Duchessa di Bal
Tabarin *and Bruno Granichstäden's* Majestät Mimi

First performance Teatro Quirino, Rome, December 14, 1919
Costantino Lombardo, conductor

Si	Gisella Pozzi
Vera	Amelia Sanipoli

Chablis   Orlando Bocci
Cleo de Mérode   Nuto Navarrini

IL PICCOLO MARAT

Original libretto by Giovacchino Forzano, using material from Les Noyades de Nantes *by Le-Nôtre (Louis Gosselin) and* Sous la terreur *by Victor Martin, with additional verses by Targioni-Tozzetti*

First performance Teatro Costanzi, Rome, May 2, 1921
Pietro Mascagni, conductor

Mariella   Gilda Dalla Rizza
Il piccolo Marat   Hipólito Lázaro
Il soldato   Benvenuto Franci
Il carpentiere   Ernesto Badini
L'orco   Luigi Ferroni
La principessa   Agnese Porter
La spia   Gino De Vecchi
Il ladro   Michele Fiore
La tigre   Luigi Nardini

PINOTTA

Libretto by Giovanni Targioni-Tozzetti, based on original libretto for Mascagni's In filanda *by Alfredo Soffredini*

First performance Teatro del Casino, San Remo, March 23, 1932
Pietro Mascagni, conductor

Pinotta   Mafalda Favero
Baldo   Alessandro Ziliani
Andrea   Ernesto Badini

NERONE

Libretto by Arturo Rossato and Targioni-Tozzetti from the play Nerone *by Pietro Cossa*

First performance Teatro alla Scala, Milan, January 16, 1935
Pietro Mascagni, conductor

Atte   Lina Bruna Rasa
Egloge   Margherita Carosio
Nerone   Aureliano Pertile
Menecrate   Apollo Granforte
Nevio   Ettore Parmeggiani
Babilio   Tancredi Passero

Faonte	Gino Del Signore
Epafrodito	Fabio Ronchi
Mucrone	Luciano Donaggio
Petronio	Giuseppe Noto
Eulogio	Franco Zaccarini
Un pastore	Nello Palai

The Music of Pietro Mascagni:
A Selective Discography

Mascagni's beginnings as a composer coincided with the birth of recording. Within less than a decade of the debut of *Cavalleria rusticana*, half a dozen renditions of the famous "Siciliana" had appeared, to be followed by over two hundred more since the dawn of the twentieth century. Today, although innumerable versions of *Cavalleria* are available, many of his other works have been largely neglected by the recording industry. Still, in contrast to only a few years ago, thanks to the generous profit margins of the CD industry and the enterprising work of a number of small Italian labels, particularly Bongiovanni, it is now possible to find at least one recording of every one of Mascagni's operas and nearly all of his nonoperatic works. Predictably, however, the recordings are wildly uneven in quality of performance and recorded sound.

Those seeking a complete Mascagni discography are urged to consult Roger Flury's admirable *Pietro Mascagni: A Bio-bibliography*, which contains well over two thousand entries. This essay offers, instead, a selective—and opinionated—guide to the principal recordings of Mascagni's music, including both his operas and his more important nonoperatic works. The opinions are those of the author, and the author alone.

297

CAVALLERIA RUSTICANA

Hundreds of recorded versions of *Cavalleria* exist, on LPs, cassettes, videos, and most recently, CDs. Flury lists thirty-eight different CD versions, the earliest dating from 1929 and the most recent from 1997. They include two noteworthy performances led by Mascagni himself, the first a live performance from a 1938 tour of the Netherlands (Bongiovanni) and the second a studio recording made with the La Scala orchestra and chorus in 1940 to commemorate the fiftieth anniversary of the work's debut (EMI and other versions). The latter has a stellar cast with Beniamino Gigli as Turridu, Lina Bruna Rasa as Santuzza, and Gino Bechi as Alfio. Giulietta Simionato, later a famous Santuzza, sings the small role of Lucia. Although Mascagni's tempi are on the slow side, the dramatic tension rarely flags, and Gigli and Rasa are both outstanding. As an added bonus, the recording includes short introductory remarks by Mascagni himself, his high-pitched voice still clear and vigorous at seventy-six.

The outstanding recording of *Cavalleria*, however, was made thirteen years later, in 1953, again with the La Scala orchestra and chorus under the baton of Tullio Serafin, with Maria Callas as Santuzza, Giuseppe Di Stefano as Turridu, and Rolando Panerai as Alfio (EMI). There is no finer Santuzza on recordings than Callas, while Di Stefano, here at his prime, is a superb, beautifully nuanced Turridu. Serafin, arguably the best Italian opera conductor of the 1950s, conducts a taut, propulsive, and beautifully shaped performance. The recording quality is not great, and the sound Serafin draws from the La Scala orchestra is sometimes rough, but these are minor defects in an otherwise remarkable rendition.

Herbert von Karajan's *Cavalleria*, dating from 1965 (Deutsche Grammophon), takes almost as long as Mascagni's and is distinguished by both Fiorenza Cossotto's fine Santuzza and the remarkable sound and precision of attack that von Karajan elicits from—once again—the La Scala orchestra and chorus. He fails, though, to imbue the work with the dramatic intensity that Mascagni and Serafin bring to it and is doomed by Carlo Bergonzi, who sings Turridu with the lassitude of a middle-aged roué for whom nothing Santuzza can say to him is new or particularly important. Far stronger dramatically, although not quite up to the Callas/Di Stefano performance, is a 1963 version with the golden-voiced Franco Corelli and Victoria de los Angeles as the unfortunate pair and Mario Sereni as Alfio (EMI). Superbly conducted by the seventy-seven-year-old Gabriele Santini at the helm of the Rome Opera orchestra and chorus, this is one of the fastest performances on record but does not feel rushed.

A 1960 performance led by Serafin with the Rome Opera orchestra and chorus (London) is worth listening to for Giulietta Simionato's Santuzza but is marred by Mario del Monaco's stentorian, uninteresting Turridu. A live recording of Simionato singing the role with Di Stefano as Turridu, taken from a 1955 performance at La Scala conducted by Antonino Votto (Opera d'oro), although inexpensive, is of far less interest. Neither singer is in particularly good voice, the sound quality is poor, and under Votto's routine time beating the La Scala orchestra sounds like a provincial pit band. It is hard to imagine that this is the same orchestra that von Karajan made sound like the Berlin Philharmonic only a few years later.

More recent performances, whatever they may offer in improved technology, fail to improve on the earlier renditions. A 1976 recording conducted by Gianandrea Gavazzeni, a famous Mascagni conductor, has an excellent Santuzza in the Romanian Julia Varady and a fine Alfio in Piero Cappuccilli, but Luciano Pavarotti is a painfully inadequate Turridu (London). With little apparent feeling for the role, he shouts, barks, and snarls intermittently but fails to give it any distinctive character. Plácido Domingo, on the other hand, is a superb Turridu in his 1982 portrayal under the baton of Georges Prêtre with—yet again—the La Scala orchestra and chorus (Philips). Elena Obraztsova's Santuzza can perhaps be best characterized as unusual. More distressing than her heavy vibrato and distinctive Slavic tone quality is the unrelenting intensity of her interpretation, in which virtually every moment is sung at fever pitch. While this approach results in a spectacular climactic duet with Turridu—in which Domingo's passion matches hers—her frenzy is wearing and ultimately undermines the work's inherent dramatic power.

Finally, a 1990 "international" performance, featuring Jessye Norman, Giuseppe Giacomini, and the Russian baritone Dmitri Hvorostovsky, with the Orchestre de Paris under Semyon Bychkov's capable leadership (Philips), while not the definitive *Cavalleria*, is a strong effort. Giacomini is a fine Turridu, while Hvorostovsky is an understated but powerful Alfio. Although Norman, with her opulent voice, is hardly the typical Santuzza, she manages to find the passion for a credible performance.

L'AMICO FRITZ

No other Mascagni opera has generated nearly as many recorded versions as *Cavalleria*. Despite *Fritz's* continued survival on the fringe of the repertory, it has rarely been recorded, and only four CD versions exist, the most recent one being a reissue of a 1968 LP. Two of the recorded versions, however, are noteworthy. The first is a 1941 recording made under Mascagni's direction, leading the RAI orchestra and chorus of Turin with the (then) husband-wife team of Fernando Tagliavini as Fritz and Pia Tassinari as Suzel, and Saturno Meletti as David (Fonit-Cetra). Tagliavini and Tassinari sang these roles often and inhabit them comfortably, although Tassinari's voice is on the thin side for the role. The elderly Mascagni's last recording, this is a loving and leisurely performance of a lyrical, warmly emotional work.

Even better, however, is the 1968 recording with Luciano Pavarotti and Mirella Freni under the baton of Gavazzeni conducting the orchestra and chorus of the Royal Opera House, Covent Garden (EMI). It is hard to imagine a finer rendition of this work. Pavarotti and Freni, both in their early thirties, sing not only with affection but also with a wonderfully appealing freshness and beauty of sound. Vincenzo Sardiniero's David matches them perfectly, while Gavazzeni's conducting is idiomatic and beautifully paced. The 1951 recording with Beniamino Gigli (Archipel), recorded live at the San Carlo in Naples, sadly has little to recommend it.

I RANTZAU

Only one version of this opera exists on CD (or any other medium), a recording of a 1992 live performance in Livorno (Fonè), which appears to have been the only performance of this opera anywhere since the late 1890s. Conducted by Bruno Rigacci with a generally competent cast and orchestra, and recorded with decent sound quality, it offers a credible version of this little-known work. Mascagni's 1927 recording of the prelude to this opera is available separately on CD, and an outstanding performance by Domingo and Renata Scotto of the score's high point, the act 4 love duet, came out on LP in 1978 but has yet to reappear on CD.

GUGLIELMO RATCLIFF

Two recordings of *Ratcliff* are available on CD, one from an early RAI broadcast (Nuova Era), and the other from a recent live performance in Livorno (Agorà). The 1963 RAI broadcast, led by Armando La Rosa Parodi, is in all but one respect an outstanding performance. The cast, including Ferruccio Mazzoli as MacGregor and Giovanni Ciminelli as Douglas, is far superior in most respects to the journeyman singers that populate the 1995 Livorno production, while La Rosa Parodi's conducting gives this often sprawling work more dramatic momentum and continuity than does his counterpart Massimo de Bernart. The great deficiency of the RAI performance is its Ratcliff, Pier Miranda Ferraro, whose strident vocal quality and unpleasant mannerisms strain the listener's patience. By contrast, the Livorno performance has Maurizio Frusoni in this challenging role, an unexceptionable tenor with an undistinguished voice, pleasant but lacking in personality. Despite Ferraro's deficiencies, the earlier performance still offers the best rendition of this important opera.

SILVANO

Two recordings of *Silvano* are available on CD. Taken from a 1973 RAI broadcast, a little-known cast led by Pietro Argento gives a rough and ready but idiomatic account of this tuneful work (Foyer). Renata Mattioli is particularly strong as the unfortunate Matilde, while Gianni Jaia is ardent but unsubtle as her swain. A more recent recording made in 1995 with Peter Tiboris leading the Bohuslav Martinů Philharmonic (a Czech orchestra, but recorded in New York) has the advantage of substantially more refined orchestral and choral forces, and a warm, appealing Silvano in the young American tenor Joseph Wolverton (Elysium). Although Wolverton shows some strain above the staff, and the other singers are not as strong as in the 1973 RAI version, Tiboris's conducting, which shows a real affection for the opera, and the quality of the orchestral and choral work make this the preferred version.

ZANETTO

A live 1986 recording from Livorno with Rita Lantieri and Ambra Vespasiani under the direction of Mauro Ceccanti (Bongiovanni) offers an unusually vigorous reading of this delicate chamber opera, with more passion than moonlight, but not unsuccessful on its terms. The best rendition I have heard comes from a 1977 Amsterdam performance under Kees Bakels, with Paola Barbieri and Elena Jankovic, unfortunately available only on cassette by mail order.

IRIS

Magda Olivero was the greatest Iris of the LP era, and two of her performances are available on CD, a 1956 Turin performance (Fonit) and a 1963 performance from Amsterdam with the Concertgebouw orchestra and chorus under Fulvio Vernizzi (GOP). The latter is not only far preferable to the former but is still, despite the appearance of a studio recording with Ilona Tokody and Plácido Domingo under the baton of Giuseppe Patanè in 1988 (CBS), the finest available recorded version of *Iris*. Olivero is superbly partnered by the little-known tenor Luigi Ottolini; although his voice lacks Domingo's richness, his higher, lighter tenor is in many ways better suited to the role of Osaka and his performance is far more nuanced and engaged. Domingo appears to have little identification with Osaka and tries to make up in volume and ringing tone what his interpretation lacks in subtlety or conviction. Vernizzi leads the superb Concertgebouw orchestra and chorus in a beautifully molded and paced performance, while Patanè's conducting is more stolid and lacking in dramatic tension.

A recent live recording from the Rome Opera features fine orchestral playing and a sensitive and powerful, although sometimes mannered, Iris from Daniella Dessi. José Cura is a stolid, disengaged Osaka, however, and the performance is further marred by conductor Gianluigi Gelmetti's occasionally wayward tempi and by an excess of noise from both stage and audience.

"Apri la tua finestra," the tenor serenade from the first act, was a staple of the tenor repertory for much of the past century, and was recorded by many of the great Italian tenors, including De Lucia, Caruso, Gigli, Martinelli, and more recently, Di Stefano and Pavarotti, all of whom can be heard singing this highly treacherous number on CD with uneven results. Another often-recorded selection is Iris's aria from the second act, "Un dì ero piccina," with CD versions by Carelli, Farneti, Bori, and Mazzoleni from the early days of recording, and Scotto, Freni, and Soviero in recent years.

LE MASCHERE

The only CD recording available of *Le Maschere* (Ricordi–Fonit Cetra) is, fortunately, an excellent one. Recorded at a live 1988 performance in Bologna, a talented young cast gives a sparkling performance of the work under the sensitive baton of Gianluigi Gelmetti. Vincenzo La Scola is particularly strong as Florindo, and the Bologna orchestra and chorus are first-rate. An old LP from a 1961 Trieste performance, for many years the only available recording of this work, is inferior to the more recent rendition in nearly every respect.

Surprisingly, the delightful overture, although frequently included in compilations of operatic overtures and intermezzi during the 78 and LP eras, is all but impossible to find on CD, with only one version listed in Flury's discography—a 1940 performance led by Gino Marinuzzi on an obscure label.

AMICA

Kicco, a small Italian label, released a studio recording of *Amica* in 1995, with the Hungarian Radio and Television Orchestra and chorus under the somewhat frenetic leadership of Marco Pace. While it is an energetic performance, which captures much of the passion and intensity of this little-known work, it is compromised by the deficiencies of two of its three leading singers. Although Fabio Armiliato as Giorgio has a bright, strong tenor voice, its timbre can be unpleasant, and his vocal mannerisms distracting. Katia Ricciarelli, who sings Amica, was already well past her vocal prime when the recording was made; although she sings with passion and beauty in her lower registers, her problems with pitch and tone above the staff are impossible to ignore. Only Rinaldo, the baritone Walter Donati, comes through unscathed.

ISABEAU

Only one CD version exists for *Isabeau*, although as of this writing, Bongiovanni has announced the forthcoming release of a Dutch performance under the Mascagni specialist Kees Bakels with the American soprano Lynne Strow Piccolo. The only current alternative is a reissue of an LP made from a 1962 San Remo performance under Tullio Serafin. Marcella Pobbè, who sang this role often, is a strong and effective Isabeau, but tenor Pier Miranda Ferraro is seriously overmatched by the role of Folco. With only passable sound, this recording nonetheless offers a general idea of what this powerful opera is about. The new Bongiovanni recording is likely to be worth waiting for.

A number of versions of Folco's famous aria "Non colombelle" are available on CD, not only by Bernardo De Muro, who originated the role in Italy, but also from Gigli, Lázaro, and Del Monaco.

PARISINA

The first and only CD of Mascagni's most ambitious opera appeared not until 2000, recorded at a live performance at the Montpellier Festival during the summer of 1999 (Actes Sud). While the performance has its virtues, including Enrique Diemecke's sensitive and propulsive leadership of the Montpellier orchestra and chorus and a fine Parisina in Denia Mazzola, it falls far short of what Mascagni's most ambitious opera deserves. Vladimir Vaneev's voice lacks the richness needed fully to capture the power and pathos of Nicolò d'Este, while Vitali Taschenko's bleating, struggling tenor is painfully inadequate for the brave but foolish Ugo. Worst of all, while making modest and acceptable cuts in the first three acts, the performance eliminates entirely the last act, which not only contains some of Mascagni's finest music but is also essential to the entire work's balance and proportion.

A solid performance that includes the fourth act was broadcast by RAI in 1976 under the direction of Pierluigi Urbini, with a capable cast including Emma Renzi as Parisina and Michele Molese as Ugo. Available at one time on LP, one hopes that it may become available eventually on CD.

LODOLETTA

A strong studio performance of *Lodoletta* appeared in 1990 with the Hungarian State Orchestra and Radio/Television Chorus under Charles Rosekrans (Hungaroton), and with Maria Spacagna as Lodoletta and Peter Kelen as Flammen repeating their roles from the successful New Jersey State Opera production of the year before. This is an attractive, well-paced rendition of the opera and is preferable to the two live versions, from Livorno performances in 1960 and in 1994, on Fonè.

IL PICCOLO MARAT

Nicola Rossi-Lemeni, a famous Italian basso of the 1950s and 1960s, was fond of the role of the Ogre in *Il Piccolo Marat* and sang it often, with his wife, Virginia Zeani, as Mariella and various tenors as the Little Marat. Two versions of his performance are available on CD, one from Livorno in 1961 (Fonè) and the other from San Remo in 1962 (Fonit). The latter has marginally better sound and in Giuseppe Gismondo has a more effective Little Marat than the vocally wayward Umberto Borsò. Far better, however, is a 1992 Dutch version led by Kees Bakels (Bongiovanni). While Frederic Vassar may lack something of Rossi-Lemeni's power as the Ogre, the rest of the cast is strong, with Susan Neves an outstanding Mariella and Daniel Galvez-Vallejo a strong, rather baritonal Little Marat. Particularly important in this opera, in which the orchestra and chorus play such a central role, the Netherlands Radio Symphony and Chorus are first-rate, performing with conviction and power under Bakels's direction. A 1989 Livorno production (Fonè), while blessed with some attractive voices, is chorally and orchestrally undernourished by comparison.

NERONE

Only one recording of *Nerone* is available, a 1986 rendition with the Hilversum Radio Symphony Orchestra and the Dutch Radio/TV Chorus under Kees Bakels (Bongiovanni). Bakels leads a strong, well-paced performance, doing more than justice to Mascagni's last opera. The two important women in the cast, Lynne Strow Piccolo as Atte and Rosanna Didonè as Egloge, are both excellent and make up for the limitations of the coarse Bulgarian tenor Georgi Tcholakov in the title role.

At least two versions of the opera's gem, Egloge's aria "Danzo notte e dì," are available on CD, as is a rendition by Plácido Domingo of Nero's act 3 "Quando, al soave anelito."

OTHER WORKS

In addition to his more substantial operas, Mascagni composed an operetta, *Si*, and late in life exhumed a student work, *Pinotta*, technically an opera but of nominal dramatic character. Both are represented by a single CD version. A recording of *Si* was taken from a 1987 summer performance in Montepulciano led by Sandro Sanna (Bongiovanni). It is an attractive, well-sung performance of this charming work, marred only by the conductor's lack of feeling for the Viennese operetta genre to which this work belongs, and for the flexible pacing it demands.

Pinotta appears in an excellent 1995 performance from Brussels under Dirk de Caluwè, which is included as part of a two-CD set by Bongiovanni along with the short opera *Zanetto*, the composer's unusual symphonic poem for orchestra and soprano *A Giacomo Leopardi*, and a short and very attractive orchestral piece written for a 1930 royal wedding entitled *L'Apoteosi della cicogna* (The stork's apotheosis). Bongiovanni has also recorded Mascagni's two most important purely orchestral works, the film score *Rapsodia satanica* and the symphonic poem *Visione lirica (Guardando la Santa Teresa di Bernini)*, both performed by the Londerzeel Youth Symphonic Orchestra under Peter Himpe.

While competent performances, they are short on the passion and energy that these works—particularly *Rapsodia satanica*—need to be fully effective. As the only available performance of the *Rapsodia*, though, this recording is an important part of any Mascagni collection.

Another performance of *Visione lirica* is also available on a highly enjoyable CD of Mascagni conducting his own works (along with Rossini's *William Tell* Overture) on VAI. This CD contains a number of orchestral excerpts from his operas, as well as his *Canto del lavoro*, a lively march written in 1928 for the Fascist trade union movement. Mascagni's other major nonoperatic work, the youthful *Messa di gloria*, has been recorded more often, and is currently available on CD in four different versions, including a studio recording featuring the tenor Fabio Armiliato and the baritone Piero Capuccilli (Kicco).

One more important Mascagni CD is a 1995 recording of the composer's songs for voice and piano, ably sung by soprano Anastasia Tomaszewska-Schepis and tenor Angel Rodriguez (Bongiovanni). Written between 1881, when the composer was in his teens, and 1917, his songs not only are consistently enjoyable but also include a number of little-known lyric gems, such as "Sera d'ottobre" and "La luna." Another Bongiovanni recording, which offers the piano music of Mascagni, Giordano, and Puccini performed by Marco Sollini, is of less interest. None of the three composers wrote anything other than trivial, occasional works for the piano, and these pieces add little to their reputations.

Notes

Page

xii   Factual errors: as an example, it is worth noting that the entry on Mascagni in the 1980 *New Grove Dictionary of Music and Musicians* 11 : 743 – 44, although making thoughtful judgments on many of his works, contains no fewer than twelve errors of fact, all dealing with readily verifiable matters.

xiii   Puccini interview: cited in Morini, ed., *Pietro Mascagni* 1 : 380.

xiv   Driving energy: Hershman and Lieb, *The Key to Genius: Manic-Depression and the Creative Life,* p. 185; Iovino, *Mascagni: L'avventuroso dell'opera* (Milan, 1987). Additional important Mascagni material appeared during the 1990s, in particular the two-volume *Epistolario* (selected letters) edited by Morini, Paloscia, and Iovino, which was published in 1997.

xvi   The Croatto oils are reproduced in *Mascagni ritrovato* [Mascagni rediscovered] (Milan, 1995), pp. 74–75.

CHAPTER 1

3   Family origins of Mascagni from E. Gragnani, "Prospetto cronologico della vita e delle opere di Pietro Mascagni" (citing Mario Morini as the source of the

information), in Comitato Onoranze nel 1° Centenario della Nascita, *Pietro Mascagni: Contributi alla conoscenza della sua opera nel primo centenario della nascita* (Livorno: Comitato Onoranze, 1963; subsequently cited as Comitato, *Contributi*), and T. Celli, "La *Cavalleria* e otto lettere," *La Scala*, June 15, 1951. Piazza delle Erbe is vividly described in A. Jeri, *Mascagni: Quindici opere, mille episodi* (Milan, 1940), pp. 5–6.

4   The discussion of the history of Livorno is based generally on Piombanti, *Guida storica ed artistica della città e dintorni di Livorno* (Bologna, 1969; reprint of 1903 edition); L. Bortolotti, *Livorno dal 1748 al 1958* (Florence, 1970); and D. LoRomer, *Merchants and Reform in Livorno, 1814–1868* (Berkeley, Calif., 1987).

5   Information on death rates in Italy by province is from E. Raseri, *Atlante di demografia e geografia medica d'Italia* (Rome, 1906). Fellow Livornese: S. De Carlo, ed., *Mascagni parla* (Rome, 1945), p. 23. This volume, which contains a wealth of both information and misinformation about Mascagni's life and career, is based on the stenographic record of a series of conversations between Mascagni and the young journalist De Carlo that took place in November and December 1942.

6   M. Clark, *Modern Italy, 1871–1982* (London, 1984), p. 38. There was a significant economic and cultural gap between elementary school teachers, who tended to have little education and be considered low in the social scale, and teachers in the *ginnasio* or especially the *liceo*, who were often university graduates and important intellectual figures in their community. Giuseppe Chiarini, principal of the Ginnasio F. D. Guerrazzi when Mascagni was there, later became a major figure in Italian education, and Mascagni became friendly with Giovanni Pascoli, one of the greatest modern Italian poets, when the poet taught at the *liceo* in Livorno. Early years of Pietro Mascagni: see A. Taddei, "Pietro Mascagni," *Liburni Civitas* 12 (1940); G. Targioni-Tozzetti, "Ricordi e rettificazioni mascagnane," *Liburni Civitas* 5, no. 6 (1932); and E. Gragnani, "Mascagni a Livorno," in M. Morini, ed., *Pietro Mascagni* (Milan, 1964), 2:49; and E. Gragnani, "Prospetto." The two-volume compilation edited by Morini includes a wide variety of critical and biographical essays, as well as reproductions of a variety of important documents, and, although published nearly four decades ago, remains the single most important published source for information about Mascagni.

7   No harm: De Carlo, ed., *Mascagni parla*, p. 26; Zilia: ibid., pp. 24–26.

8   Description of Soffredini cited in Gragnani, "Prospetto cronologico," 571. The description of Soffredini's early encounter with Mascagni is from an account written by Soffredini and published in the magazine *Natura e Arte*, July 15, 1892, reprinted in E. Pompei, *Pietro Mascagni nella vita e nell'arte* (Rome, 1912), pp. 18–19. Interestingly, Soffredini's account reappears almost word for word in Mascagni's own much later recollections. Although Soffredini writes that this episode took place in 1876, the certificate that Soffredini prepared in 1882 for Mascagni to submit with his application for admission to the Milan Con-

servatory indicates that Mascagni studied with him for four years, which would place the beginning of his studies in early 1878, or at the earliest the fall of 1877, instead of 1876.

9　An itinerant musician appears on occasion as a figure symbolic of poverty and improvidence in nineteenth-century Italian folk art, e.g., a hand-painted fan with such a figure, captioned "the way to bankruptcy" (collection of Aldo Dente, Bologna).

10　The story of the three-way confrontation between Soffredini, Mascagni's father, and Mascagni's uncle Stefano appears in various sources in various forms, and the version presented here is what appears to be the most plausible. Since Mascagni did not continue into the *liceo* after graduating from the *ginnasio* in 1879, it is clear that the decision to focus on music and abandon thoughts of a legal career must have taken place before then. Quotations from De Carlo, ed., *Mascagni parla*, pp. 27–28. Operas in Livorno: from F. Venturi, *L'opera lirica a Livorno, 1847–1999* (Livorno, 2000), pp. 180–81.

11　It is likely that the Symphony in C Minor, in contrast to the later Symphony in F Major, is a sinfonia in the early sense, i.e., a single-movement overture with sections of contrasting tempi. Mass: De Carlo, ed., *Mascagni parla*, p. 27. Collaboration: T. Celli, "La *Cavalleria*." The description of the Symphony in F Major is based on Gragnani, "Mascagni a Livorno," pp. 51–55. The score of the symphony appears to have disappeared since the 1960s. Soffredini quotation: Pompei, *Pietro Mascagni*, p. 20.

12　Write symphonies: quoted in A. Fraccaroli, *Celebrità e quasi* (Milan, 1923), p. 177. Uncle Stefano and *In filanda*: De Carlo, ed., *Mascagni parla*, p. 33. In Mascagni's reminiscences he links his uncle to the first performance of *Alla gioia* early in 1882. This is not possible, since Stefano Mascagni died in 1881, either on October 10 (Gragnani, "Prospetto," p. 576) or June 20, according to R. Iovino, *Pietro Mascagni: L'avventuroso dell'opera* (Milan, 1987), p. 10 (citing the civil register of the city of Livorno). First performance of *In filanda*: Jeri, *Mascagni*, p. 12.

13　A program of the March 30 performance is reproduced in Morini, ed., *Pietro Mascagni*, vol. 1, following p. 32. *Il Telegrafo* review: Jeri, *Mascagni*, p. 13. *Il Popolano* review: Gragnani, "Mascagni a Livorno," p. 56. Dedication of *In filanda*: N. Gallini, "Mascagni a Milano," in Morini, ed., *Pietro Mascagni* 2:79. Performance in Milan: De Carlo, ed., *Mascagni parla*, pp. 27–28; Iovino, *Pietro Mascagni*, p. 9.

14　*In filanda* has never been published. The discussion is based on study of the manuscripts of the initial piano-vocal score and the subsequent orchestral version, both of which are in the music manuscript collection of the Pierpont Morgan Library in New York. Performance of Symphony in F Major, additional works: Gragnani, "Prospetto," p. 575.

15　Description of Mascagni: from *L'illustrazione toscana e dell'Etruria*, April 1941, cited in Gragnani, "Prospetto," p. 573. Letter to Soffredini: Gallini, "Mascagni a Milano" 2:77. Periods of zeal: Pompei, *Pietro Mascagni*, p. 22.

16   "Ode to Joy": De Carlo, ed., *Mascagni parla,* pp. 32–33. Tchaikovsky actually wrote his setting of the "Ode to Joy" at twenty-five, as his graduation piece at the Saint Petersburg Conservatory. It was not well received. *Alla gioia* first performance: Gragnani, "Mascagni a Livorno" 2:57. I have reviewed a bound volume containing the piano-vocal versions of eight of the fourteen sections of this work, including most of the major choral and ensemble pieces, but only one solo aria, in the music manuscript collection of the Pierpont Morgan Library in New York. The orchestral score has disappeared. In view of the last-minute rush to complete the work, it is possible that the missing sections were composed directly in orchestral score rather than first in short score (as was Mascagni's customary practice), and then orchestrated.

17   Preparations for and departure from Livorno: Gallini, "Mascagni a Milano" 2:78.

CHAPTER 2

19   L. Barzini, "Milan: A Native's Return," in *Memories of Mistresses* (New York, 1986), pp. 168–69. Tenements: P. Valera, *Milano sconosciuto* (1879), cited in E. Gioanola, *La Scapigliatura: Testi e commento* (Turin, 1975), p. 112. N. Gallini, "Mascagni a Milano," in Morini, ed., *Pietro Mascagni* 2:78.

20   Write an opera: letter (undated) to Soffredini in Morini, ed., *Pietro Mascagni* 2:79. Lucca: letter, May 11, 1882, ibid., pp. 80–81.

21   Tear my hair: letter to Soffredini, May 13, 1882, ibid., p. 79. *Preludio:* see Gragnani, "Prospetto," p. 579. Other works: Morini, ed., "Composizione varie," in *Pietro Mascagni* 2:202. Concerts: Gragnani, "Prospetto," p. 580. Wedding: Gallini, "Mascagni a Milano" 2:81. This is, however, inconsistent with Gragnani, "Prospetto," who states that the Coro Nuziale was written for a concert at the Istituto Cherubini late in August of that year. Brother's death: Gragnani, "Prospetto," p. 581.

22   Mascagni's sister died on January 9, 1883, which he mentions in a letter to Cav. Jacopo Magroni, March 23, 1883; J. Magroni, *Del Maestro Pietro Mascagni— (Memorie)* (Livorno, 1890). The cause of death of Mascagni's two siblings is unknown but, in view of their mother's illness and their living conditions, might well have also been tuberculosis. Stipend: Gallini, "Mascagni a Milano" 2:81. Domenico Mascagni's letter seeking his son's admission and other documents submitted to the conservatory are reproduced in Morini, ed., *Pietro Mascagni,* vol. 1. Committee: letter to Soffredini, October 12, 1882, in Gallini, "Mascagni a Milano" 2:81–82. First-year courses: from Mascagni's record on file at the Milan Conservatory. Competing: letter to father, October 12, 1882, in Pompei, *Pietro Mascagni,* p. 28.

23   Letter to Giuseppe Soffredini, November 29, 1882, in Gallini, "Mascagni a Milano" 2:83. Young man about town: ibid., p. 84. The discussion of the Scapigliati and the Scapigliatura is based generally on Gioandola, *La Scapiglatura;*

E. Gennarini, *La Scapigliatura Milanese* (Naples, 1961); R. Tedeschi, *Addio, Fiorito Asil* (Milan, 1978), chapter 1, "Boito e gli scapigliati"; Cleto Arrighi [pseud. of Carlo Righetti], *La Scapigliatura* (Milan, 1977), p. 117. Poem by Praga: cited in Tedeschi, *Addio*, p. 9 (my translation). Praga was also a librettist and rewrote the libretto for the revised version of Ponchielli's *I Promessi sposi*.

24 Mascagni's *Elegy* on Wagner's death: see Gallini, "Mascagni a Milano" 2:85. Puccini and Mascagni: see Iovino, *Pietro Mascagni*, 18–20. Puccini biographies tend to contain a variety of anecdotes of uncertain veracity about the two composers' year together.

25 Score of *Parsifal*: cited in Jeri, *Mascagni*, p. 24. Trousers: letter to father, November 5, 1883, in Pompei, *Pietro Mascagni*, p. 30. Coaching and piano lessons: Gallini, "Mascagni a Milano" 2:84. Romance: letter to Soffredini, April 4, 1883, ibid., p. 86.

26 The discussion of revisions is based on comparison between the manuscript of *In filanda* and the published score of *Pinotta*, which was published after Mascagni's final revisions to the work in 1932, also M. Morini, "Mascagni prima della *Cavalleria*: Da *In filanda* a Pinotta," *Rassegna Musicale Curci* 41 (May 1988): 3–7.

27 One other entry: Gallini, "Mascagni a Milano" 2:89. Grades: from Mascagni's records on file at the Milan Conservatory. Ponchielli letter: Gallini, "Mascagni a Milano" 2:89. My first thought: letter to father, June 18, 1883, in Pompei, *Pietro Mascagni*, p. 29. What air: letter to Guido Cave et al., July 11, 1883, unpublished material in Biblioteca Livia Simoni at La Scala Opera House, Milan (henceforth cited as BLS).

28 Grand opera: letter to father, July 14, 1884, unpublished material in Museo Mascagnano, Livorno (henceforth cited as MM). Other writers have placed the genesis of *Guglielmo Ratcliff* in 1882, based in large part on an article by Mascagni entitled "Prima di *Cavalleria*" (Before *Cavalleria*), which appeared in the magazine *Fanfulla della Domenica* on December 1, 1892, in which he describes working on the opera in the summer of 1882, after having first encountered it the previous spring in Milan. Because Mascagni was notoriously unreliable about dating events in his earlier life, however, this evidence should perhaps not be given great weight. More important is the evidence of Mascagni's correspondence. In view of the important role that *Ratcliff* plays both in his life and in his correspondence from mid-1884 on, the complete absence of references to the work in his considerable correspondence during the earlier years is inconsistent with any date earlier than late 1883 or 1884 for his initial exposure to Heine's play. Moreover, his search for an operatic libretto is a central theme of his letters in 1882 and 1883. He would at least have contemplated entering *Ratcliff* in the competition at the conservatory, or bemoaned his inability to do so, had he indeed already been working on the piece. Maffei's verses: *Fanfulla* article, cited in Pompei, *Pietro Mascagni*, p. 31. Grand passion: De Carlo, ed., *Mascagni parla*, p. 89.

29 Dearest friend: Jeri, *Pietro Mascagni*, p. 26.

30 "Pigmeo Sarcanti": Gallini, "Mascagni a Milano" 2:84. "Ratcliff's Dream" episode: ibid., pp. 90–91. "Il Re a Napoli": Morini, ed., *Pietro Mascagni* 1:256. Letter to father, March 21, 1885, in MM; letter to Gianfranceschi, March 24,
1885, in Morini, ed., *Pietro Mascagni* 1:256.

31 Notation regarding withdrawal on Mascagni's record on file at Milan Conservatory. Most writers have asserted, without any supporting evidence, that Mascagni flunked out, or was thrown out, of the conservatory. Actually, Mascagni's grades in his major field for his first two years were more than adequate;
his poor grades in other areas, however, meant that he was unable to accumu-
late enough points to receive his diploma at the end of the minimum three-year
period and would have had to remain a fourth year in order to graduate. Operetta in Italy generally: see E. Opicelli, "L'operetta italiana," in *L'Operetta da
Hervé al Musical* (Genoa, 1985), and V. Terenzio, *La musica italiana nell'ottocento*
(Milan, 1976), pp. 683–87. Astonishingly little has been written about the
picaresque world of nineteenth-century Italian operetta, even in Italian. Strolling players: W. Weaver, *Duse* (New York, 1984), p. 15.

32 Packed up: *Fanfulla* article, quoted in Pompei, *Pietro Mascagni*, pp. 37–38. Can't
go back: letter to Gianfranceschi, May 18, 1886, in Morini, ed., *Pietro Mascagni*
1:262. Sconamiglio company: Opicelli, "L'operetta," p. 178. Genoa season:
Iovino, *Mascagni*, p. 26.

33 Mechanical: letter to Gianfranceschi, February 13, 1886, in Morini, ed., *Pietro
Mascagni* 1:258. Giuseppina: letter to Gianfranceschi, July 10, 1887, in BLS.
There are many other shorter references to her in his other letters to Gian-
franceschi. Turn sour: letter to Gianfranceschi, May 9/18, 1886, in Morini, ed.,
Pietro Mascagni 1:261–62. Fourth act: ibid., p. 262. Conditions in Ancona,
from *Fanfulla* article, quoted in Pompei, *Pietro Mascagni*, p. 39.

34 Production of *Il grande mogol*: Morini, ed., *Pietro Mascagni* 1:263; see also Opicelli, "L'operetta, p. 46, where the operetta is referred to as a "brilliant score."
Days of sickness: letter to Gianfranceschi, July 10, 1886, in Morini, ed., *Pietro
Mascagni* 1:264. Wanted to write: letter to Gianfranceschi, August 2, 1886,
ibid., p. 265. Letter from father: letter to Gianfranceschi, September 30, 1886,
ibid., p. 268.

35 The description of Mascagni's meeting with Lina is from an unattributed biographical sketch that appears in G. Cenzato, ed., *Nascita e gloria di un capolavoro
italiano: Cinquantenario della "Cavalleria rusticana"* (Milan, 1940), p. 6. Sweet: letter
to Gianfranceschi, July 10, 1887, in BLS.

36 Visit to Parma: letter to Lina, April 18, 1897, in MM. Despised: letter to Gianfranceschi, August 11, 1886, in Morini, ed., *Pietro Mascagni* 1:267. Maresca
company travels: *Fanfulla* article, quoted in Pompei, *Pietro Mascagni*, p. 39.

CHAPTER 3

39   Cerignola: see D. Cellamare, *Pietro Mascagni: "Cerignola, culla della mia musica"* (Rome, 1965), and D. Cellamare, *Mascagni e la "Cavalleria" visti da Cerignola* (Rome, 1941). Theater: Cellamare, *Pietro Mascagni*, pp. 18–20.

40   Creuze de Lesser, in his *Voyage en Italie et en Sicile* (Paris, 1806), p. 86, wrote: "L'Europe finit a Naples, et même elle y finit assez mal." Friendship with Cannone: Cellamare, *Pietro Mascagni*, p. 38, Iovino, *Mascagni*, 31. Letter to father: Cellamare, *Mascagni*, p. 36. Escape: Pompei, *Mascagni*, pp. 40–41; Cellamare, *Mascagni*, p. 33. Quotations from *Fanfulla* article in Pompei, *Mascagni*, pp. 40–41. A particularly vivid description of the escape story is found in Jeri, *Pietro Mascagni*, pp. 36–38. At least one source has cast some doubt on whether the escape happened at all; Arnaldo Marchetti, in "Da Cerignola a Roma sulle ali della gloria," *Musica e Dischi* (September 1963), writes that the Maresca company broke up at the end of their stay in Cerignola, instead of continuing on with the tour to Sicily, and that Mascagni simply decided to stay behind rather than return to Naples with the rest of the company. While this article is hardly definitive and contains a number of errors about other aspects of the subject, it is worth noting that in letters to his father and to his friend Gianfranceschi on February 16 and 17 respectively, or close to the date of the "escape," Mascagni makes no mention of any of the adventures or any particular conflict with Maresca, as later retold in the *Fanfulla* article. On the other hand, a letter from Maresca taking issue with certain particulars of Mascagni's account, which was published in *La Lombardia* in 1895, appears implicitly to support the overall story; see Morini, ed., *Pietro Mascagni* 1:270.

41   Reopening of music school: Cellamare, *Pietro Mascagni*, pp. 24–26. Pianos in Cerignola: Cellamare, *Pietro Mascagni*, p. 56. Cellamare is making the point that this was an unusually large number of pianos to be found in a small city in those days, given the cost of a piano and the general economic level of the community. This is undoubtedly true; the fact remains, however, that it offers a small economic base for a professional piano teacher. Piano lessons: De Carlo, ed., *Mascagni parla*, p. 42. Instruments: ibid., p. 47. From contemporary accounts it is clear that Mascagni was a very good although perhaps unpolished pianist. During all his travels up to this point, when he rarely had access to a piano, he carried a violin, which he played regularly, both for his own entertainment and when composing. The "club" is referred to by that word in Mascagni's letter to Gianfranceschi of March 22, rather than in Italian, e.g., *circolo*. Behavior *all'inglese* was popular among late nineteenth-century Italian aristocrats, even in out-of-the-way Cerignola. Go to Rome: letter to Gianfranceschi, April 8, 1887, in Morini, ed., *Pietro Mascagni* 1:273.

42   Vegetates, love Lina: letter to Gianfranceschi, July 10, 1887, in BLS. The house on Via Assunta (number 15) and the street, except for the plaque, are almost exactly the same today as in Mascagni's time. Child's illness and death: Morini,

ed., *Pietro Mascagni* 1 : 275–77. The *Messa da Requiem* is mentioned and a facsimile of a few pages reproduced in Cellamare, *Mascagni,* pp. 40– 42; there appears to be no more recent record of the manuscript. Trip to Naples: see letter to Gianfranceschi, March 7, 1889, in Morini, ed., *Pietro Mascagni* 1 : 279; also A. Fraccaroli, *La vita di G. Puccini* (Milan, 1925), p. 53. Review of performance: Cellamare, *Mascagni,* pp. 43– 45. Letter to Galli, in Morini, ed., *Pietro Mascagni* 1 : 295.

43   Get out, countryside: De Carlo, ed., *Mascagni parla,* pp. 53–54. By the time of the second competition only two major firms were still active in the industry, the firm of Lucca having been purchased by Ricordi in 1888. First competition: Carner, *Puccini* (New York, 1958), pp. 36–38.

44   By Jove: from *Fanfulla* article, in Pompei, *Pietro Mascagni,* p. 51. Letter to Pagliara, in Cellamare, *Pietro Mascagni,* p. 48. Fontana: De Carlo, ed., *Mascagni parla,* 173.

45   The story about the fateful death of the deputy making it possible for Mascagni to afford the trip to Livorno, thereby securing a libretto and making *Cavalleria* happen, is another classic Mascagni story. It appears in the *Fanfulla* article, is reproduced in Pompei, *Pietro Mascagni,* p. 51, and is accepted by Iovino, *Mascagni,* p. 35. It does not appear, however, in Jeri, who usually does not shrink from melodrama; he describes the trip as having been made possible by stringent economies on Lina's part (*Mascagni,* p. 43). Although it cannot be proven, it may well be true. Adriano Novi-Lena, the undistinguished Liberal deputy for Livorno, did indeed die on May 12, 1888, appropriate timing for a fall by-election. Letter of October 26 to Targioni-Tozzetti: in Cenzato, ed., *Nascita e gloria di un capolavoro Italiano* (Milan, 1940), p. 10. Mascagni notes having seen *Cavalleria* in the theater as a student (De Carlo, ed., *Mascagni parla,* p. 172), but indicates that he saw it done by Flavio Andò and not by Duse; actually, the two were in the same production, as Turridu and Santuzza, respectively; see Weaver, *Duse,* p. 42. "Husband and Priest" (Marito e sacerdote), in Morini, ed., *Pietro Mascagni* 1 : 279. Letter to Targioni-Tozzetti, December 14, 1888, in Cenzato, ed., *Nascita,* p. 11. The original piano manuscript of the Intermezzo is reproduced ibid., following p. 39; it is dated October 26, 1888.

46   Some later editions of *Vita dei campi* were published with the subtitle *Cavalleria Rusticana and Other Stories.* First performance of the play: Weaver, *Duse,* pp. 40– 43. Account of (possible) historic incident: L. LaRosa, "Leggenda e storia nella 'Cavalleria,'" *Rassegna Melodrammatica,* July 1–18, 1957. The closing phrase, "hanno ammazzato compare Turridu," is impossible to translate precisely, as there is no idiomatic English equivalent for *compare* as used by Verga. While the literal translation of the word, in standard Italian dictionaries, is "godfather"— in the sense of the baptismal relationship, not in the sense popularized by Mario Puzo—it has both a lesser and a deeper meaning in Verga's Sicilian village setting. I have followed a suggestion by Arthur Joseph Slavin in translating the word as "comrade," which appears to come closer to the essence of the word than either "friend" or "neighbor," recognizing that to some, the term may still be suggestive of communism.

47 Comment on characters: M. Vallora, "Per un'analisi delle tre 'Cavallerie,'" in G. Aulenti and M. Vallora, eds., *Quartetto della maledizione* (Milan, 1985), p. 62. The reference to the opera's being based on the story rather than the play, which can be refuted by the most cursory glance at both, is in *The Simon & Schuster Book of the Opera* (New York, 1985), p. 299. H. E. Krehbiel, in *The Second Book of Operas* (Garden City, N.Y., 1917), makes the same error, attributing important differences between the libretto and the story to the librettists, when the changes were actually made first in the play and adopted in the libretto; see pp. 136–37.

48 Piano rental: Cellamare, *Pietro Mascagni*, pp. 56–57. Letter to aunt: Celli, "La Cavalleria," p. 34.

49 Birth of son and marriage: Cellamare, *Pietro Mascagni*, pp. 57–58. Certain sources date the marriage in 1888, but the version in Cellamare is the most detailed and provides the most corroborative information. Mascagni makes clear in his letter to Gianfranceschi of July 10, 1887, in BLS, that he and Lina were known as man and wife in Cerignola. Description of Lina: Iovino, *Mascagni*, p. 30. An anecdote illustrating Lina's reliance on soothsayers is found in Tom Antongini, *D'Annunzio* (Boston, 1938), p. 237. Description of mother: Emy Mascagni, *Si inginocchi la piu piccina* (Milan, 1936), p. 43. Madly in love: letter to Lina, March 3, 1890, in Mascagni/Farinelli collection (henceforth cited as MFC).

50 Letters to Targioni-Tozzetti of March 2 and March 18: Cenzato, ed., *Nascita*, pp. 13, 15–19. First version of ending: ibid., pp. 14–15. The penultimate version of the finale from the original manuscript is reproduced in N. Fiorda, *Arte beghe bizze di Toscanini* (Rome, 1969), p. 177. Despite the title, this book is not entirely or even principally about Toscanini, but is a collection of reminiscences of various famous musicians whom Fiorda knew (or claimed to know). That version is largely identical with the professionally copied piano-vocal score that was used for the first performance and is now in MM. Origin of Siciliana: De Carlo, ed., *Mascagni parla*, pp. 177–78, also Ricci, *34 Anni con Mascagni* (Milan, 1976), p. 26. The author of the poem was Giacomino de Zerbi, the younger brother of the prominent writer and politician Rocco de Zerbi, whose historical novel *Vistilia* nearly became a Mascagni opera. Giacomino was of a different stripe; a ne'er-do-well, he was a remittance man in Cerignola, under orders from his brother to engage in agricultural pursuits and keep away from cards and horses, easier in Cerignola than in Milan. He was also a poet of a modest sort and provided Mascagni with a collection of his verses, in which the composer found the one he used for the Siciliana.

51 Doubts: Jeri, *Mascagni*, p. 46. Rescue of Lina: Pompei, *Pietro Mascagni*, p. 55; Iovino, *Mascagni*, p. 36. A variant appears in Cellamare, *Pietro Mascagni*, pp. 58–59, including the statement "this is a true story." Description of actual dispatch of opera: letter to Targioni-Tozzetti and Menasci, May 28, 1889, in U. Bernardini-Marzolla, "Spunta di storia delle opera di Pietro Mascagni da un carteggio

perduto," in Comitato, *Contributi*, pp. 64–67. Everything seemed rosy: ibid., p. 65.

52   Lost lessons: letter to Targioni-Tozzetti, August 3, 1889, in Cenzato, *Nascita*, pp. 21–22. Attacks in *Risveglio*: Pompei, *Pietro Mascagni*, pp. 49–50. Letter to Puccini: Cellamare, *Pietro Mascagni*, p. 60. Thunderclap: letter to Targioni-Tozzetti, August 3, 1889, in Cenzato, *Nascita*, p. 21. Telegram and reaction: letter to Targioni-Tozzetti, February 22, 1890, ibid., p. 25.

CHAPTER 4

53   The original list of jurors included Eugenio Terziani, who died during the early part of the competition and was replaced by Platania. Platania, perhaps because he was a replacement juror, did not sign the jury report. Biographical information on jurors is from *New Grove*, which contains entries for all five jurors. Albergo del Sole: De Carlo, ed., *Mascagni parla*, p. 52. The Albergo del Sole, facing the Pantheon, is today one of Rome's most elegant small hotels. In Mascagni's day it was little more than a flophouse.

54   Prelude: De Carlo, ed., *Mascagni parla*, pp. 55–56. Mascagni's 1892 and 1942 versions of this important episode in his life vary in small details but are generally consistent. Superior mind: letter to Lina, March 4, 1890, in M. Morini, R. Iovino, and A. Paloscia, eds., *Pietro Mascagni: Epistolario* 1:111. Conversation with Galli: letter to Lina, March 3, 1890, in MFC. Jury procedures: "La relazione della commissione giudicatrice del concorso Sonzogno," reprinted in Cenzato, ed., *Nascita*, pp. 41–46.

55   Sonzogno interview: De Carlo, ed., *Mascagni parla*, pp. 62–64. Meeting with Puccini: De Carlo, ed., *Mascagni parla*, p. 65. Meeting with Saladino: ibid., pp. 67–68, also Pompei, *Mascagni*, pp. 71–75. Error: De Carlo, ed., *Mascagni parla*, p. 66.

56   Flea in ear: letter to Targioni, January 5, 1889, in Cenzato, ed., *Nascita*, p. 12. Salvestri: see also Morini, ed., *Pietro Mascagni* 1:290n. Postcard: reprinted in G. Targioni-Tozzetti, "Da *Cavalleria rusticana* a *Vistilia*," *La Rivista di Livorno* 1, no. 3 (1926): 117. Letter to Verga, March 9, 1890: quoted in Iovino, *Mascagni*, p. 37. Letter of March 27, 1890: ibid., p. 38. The actual letter from Verga has been lost; this part is quoted by Mascagni in a letter to Targioni-Tozzetti of April 5, 1890, in Bernardini-Marzolla, "Spunta di storia," p. 68.

57   Verga-Mascagni-Sonzogno litigation: see Morini, ed., *Pietro Mascagni* 1:290n, also Iovino, *Mascagni*, pp. 38–39, and G. Cecchetti, *Giovanni Verga* (Boston, 1978). The litigation had a nasty epilogue more than ten years later when Verga authorized another composer, Domenico Monleone, to set *Cavalleria*. When Monleone's opera, after a moderately successful Amsterdam production in 1907, was considered for production by some Italian houses, Sonzogno and Mascagni brought suit to block productions of the work. The court of appeals

found for Sonzogno and Mascagni, forbade any further performances, and ordered Verga and Monleone to pay the costs of the case. Arrival in Rome, posters, entrance: letter to Lina Mascagni, May 2, 1890, in Pompei, *Mascagni*, pp. 77–79. Difficulties with *Rudello:* letter to Lina, May 3, 1890, suggesting that this information came to him from Mugnone, in Cellamare, *Pietro Mascagni*, pp. 73–74. Visit with Spinelli: Pompei, *Pietro Mascagni*, p. 79. Add dances: Cellamare, *Pietro Mascagni*, p. 72. Roberto Stagno: E. Gara, "Cantati mascagnani tra pregiudizio e verita," in Morini, ed., *Pietro Mascagni* 1:206.

58   Sublime: letter to Lina, May 3, 1890, in Cellamare, *Pietro Mascagni*, p. 72. Dear Maestro: Ricci, *34 anni*, p. 31. The performance cuts made to *Cavalleria* are discussed generally in Fiorda, *Arte beghe*, pp. 171–77. I reviewed the piano-vocal score of *Cavalleria* prepared by Sonzogno's copyist, with the changes made for the first performance in Mugnone's hand, in the Museo Mascagnano in Livorno. Aside from the two major cuts noted, more than a dozen smaller changes, many of some importance, were made to the initial manuscript before the first performance. Other changes involved transposing arias, generally a semitone downward, for the convenience of the artists. Many of the cuts to the drinking song were restored in the published version of the opera. Principal object: letter to Lina, May 3, 1890, in Cellamare, *Pietro Mascagni*, p. 72. Criminally provincial clothes: interview with Alberto Gasco, quoted in M. Rinaldi, "Mascagni a Roma," in Morini, ed., *Pietro Mascagni* 2:98. Work seriously: letter to Targioni-Tozzetti and Menasci, in Cenzato, ed., *Nascita*, p. 33. Fiftieth anniversary comment: article in *Domenica della Corriere*, March 17–23, 1940.

59   Checchi article: quoted in Pompei, *Pietro Mascagni*, p. 81. Description: G. Kobbe, *The Compete Opera Book* (New York, 1935), pp. 610–11. Bellincioni interview: Rinaldi, "Mascagni a Roma" 2:97. White as a sheet (bianco come un panno lavato): Checchi, quoted in Pompei, *Pietro Mascagni*, p. 84. *Capitan Fracassa*, ibid.

60   D'Arcais: ibid., p. 85. *Il Diritto:* ibid., pp. 89–90. Checchi: ibid., p. 90. Pannain: "*Cavalleria rusticana*," *Rassegna Musicale Curci* 17, no. 4 (December 1963): 2 (this article was initially written in 1940).

61   Even the queen: letter to father, May 19, 1890, in Pompei, *Pietro Mascagni*, p. 93; Primo Levi (L'Italico): "La *Cavalleria rusticana* e il maestro del giorno," in *Paesaggi e figure musicali* (Milan, 1913), p. 266. Historic moment: A. Nicastro, *Il melodramma e gli italiani* (Milan, 1982), p. 15.

62   Perhaps the best extended discussion of this period is the chapter "A Problem of Identity (Italian Opera, 1870–1890)" in Julian Budden, *The Operas of Verdi* (New York, 1981), 3:263–92. Weber's *Der Freischütz*, the most popular German opera of the time, waited twenty-two years for a single isolated Italian performance and did not appear regularly on Italian stages until the 1870s. During this entire fifty-year period the only two foreign operas, performed in Italian, of course, that obtained any real Italian success were Auber's 1828 *La muette de*

Portici and Herold's 1831 *Zampa*. Both of these operas have Italian settings, which may account for part of their acceptance.

63   In 1875 only twelve of seventy-seven operas performed in Italy that year were by foreign composers; *Gazzetta musicale di Milano*, quoted in D. Pistone, *L'opéra italien au XIX siècle de Rossini à Puccini* (Paris, 1986), p. 99. By 1903 the proportion of foreign works in the repertory had increased but was still a modest 25 percent; ibid., p. 103.

64   Toscanini was passionately devoted to Catalani and his music, particularly *La Wally*, naming his two children after characters from that opera. Pallid: Budden, *The Operas of Verdi* 3 : 290. Excerpts from Catalani's letters, which make depressing reading, are found in N. Zurletti, *Catalani* (Turin, 1982), pp. 194–95.

65   Verismo: G. Viti, *Verga verista* (Florence, 1981), p. 27; Verga, "L'amante di Gramigna," in *Tutte le novelle*, Mondadori edition, p. 192. Definition of verismo: *New Grove* 19 : 670.

66   Brilliant stroke: Stephen Oliver, "*Cav*: Is It Really 'Verismo'?" *Opera* 37 (October 1986): 1130. A great deal has been written about *Cavalleria*, and it is difficult to come up with an idea about the opera that has not been expressed in some fashion before. Among relevant articles, it is worth noting Matteo Sansone, "Verga and Mascagni: The Critics' Response to *Cavalleria rusticana*," *Music and Letters* 71, no. 2 (May 1990): 198–214; Pannain, "*Cavalleria*"; Renato Mariani, "Mascagni ieri e oggi," in *Verismo in musica e altri studi* (Florence, 1976); Nicola Melchiorre, "Il significato della *Cavalleria*," *Il mondo della musica* 1, no. 16 (September 1, 1945); Guido Salvetti, "Il teatro d'opera tra verismo e decadentismo," in *Storia della musica: Il novecento I* (Turin, 1977).

67   Orgiastic: E. Checchi, "*Cavalleria rusticana*," in *Pietro Mascagni 1890–1920: Dalla "Cavalleria" al "Piccolo Marat"* (Milan, 1920), unpaged.

69   The distinguished Italian musicologist Roman Vlad has written an extended analysis of the motivic relationships in *Cavalleria*: "Modernità di *Cavalleria*," in Piero Ostali and Nandi Ostali, eds., "*Cavalleria rusticana*," *1890–1990: Cento anni di un capolavoro* (Milan, 1990), pp. 15–40. Puccini, in a bitter moment, commented rather unfairly that "*Le Villi* initiated the style that is now called 'Mascagnian,' and no one has ever done that fact justice"; letter, August 9, 1895, in E. Gara, ed., *Carteggi Pucciniani* (Milan, 1958), p. 117. Notwithstanding the borrowings in *Cavalleria*, this is an absurd exaggeration.

70   Victory: letter to Gianfranceschi, July 4, 1889, in Morini, ed., *Pietro Mascagni* 1 : 280.

CHAPTER 5

71   Valletta: quoted in Pompei, *Pietro Mascagni*, p. 92. Gray, ignoble business: Clark, *Modern Italy*, p. 44.

72 Transformation: G. Confalonieri, "Mascagni e Verdi," In Morini, ed., *Pietro Mascagni* 1:51. Reception in Cerignola: Pompei, *Pietro Mascagni,* pp. 100–102; Cellamare, *Pietro Mascagni,* pp. 85–86; Jeri, *Mascagni,* pp. 69–70. Genre: letter to Targioni and Menasci, April 19, 1890, in Cenzato, ed., *Nascita,* p. 36. Corday: letter to Galli, April 30, 1890, in Morini, ed., *Pietro Mascagni* 1:291. *Beatrice Cenci* and *Vistilia:* ibid., p. 292n. Targioni and Menasci, apparently with the composer's approval, published the libretto in 1900 with the subtitle "Scene lyriche per la musica di Pietro Mascagni." Some sources inaccurately date this publication as 1902. Subsequent *Vistilia* history: see also Morini, ed., *Pietro Mascagni* 1:416–19. Reference to work as completed opera: H. E. Krehbiel, *A Second Book of Operas* (New York, 1917), p. 159.

73 The first known reference to *Nerone* appears in a letter to Sonzogno, November 25, 1890, cited in G. Amici et al., *Mascagni contro Sonzogno: Comparsa conclusionale del maestro Pietro Mascagni* (Livorno, 1915), p. 15. This document, which is an extended legal brief stating the composer's position in contract litigation between Mascagni and the Sonzogno firm, is an exceptionally valuable, if tendentious, source on the composer's dealings with his publisher between 1890 and 1915. Plenty of time: Morini, ed., *Pietro Mascagni* 1:415. Contract with Ricordi: letter to Bergamini, January 30, 1914, in MM. See also Jeri, *Mascagni,* pp. 107–10, for a somewhat confused account, and Amici et al., *Mascagni contro Sonzogno,* p. 22, which suggests that the Ricordi contract may have been executed in Rome prior to Mascagni's executing his first contract with Sonzogno. Popularity of Erckmann-Chatrian: L. Schoumacker, *Erckmann-Chatrian, étude biographique et critique d'après des documents inédits* (Paris, 1933), p. 5. *Les deux frères:* ibid., p. 155. Choice definite: letter to Lina, August 6, 1890, in Pompei, *Pietro Mascagni,* p. 148. Arrival in Livorno: ibid., p. 104; see also Jeri, *Mascagni,* pp. 70–73. Gragnani, "Prospetto": in Comitato, *Contributi,* pp. 599–600.

74 Pitts Sanborn: "*Cavalleria rusticana,*" in L. Biancolli, ed., *The Opera Reader* (New York, 1953), p. 216. Catalogue of performances: R. Celletti, "I primi tre anni di *Cavalleria,*" parts 4–7 of "La *Cavalleria rusticana* e il mito di Mascagni," *Musica e Dischi* (April–July 1963); Arturo Colautti, writing in *Il Corriere di Napoli:* quoted in Cenzato, ed., *Nascita,* p. 54. Mascagni's first apartment in Livorno was along the principal downtown street, Via Vittorio Emmanuelle (now Vio Grande): N. Benvenuti, *Pietro Mascagni nella vita e nell'arte* (Livorno, 1981), p. 52.

75 Cerignola house: Pompei, *Pietro Mascagni,* p. 122. The "Pifferata di Natale" is reproduced in Comitato, *Contributi,* p. 603. The serenades of the Abruzzi shepherds were a famous part of Christmas season in Rome in the nineteenth century but are rare today. Dedicated: letter to Galli, December 14, 1890, in Morini, ed., *Pietro Mascagni* 1:296. Birth: Gragnani, "Prospetto," p. 601; Naples production: Celletti, "La *Cavalleria rusticana*" (April 1963); Pompei, *Pietro Mascagni,* pp. 106–7; Michael Henstock, *Fernando De Lucia* (Portland, Ore., 1990), pp. 106–9. Sonzogno generally: M. Morini, N. Ostali, and P. Ostali Jr., eds.,

Casa Musicale Sonzogno: Cronologie, saggi, testimonianze (Milan, 1995), pp. 9–10. Not to worry: quoted in letter to Domenico Mascagni, May 22, 1890, in Amici et al., *Mascagni contro Sonzogno*, p. 8. Feelings of gratitude: letter to Bergamini, January 30, 1914, MM.

76   Contract: Amici et al., *Mascagni contro Sonzogno*, p. 10. Bless your name: letter to Sonzogno, February 13, 1891, ibid., p. 16. Like a son: letter to Sonzogno, June 20, 1891, ibid., p. 19; Sonzogno and *Ratcliff:* De Carlo, ed., *Mascagni parla*, pp. 71–74. Letter to Bergamini, January 30, 1914; see also Henstock, *Fernando De Lucia*, p. 257. This episode probably took place in the fall of 1892, before Mascagni began his serious reworking of that opera. In return for his ceding *Ratcliff* to Sonzogno, Mascagni agreed to sell his next opera to Ricordi, which turned out to be the considerably more lucrative (for both composer and publisher) *Iris*. A different and rather unlikely version, in which Mascagni asked Ricordi for the return of the opera voluntarily, without any pressure from Sonzogno, appears in G. Adami, *Giulio Ricordi e i suoi musicisti* (Milan, 1933), pp. 171–72. Train scene: Pompei, *Pietro Mascagni*, pp. 120–21. The same episode appears, described in similar fashion, in De Carlo, ed., *Mascagni parla*, pp. 113–14. It appears in many writings about Mascagni, e.g., Henstock, *Fernando De Lucia*, p. 123.

77   June 1890: letter to Targioni and Menasci, April 21, 1891, in M. Morini, "Nascita dell'*Amico Fritz*," in P. Ostali and N. Ostali, eds., *"L'Amico Fritz" nel centenario della prima rappresentazione: Atti del 4° convegno di studi su Pietro Mascagni* (Milan, 1994), p. 11. Loved the subject: ibid. First notes: Rubens Tedeschi, "*L'Amico Fritz:* Romanzo, commedia, libretti," ibid., p. 45. Daspuro, *Memorie* (unpublished): quoted in Morini, "Nascita," p. 12. Mass in Orvieto: Pompei, *Pietro Mascagni*, pp. 113–15; Morini, ed., *Pietro Mascagni* 1:295n. Description of Orvieto scene: *Teatro Illustrato*, June 1891.

78   Princely room: letter to Lina, June 2, 1891, in Pompei, *Pietro Mascagni*, p. 124. Letter to aunt: quoted in M. Morini, "Profilo di Mascagni," in Morini, ed., *Pietro Mascagni* 2:27. Morini refers to the letter as having been written in June 1891; if so, it clearly must date from late in the month, since the letter refers to the trip to Como as imminent. The Como performance was in July (see Celletti, "La *Cavalleria rusticana*," part 5 (May 1963); this letter thus may have been written early in July. Role of Targioni and Menasci: see G. Targioni-Tozzetti, "Da *Cavalleria rusticana* a *Vistilia*," in *La rivista di Livorno* 1, no. 3 (1926): 117; Tedeschi, "*L'Amico Fritz*," p. 45, including a comparison of the Cherry Duet as originally written by Daspuro and as revised by Targioni and Menasci. Worked miracles: letter to Galli, September 7, 1891, in Morini, ed., *Pietro Mascagni* 1: 298. Face-saving: Henstock, *Fernando De Lucia*, pp. 125–26. Second masterpiece: Celletti, *L'Amico Fritz*, part 1 (August 1963). Biaggi: Pompei, *Pietro Mascagni*, p. 132.

79   Calvé and De Lucia: E. Gara, "Cantanti mascagnani tra pregiudizio e verità," *Pietro Mascagni* 1:214–15. Lhérie: Celletti, *L'Amico Fritz*, part 3 (January 1964). Checchi: Pompei, *Pietro Mascagni*, p. 130. De Barga: ibid., p. 131. Levi: "*L'Amico*

Fritz e il maestro aspettato" (review of November 2, 1891), in *Paesaggi e figure musicali,* p. 275. Performances: Celletti, *L'Amico Fritz,* part 3 (January 1964).

80   *Falstaff:* Celletti, *L'Amico Fritz,* part 1 (August 1963).

82   Train ride: De Carlo, ed., *Mascagni parla,* p. 114. Tedeschi, *"L'Amico Fritz,"* p. 47. Livorno production: Gragnani, "Mascagni a Livorno," in Morini, ed., *Pietro Mascagni* 1:59.

83   Inspiration, challenge: letter to Lina, February 15, 1892, in Pompei, *Pietro Mascagni,* p. 152. Audacious: letter to Lina, February 24, 1892, ibid. *Ratcliff:* ibid.

84   It is not clear precisely when Mascagni finished *I Rantzau;* in his letter of June 19 to Galli, he comments, "Now I am setting about the instrumentation, which I hope to wrap up in August"; in Morini, ed., *Pietro Mascagni* 1:299–300. Benvenuti also indicates that the opera was finished in August; *Pietro Mascagni,* p. 56. Vienna tour: see generally Pompei, *Pietro Mascagni,* pp. 134–43; De Carlo, ed., *Mascagni parla,* pp. 107–10. Opera house: letter to Lina, September 12, 1892, in Pompei, *Pietro Mascagni,* p. 138. Saw little: letter to Lina, September 13, 1892, ibid. Autographs: De Carlo, ed., *Mascagni parla,* p. 108. Mascagni notes that he accumulated "quite a gallery of feminine masterworks" from the photographs enclosed in these letters, but that he felt obligated to destroy them; ibid., p. 109. Hanslick: quoted in Morini, "Profilo" 2:18.

85   Letter from Mahler: H.-L. de La Grange, *Mahler* (New York, 1973), 1:264. Singers in *I Rantzau:* Gara, "Cantanti" 1:217–18. *Fieramosca* and *Corriere:* Pompei, *Pietro Mascagni,* p. 160. Critical summary: *Teatro Illustrato,* December 1892. Toscanini: H. Sachs, *Toscanini* (New York, 1978), p. 42. The conflict between Mascagni and Toscanini was prompted initially by the members of the Costanzi orchestra's telegraphing their congratulations to Mascagni in Florence without, as it happened, Toscanini's knowledge. Mascagni had responded with his thanks, adding, "I will be proud to lead the famous Roman orchestra in the first performance of my opera." See also M. Rinaldi, "Mascagni a Roma," in Morini, ed., *Pietro Mascagni* 2:101.

86   Rome reaction: *Teatro Illustrato,* December 1892. Berlin: Sonzogno letter to Menasci, October 6, 1893, in Bernardini-Marzolla, "Spunti di storia," p. 106. Hanslick: *Fünf Jahre Musik, 1891–1895,* quoted in Morini, ed., *Pietro Mascagni* 1:101–2. *I Rantzau* was given a single concert performance broadcast by EIAR (Italian radio) in 1930.

87   It is worth noting that in 1892 neither Debussy nor Mahler, let alone Schoenberg or Stravinsky, had emerged as significant influences on their fellow composers. It is likely that Mascagni's familiarity at this point with any non-Italian composers other than German ones was quite limited. Mascagni can sing: Giannotto Bastianelli, *Pietro Mascagni,* p. 63. Illusions: letter to Lina, November 21, 1892, in Pompei, *Pietro Mascagni,* p. 163; Campidoglio: letter to Sonzogno, January 26, 1893, in Amici et al., *Mascagni contro Sonzogno,* p. 20. Boss: letter to Sonzogno, May 16, 1893, ibid., p. 21.

CHAPTER 6

89   House and furnishings: Benvenuti, *Pietro Mascagni,* pp. 52–53. Collections: Iovino, *Mascagni,* p. 65; Emy Mascagni, *S'inginocchi,* pp. 173, 175.

90   Marconi: Morini, "Profilo di Mascagni," *Pietro Mascagni* 2:19. Conversationalist: Fraccaroli, "Mascagni e il capolavoro," in G. Cenzato, ed., *Nerone* (Milan, 1935), p. 30. Immense rewards: letter to Luigi Manzari, in Morini, "Profilo" 2:27. World knows: quoted ibid., p. 12. This insightful but tendentious psychological profile was written, strangely enough, by Mascagni's attorneys in support of his litigation against the Casa Sonzogno (Amici et al., *Mascagni contro Sonzogno,* p. 13).

91   His manic pattern is described in A. Fraccaroli, *Celebrita e quasi,* p. 176. Claque: letter of Domenico Mascagni to Maria Mascagni, quoted in Morini, "Profilo" 2:31, also review of *Silvano* in *Gazzetta Musicale di Milano,* March 31, 1895. "Il capobanda" appeared on September 2 and 3, 1892, in the Neapolitan newspaper *Il Mattino;* it is reprinted in R. Tedeschi, *D'Annunzio e la musica* (Scandicci, 1988), pp. 192–95. Mascagni's rejoinder: De Carlo, ed., *Mascagni parla,* p. 100. Emy Mascagni's memoir provides a warm, detailed, although somewhat fanciful picture of the relationship between the two men during the period of the composition of *Parisina* in 1912.

92   Mascagni's feelings about Leoncavallo are reflected in an anecdote in M. Morini, "Anedotti mascagnani," *Corriere degli Artisti,* n.d. "Verdi's heir": see comment in Alexander, *Giovanni Verga,* p. 159. *Gazzetta del Popolo:* quoted in G. Tarozzi, *Puccini: La fine del bel canto* (Milano, 1972), p. 40. Shaw: Mosco Carner, *Puccini,* p. 64. *Le passant:* G. Ferrières, *François Coppée et son oeuvre* (Paris, 1908), p. 13. Letter from Sonzogno to Menasci: Bernardini-Marzolla, "Spunti di storia," p. 103. Letter to Gianfranceschi: Morini, ed., *Pietro Mascagni* 1:282. London trip generally: Pompei, *Pietro Mascagni,* pp. 175–89. Queen Victoria: ibid., p. 189.

93   I don't care: letter to Lina Mascagni, July 5, 1893, in MFC. Affair: Iovino, *Mascagni,* p. 68. The family anecdote that Iovino recounts in support of this suggestion is entertaining but makes more sense as supporting the proposition that Lina *believed* that her husband had had an affair with Melba, than that the affair actually took place. Letter from Sonzogno to Menasci: Bernardini-Marzolla, "Spunti di storia," p. 106. In *Labilia* the basic situation recurs: Labilia is pledged in marriage to Volello, who goes off to the army. Hearing that he has died in battle, she agrees to marry another. He returns, having only been wounded, spurns her offer to return to him, and ends up throwing himself and her into a gorge; see Cenzato, ed., *Nascita,* p. 48. The first reference to *Silvano/Romano* appears in a letter to Lina Mascagni, July 22, 1893, in MFC.

94   Rumors of operas, "Sera d'ottobre": Gragnani, "Prospetto," in Comitato, *Contributi,* p. 610. Mascagni was a personal friend of Pascoli, one of the most important Italian poets of the nineteenth century, who taught during this period at the *liceo* in Livorno. Dates of completion of various sections of *Silvano* are

noted by the composer on the original manuscript, a photocopy of which is in MM. Death: letter to Galli, in Morini, ed., *Pietro Mascagni* 1 : 300. Pistol shot: *Gazzetta dei teatri* 57, no. 12 (March 28, 1895): 1.

95   Letter to Checchi: Pompei, *Pietro Mascagni*, p. 198. Heldentenor: Gara, "Cantanti," in Morini, ed., *Pietro Mascagni* 1 : 219. Nappi comments on De Negri and Della Rogers: ibid., p. 220.

96   Ricordi: *Gazzetta Musicale di Milano,* February 24, 1895, p. 123; "Leporello": *L'Illustrazione Italiana,* February 24, 1895; *Gazzetta dei Teatri,* February 21, 1895.

97   Verdi comment: G. Confalonieri, "Mascagni e Verdi," in Morini, ed., *Pietro Mascagni* 1 : 56. Fellowship: ibid., p. 66; see also M. Conati, ed., *Encounters with Verdi,* pp. 310–16. Sweetest man: De Carlo, ed., *Mascagni parla,* p. 199.

98   Pope: letter to Gianfranceschi, April 8, 1887, in Morini, ed., *Pietro Mascagni* 2:273. Closed my eyes: letter to Gianfranceschi, May 18, 1886, ibid., p. 262.

99   Grand passion: De Carlo, ed., *Mascagni parla,* p. 89; Guido Salvetti, "Mascagni: La creazione musicale," in *Mascagni* (Milan, 1984), p. 75.

100   *Gazzetta dei Teatri:* Gara, "Cantanti," in Morini, ed., *Pietro Mascagni* 1 : 223. *Gazzetta Musicale di Milano,* March 31, 1895, p. 212.

101   Colombani: *Corriere della Sera,* March 26–27, 1895. Rinaldi, *Musica e verismo,* p. 212. Bastianelli, *Pietro Mascagni,* p. 80.

102   Genre: letter to Targioni and Menasci, April 19, 1890, in Cenzato, ed., *Nascita,* p. 36; see also comment on Targioni-Tozzetti and Menasci as librettists in Alexander, *Giovanni Verga,* pp. 159–60.

CHAPTER 7

105   Contract provisions: Amici et al., *Mascagni contro Sonzogno,* p. 25. The first contact between Mascagni and Illica took place during a performance of *Ratcliff:* see M. Morini, "*Iris* e i progetti non realizzati," in Comitato, *Contributi,* p. 201. On Illica generally, see M. Morini, "Profilo di Illica," *La Scala,* October 1956.

106   Note on new form of opera: Morini, "*Iris,*" p. 193.

107   Guidi-Carnevali visit described in letter to Amintore Galli, October 26, 1895, in Morini, ed., *Pietro Mascagni* 1 : 300–301. Pedrotti died a few months after resigning from the position of director in Pesaro, when, suffering from depression, he threw himself into the Adige River in his home city of Verona; he is still known for his comic opera *Tutti in maschera.* The end of *Zanetto* appears on the manuscript, in MM. In marked contrast to other Mascagni scores, no earlier dates for completion of any sections of the opera appear elsewhere in the manuscript. Mistreated: letter to Galli, October 26, 1895, in Morini, ed., *Pietro Mascagni* 1 : 301.

108   Conservatory education: cited in Morini, "Profilo di Mascagni," in Morini, ed., *Pietro Mascagni* 2 : 39–40. Terms of employment: Pompei, *Pietro Mascagni,* 235–

36. Enrollment: *Annuario 1894–1895* (Pesaro, 1895). Letter to Galli, October 26, 1895, in Morini, ed., *Pietro Mascagni* 1 : 301.

109   The description of Mascagni's activity at the Liceo Rossini is based principally on my review of material contained in the issues of *La Cronaca Musicale* between 1896 and 1902; see also Morini, "Profilo di Mascagni," in Morini, ed., *Pietro Mascagni* 2 : 40. Statistics: *Annuario* of Liceo Rossini for 1894–95 through 1898–99. The Liceo, at Mascagni's suggestion, discontinued publication of the *Annuario* after 1899, publishing statistical information in *La Cronaca Musicale*. Zanetto reception: Pompei, *Pietro Mascagni*, p. 231.

111   Ferrari Trecate: quoted in Morini, "Profilo di Mascagni" 2 : 38. Mascagni maintained a paternal interest in the lives of many of his pupils; some years after leaving Pesaro, while visiting Vienna, he interceded with the Emperor Franz Josef to obtain Hatze's exemption from military service; De Carlo, ed., *Mascagni parla*, pp. 119–20. Mascagni also offered encouragement and support to enable Hatze to reestablish his professional career after World War I; see letter to Anna Lolli, November 12, 1925, Museo Mascagnano, Bagnara di Romagna (henceforth cited as BdR). Fell in love: Pompei, *Pietro Mascagni*, p. 236.

112   Long live Japan: Morini, *"Iris,"* p. 203. Novelty: Illica letter of April 1, 1896, ibid., p. 204. Letters to Ricordi and Illica: ibid.

113   An amusing description of the country cottage is found in the letter to Illica of July 24, 1896, in Morini, Iovino, and Paloscia, eds., *Epistolario* 1 : 176–77. Yesterday: Illica to Ricordi, in Morini, *"Iris,"* pp. 204–6.

114   The first reference to the opera that was to become *Le Maschere* is in a note from Mascagni to Illica during Illica's August stay in Pesaro; M. Morini, "Preparazione dei sette fiaschi delle *Maschere*," *La Scala*, February 1956, p. 50; see also letter of August 18, 1896, in Morini, ed., *Pietro Mascagni* 1 : 310. Sonzogno acceptance: letter to Illica, October 3, 1896, ibid., p. 311. At times: letter to Illica, October 27, 1896, ibid., p. 314.

115   Letter to Gianfranceschi, October 27, 1896; ibid. Dietze story: Cellamare, *Mascagni*, pp. 122–23. Trip to Castellarquato: Pompei, *Pietro Mascagni*, pp. 251–52.

116   Masterpiece: letter to Illica, April 20, 1897, in Morini, ed., *Pietro Mascagni* 1 : 316. Epilogue: Illica to Ricordi, September 1896, in Morini, *"Iris,"* p. 208. Do as you want: letter to Illica, August 27, 1897, in Morini, ed., *Pietro Mascagni* 1 : 317. Not opposed: letter to Ricordi, February 7, 1898, in Morini, *"Iris,"* p. 215.

117   Post: A. Colombani, *Corriere della Sera*, March 28–29, 1898. Programs: G. Tintori, *Duecento anni di Teatro alla Scala: Cronologia opere-balletti-concerti, 1778–1977* (Milan, 1979), p. 266. Tintori specifies which performances were Milan premieres, but not which were also Italian premieres; with respect to these works, the two are probably the same. Interestingly, this performance of the Grieg Concerto appears to be the only time in his conducting career that Mascagni programmed a solo concerto on an orchestral program. The soloist was the highly regarded Italian pianist Ernesto Consolo. Colombani, *Corriere della Sera*, April 25–26, 1898.

118   Studied intensively: letter to Ricordi, June 1, 1898, in Morini, *"Iris,"* p. 217. Orchestra reinforced: ibid., p. 219; *Corriere della Sera,* July 1, 1898. It is not clear precisely when Mascagni actually wrote the *Poema,* since there hardly appears to have been time between his return to Pesaro at the end of April and the first performance at the end of June. It is more likely that the *Poema* was written before Mascagni's departure from Pesaro in early March 1898, perhaps as early as the fall of 1897. Death: letter to Filippo Mariotti, in MM.

119   Lacks faith: letter to Illica, July 7, 1898, in Morini, ed., *Pietro Mascagni* 1:320; this letter was written at least in part for Illica to pass on to Sonzogno (see Morini, "Preparazione," p. 51). Contract amendment: Amici et al., *Mascagni contro Sonzogno,* pp. 36–38.

120   Not a saint: letter to Ricordi, June 24, 1898, in Morini, *"Iris,"* p. 224. Rehearsals: letter from Illica to Ricordi, ibid., p. 222. Fight with Mascheroni: ibid., pp. 223–24; also Henstock, *Fernando De Lucia,* p. 260. *Tribuna:* quoted in Morini, *"Iris,"* pp. 223–24. Rapprochement: letters to Anna Lolli, June 7 and 13, 1920, in BdR: G. Adami, *"Iris 'opera da manicomio,'"* *Popolo d'Italia,* January 15, 1945, quoted (paraphrased?) in Morini, *"Iris,"* p. 225.

121   Weak De Lucia performance: Gara, "Cantanti," in Morini, ed., *Pietro Mascagni,* 1:227. Complaints about singers: letter to Toscanini, January 16, 1899, in G. Barblan, *Toscanini e La Scala* (Milan, 1972), p. 322. Attendance at premiere: Morini, *"Iris,"* p. 226; *La Gazzetta dei Teatri* 60, no. 45 (November 24, 1898): 4. Telegraphic office: ibid. Mascagni had used his influence to get Sonzogno to put *Andrea Chénier* back on the La Scala schedule for 1896, after Amintore Galli, Sonzogno's musical advisor, had recommended rejection of the opera; P. Alvera, *Giordano* (Milan, 1986), p. 31.

122   Comment to Checchi: Morini, *"Iris,"* p. 225. The prelude to *Iris* is often referred to incorrectly as the Hymn to the Sun. Description of premiere: A. Gasco, *"Iris,"* in *Da Cimarosa a Stravinsky* (Rome, 1939), p. 187. Faithful Livornese: *Gazzetta dei Teatri,* November 24, 1898, p. 5; also Pompei, *Pietro Mascagni,* pp. 269–70. Summaries of the critical reaction were published in brief form in *Corriere della Sera,* November 24–25, 1898, and in substantially more extended form in the *Gazzetta Musicale di Milano,* December 1, 1898. The latter, however, given the way in which Ricordi used the gazette for promotional purposes, is probably somewhat tendentious, particularly in the choice of which passages to cite from each review.

123   Valetta: quoted in Pompei, *Pietro Mascagni,* pp. 270–71; *Gazzetta dei Teatri,* November 24, 1898, p. 5. Parisotti: quoted in Gallini, "Mascagni a Roma," in Morini, ed., *Pietro Mascagni* 2:104–5. Parisotti had been the secretary of the Sonzogno competition won by Mascagni in 1890. *L'Opinione: Gazzetta Musicale di Milano,* December 1, 1898, p. 690. Spada: ibid., 689–90.

124   The complicated and confusing story of the dealings between Mascagni, his attorney Cassuto, Ricordi, and Toscanini leading up to and including the Milan premiere of *Iris* is given in detail in Henstock, *Fernando De Lucia,* pp. 264–

73; letters to Ricordi of January 26, 1899, in Morini, *"Iris,"* p. 231. Toscanini disliked *Cavalleria*; during his first period as director at La Scala the wretched quality of the only performances of *Cavalleria* that he directed, both in 1907, attracted unusual notice; see Barblan, *Toscanini*, pp. 138–39. During both of Toscanini's periods as director of La Scala, the number of performances of Mascagni operas dropped dramatically by comparison with periods both preceding and following those years. Productions of *Iris* are listed in Tom Kaufman et al., "Cronologia delle rappresentazioni e delle esecuzioni," in Fulvio Venturi, ed., *"Iris," 1898–1998: Il centenario* (Livorno, 2000), pp. 191–220. Bastianelli, *Pietro Mascagni*, pp. 85–86. An article on the one hundredth anniversary of *Iris*, Paula Dietz, "Reviving an Operatic Immortal," *New York Times*, November 22, 1998, asserts that the source for the opera is to be found in *Le livre de jade*, a late nineteenth-century anthology of Chinese (not Chinese and Japanese, as stated in the article) poetry. This is without foundation, and there is no connection between the two; letter of Donald Keene to the author, January 25, 1991.

125 Cesare Orselli, "Inquietudini di *Iris* nell'Italia umbertina," in Venturi, ed., *"Iris," 1898–1998*, p. 34; J.-K. Huysmans, *Against the Grain (À rebours)* (New York, 1969), p. 100. Art nouveau, the iris: see "The Art Nouveau Iris," in Siegfried Wichmann, *Japonisme* (New York, 1985), pp. 86–89. *Iris* as art nouveau opera: see Giampiero Tintori, quoted in Gianni Gori, "Il fascino perverso della piovra nel 'teatro di poesia' post-romantico," in M. Morini and P. Ostali, eds., *Mascagni e "l'Iris" fra simbolismo e floreale* (Milan, 1989), p. 72.

127 Gori, ibid., discusses the symbolism of the octopus in the poetry of the time. It is tempting to speculate that Illica's image of the octopus encircling the young woman with its tentacles was inspired by seeing the famous Hokusai print *The Dream of the Fisherman's Wife*. In the print, however, the octopus's intentions are clearly sexual, rather than murderous.

CHAPTER 8

129 The composer acknowledged receipt of the third act from Illica on March 10, 1899; Morini, ed., *Pietro Mascagni* 1 : 320. He died: letter to Illica, June 10, 1899, in ibid., p. 323.

130 Ten lire: letter to Domenico Mascagni, December 31, 1884, in MM. During 1890 and 1891 Mascagni was approached by a number of his father's creditors, to whom his father owed more than four thousand lire, an amount probably substantially greater than his father's annual earnings; see letters to Domenico Mascagni, November 11, 1890, and September 18, 1891, in MM. Letter of Domenico Mascagni to Maria Mascagni of February 16, 1892, quoted in Morini, "Profilo di Mascagni," in Morini, ed., *Pietro Mascagni* 2 : 31. The only debatable exception to this characterization of Mascagni's operatic fathers is Antonio in *Lodoletta*. He is, however, Lodoletta's adoptive rather than her biological father (a distinction given some emphasis in the opera) and, in any event, is killed off

little more than halfway through the first act, thereby making her an orphan, another Mascagni archetype. Can't go on: letter to Illica, June 10, 1899, in Morini, ed., *Pietro Mascagni,* 1 : 322. Going magnificently: letter of August 23, 1899, ibid., p. 324.

131 Luigi Baldacchi, "I libretti di Mascagni," *Nuova Rivista Musicale Italiana* 3 (July–September 1985): 397. New powder: letter to Illica, October 1, 1899, in Morini, ed., *Pietro Mascagni* 1 : 325. Letter from Illica to Sonzogno, ibid., p. 328. Complexity of intrigues in commedia dell'arte: see A. Nicoll, *The World of Harlequin* (Cambridge, 1963), pp. 9–14, 127–44. Letter to Illica, December 22, 1899, in Morini, ed., *Pietro Mascagni* 1 : 329. Pesaro: see Pompei, *Pietro Mascagni,* p. 240; De Carlo, ed., *Mascagni parla,* pp. 92–95; and G. Orsini, . . . *di Pietro Mascagni* (Milan, 1912), p. 49.

132 February, theaters: letter to Illica, February 6, 1900, in Morini, Iovino, and Paloscia, eds., *Epistolario* 1 : 227; also Morini, "Preparazione dei sette fiaschi delle 'Maschere,'" *La Scala* (February 1956): 55. Pietro Mascagni, *L'evoluzione della musica nel secolo decimonono* (Rome, 1900). This pamphlet is an abridged version of the lecture; those parts of the lecture that have been deleted, however, are in all cases either paraphrased or summarized.

133 Letter to Gianfranceschi, October 5, 1903, in BLS. Five thousand lire: Morini, "Preparazione," p. 55. Commission: letter to Sonzogno, May 19, 1900, in Amici et al., *Mascanni contro Sonzogno,* pp. 39–40. Thousand pages: letter to Illica, September 22, 1900, in Morini, "Preparazione," p. 56.

134 Tebaldini report: "Mascagni pel Liceo Rossini" (open letter from Pietro Mascagni), *Gazzetta Musicale di Milano,* September 27, 1900. Sgambati report: from D. Cassuto, *Difesa del Maestro Pietro Mascagni* (1902), quoted in Iovino, *Mascagni,* pp. 91–92. Tebaldini letter: Gragnani, "Prospetto," in Comitato, *Contributi,* p. 629. The Pesaro council may have miscalculated in their choice of Tebaldini. If he and Mascagni were friends, as is suggested by Tebaldini's use of the intimate *tu* in his letter, it is unlikely that Tebaldini would have written anything to Mascagni's disadvantage in his report. Giolitti: quoted in De Carlo, ed., *Mascagni parla,* p. 94. Costanzi and La Scala: Pompei, *Pietro Mascagni,* p. 312; also Jeri, *Mascagni,* p. 120. Jeri states that the multiplicity of theaters was simply a product of more theaters' asking for it, and Mascagni's and Sonzogno's obliging. This can be dismissed, as can Mascagni's later musings.

135 La Scala and Carlo Felice: E. Zorzi, *"Le Maschere"*: *Album-ricordo* (Rome, 1901), unpaged. Enable: Pompei, *Pietro Mascagni,* pp. 308–9. Dedication of opera to self: see Gragnani, "Prospetto," pp. 630–31; also Jeri, *Mascagni,* pp. 120–21. Jeri reproduces a satirical cartoon on the subject that appeared in *L'Italia che ride.* Interestingly, this canard periodically reappears as fact in otherwise respectable sources; see, e.g., M. Rinaldi, "Fu sempre caro a Mascagni il sensibile e generoso pubblico romano," *Il Messaggero,* August 2, 1955.

136 Cast lists appear in Gara, "Cantanti," in Morini, ed., *Pietro Mascagni* 1 : 230–31. Arrival at rehearsal: E. Checchi, "I capricci della cronaca," in *Gazzetta Musicale*

di Milano, January 17, 1901, p. 29. Modest but useful: Zorzi, *"Le Maschere."* The fastest trains between Rome and Milan took twelve to fifteen hours, not including frequent layovers and changes of train in Bologna and Florence; they were often late. Traveling: Zorzi, *"Le Maschere."*

137   The first-night outcome in all six theaters is summarized in *Corriere della Sera,* January 18–19, 1901; *La Tribuna,* January 19, 1901; and *Il Trovatore,* January 19, 1901. Description of Milan performance: Giovanni Pozza, *Corriere della Sera,* January 18–19, 1901.

138   Montefiore: *La Tribuna,* January 19, 1901. Cametti: *Gazzetta Musicale di Milano,* January 24, 1901. Levi, *Paesaggi,* p. 299. *Messaggero:* in "Le critiche alle *Maschere* di Mascagni," *Corriere della Sera,* January 19–20, 1901. Cuts: M. Morini, ed., *"Le Maschere* di Pietro Mascagni nell giudizio della critica," in concert program for Bologna production of the opera, December 1987, p. 39. My comparison between the changes in the three versions is based on an analysis of the three published libretti.

139   Review: Baron Charles de Platen, *Souvenirs musicaux et dramatiques* (Rome, 1911), p. 143.

141   Valetta, *"Le Maschere* di Pietro Mascagni," *Nuova Antologia,* February 1, 1901, p. 557.

142   The story of how Wolf-Ferrari's artistic direction was influenced by *Le Maschere* is found in E. Piamonte, "Ermano Wolf-Ferrari e *I quattro rusteghi,"* notes to Fonit-Cetra recording. Gavazzeni, "La musica di Mascagni, oggi," in Morini, ed., *Pietro Mascagni* 1:29. Rupture with Sonzogno: see Morini, *"Iris,"* p. 254

143   Ricordi overtures: ibid., pp. 236–37. Giacosa: ibid., pp. 238, 241. Sidelines: ibid., p. 238. *House of the Dead:* ibid., p. 242. Nihilism: ibid., p. 243.

144   Giordano letter: M. Morini, ed., *Umberto Giordano* (Milan, 1968), p. 295. Dark, gray drama: letter to Ricordi, in Morini, *"Iris,"* p. 250 (Morini does not date this letter, but it is clear that it was written on or about September 20, 1901). *Butterfly:* ibid., p. 253. Huddling: letter to Illica, November 22, 1901, ibid. Lose time: letter to Ricordi, February 5, 1902, ibid., p. 262. Simpleminded: letter to Illica, March 28, 1902, ibid., p. 264.

145   Letter from Budapest: see G. Cenzato, "Mascagni, genio fastidioso," *La Scala,* October 1956, p. 55. Spain trip: De Carlo, ed., *Mascagni parla,* pp. 131–36. Letter to Passeri-Modi, May 20, 1902, in Commissione Consultativa, Ministero della Pubblica Istruzione, *Parere sul ricorso del Maestro Pietro Mascagni* (Rome, 1902), p. 7. Confessed: ibid., p. 8. The Florence concerts, the Santa Croce events, *Corriere Italiano* review, and Mascagni's message are all from "Le solenni onoranze a Rossini in Firenze," *La Cronaca Musicale* 7, nos. 1–2 (1902): 13–21. Marconi was one of the most popular Italian tenors of the period; owner of a light voice, he resisted Mascagni's efforts to get him to sing the role of Ratcliff, writing their mutual friend Angelo von Eisner on September 17, 1901, "Mascagni is so dear as a person, so impossible as a composer. He would cut off his balls before cutting a note" (in BLS).

146   Family celebrations: Cenzato, "Mascagni," p. 56. At least for part of this ab-
      sence, according to Cenzato, newspapers reported that he was conducting
      Cavalleria in Terni. Ceccarelli: N. Tabanelli, "La questione Mascagni–Liceo di
      Pesaro dal punto di vista giuridico," *Rivista Musicale Italiana* 9, no. 4 (1902): 9
      (page numbers are from a reprint). Fine behavior: letter to Passeri-Modi,
      June 9, 1902, in Commissione, *Parere*, pp. 8–9. Sign: Tabanelli, "Questione,"
      p. 9. Letters to Passeri-Modi, July 11 and 14, 1902, ibid., p. 10; Tabanelli cites
      a deficit of 16,528 lire, which appears to be the cumulative deficit for the two
      years. Exercises: Cenzato, "Mascagni," p. 56.

147   Proposal: Tabanelli, "Questione," p. 10. Divert funds: Commissione, *Parere*,
      p. 11. Two Foscaris: Cassuto, *Difesa*, in Iovino, *Mascagni*, p. 93. Student ultima-
      tum: Commissione, *Parere*, p. 11. Letter for students to sign: Tabanelli, "Que-
      stione," p. 11. Good name: letter to Passeri-Modi, July 20, 1902, quoted by
      Cassuto, in Iovino, *Mascagni*, pp. 93–94. Rejection of offer: Tabanelli, "Que-
      stione," p. 11. Letter of Passeri-Modi to Mascagni, July 24, 1902, quoted by
      Cassuto, in Iovino, *Mascagni*, p. 94.

148   Vulgar menu: Tabanelli, "Questione," p. 11. Mascagni certificates: *Il Trovatore*,
      October 19, 1902. Three issues: "Renato," *L'Illustrazione Italiana*, August 31, 1902.
      Telegrams: Orsini, . . . *di Pietro Mascagni*, p. 56. Acknowledged: Passeri-Modi to
      a reporter from *La Tribuna*, quoted in Tabanelli, "Questione," p. 8.

149   Supremacy: Commissione, *Parere*, p. 15. Cinotti address: *La Cronaca Musicale* 7,
      no. 10 (1903): 171–72. Zanella did eventually write an opera, but not until he
      had been at Pesaro for a number of years; see J. C. G. Waterhouse, "Amilcare
      Zanella," *New Grove* (1980) 20:639.

150   Simpleton: De Carlo, ed., *Mascagni parla*, p. 95.

CHAPTER 9

151   *L'Illustrazione Italiana*, August 24, 1902, p. 142. The commission was reported in
      the *Corriere dei Teatri*, June 29, 1902, although Tyler's name was misspelled Eyler;
      Tyler was acting for the firm of Liebler & Co.

152   Repression: see, e.g., G. Candeloro, *Storia dell'Italia moderna* (Milan, 1974), 7:
      59–60. Seventy-eight demonstrators or bystanders were killed in Milan alone
      in 1898. Mascagni: quoted in *Il Trovatore*, August 24, 1902. Mascagni's music
      was characterized in a review of the Washington debut of *The Eternal City* as
      "a notable feature of the performance," *New York Herald*, October 7, 1902. Li-
      vorno orchestra: interview with Maestro Nedo Benvenuti, July 1989; also
      E. Gragnani, "Miscellanea mascagnana," *Rivista di Livorno* 2, no. 4 (July–August
      1952): 205–6. Contract: *Musical Courier*, July 23, 1902. Opera in America: see
      R. L. Davis, "Grand Opera and the 'Nouveau Riche,'" in *A History of Music in
      American Life*, Vol. 2, *The Gilded Years: 1865–1920* (Huntington, N.Y., 1980).

153   Star system: *Musical Courier*, October 15, 1902. His operas: *Musical Courier*,
      July 23, 1902. As many as thirty members of Mascagni's orchestra were pres-

ent or former Pesaro students; *Gazzetta Musicale di Milano,* September 25, 1902. Bianchini-Cappelli was incorrectly described as Mascagni's wife by the *New York Times* on his arrival, October 5, 1902, an error carelessly transmitted by G. R. Davis in "The Maestro Comes to Town," *Opera News,* January 17, 1981.

154   Chaotic greeting, businessman: *New York Times,* October 5, 1902. Two orchestras: *New York Herald,* October 6, 1902. Complaint: *New York Times,* October 6, 1902. Music: letter to Hirsch, October 31, 1902, in Pompei, *Pietro Mascagni,* p. 325.

155   Reviews: *Musical Courier,* October 15, 1902; *New York Times,* October 9, 1902; *New York Herald,* October 9, 1902. Downpour: *New York Times,* October 12, 1902. A summary report on the Philadelphia premiere of *Iris,* with a brief note of local critical reaction, appeared in the *New York Herald,* October 15, 1902; the *Times* did not even mention the Philadelphia performance. *Musical Courier* review, October 22, 1902. *Tribune* review: quoted in "The Press and *Iris,*" *Musical Courier,* October 22, 1902.

156   Review: *New York Times,* October 17, 1902. Withdrawal of *Ratcliff:* ibid., October 18, 1902. Arrival in Philadelphia: ibid., October 14, 1902. Smaller crowds: *Musical Courier,* October 29, 1902. Musicians unpaid: *Boston Herald,* November 6, 1902, also *Il Trovatore,* December 14, 1902. Review: *Boston Herald,* November 4, 1902. Mittenthal: ibid., November 6, 1902.

157   Letter to friend written November 6, 1902, original in Library of Congress. I have been unable to establish to whom this letter was sent. It is clearly written to a close male friend; the affectionate salutation is headed "Gigione di mio cuore," "Gigione" being theatrical slang for a ham or scene stealer, but also an affectionate way of saying "big Luigi." The letter is signed, unusually, "Cav. Genio," or "Sir Artist," apparently a nickname by which Mascagni was known in some circles; the composer also used this as a nom de plume when publishing humorous or satirical pieces in the 1890s (see Morini, "Profilo" 2:17). Mittenthal statements: *Boston Herald,* November 6, 1902. Arrest, warrants: ibid., November 9, 11, 12, 1902. Condition of orchestral players: *Il Trovatore,* December 14, 1902. Editorial: *Musical Courier,* November 12, 1902. Captain Dreyfus: U. Ojetti, "Mascagni, l'America e i quattrini," first published in *Il Resto del Carlino,* reprinted in *Il Trovatore,* November 16, 1902.

158   Troubles of second tour: *New York Times,* December 10, 19, 1902. Mascagni in Chicago: ibid., December 23, 24, 25, 26, 1902. Chicago concerts: Pompei, *Pietro Mascagni,* p. 337; *New York Times,* January 13, 1903. Arrival in San Francisco: *San Francisco Chronicle,* February 8, 1903.

159   Bohemian Club: Pompei, *Pietro Mascagni,* pp. 341–43. A parchment scroll presented to the composer on that occasion is on display in MM. *Examiner* quotation: Pompei, *Pietro Mascagni,* p. 338. Critical: *San Francisco Chronicle,* February 14, 1902. Dinner at Italian Chamber of Commerce, Mascagni statement: Pompei, *Pietro Mascagni,* pp. 338–40. I discovered the "Pensiero," which does not appear

in any published list of the composer's works, in the Library of Congress. Additional concerts: *San Francisco Chronicle,* March 1, 5, 1903. Massachusetts courts: *New York Times,* February 27, 1903. Letter to Hirsch, March [24?], 1903, in Pompei, *Pietro Mascagni,* p. 345. Arrival in Rome: Orsini, . . . *di Pietro Mascagni,* p. 60.

160 F. Ritter, *Music in America* (New York, 1895), pp. 198–99. Ritter was the head of the music department at Vassar College; Davis, "Maestro," p. 15.

161 During the next three years, Mascagni had at least two lawsuits going on simultaneously: one that involved an effort to have the minister's action removing him from the directorship overturned, and then an action for damages against the Liceo Rossini, and the second an action to block the Liceo from removing him and his possessions from the apartment he had occupied as director. As he clearly had no intentions of returning to the directorship or living in the apartment, these lawsuits were at best matters of principle. He was unsuccessful in his efforts for reinstatement, largely because the courts ruled that they lacked jurisdiction over such administrative matters; see Tabanelli, "Questione" (1903), and "Ancora la questione Mascagni," *Rivista Musicale Italiana* 11, no. 3 (1904): 573–77. He was also unsuccessful, in the end, to prevent having to remove his effects from the Pesaro apartment, although he was able to prolong the matter for nearly four years. He did, however, in 1906 win an award of damages against the Liceo Rossini and a form of vindication; *Il Trovatore,* August 4, 1906. Mascagni and National School of Music: see Rinaldi, "Mascagni a Roma," in Morini, ed., *Pietro Mascagni* 2:109; E. D'Harcourt, *La musique actuelle en Italie* (Paris, 1906), pp. 214, 217. Lessons: Ezio Carabella, quoted in Rinaldi, "Mascagni a Roma," p. 109. An interview that discusses Mascagni's work at the school in detail is Ugo Falena, "Conversando con Pietro Mascagni," *Il Tirso* 1, no. 3 (May 29, 1904). D'Harcourt, *Musique actuelle,* noted that "la local de la via Santa Chiara est très misérable," p. 217. Bastogi: *Musica,* July 10, 1910.

162 Move to Corso Vittorio Emmanuelle: Rinaldi, "Mascagni a Roma" 2:109. Had thought: letter to Illica, June 5, 1903, in Morini, "Iris," p. 266. Love interest: letter to Ricordi, June 16, 1903, ibid., p. 267. No satisfaction: letter to Ricordi, August 14, 1903, ibid., p. 271. Description of libretto, "symphonic prologue": ibid., pp. 272, 274.

163 P. Mascagni, *Per le opere dell'ingegno* (Rome, 1905), p. 8; this pamphlet initially appeared as two articles in the magazine *Vita* earlier in 1905. Fledgling: ibid., p. 9.

164 Wolf-Ferrari: letter to Mascagni quoted ibid., p. 11. Rental fees: see D'Harcourt, *Musique actuelle,* p. 41. Typical rental fees for a major theater for a Verdi opera ranged from two thousand to four thousand lire; the rental fee for Giordano's *Siberia,* a major novelty at the time of its writing, was eleven thousand lire. Fees: Mascagni, *Per le opere dell'ingegno,* passim, also Mascagni interview in *Il Momento* (Turin), May 22, 1904, quoted in Morini, "Iris," p. 278. Terms: ibid. The substantial disparity in fees between Ricordi and Sonzogno was made possible by the essentially cartel-like nature of their relationship; with the excep-

tion of the unusual circumstances of Mascagni's relationship with Ricordi, a composer typically "belonged" to one publisher or the other. Publishers did not steal from each other.

165 Waited too long: letter to Illica, April 5, 1904, in Morini, *"Iris,"* p. 275. Bad faith: Illica to Ricordi, ibid. Meeting, Don Pietro: Ricordi to Illica, ibid., pp. 276–78.

166 Revisions to *Amica* by Menasci: U. Bernardini-Marzolla, "Spunti di storia," in Comitato, *Contributi,* pp. 114–31; Menasci, unlike Targioni-Tozzetti, spoke and wrote fluent French. Paris trip, including the critical polemic prompted by the Lamoureux concerts: *Corriere della Sera,* January 24, 31, 1905; also De Carlo, ed., *Mascagni parla,* p. 131. Sardou visit: Morini, *"Iris,"* p. 279n. Sopranos: Gara, "Cantanti," in Morini, ed., *Pietro Mascagni* 1:233–34. Paris reviews: quoted in *Corriere della Sera,* March 18, 1905.

167 Pozza review: ibid., March 17, 1905. Plans to stage *Amica:* ibid., April 4, 1905. Rome premiere review: ibid., March 14, 1905. Subsequent performances: Platen, *Souvenirs,* p. 136; also *Tribuna,* May 16, 25, 1905. Serata d'onore: ibid., June 1, 1905.

168 Small steps, dropped from Costanzi season: Mascagni, *Per le opere dell'ingegno,* pp. 21–22; see also letter to Gianfranceschi, February 22, 1906, in BLS. There are records of four productions, all conducted by Mascagni, in Italy between 1928 and 1939. Pompei, *Pietro Mascagni,* p. 351. Mascagni's relationship to Wagner, whose pervasive influence was unavoidable during his early and middle years, was an ambivalent one. With his almost obsessive preoccupation with the distinctive character of Italian music and his own *italianità,* he found it difficult if not impossible to acknowledge his immense debt to the German master. While ready enough to write and speak of Wagner's genius, he rarely did so without qualifying his words in some fashion and reminding his audience that for all Wagner's greatness, his influence was either irrelevant or even harmful to the Italian musical world.

CHAPTER 10

171 Meeting with Tito Ricordi: letter to Gianfranceschi, January 23, 1906, in BLS. Mocchi overtures: Amici et al., *Mascagni contro Sonzogno,* p. 43. Contract provisions: ibid., pp. 47–49.

172 Reading of libretto; Orsini, *. . . di Pietro Mascagni,* p. 69. Letter to Sonzogno, December 13, 1906, in Amici et al., *Mascagni contro Sonzogno,* p. 54. Letter to Sonzogno, August 7, 1907, ibid., p. 57. Abandoning libretto: Orsini, *. . . di Pietro Mascagni,* p. 72. Thirty-two hundred libretti: letter to Angelo Eisner von Eichendorf, August 8, 1907, in BLS. Illica approach in May 1908: Iovino, *Mascagni,* p. 149. Illica's initial efforts with *Isabeau:* Morini, ed., *Pietro Mascagni* 1:341–42. Substitution of operas: Amici et al., *Mascagni contro Sonzogno,* pp. 55–

56. On own account: letter to Illica, July 16, 1908, in Morini, ed., *Pietro Mascagni* 1:341.

173   More and more convinced: letter to Illica, October 2, 1908, ibid., p. 342. "I need you": letter to Illica, July 19, 1909, ibid., p. 345. Targioni: letter to Renzo Sonzogno of July 13, 1909, ibid.

174   Rent increases, purchase of land: letter to Gianfranceschi, March 16, 1909, in BLS. This was an expensive piece of land, 900 square meters (9,800 square feet) for 100 lire per square meter, equivalent to $23 per square foot in current dollars. De Rensis: *Musica*, January 17, 1909. Pergolesi observances: ibid., January 29, 1910. Lecture: Pietro Mascagni, "Grandezza di Pergolesi," excerpts in Morini, ed., *Pietro Mascagni* 2:159. STIN: see Nicolodi, "Musica italiana," p. 184; also *Musica*, various issues.

175   Orefice season: *Musica*, January 24, 1909. Operettas: M. Rinaldi, "Mascagni salvò il Costanzi," *Il Messaggero*, December 7, 1963. Hiring of Mascagni: *La Tribuna*, July 28, August 7 (first formal announcement), 1909. Quotation: "Lo czar del teatro Costanzi in Roma," *Ars et Labor* 64, no. 11 (November 1909). Rebuilding of theater: *La Tribuna*, November 22, 1909.

176   *Elektra: Musica*, November 7, 1909. According to Mascagni, the publishers were asking thirty-six thousand lire for a package permitting the opera to be performed at the Costanzi, the Pergola (Florence), and the San Carlo. This was between two and three times the going rate for a desirable new opera. *Elektra* had been performed only once before in Italy, in the spring of 1909 in Milan. *Tristan*, king and queen: *La Tribuna*, December 18, 1909. Barini: ibid. Belli: quoted in Rinaldi, "Mascagni." Barini on *Bohème: La Tribuna*, January 23, 1910. Puccini telegram in Rinaldi, "Mascagni." *Messaggero:* quoted ibid.

177   Rarity of *Don Carlos* performances: ibid. Incagliati in *Musica*, February 5, 1910. Mascagni's plans for the 1911 season were outlined by the composer as early as August 1909; see S. Savarino, "Parlando col maestro Mascagni al Costanzi," *La Tribuna*, August 10, 1909. Board action: *Musica*, February 20, 1910. Replace with Visconti: letter to Lina Mascagni, October 1, 1909, in Morini, Iovino, and Paloscia, eds., *Epistolario* 1:317. The hostility between Mascagni and San Martino was widely known and was ventilated in a series of pieces that appeared during 1910 in the Roman musical magazine *Orfeo*. San Martino had a sort of delayed revenge on Mascagni in 1943, when he published his memoirs; in a book 319 pages long largely devoted to musical life in Rome from the 1890s to the 1920s, Mascagni's name does not appear even once.

178   Resolution, new contract: Rinaldi, "Mascagni," and *Musica*, February 27, 1910. Closing night: Rinaldi, "Mascagni." Profit: Orsini, . . . *di Pietro Mascagni*, p. 79. Announcement of 1911 season: *Musica*, July 24, 1910. Only preoccupation: letter to Gianfranceschi, January 23, 1906, in BLS.

179   Melba: see Iovino, *Mascagni,* p. 68, also letters from Mascagni to Lina during his 1893 London visit. According to Mario Morini (in a conversation with me), rumors of a liaison between Mascagni and Farneti were widespread during the early years of the century. A. Lualdi, *Tutti vivi* (Milan, 1955), pp. 83–84. Letter to Rosina Lolli, September 5, 1910 (all of the letters to Anna and Rosina Lolli are in BdR).

180   The April 4 date is based on Mascagni's dedicatory note in the score of *Isabeau,* written April 4, 1911. Terrible crisis: letter to Illica, April 22, 1910, in Morini, ed., *Pietro Mascagni* 1 : 349–50. How can you: letter to Lolli, April 29, 1910. Lolli's letters from this period have not survived. Their content can easily be inferred from Mascagni's responses, which often quote or paraphrase her letters at length. Concert: letter to Lolli, May 1, 1910. Not understood: letter to Lolli, May 3, 1910.

181   Suicide attempt: undated letter to Lolli, probably written between May 12 and May 15. Leaving Rome: letter to Anna Lolli, May 24, 1910. Initial approach from United States: *Musical America,* October 23, 1909; see also Morini, ed., *Pietro Mascagni* 1 : 350n. Americans: letter to Illica, May 3, 1910, ibid., p. 350. Saintly and good: letter to Lolli, June 1, 1910.

182   Slave: letter to Lolli, June 10, 1910. Ecstasy: letter to Lolli, June 24, 1910. In his letter of June 29, Mascagni refers to her having "given him the sacred flower of [her] virginity." Completion of opera: letters to Lolli, August 21, 27, September 2, 1910 ("*Isabeau* is completed! Completed with thoughts of you!"). The draft of the intermezzo is in BdR. Go out: letter to Lolli, August 19, 1910.

183   Suspicions, Lodi: letter to Lolli, August 28, 1910. Edmunds: letter to Lolli, September 7–8, 1910. Moving: letter to Lolli, August 29, 1910. It was, ironically, Lina, who probably did not want him underfoot, who suggested that he orchestrate the opera in Milan. Travel arrangements: letter to Lolli, September 9, 1910. His instructions were in great detail, citing schedules, alternatives, etc. Repairs: letter to Lolli, November 15, 1910. A drawing of Mascagni in his pajamas working on the orchestration of *Isabeau* at the Hotel Regina appeared in *L'Illustrazione Italiana,* October 30, 1910. Mascagni cut it out and gave it to Lolli, with the inscription "To good Annuccia, so she can always watch her Pietro at work." Visit to Francesco: letter to Lolli, November 29, 1910. Encounter with Puccini: Pompei, *Pietro Mascagni,* pp. 382–83.

184   Fake success: letter to Lolli, July 19, 1911. Mascagni did not think highly of *Fanciulla,* writing Lolli on December 2, 1910, "Here we are, as usual: from one salon aria he's made an entire opera . . . even less music than in his others." Letter from Puccini to Simoni and Adami, June 20, 1921, in E. Gara, *Carteggi Pucciniani* (Milan, 1958), p. 508. Scene: letter to Lolli, November 28, 1910. American tour: Morini, ed., *Pietro Mascagni* 1 : 351n, also Orsini, . . . *di Pietro Mascagni,* pp. 81–82, and, for the American perspective on this episode, J. McPherson, "Bessie Abott and the Naked Lady," *Opera Quarterly* 17, no. 2 (spring 2001):

218–34. Private performance of *Isabeau:* Rinaldi, "Mascagni a Roma," in Morini, ed., *Pietro Mascagni* 2 : 111. Among the listeners were the Roman critics Nicola d'Atri and Alberto Gasco.

185 Stivender, "Illica, Mascagni, and the Writing of *Isabeau*," p. 11.

CHAPTER 11

189 Beacon: G. M. Gatti, *Ildebrando Pizzetti* (Milan, 1954), p. 13. Nineteenth-century chromaticism: G. Bastianelli, *La crisi musicale europea* (Florence, 1976), p. 139.

190 Junk shop: quoted in Salvetti, *Storia della musica*, p. 176. Marinetti: quoted in O. Calabrese, ed., *Modern Italy: Images and History of a National Identity* (Milan, 1984), 2 : 414. Futurist musical manifesto: reproduced in Salvetti, *Storia della musica*, pp. 205–7. Technical manifesto: conclusion reproduced ibid., pp. 207–8. Mascagni's feelings about the Futurist adventure can perhaps be inferred from a letter from Marinetti to Pratella, November 27, 1910, referring to "the allusion made by Mascagni to you, with the usual 'strong, acute sorrow' that men who are both famous and showing signs of softening experience when they see young men of an innovative spirit, tired of playing disciple, slip out of their heavy hands," in F. T. Marinetti, *Lettere Ruggente a F. Balilla Pratella ed altri.* Pizzetti: quoted in Salvetti, *Storia della musica*, p. 177; Bastianelli, *Crisi*, pp. 140–41. Memoirs: A. Casella, *Music in My Time.* His mission: see also A. Casella, "Poderosa immissione di sole" (obituary appreciation of Mascagni), *Il Mondo Musicale*, September 1, 1945.

191 Pure representative: Bastianelli, *Pietro Mascagni* (Naples, 1910), p. 24. Sought to innovate: Pratella, quoted in Salvetti, *Storia della musica*, p. 207. Marinetti did not share Pratella's feelings, concluding the letter to Pratella cited above, "Mascagni makes me nauseous!" Quotation: Casella, "Poderosa immissione di sole."

192 Work of art: in "Impressioni d'arte e ricordi di Pietro Mascagni," *Il Piccolo della Sera* (Trieste), February 27, 1924. Fundamental essence: Mascagni, "Grandezza del Pergolesi," in Morini, ed., *Pietro Mascagni* 2 : 159. Wave of madness: "Impressioni d'arte." Requests to produce *Isabeau* came from Turin, Milan, Naples, Florence, and Rome. Offer from Mocchi and acceptance: Orsini, . . . *di Pietro Mascagni*, p. 84.

193 Cold fish: letter to Lolli, April 11, 1911. Arrival at Buenos Aires: *La Patria degli Italiani*, May 3, 1911, quoted in Pompei, *Pietro Mascagni*, pp. 401–4, also letter to Lolli, May 8, 1911. Letter to Pompei, May 8, 1911, quoted in Pompei, *Pietro Mascagni*, p. 404. Population, Italian born: F. Latzina, *Sinopsis estadística Argentina* (Buenos Aires, 1914). Between 1880 and 1910 more than 1.5 million Italians emigrated to Argentina. Rehearsal: letter to Lolli, May 31, 1911.

194 Description of premiere: Pompei, *Pietro Mascagni*, pp. 405, 408. Ovation: *L'Illustrazione Italiana*, June 11, 1911, p. 597. *Diario*, Romaniello: both quoted in Pom-

pei, *Pietro Mascagni*, p. 410. A contemporary article from *Il mondo argentino* summarizing the diverse Argentinian critical reaction appears in Morini, ed., *Pietro Mascagni* 1 : 353–54. Working constantly: letter to Lolli, June 16, 1911. Anniversary: described in letter to Lolli, June 27, 1911.

195   Students: letter to Lolli, July 27, 1911. Nerves: letter to Lolli, September 16, 1911. The count of performances appears in Pompei, *Pietro Mascagni*, p. 418. The repertory included fifteen different operas; *Isabeau*, the most frequently done, was performed twenty-five times. Correspondence with Riccardo Sonzogno: Amici et al., *Mascagni contro Sonzogno*, pp. 69–74. January 10 opening: "La lunga polemica fra La Scala e Mascagni," *Corriere della Sera*, January 21, 1912. Contract, Sonzogno and La Scala: Amici et al., *Mascagni contro Sonzogno*, pp. 78–79.

196   Offers from Venice: letters to Lolli, December 11, 23, 1911. Conflicts: "La lunga polemica"; Amici et al., *Mascagni contro Sonzogno*, pp. 79–83. Despite minor differences, the two accounts are generally consistent.

197   Pozza: *Corriere della Sera*, January 21, 1912. Barini: *Nuova Antologia*, February 1, 1912, p. 556. Financial success: *Corriere della Sera*, April 21, 1912. Casa Sonzogno: see Morini, ed., *Pietro Mascagni* 1 : 359–61, also Amici et al., *Mascagni contro Sonzogno*, p. 66. Letter to Renzo Sonzogno, July 5, 1910, in Morini, ed., *Pietro Mascagni* 1 : 359–60.

198   Riccardo: letter to Illica, August 10, 1911, Amici et al., *Mascagni contro Sonzogno*, p. 71. Success of Renzo Sonzogno: Morini, ed., *Pietro Mascagni* 1 : 360. Sale of assets: letter from Count Suzani to Illica, June 1912, ibid., pp. 360–61; letter of E. Sonzogno to Illica, ibid., p. 361. Mascagni was not acting entirely on his own; Renzo went to Venice in February to ask Mascagni to intercede with his uncle; letter to Lolli, February 12, 1912. Origins of *Parisina* venture: M. Morini, "Nascita e vicenda di *Parisina*," *Rassegna Musicale Curci*, January 1979, pp. 3–8. A different version of the same essay appeared earlier in the program book for the 1978 Rome performance of *Parisina*. Dates: L. Campolonghi, "D'Annunzio e Mascagni esalanto *Parisina*," *Il Secolo*, May 3, 1912. In contrast to Morini's definite statement that the initial contract between Sonzogno and D'Annunzio was signed in May 1911, this article states that "nothing definite was concluded during those days."

199   Profile: E. Checchi, "Mascagni e D'Annunzio," *Gazzetta Musicale di Milano*, May 30, 1901. Checchi's profile of Mascagni is equally vivid. D'Annunzio at *Iris*: R. Tedeschi, *D'Annunzio e la musica*, p. 93. While many sources, including Morini, ed., *Pietro Mascagni* 1 : 367, describe this meeting as having taken place during the first Naples performances of *Iris* in March 1899, Gelati has pointed out that D'Annunzio spent all of March 1899 with Eleanora Duse in Corfu (*Il vate e il capobanda* [Livorno, 1992], pp. 28–29). Separation: letter to Lolli, February 15, 1912 (the subject is discussed in various letters, beginning on January 28).

200   London fee: *L'Illustrazione Italiana*, March 10, 1912. This article describes this episode in Mascagni's conducting career in some detail; some negative Italian

reaction to the music-hall quality of the event is recorded in "Mascagni all'Hip-podrome," *La Stampa*, March 4, 1912. Sleep alone: letter to Lolli, March 6, 1912. Trip to Paris: Campolonghi, "D'Annunzio e Mascagni esaltano *Parisina*"; "L'impressioni di Mascagni sulla *Parisina*," *Corriere della Sera*, May 8, 1912. Fusion of souls: T. Antongini, "D'Annunzio e Mascagni a Parigi," *L'Illustrazione Italiana*, May 19, 1912, p. 495. Don't touch: quoted in Morini, ed., *Pietro Mascagni* 1 : 368. Letter from Farinelli to Mascagni, June 19, 1912, in BdR. Waylaid: letter to Lolli, July 5, 1912. Archachon: Morini, ed., *Pietro Mascagni* 1 : 369. The expectation that Mascagni would resettle in Archachon to write the opera was widely reported in the newspapers in May 1912. Events: letters and telegrams to Lolli, July 9, 10, 11, 1912.

201 Front-page articles on the elopement appeared on July 12 and 13 in the *New York Times*, the latter article denying statements made in the former; see also *La Tribuna*, July 13, 1912. Routine: E. Mascagni, *S'inginocchi la piu piccina* (Milan, 1936), pp. 35–36. This charming and entertaining book, which purports to be a memoir of their stay in France during 1912, is highly fanciful and, on factual matters, utterly unreliable. For understandable reasons, Anna Lolli's presence is never mentioned; less explicably, Emy Mascagni, who was nearly twenty at the time, refers to herself throughout as being fifteen. Indeed, almost every factual statement in this book that can be checked from a contemporary source is found to be either distorted or simply incorrect. There is little doubt that Emy made much of the book up, basing it on her hazy recollections more than twenty years later. Just the same, it offers much of the flavor of their stay in France.

202 Letter of D'Annunzio to Mascagni, August 12, 1912, in BdR (Mascagni gave Lolli his letters from D'Annunzio as a memento of their stay in France). Letter of Mascagni to D'Annunzio, August 23, 1912, in A. Lualdi, "Mascagni, D'An-nunzio e *Parisina*," *Quaderni d'annunziani* 30–31 (Gardone Riviera: Fondazione il Vittoriale degli Italiani, 1965), p. 73. All letters from Mascagni to D'Annunzio subsequently cited are from this source. Duncan: G. Gatti, *Vita di Gabriele D'An-nunzio* (Florence, 1988), pp. 252–53. Void: letter to D'Annunzio, August 13, 1912, in Lualdi, "Mascagni." D'Annunzio's side of relationship: see Tom Antongini, *Vita segreta di D'Annunzio*, quoted in Gelati, *Vate*, pp. 76–77. Ecstasy: letter to Gianfranceschi, October 4, 1912, in BLS. Role of Renzo Sonzogno: ibid. Letter from D'Annunzio, September 11, 1912, in BdR.

203 Keeping her word: letter to Lolli, October 11, 1912. One thousand thirty lines: letter to D'Annunzio, November 2, 1912, in Lualdi, "Mascagni." Inordinate length: ibid. Human endurance: letter to D'Annunzio, November 24, 1912, ibid. Dear hopes: letter to D'Annunzio, December 1, 1912, ibid.

204 Tomb: letter to D'Annunzio, December 26, 1912, ibid. Without life: letter to D'Annunzio, January 29, 1912, ibid. House in Milan: letter to Lolli, March 5, 1913. Wedding witnesses (*padrini*): letter to Gianfranceschi, October 12, 1913, in BLS; there are repeated references in the letters to Lolli regarding Mimi's difficulties during this period.

205   Opening night: in view of the importance attributed to the length of *Parisina*, the actual timings of the acts on opening night may be of interest:

	START	END	DURATION
Act 1	8:30	9:35	1:05
Act 2	10:00	11:20	1:20
Act 3	11:50	12:40	0:50
Act 4	12:55	1:35	0:40

The opera, exclusive of intermissions, was three hours and fifty-five minutes long; *Corriere della Sera*, December 16, 1913; *Observer*, December 16, 1913. Pozza: *Corriere della Sera*, December 16, 1913. Gasco: quoted in "Antologia critica," section of program book for Rome Opera production of *Parisina* in 1978. Nappi: ibid.

206   Gasco: Morini, ed., *Pietro Mascagni* 1 : 380. Cuts: *Corriere della Sera*, December 18, 1913. Crescendo of success: *Corriere della Sera*, December 28, 1913. A La Scala production in the 1930s was contemplated but apparently abandoned because of casting difficulties. RAI gave a largely intact unstaged broadcast performance in 1976, which (in private recordings) represents the closest approximation to the complete score available. The extent to which *Parisina* is dominated by the shade of *Tristan* can hardly be overstated. Not only does Parisina refer to the Tristan legend repeatedly in D'Annunzio's text, but the third act is clearly closely modeled on the second act of Wagner's opera.

208   Puccini: interview with Enrico Cavacchioli, in Morini, ed., *Pietro Mascagni* 1 : 380. Constant thought: quoted in Fraccaroli, *Celebrità e quasi*, p. 180.

210   Berlioz's *Les Troyens* may be considered an exception to this statement.

CHAPTER 12

211   There is no direct evidence of the winter meetings between Mascagni, Forzano, and Sonzogno, but they can reasonably be inferred from the subsequent events. Marie Louise de la Ramée lived most of her life in Italy, in Viareggio, and her novel had been published in Italy under the title *Due zoccoletti*. Puccini letter to Schnabl, in Gara, *Carteggi Pucciniani*, p. 420. Auction: Ashbrook, *The Operas of Puccini*, pp. 153–55. Contrary to Ashbrook, Mascagni was not present at the auction. Forzano played a minor part in this episode, acting as a consultant to the magistrate charged with evaluating the value of the operatic rights to the book from a literary standpoint. In that capacity, he presented a report in which he concluded, with little apparent basis for his opinion, that the rights were worth twenty thousand lire (copy in BdR). The manuscript of Forzano's first draft for the first two acts of *Lodoletta* is in BdR. The differences between this draft and the final libretto are considerable.

212 Cines, *Enciclopedia dello spettacolo* 3 : 859. *Cabiria:* G. Rondolino, "Storia del cinema italiano dalle origini agli anni trenta," in *Storia sociale e culturale d'Italia*, vol. 3,
Lo spettacolo, p. 421. Intermarriage: G. P. Brunetta, "Comets and Fireflies: The
Shining Dreams Great and Small of Forty Years of Italian Cinema," in Hulten
and Celant, eds., *Italian Art, 1900–1945* (New York, 1989), p. 193. Garibaldi: letter to Lolli, March 20, 1914. The Garibaldi film with music by Mascagni was
announced but abandoned for obscure reasons; see C. Piccardi, "Mascagni
e l'ipotesi dell 'dramma musicale cinematografico,'" *Musica/Realtà* 11 (August
1991): 89–90, and M. A. Prolo, *Storia del cinema muto italiana* (Milan, 1951), p. 75.
Contract: letter to Lolli, May 7, 1914. Martini's poem contains a number of
points where the character of Tristan is associated with the story of Tristan
and Isolde. Oxilia: G. Livoni, *Il tragico Fato*, quoted in Prolo, *Storia del cinema*,
pp. 109–10.

213 Borelli: see *Enciclopedia dello spettacolo* 2 : 830, also Rondolino, "Storia del cinema,"
p. 424, Prolo, *Storia del cinema*, p. 57. References to timings, notebook, initial
sketches, in letters to Lolli, October 3, 15, 17, 1914. Purchase of villa: letter to
Lolli, June 5, 1914, also slightly different version in Benvenuti, *Pietro Mascagni*,
p. 53. Emy and Farinelli: letters to Lolli, August 15, 16, 21, 1914.

214 Feelings about European war: letter to Lolli, August 10, 1914. Lunch with Lina:
letter to Lolli, December 8, 1914. Family battles: letters to Lolli, August 15,
September 15, 1914. Projector: letter to Lolli, September 17, 1914. Dino: let-
ter to Lolli, September 25, 1914. Finished prologue and second part: letter to
Lolli, October 16, 1914. Hundreds of times: letter to Lolli, November 15, 1914.
Date on score in MM.

215 Costanzi production: letters to Lolli, April 10, 16, 21, 1916. Disturbance: *Musical Times*, August 1, 1917, p. 369. Reviews: *Musica*, July 15, 1917, *Musical Times*,
August 1, 1917, p. 370.

216 Turin performances: letter to Lolli, January 8, 1918. A. Salandra, "L'intervento,"
in S. Clough and S. Saladino, eds., *A History of Modern Italy* (New York, 1968),
p. 307. Treaty of London: ibid., pp. 308–10. Although the treaty was secret,
reasonably accurate rumors of its existence began to circulate in Italy within
little more than a week of its signing. Transformation of theater: *La Tribuna*,
February 20, 1915. Preparations for *Mosè*: essay by Alberto Gasco in *La Tribuna*,
April 2, 1915.

217 Review: *La Tribuna*, April 5, 1915. Mascagni and Rossini: M. Morini, "Masca-
gni e Rossini," *L'Opera* 4 (1968): 12–13. Collapse: letter to Lolli, May 7, 1915.
In Livorno: letter to Lolli, May 7, 1915. Suffering: letter to Lolli, May 9, 1915.
Mobilization, war will not be: letter to Lolli, May 11, 1915. Delirium: letter to
Lolli, May 15, 1915. Treatments: letter to Lolli, May 16, 1915.

218 Lunatics: letter to Lolli, May 16, 1915. Leoncavallo: W. Weaver, *The Golden Century of Italian Opera*, p. 235. Illica: M. Morini, "Profilo di Illica," *La Scala*, October 1956, p. 48. Puccini: Weaver, *Golden Century*, pp. 234–35, Ashbrook, *The
Operas of Puccini*, pp. 157–58. Urbino: letter to Lolli, February 6, 1915. Car and

219   chauffeur: letter to Lolli, June 11, 1915. Motorcycle: letter to Lolli, June 17, 1915. Naples concert: letter to Lolli, January 19, 1916. Franco-Italian League: Morini, ed., *Pietro Mascagni* 1 : 389. Cappa: ibid., p. 391.

219   On the copy of "Bimba bionda" in the Red Cross album that Mascagni gave Anna Lolli he wrote, "Anna and Pietro make up the name Nino Pareto." "To the Sources of Melody" appeared in *Il Mondo,* November 7, 1915; it appears in its entirety in translation in Stivender, "Mascagni's *Lodoletta,*" pp. 2–4, and in part in Morini, ed., *Pietro Mascagni* 1 : 388–90.

220   Litigation: Amici et al., *Mascagni contro Sonzogno,* pp. 113–17. Order attaching property: letter to Lolli, July 9, 1915. Afraid of lawsuit: letter to Lolli, August 13, 1915. Telling Walter: letter to Lolli, November 5, 1915. Forzano approach to Puccini: letter to Lolli, March 12, 1916. Although this episode is not corroborated by other sources, it is nonetheless consistent with the writer's personality. Mascagni acknowledged Forzano's return in his letter to Lolli of April 19, 1916. Bit of relief: letter to Lolli, May 22, 1916.

221   Working against me: letter to Lolli, January 31, 1917. Mammismo: L. Baldacci, "I libretti di Mascagni," *Nuova Rivista Musicale Italiana* (July–September 1985): 402. Show our romance: letter to Lolli, November 4, 1916. Contaminates: letter to Lolli, November 18, 1916.

222   I have reconstructed the intrigues between Mascagni, Sonzogno, Mocchi, Carelli, and others with respect to the premiere of *Lodoletta* from a long series of letters to Lolli written between November 1916 and March 1917. Letter from La Scala: quoted in letter to Lolli, February 21, 1917. Telegrams: letter to Lolli, February 24, 1917. Letter to Sonzogno: paraphrased in letter to Lolli, March 6, 1917. Never: letter to Lolli, March 25, 1917.

223   Forzano: letter to Lolli, December 31, 1916. Changes in closing scene: letters to Lolli, January 13, 19, 1917. Gentle feeling of comfort: *Corriere della Sera,* April 24, 1917; Barini: *La Perseveranza,* May 3, 1917. Bastianelli: quoted in Gragnani, "Prospetto," p. 686.

224   Lualdi: *Musica,* April 30, 1917. Forty-five: letter to Lolli, January 13, 1917. Livorno triumph: letter to Lolli, July 29, 1917. Off and flying: letter to Lolli, September 24, 1917. *New York Herald,* January 13, 1918. The *New York Times* critic was also favorably disposed, writing on January 13 that Mascagni's "spell of ill luck is broken at last, shattered for the moment as indubitably as the little pitcher in Greuse's famous painting." The Metropolitan Opera performance was conducted by Mascagni's former pupil Robert Moranzoni.

225   Baby: letter to Lolli, August 31, 1917. Beautiful brown harlot: Ouida, *Two Little Wooden Shoes,* p. 232.

226   Serenity: Stivender, "Mascagni's *Lodoletta,*" p. 37.

227   Among echoes of *Iris,* which may or may not be deliberate, are Flammen's "Sorridi . . . sorridi ancora!" in act 2, which recalls Osaka's "Ridi . . . Ridi ancora!" from act 2 of *Iris,* and Lodoletta's plaintive "Perchè? . . . perchè?"

CHAPTER 13

229   Caporetto: Candeloro, *Storia dell'Italia moderna* 8:182–94; Dino alive: letter to
       Lolli, November 29, 1917. Activity: letters to Lolli, November 30, Decem-
       ber 3, 15, 1917. Movie theater: letter to Lolli, January 8, 1918.

230   Horns: letter to Lolli, April 8, 1918. Visit from Lombardo: letter to Lolli, July 2,
       1918 (emphasis in original). Mascagni later (probably during August 1918) de-
       scribed this visit to the young Livornese musician and *mascagnano* Emilio Gra-
       gnani in identical terms, with one significant exception: Mascagni told Gra-
       gnani that it had been Lombardo rather than himself who had proposed a new
       operetta after Mascagni had rejected the *Silvano* pastiche; quoted in Morini,
       ed., *Pietro Mascagni* 1:393. Mascagni had previously authorized an operetta
       adaptation of *Le Maschere*, described in *Il Tirso*, February 16, 1916 (this entire
       issue of the magazine was devoted to the premiere of the operetta version of *Le
       Maschere*). Letter to Orsini, July 21, 1918, in Morini, ed., *Pietro Mascagni* 1:385.
       Teach Italians: letter to Lolli, July 16, 1918.

231   Origins of libretto: Morini, ed., *Pietro Mascagni* 1:394. Although *Sì* is not iden-
       tical to its predecessor, there is enough similarity to make clear that Lombardo
       borrowed not only a good deal of the plot but many of the lyrics as well; see
       Oppicelli, *L'operetta*, p. 205. No profound concept: letter to Lolli, August 7,
       1918. Dates of composition of sections on manuscript of *Sì* in MM. Influenza:
       letters to Lolli, October 10, 17, 1918.

232   "Bimba bionda": letters to Lolli, October 18, 19, 1918. Trip to Turin: letter to
       Lolli, November 9, 1918. Dino's return: letter to Lolli, November 27, 1918. San
       Carlo season, revival: letter to Giovanni Orsini, March 24, 1919, in Orsini,
       Vangelo d'un mascagnano (Milan, 1926), no page numbers. Death of Maria Tafi:
       letter to Lolli, February 8, 1919.

233   Aunt's help with *Cavalleria*: letter to Maria Tafi [Mascagni], February 1, 1889,
       in Celli, "La *Cavalleria*," pp. 33–34. Maria Tafi's two sons, Mario and Luigi Ma-
       scagni, and Mario's son Andrea are the only other members of Pietro Masca-
       gni's family known to have become musicians. Mario Mascagni had a distin-
       guished career as director of the Bolzano Conservatory. Luigi had a more
       modest career as music teacher and conductor in various small towns in North-
       ern Italy. Good man: letter to Lolli, August 9, 1919. Puccini: letter to Lolli, Au-
       gust 12, 1919. Myth: Gregor, *Italian Fascism and Developmental Dictatorship* (Prince-
       ton, N.J., 1979), p. 175. Situation: letter to Lolli, July 12, 1919. Blend politics:
       Morini, ed., *Pietro Mascagni* 1:400.

234   Libretto: interview with A. Belli, *Il Corriere d'Italia*, June 22, 1920, reprinted ibid.
       It seems clear that all of this took place during Mascagni's stay in Milan between
       September and December 1918; not long after arriving in Naples, Mascagni
       wrote Lolli, "I have something going with Forzano," presumably referring to
       Marat: letter of January 14, 1919. According to a later letter of Mascagni's,
       Forzano first offered *Marat* to Puccini, which may or may not be true; letter to

Lolli, November 13, 1919. Boring travels: letter to Armando Tanzini, June 21, 1919, in MM. Tanzini, a prosperous Livorno merchant who was actively involved in operatic promotions in his city, was a close friend of Mascagni as well as his regular partner in tamburello, a game similar to badminton played with tambourinelike objects rather than rackets.

235   Separate rooms: letter to Lolli, August 16, 1919. Arrival of Mario: letter to Lolli, August 16, 1919. Freedom: quoted ("you've written me") in letter to Lolli, September 7, 1919.

236   Go on writing: letter to Lolli, May 17, 1920. Stayed as it was: letter to Lolli, September 22, 1919. Working without words: letter to Lolli, November 12, 1919. Ferocity: letter to Lolli, November 25–26, 1919.

237   Review: *La Tribuna*, December 15, 1919. The feeling that Mascagni was demeaning himself and his public by writing an operetta was widespread. The important critic Giorgio Barini wrote in the magazine *Il Pianoforte* (February 1923) that "it is unforgivable for an artist such as the composer of *Cavalleria, Iris,* and *Parisina* to make a foray into the tired, commercialized realm of operetta"; the composer himself wrote Lolli on October 24, 1919, "Imagine, I am finishing my artistic career, after so many dreams of glory, with an . . . *operetta!*" Illica funeral: *Nuovo Giornale* (Piacenza), quoted in *Musica d'Oggi*, January 1920. Giordano condescended: letter to Lolli, December 10, 1919.

238   Forzano, "Un caro ricordo di Pietro Mascagni" (a title chosen perhaps with sarcastic intent), *Il Giornale d'Italia*, March 10, 1960. An account similar in substance but with somewhat less detail appears in Forzano's *Come li ho conosciuti*, pp. 30–31. Brackets: ibid., p. 31. Forzano scene: letter to Lolli, February 23, 1920. Edoardo Sonzogno, letter of March 15, 1920. Death of Renzo in mistress's apartment: letter to Lolli, April 7, 1920.

239   Speculators: letter to Lolli, April 7, 1920. Death going round: letter to Lolli, April 3, 1920. Four hundred thousand workers: Clark, *Modern Italy*, p. 208; see also T. Abse, "The Rise of Fascism in an Industrial City: The Case of Livorno, 1918–1922," in D. Forgacs, ed., *Rethinking Italian Fascism* (London, 1986), pp. 62–66. Although the story of Mascagni's visit to the Orlando shipyards appears in innumerable sources, the most detailed account appears to be that in Santini, *Mascagni*, pp. 109–11. Words on scroll: from *Il Mattino*, September 10–11, 1920. The wording differs slightly from that quoted in Santini, *Mascagni*, p. 110. *Popolo d'Italia*, September 20, 1920.

240   Puccini: in C. Paladini, *G. Puccini* (Florence, 1961), p. 142. Letter to Balilla Pratella, September 25, 1920, in *Il Messaggero* (Lugo), September 6, 1980. "Iron Fist": quoted in H. Sachs, *Music in Fascist Italy*, p. 104. Prezzolini: in Morini, ed., *Pietro Mascagni* 1 : 404–5. Mascagni was responding to Prezzolini's criticism of his behavior in Livorno. An example of Mascagni's obliviousness to politics, and arguably to reality, was his hounding of the Livorno prefect and prosecutor in July 1920, at the height of the wave of strikes and demonstrations, demanding that they take immediate action against various operetta companies and their

promoters and resenting bitterly their failure to give his concerns immediate and thorough attention: see letter to Lolli, July 24, 1920. The point about the Senate seat is made by too many different figures not to be taken seriously, including Goetz, "Die Beziehungen zwischen Pietro Mascagni und Benito Mussolini," p. 216; Santini, *Mascagni*, p. 108; Gragnani, "Mascagni a Livorno," in Morini, ed., *Pietro Mascagni* 1:68; and M. Morini, "Attribuivano a Mascagni le barzellette antifasciste," *Nazione Sera*, October 3, 1953.

241 Mocchi: letter to Lolli, January 18, 1921. Death of Paolo Mascagni: letters to Lolli, February 2, 3, 1921. Copyists: Ricci, *34 anni*, p. 86.

242 *Giornale d'Italia:* in Morini, ed., *Pietro Mascagni* 1:409. "Viva l'Italia": ibid. Carelli: L. Lodi, "*Il Piccolo Marat*," in *Pietro Mascagni 1890–1920*, no page number; Gasco: in *La Tribuna*, May 4, 1921. Bastianelli, *Il Resto del Carlino*, November 15, 1923, reprint in Morini, ed., *Pietro Mascagni* 1:143–44. Alaeona: *Musica d'Oggi*, May 1921, p. 145. Celletti has suggested that "the vogue that [*Marat*] had for roughly a decade was largely thanks to Lázaro" (*Le Grandi Voci* [Rome, 1964], p. 462). *Marat* also benefited from the championship of the bass Nicola Rossi-Lemeni and his wife, Virginia Zeani, who sang the Ogre and Mariella, respectively, in a number of productions during the 1960s.

243 Petronio: *L'Illustrazione Italiana*, May 22, 1921, p. 620. Gasco: *La Tribuna*, May 4, 1921.

244 Letter to Orsini, November 2, 1919, in Orsini, *Vangelo d'un mascagnano*, p. 190.

CHAPTER 14

247 In a famous quotation, General Diaz, when asked by the king if the army could be counted on to put down a Fascist coup, said, "The army will do its duty, but it would be better not to put it to the test"; quoted in Lyttleton, *The Seizure of Power: Fascism in Italy, 1919–1929* (Princeton, N.J., 1973), p. 92. Marcia Reale: Mascagni interview, "Mascagni vorrebbe spiegare!!" *Musica*, January 15, 1921.

248 Attacks by Fascists in Verona: letter to Lolli, July 25, 1921. Turin: letter to Lolli, December 9, 1921. Mascagni changed the time of his departure from Livorno to Verona "to avoid the darkness in these days of Communists and Fascists"; letter to Lolli, July 16, 1921. New libretto: letter to Lolli, August 27, 1921. Rebuff from D'Annunzio: letter to G. M. Viti, April 28, 1922, in Remo Giazotto, "Quattordici lettere inedite di Pietro Mascagni," *Nuova Rivista Musicale Italiana* 4 (1970): 494; see also Gelati, "*Cavalleria*," pp. 108–11. Funeral: letter to Lolli, March 4, 1938. Mimi rejoining army: letter to Lolli, August 10, 1921. Gemma Risgalla: letter to Lolli, September 14, 1921; also "Quanti segreti nelle sue lettere: Incontro con la nuora di Pietro Mascagni," *Gente*, April 20, 1979.

249 Darling young woman: letter to Lolli, September 18, 1921. Such a mess: letter to Lolli, February 18, 1922. Shocked dizzy: letter to Viti, August 4, 1922, in Giazotto, "Quattordici lettere," p. 497. Prompted enthusiasm: ibid. Without

any documentation of Mocchi's side of this controversy it is difficult to estab-lish the facts of the dispute, given Mascagni's elevated emotional temperature throughout the episode.

250   *Rigoletto:* letter to Lolli, June 23, 1922. Rio: letter to Lolli, September 19, 1922. God knows: letter to Lolli, November 8, 1922. Moment: letter to Viti, No-vember 10, 1922, in Giazotto, "Quattordici lettere," p. 501. Puccini congratu-latory message: Fiamma Nicolodi, *Musica e musicisti nel ventennio fascista* (Fiesole, 1984), p. 36. Disaster: G. Marotti and F. Pagni, *Giacomo Puccini intimo* (Florence, 1926), pp. 172–73.

251   Meeting with Arpinati: letter to Viti, December 29, 1922, in Giazotto, "Quat-tordici lettere," p. 502. The same letter describes an unusual event that also took place in Bologna. Mascagni was approached by representatives of D'An-nunzio, who advised the composer to avoid Arpinati and suggested that the poet was planning to come out openly against Fascism. Not surprisingly, Ma-scagni's feelings toward D'Annunzio being what they were at the time, the poet's emissaries were rebuffed. Squadristi: Goetz, "Beziehungen," p. 213. Audience: ibid., p. 214. Interview: Rafaello de Rensis, *Musica vista*, p. 78. Count on me: quoted in Goetz, "Beziehungen," p. 214. Denunciation, fight: Rensis, *Musica vista*, p. 79; Saint Teresa: letter to Lolli, January 4, 1923. The manuscript of *Vi-sione lirica* (short score) is in BdR.

252   Review: *Musica d'Oggi,* February 23, 1923, p. 59. Emy: letter to Lolli, Septem-ber 11, 1923. Dino: letter to Lolli, August 10, 1923. Day and night: letter to Lolli, August 11, 1923. Haven't touched: letter to Lolli, August 19, 1923. Most beautiful music: letter to Lolli, August 30, 1923. The following table outlines Mascagni's activities between November 1923 and June 1924, reconstructed largely from information in his letters to Lolli. Figures in brackets represent es-timates of the number of performances where they were not possible to deter-mine precisely.

DATES	CITY	ACTIVITY	PERFORMANCES
11/1–12	Treviso	*Isabeau*	8
11/12–17	Bologna	*Marat*	3
11/18–24	Rome	*Aida*	1
11/24–26	Bologna	*Marat*	2
11/26–27	Milan	Brother's funeral	
11/27–28	Bologna	*Marat*	[1–2]
11/29–12/12	Venice	*Marat*	[4–5]
12/13–17	Mestre	*Marat*	2
12/30–1/15	Rome	Augusteo concerts	3
1/16–2/17	Bari	*Marat*	11

DATES	CITY	ACTIVITY	PERFORMANCES
2/19–3/6	Trieste	*Marat*	[10–12]
3/7–27	Fiume	*Marat*	[6–9]
3/28–30	Venice	*Marat*	2
3/31	Ferrara	*Marat*	1
4/1–2	Venice	*Marat*	1
4/3–7	Milan	Business meetings	
4/11–29	Catania	*Iris*	[6–8]
4/30–5/7	Florence	*Isabeau*	3
5/8–12	Catania	*Iris*	1
5/13–25	Florence	*Isabeau*	4
6/10–30	Fabbriano	*Isabeau*	[9–11]

Puccini: letter to Lolli, November 24, 1923.

253   Brother's death: letter to Lolli, November 26, 1923. Grave: letter to Lolli, November 27, 1923. Christmas: letter to Lolli, December 27, 1923. Tchaikovsky: letter to Lolli, January 14, 1924. Cerignola: letter to Lolli, February 15, 1924. Ostali and Sonzogno: letter to Lolli, April 8, 1924.

254   Apartment: letter to Lolli, June 4, 1924. Mascagni would eventually buy Lolli an apartment, as well as farmland in her home village of Bagnara di Romagna. A partial statement of Mascagni's accounts for 1931, which includes his business manager's disbursements to Mascagni's three children, is in MFC; see also letter to Lolli, February 13, 1927. By this point, Mascagni was heavily subsidizing Dino's motorcycle business as well. The relative partiality of the smaller provincial theaters to Mascagni's works was not a new phenomenon; a published list of operas planned for the 1908 winter/spring season, listing offerings in twenty-nine theaters, showed a remarkable dichotomy. Among forty operas to be presented by the five principal houses (Costanzi, La Scala, San Carlo, Fenice, and Regio, the Carlo Felice being closed that year) no Mascagni operas were planned; among ninety-four productions scheduled in twenty-four smaller houses, sixteen were Mascagni operas, including six different works: *Musica*, December 15, 1907. One can suggest a number of at least plausible reasons for this marked difference, including idiosyncratic conditions such as the dislike that Toscanini, who headed La Scala at the time, had for Mascagni. More important, it reflects the extent to which Mascagni's popular appeal exceeded his critical respectability. Forty years after its debut, during the 1930–31 season, *Cavalleria* had 264 performances in Germany, behind only *Tannhäuser* (301), *Der Freischütz* (295), and *Die Zauberflöte* (295). Known everywhere: letter to Lolli, August 10, 1924. Camels: *Musical Courier*, October 28, 1924.

255   Arrival in Berlin: letter to Lolli, September 7, 1924. Collapse of tour: letter to Lolli, September 27, 1924. Canceled engagements, base: letter to Lolli, No-

vember 20, 1924. Humiliation: letter to Lolli, November 2, 1924. It is impossible to establish precisely what this letter refers to. Although it might represent Mascagni's reaction to Puccini's nomination as senator, a nomination that both musicians craved, this seems unlikely; not only does it seem excessive even for Mascagni, but the state of excitement would seem particularly inappropriate coming nearly two months after the event. Anti-Italian: letter to Lolli, February 16, 1925. Letter to Belli: in Gragnani, "Prospetto," p. 663.

256   Best conditions: letter to Lolli, April 18, 1925. Passport: letter to Lolli, August 3, 1925. Blackmail: S. Benelli, *Schiavitù* (Milan, 1945), p. 15; see also letter to Hirsch, July 22, 1925, in Donati, *Mascagni in cartolina* (Livorno, 1990), p. 13. Separation: letter to Lolli, October 30, 1924. Telegram from Dino: letter to Lolli, November 13, 1924. Ciano and Campana: Goetz, "Beziehungen," pp. 216–17, quoting Aleardo Campana, "Mascagni e Mussolini," *Il Terreno*, August 7, 1955. Costanzo Ciano, a naval hero of World War I, served in various cabinet positions under Mussolini and was the de facto Fascist boss of Livorno. His son Galeazzo was later foreign minister and Mussolini's son-in-law.

257   The telegram was reprinted in *Il Giornale d'Italia*, November 17, 1925. Meeting with Mascagni and Federzoni; interview: Goetz, "Beziehungen," pp. 217–18.

258   Telegram: Nicolodi, *Musica e musicisti*, p. 372. Mussolini affectionate: letter to Lolli, March 28, 1927. Not a Fascist: letter to Orsini, June 12, 1934, in Nicolodi, *Musica e musicisti*, p. 399.

259   Rossoni was an interesting figure; a prominent anarcho-syndicalist leader in 24 United States in the 1910s, working closely with Big Bill Haywood and Eugene Debs, he returned to Italy when war broke out and became one of the first union leaders to join forces with Mussolini in the early days of Fascism; see John P. Diggins, *Mussolini and Fascism*, p. 87. Venice performance: letter to Lolli, March 1, 1928. Totally stunned: letter to Lolli, January 13, 1927. Academy, compromise: Philip V. Cannistraro, quoted in G. Gembillo, "La politica culturale," in S. Fedele and G. Restifo, eds., *Il fascismo: Politica e vita sociale*, p. 134. An extensive file on the Royal Academy, maintained by Domenico Mascagni on his father's behalf, is preserved in MM, from which this description is derived.

260   Letter from Lina Mascagni to Vittorio Gianfranceschi, October 23, 1929, in BLS. Donkeys: De Carlo, ed., *Mascagni parla*, pp. 147–48. Description of Via Po house: A. Lancellotti, "Mascagni a casa sua," *Noi e il Mondo*, July 1917, p. 478. Description of Plaza suite, dreariness: Rinaldi, "Mascagni a Roma." Luigi Ricci, who worked closely with the composer during this period, wrote that the furnishings "were so simple and modest that many could never figure out why the Maestro, owning a villa in Livorno and another in Rome, preferred living there" (Ricci, *34 Anni con Pietro Mascagni*, p. 124). Mascagni still owned his villa in Milan as well, but for years had spent little time there.

261   Scopone: see Rinaldi, "Mascagni a Roma" 2:117. Bricks: P. Mascagni, "I miei settantun anni," in G. Cenzato, ed., *Nerone*, p. 72. Vermouth: Raimondo Collino Pansa, "Mascagni all'aperta," *Panorama*, August 27, 1939, p. 443. Not only with

pepper: ibid. Mascagni's wit is discussed in many sources, including M. Morini, "Profilo di Mascagni," in Morini, ed., *Pietro Mascagni* 1 : 11, and "Mascagni umorista," *La Scala*, August 1955. Overwhelmed: letter to Lolli, March 10, 1932.

262 Emy received 64,268.70 lire from her father to support herself and Piermarcello in 1931 (accounts in MFC); the range of white-collar salaries in Italy at the time was 7,000 to 15,000 lire per year. The letters to Lolli are full of loving, playful references to his grandchildren. Mimi in militia: letter from Achille Starace to Lina Mascagni, May 3, 1937, in MFC. Mimi's bills: letter from Peppino Hirsch to Pietro Mascagni, January 20, 1936, in MFC. Dino, first difficulties: letter to Lolli, March 13, 15, 1927. Tragic dimensions: letter to Lolli, September 25, 1931.

263 Refusal to cooperate: letter to Lolli, June 25, 1934. Flight and return: letters to Lolli, September 7, October 22, 26, November 6, 30, 1934. Mario Labroca, "Il musicista del 'cantar continuo,'" *Radiocorriere*, May 1955. Labroca, it should be stressed, was far from a *mascagnano*; indeed, as a composer during the 1920s and 1930s he was very much part of the modern movement. A. Casella, "Mascagni and Jazz," *Christian Science Monitor*, September 4, 1926. Victory: quoted in Casella, *21 + 26* (Rome, 1931), p. 224.

264 Occult forces: letter to Lolli, February 10, 1927. Boycott: letter to Giovanni Orsini, August 22, 1929, in M. Morini, "Intorno a P. Mascagni: Faville polemiche," *Viator*, January–February 1949. Letter to Mussolini: Nicolodi, *Musica e musicisti*, p. 402. Both Morini, in "Intorno," and Goetz, in "Beziehungen," accept the existence of a boycott. The post-Toscanini management at La Scala was substantially more hospitable to Mascagni's works. During the 1930s La Scala presented a total of sixteen productions of ten different Mascagni operas, including major revivals of *Le Maschere* (1931) and *Ratcliff* (1932). Mascagni conducted nine of the sixteen productions. The pattern was similar in Rome. During the last ten years of the Carelli-Mocchi era at the Costanzi, particularly after Mascagni's rupture with Walter Mocchi, he was little performed. From 1929 to 1939, under the new management set up by the government, which had taken over the theater in 1928, there were seventeen productions of nine Mascagni operas, of which twelve were conducted by the composer. Mascagni's denunciations of SIAE are reproduced in Nicolodi, *Musica e musicisti*, pp. 384– 86, 391–98. Episode: ibid., p. 49. Disdainful isolation: Casella, *21 + 26*, p. 237.

265 Who knows: letter to Lolli, December 4, 1926. Intervention: letter to Lolli, February 11, 1928. *I Promessi sposi:* letter to Lolli, December 23, 1927. Forzano and *Le Maschere:* letter to Lolli, October 21, 1930. The story of Caniglia and the 1931 La Scala production is in Ricci, *34 anni*, pp. 125–29.

266 Public: G. M. Ciampelli, *"Le Maschere* di Mascagni alla Scala," *Musica d'Oggi*, March 1931. Subsequent productions took place in Rome (1931, 1940), Livorno (1931), Genoa (1933), San Remo (1935), and Milan (1941). Suitcase: Giovanni Cenzato, "Come Mascagni pagò un debito di cinquant'anni fa," *Corriere della Sera*, September 12, 1931. A second account of this episode, similar but

differing in a number of significant details, appears in Ricci, *34 anni,* pp. 133–37. Morini has provided some useful corroborative details in "Mascagni prima della *Cavalleria:* Da *In filanda* a *Pinotta*," *Rassegna Musicale Curci,* May 1988. Both Cenzato and Ricci reported that the score that Mascagni found in his suitcase was the 1883 *Pinotta;* Mascagni specifically corrected that mistake in a letter to Targioni-Tozzetti, March 15, 1932, ibid., p. 5.

267   Pigna: ibid., pp. 6–7. Little nothing: letter to Lolli, December 11, 1931. Description of premiere: letter to Lolli, March 24, 1932. The composer's description of the scene is consistent with the account in the *Corriere della Sera.* Review: "La prima di *Pinotta* a San Remo," *Corriere della Sera,* March 24, 1932.

268   Mascagni conducted *Pinotta* in Florence, Pisa, Livorno, and Novara in 1932, and in Naples, Rome, and Turin in 1933.

CHAPTER 15

269   Rossato was best known for his collaborations with Zandonai, including *Giulietta e Romeo* (1922), *I Cavalieri di Ekebu* (1925), and *La Farsa amorosa* (1933). He was not necessarily a great writer; Morini characterizes him as "a librettist well regarded in those years notwithstanding his construction of libretti that were stale imitations of D'Annunzio and Benelli" (*Pietro Mascagni* 1:420). Subject: letter to Lolli, July 30, 1932. Cossa's Nero: P. Mascagni, "Perchè ho scritto il *Nerone,*" *La Lettura,* November 1, 1933. Delivered libretto: letter to Tanzini, October 26, 1932, in MM.

270   The closing words are a translation of "Sero, haec est fides?," Nero's last words as reported in Suetonius, *The Twelve Caesars.* Hymn: letter to Lolli, August 15, 1932. A number of these adaptations (attributed to Targioni rather than Rossato) are described in Gragnani, "Miscellanea mascagnana." Discussion of the dates on the various passages in the original manuscript short score are based on my analysis of the score in MM. Rossato trouble: letter to Lolli, May 18, 1933. *Nerone* comes out: letter from Rossato to Mario Mascagni, June 8, 1933, response by Mascagni to Mario Mascagni, both in Morini, ed., *Pietro Mascagni* 1:420. Interview: Arnaldo Bonaventura, "Mascagni parla del *Nerone,*" *La Nazione,* November 29, 1934. The phrase Mascagni used, "il Rossato non c'entra," has a particularly dismissive quality.

271   Worked eleven hours: letter to Lolli, August 7, 1933. Obsession: Philip V. Cannistraro, "Romanità," in P. Cannistraro, ed., *Historical Dictionary of Italian Fascism,* p. 461. Petrolini: see Nicolodi, *Musica e musicisti,* p. 55. The Mussolini/Mascagni anecdote is retold in Morini, "Formiggini e Mascagni erano l'incubo di Mussolini," *Il Tirenno,* March 25, 1952.

272   Total idiot: letter to Tanzini, October 20, 1933, quoted in Morini, ed., *Pietro Mascagni* 1:423. Supreme word: letter to Lolli, October 28, 1933. Mascagni cites Bologna's interest in the premiere of *Nerone* in his letter to Lolli, October 26,

1933. Mascagni worked with Targioni for roughly a week: letters to Lolli, May 2, 4, 6, 8, 1934. Eulogy: *Il Telegrafo*, May 31, 1934, quoted in Gragnani, "Prospetto," p. 690. Targioni: see Bianca Flury Nencini, "Giovanni Targioni-Tozzetti," *Liburni Civitas* 10, no. 3 (1937). One concern: A. Taddei, "Pietro Mascagni," *Liburni Civitas* 13 (1940): 26. Unexpected offer: letter to Lolli, June 11, 1934. Contract: letter to Lolli, June 20, 1934. Mascagni's first choice for the role of Nerone had been Giacomo Lauri-Volpi. According to Lauri-Volpi, he had recommended Pertile, considering his own voice unsuitable; quoted in Bruno Tosi, *Pertile: Una voce, un mito* (Venice, 1985), p. 176. Mount guard: letter to Lolli, October 27, 1934.

273   Overgrown Balilla: letter to Lolli, November 1, 1934. The Mostra della Rivoluzione Fascista was the Fascist regime's most ambitious effort at both self-promotion and self-definition; as such, no one was immune to being required to participate in some fashion; see Stone, *The Patron State: Culture and Politics in Fascist Italy*, pp. 128–76. The Balilla were the Fascist equivalent, more or less, of the Boy Scouts. Not looked on favorably: letter to Lolli, September 20, 1934. Description of scene: "L'Indimenticabile serata," *Corriere della Sera*, January 17, 1935. Anna Lolli also attended the premiere. As is customary, the count of the number and type of curtain call varies slightly among the different accounts of the evening; this is based on the account by G. C. Paribeni in *L'Ambrosiano*, January 1935. Copies of many of the telegrams, including that from Sibelius, are in MFC. Ceremonies after the opera, Mussolini telephone calls: *Corriere della Sera*, January 17, 1935. Alberto Gasco review: reprinted in Morini, ed., *Pietro Mascagni* 1 : 159–64.

274   Abbiati, *Corriere della Sera*, January 17, 1935. La Regime Fascista review: Morini, ed., *Pietro Mascagni* 1 : 425–26. *Nerone* broadcasts: letters from Enrico Carrara (general secretary of EIAR in Turin) to Mascagni, January 14, 22, 1935, in MFC. Secret reasons: letter to Tanzini, June 10, 1935, in MM. The reluctance of opera houses to perform *Nerone* is even less easily understood in light of the generous financial terms offered by the composer; instead of requiring payment for author's rights and rental of materials over and above his personal appearance fee, he included those costs within his usual fee of ten thousand lire per performance. Report, Mascagni saying: Nicolodi, *Musica e musicisti*, pp. 404–5.

275   Obstinate chatterbox: P. Mascagni, "I miei settantun anni," in G. Cenzato, ed., *Nerone*, p. 72. Fool's freedom: Goetz, "Beziehungen," p. 249. A comparison of the two libretti makes it possible to establish that many key sections of *Nerone* come from *Vistilia*, although it is possible that *Vistilia* was the source of additional music as well; from a stylistic standpoint, Nero's lament for Egloge, "Tu soffri, o mio tesoro," would appear to have been written long before 1933 but cannot be pinned down to a specific *Vistilia* source. Most of the *Vistilia* music can be dated to 1903–8 on both stylistic grounds and what is known about when Mascagni worked on the opera. One section, however, Atte's "Io posso per forza d'incanti," can clearly be dated on stylistic grounds to the early 1890s.

276   "Per l'Italia voluta da Mussolini," *Il Resto del Carlino*, November 18, 1935. The article was written, or perhaps dictated, while Mascagni was in Bologna conducting *Nerone*. End of year: letter to Lolli, December 27, 1935. It is unclear precisely what killed Dino; Nicolodi, *Musica e musicisti*, p. 405, writes that "he died of blood poisoning after a short illness." Lucio d'Ambra, in a lengthy article entitled "Il tenente [Lieutenant] Mascagni" in *Corriere della Sera* (date uncertain, clipping in BdR), wrote that after having been "submerged in water up to his waist," he was "struck down by the rheumatic fevers." The term "rheumatic fever" was used much more loosely at the time than it is today.

277   Never see him again: letter to Lolli, July 1, 1936. Twenty months: letter to Lolli, January 27, 1938. The summary of Mascagni's finances is based on my analysis of the composer's many financial references in his letters to Lolli, as well as the contracts, balance sheets, etc., in MFC. Mascagni had two rental apartments in the Via Po house above his own quarters, which brought three thousand lire per month each, as well as a rental property on the Via Salaria in Rome. In the 1930s members of the Augusteo orchestra in Rome, arguably the best orchestra in Italy, received seventy lire per performance: letter to Lolli, August 20, 1936. The Costanzi, a representative major company, produced on the average seven to eight different operas annually in the 1890s, twelve to fourteen in the 1910s, and twenty-four in the 1930s, without increasing the actual number of performances. The effect of the trend in Bari, one of the more important provincial cities, specifically on Mascagni's operas, is shown in the following table:

PERIOD	NUMBER OF PRODUCTIONS	NUMBER OF PERFORMANCES	PERFORMANCES PER PRODUCTION
1900–1909	6	55	9.2
1910–19	9	46	5.1
1920–29	10	58	5.8
1930–39	13	52	4.0
1940–45	6	16	2.7

278   American tour: see letters to Lolli, June 29, July 29, 1936, June 25, June 27, August 29, September 5, 1937; also letter to Mascagni from Francis P. Loubet, March 16, 1936, letter to Loubet, May 12, 1937, and other materials in MFC. The tour was announced in the *New York Herald Tribune* on May 7, 1937. German tour: letters to Lolli, September 25, 27, 1940. Propaganda Ministry: transcript of telephone conversation in Nicolodi, *Musica e musicisti*, p. 409. In my soul: letters to Lolli, May 19, 1941. Unsteady: d'Ambra, *Gli anni della feluca*, p. 63. Emy: handwritten note on May 20, 1938, opera program, in MFC. Symptoms: letter to Lolli, July 6, 1938. In 1938 a marked deterioration can be seen in Mascagni's handwriting, reflecting the apparent beginnings of a tremor in his hands.

279 Ciano funeral: letter to Lolli, June 29, 1939. Franchetti: Ardengo Soffici, "Fogli di diario: Ricordi di Mascagni," *Corriere della Sera*, August 3, 1955. Franchetti died in 1942; he and Mascagni maintained a touching correspondence during his last year, and his letters to Mascagni are in MFC. Between 1890 and 1910 Franchetti was performed more often at La Scala than any other composer except Verdi and Wagner. Soria: letter to Lolli, June 5, 1941. Rafaello Soria was not only Mascagni's banker but also a regular companion at scopone. Other close Jewish friends of Mascagni's included his librettist Guido Menasci, the Livorno hotelkeeper Chayes, the dramatist Sabatino Lopez, the publisher A. F. Formiggini, and the Roman dialect poet (and scopone partner) Trilussa. Be calm: letter to Lolli, September 11, 1939. Alfieri: letter to Lolli, July 24, 1939.

280 Rasa: see Orio Vergani, "Bruna Rasa cantante folle," *Il Messaggero*, December 31, 1947. National celebration: Mauro Calvetti, *Galliano Masini*, p. 136. The description of the fiftieth-anniversary gala in Rome is based on descriptions in *La Tribuna*, *Il Giornale d'Italia*, and *Il Lavoro Fascista*, all March 7, 1940. Now we must live: letter to Lolli, June 11, 1940. Cancellation of tour: letter to Lolli, June 14, 1940.

281 Enthusiasm: Gragnani, "Mascagni a Livorno," in Morini, ed., *Pietro Mascagni* 2:70. Except for legs: A. Belli, "Gli ottanta anni di Pietro Mascagni," *L'Avvenire*, December 7, 1943. Incontinence: letter to Lolli, August 7, 1941. Prostate condition: Edilio Leoni, *Un medico e un teatro* (Milan, 1987), p. 51. Brahms symphony: Gragnani, "Mascagni a Livorno," p. 70.

282 After the intermezzo: *L'Avvenire*, February 10, 1944. Taken up: letter to Lolli, June 5, 1941. Milan house: letter to Lolli, June 13, 1941 (it sold for the considerable price of 532,000 lire). Rental of Via Po house: Rinaldi, "Mascagni a Roma," p. 121. Ten thousand lire: letter to Lolli, August 14, 1943: "With the fall of Fascism, I've lost 120,000 lire per year, but God will provide." Sachs cites sources reporting that Mascagni received a total of 1,290,000 lire in subsidies from the regime (*Music in Fascist Italy*, p. 119); in the context of what is known about Mascagni's finances, however, this figure seems high. I alone: letter to Lolli, June 21, 1941. Papal audience: P. Mascagni, "Il cuore di S. S. Pio XII," *L'Avvenire*, June 2, 1942. Linina made a partial recovery and was still in the clinic in August 1943: letter to Lolli, August 19, 1943. She died in 1957, aged only thirty-two. Since the pope was a bright fourteen-year-old Roman schoolboy in 1890, it is not implausible for him to have retained vivid memories of *Cavalleria*'s debut. After his initial audience, Mascagni visited the pope at least three (perhaps four) times during 1943, and at least once in 1944 and once in 1945, shortly before his death.

283 "O Roma Felix" was published in facsimile in *L'osservatore romano della domenica* 11, no. 40 (October 1945). Mascagni had speculated about writing a musical homage to Saints Peter and Paul eleven years before; Agostino Stocchetti, "La Fede nella vita e nell'arte di P. Mascagni," *L'Italia*, December 25, 1934. Photograph dedication: *L'Avvenire*, December 18, 1943. Every Sunday: M. Rinaldi, "Il Ponte-

fice gli mandava le provviste al tempo del razionamento," *Il Telegrafo*, June 16, 1963. Confessed: letter to Lolli, July 20, 1943. Rome exploded: Richard Collier, *Duce: The Rise and Fall of Benito Mussolini*, p. 236. Fascism is finished: letter to Lolli, July 26, 1943.

284   Emy: letter to Lolli, August 19, 1943. Mimi: Domenico Mascagni, "Mascagni mio padre," *Il Borghese*, August 30, 1975. Mimi's status was noted in some American obituaries of the composer; the *Herald Tribune* wrote, "'He got tangled up with the Fascists,' his father explained recently" (August 3, 1945). Piermarcello: interview with Edoardo Farinelli, also C.P., "Intervista inedita con lo scomparso," *Libera Stampa*, August 3, 1945. This article also notes that Mimi's activities "thoroughly embittered the last months of his father's life." Franco Casavola, "La Fine di Mascagni," in E. Gragnani, ed., *Pietro Mascagni, 1863–1945*. Mascagni made the same comment about his miserable old age to Ricci, *34 anni*, p. 161. Hotel taken over: Rinaldi, "Mascagni a Roma," p. 122. Listening to mass: Casavola, "La fine di Mascagni," p. 30.

285   Emy, Tonino, and Lolli: A. Lolli, "Come morì Pietro Mascagni," in Angelo Anselmi, *Pietro Mascagni* (Milan, 1959), p. 70; also Iovino, *Mascagni*, p. 229. Lina, however, despite her advanced senility, is known to have objected to Anna's presence on at least one occasion; Franco Mannino recounts an extended and rather grim anecdote to that effect in *Genii* (Milan, 1987), p. 36. The young musicians' visits are described by Mannino, ibid., and Rinaldi, in "Il Pontefice." Casavola, "La fine di Mascagni," p. 30. Malipiero: Mannino, *Genii*, p. 36. Last visit to pope: *La Capitale*, August 2, 1945. Ricci, *34 anni*, p. 164.

286   The most detailed description of Mascagni's last hours is "Mascagni e morto," *Tribuna del Popolo*, August 3, 1945. Half mast: Santini, *Mascagni*, p. 43. Casella: R. de Rensis, *Musica vista*, p. 109. Rossellini, "È Morto Mascagni," *Il Giornale del Mattino*, August 3, 1945. Lina: Ricci, *34 anni*, p. 165. The account of Mascagni's funeral is based on articles in *L'Italia Libera* and *Il Giornale del Mattino*, August 5, 1945, and T. Celli, "Duecentomila attorno a Mascagni," *Il Messaggero*, August 3, 1975.

DISCOGRAPHY

297   Roger Flury's discography appears on pages 231–331 of his *Pietro Mascagni: A Bio-bibliography* (Westport, Conn: Greenwood Press, 2001).

298   Two selective discographies of *Cavalleria rusticana* are William Albright, "Chivalry in the Round: *Cavalleria* on Disc," *Opera Quarterly* 7, no. 2 (summer 1990): 90–103, and Charles Osborne, "*Cavalleria rusticana* and *Pagliacci*," in Alan Blyth, ed., *Opera on Record* (New York: Harper, 1982). Mascagni's 1940 *Cavalleria* is the longest of those reviewed in this essay, coming in at nearly eighty-two minutes, more than two minutes longer than his 1938 version. Von Karajan's performance takes 80'48", while Santini's takes only 70'23".

300 Mascagni takes 102'31" to get through *L'Amico Fritz*, while Gavazzeni manages it in 92'43".

305 As the notes to the Montpellier recording point out, the deletion of the fourth act of *Parisina* was authorized by the composer, but the deletion took place under duress, in response to complaints following the work's premiere. In the context of a concert performance at an important festival, this is no excuse.

Bibliography

The bibliography is presented in three sections: (1) principal collections of manuscripts and other unpublished material used by the author; (2) books; and (3) articles. In the last category are included some articles that, although contained within books cited in the previous section, are of enough significance to merit separate citation. Articles in daily newspapers, such as reviews, interviews, and news articles, although forming a substantial part of the source material I used, are not included in the bibliography.

PRINCIPAL COLLECTIONS OF MANUSCRIPTS
AND UNPUBLISHED MATERIAL

Biblioteca Livia Simoni, Museo Teatrale alla Scala, Milan (BLS)
Museo Mascagnano, Chiesa Arcipretale, Bagnara di Romagna (BdR)
Museo Mascagnano, Livorno (MM)
Mascagni/Farinelli collection, Rome (MFC)

BOOKS

Abbiati, Franco. *Storia della musica,* vol. 4, *Il novecento.* Milan: Garzanti, 1968.
Adami, Giuseppe. *Giulio Ricordi e i suoi musicisti.* Milan: Treves, 1933.

————, ed. *Letters of Giacomo Puccini.* New York: Vienna House, 1973.

Amici, Giovanni, et al. *Mascagni contro Sonzogno: Comparsa conclusionale del maestro Pietro Mascagni.* Livorno: Arte Grafiche S. Belforte, 1915.

Anselmi, Angelo. *Pietro Mascagni.* Milan: Castaldi, 1959.

Ashbrook, William. *The Operas of Puccini.* Ithaca, N.Y.: Cornell University Press, 1968.

Aulenti, Gae, and Marco Vallora. *Quartetto della maledizione.* Milan: Ubulibri, 1985.

Barblan, G. *Toscanini e la Scala.* Milan: Edizioni della Scala, 1972.

Bastianelli, Gianotto. *La crisi musicale europea.* Florence: Vallecchi, 1976.

————. *Pietro Mascagni.* Naples: Ricciardi, 1910.

Beecham, Sir Thomas. *A Mingled Chime.* New York: Putnam, 1943.

Bellincioni, Gemma. *Io e il palcoscenico.* Milan: Quintieri, 1920.

Benelli, Sem. *Schiavitù.* Milan: Mondadori, 1945.

Benvenuti, Nedo. *Pietro Mascagni nella vita e nell'arte.* Livorno: La Fortezza, 1981.

Bianchini, Roberto. *Una vita per Mascagni.* Siena: Barbablù, 1991.

Bianconi, Lorenzo, and Giogio Pestelli, eds. *Storia dell'opera italiana.* Vol. 4. *Il sistema produttivo e le sue competenze.* Turin: EDT/Musica, 1987.

Bonaventura, Arnaldo. *Ricordi e ritratti: Fra quelli che ho conosciuto.* Siena: Quaderni dell'accademia Chigiana, 1950.

Bracco, Roberto. *Tra le arti e gli artisti.* Naples: Giannini, n.d.

Brancati, Antonio, ed. *I centodieci anni del Liceo Musical Rossini (1882–1982) oggi Conservatorio in Pesaro.* Pesaro: Conservatorio di Musica "G. Rossini," 1992.

Budden, Julian. *The Operas of Verdi.* Vol. 3. *From "Don Carlos" to "Falstaff."* New York: Oxford University Press, 1981.

Calabrese, Omar, ed. *Modern Italy: Images and History of a National Identity.* Milan: Electa, 1984.

Calvetti, Mauro. *Galliano Masini.* Livorno: Belforte, 1986.

Candeloro, Giorgio. *Storia dell'Italia moderna.* Milan: Feltrinelli, 1974.

Cannistraro, Philip V., ed. *Historical Dictionary of Fascist Italy.* Westport, Conn.: Greenwood Press, 1982.

Cappellani, Nino. *Vita di Giovanni Verga.* Florence: Le Monnier, 1940.

Carelli, Augusto. *Emma Carelli.* Rome: Maglione, 1932.

Carner, Mosco. *Puccini: A Critical Biography.* 1958. 3d ed. New York: Holmes & Meier, 1992.

Casella, Alberto. *Music in My Time.* English translation of *I segreti della giara.* Norman: University of Oklahoma Press, 1955.

————. *21 + 26.* Rome: Augustea, 1931.

Casini, Claudio, et al., eds. *Mascagni.* Milan: Electa, 1984.

Cellamare, Daniele. *Mascagni e la "Cavalleria" visti da Cerignola.* Rome: Palombi, 1941.

————. *Pietro Mascagni: "Cerignola, culla della mia musica."* Rome: Palombi, 1965.

Celletti, Rodolfo. *Le Grandi Voci.* Rome: Istituto per la Collaborazione Culturale, 1964.

Cenzato, Giovanni, ed. *Nascita e gloria di un capolavoro italiano: Cinquantenario della "Cavalleria rusticana."* Milan: Bestetti, 1940.

————. *Nerone.* Milan: Sindacato Interprovinciale Fascista dei Giornalisti, 1935.

Clark, Martin. *Modern Italy, 1871–1982.* London: Longman, 1984.

Clough, S., and S. Saladino, eds. *A History of Modern Italy.* New York: Columbia University Press, 1968.

Cogo, Guido. *Il nostro Mascagni.* Vicenza: Cristofari, 1931.

Comitate Onoranze nel 1° Centenario della Nascita. *Pietro Mascagni: Contributi alla conoscenza della sua opera nel 1° centenario della nascita.* Livorno: Comitato Onoranze, 1963.

Commissione consultativa, Ministero della Pubblica Istruzione. *Parere sul ricorso del Maestro Pietro Mascagni.* Rome, 1902.

Conati, Marcello, ed. *Encounters with Verdi.* Ithaca, N.Y.: Cornell University Press, 1984.

Corazzol, Adriana Guarnieri. *Musica e letteratura in Italia tra ottocento e novecento.* Milan: Sansoni, 2000.

Criscione, Caterina, and Learco Andalò, eds. *Mascagni ritrovato, 1863–1945: L'uomo, il musicista.* Milan: Casa Musicale Sonzogno di Piero Ostali, 1995.

De Carlo, Salvatore, ed. *Mascagni parla.* Milan: De Carlo, 1945.

De Donno, Alfredo. *Mascagni nel 900 musicale.* Rome: Casa del Libro, 1935.

———. *Modernità di Mascagni.* Rome: Pinciana, 1931.

D'Ambra, Lucio [Renato Manganella]. *Gli anni della feluca.* Rome: Lucarini, 1989.

Donati, Paolo Luca. *Mascagni in Cartolina.* Livorno: Nuova Fortezza, 1990.

Fiorda, Nuccio. *Arte beghe e bizze di Toscanini.* Rome: Palombi, 1969.

Flury, Roger. *Pietro Mascagni: A Bio-bibliography.* Westport, Conn.: Greenwood Press, 2001.

Forzano, Giovacchino. *Come li ho conosciuti.* Turin: Radio Italiana, 1957.

Fraccaroli, Arnaldo. *Celebrità e quasi.* Milan: Sonzogno, 1923.

Frajese, Vittorio. *Dal Costanzi all'Opera.* 4 vols. Rome: Capitolium, 1977.

Gara, Eugenio, ed. *Carteggi Pucciniani.* Milan: Ricordi, 1958.

Gatti, Guglielmo. *Vita di Gabriele D'Annunzio.* Florence: Sansoni, 1988.

Gatti, Guido M. *Ildebrando Pizzetti.* Milan: Ricordi, 1954.

Gavazzeni, Gianandrea. *I nemici della musica.* Milan: Scheiwiller, 1965.

Gelati, Giovanni. *Il vate e il capobanda.* Livorno: Belforte Editore Libraio, 1992.

Gervasio, Roberto. *Come una coppia di champagne: Storia, vita e costume dell'Italia del nuovo secolo, 1900–1920.* Milan: Rizzoli, 1985.

Ghirardini, Gherardo. *Invito all'ascolto di Mascagni.* Milan: Mursia, 1988.

Gragnani, Emilio, ed. *Pietro Mascagni, 1863–1945.* Livorno: Comitato Onoranze a Pietro Mascagni, 1947.

Gregor, A. James. *Italian Fascism and Developmental Dictatorship.* Princeton, N.J.: Princeton University Press, 1979.

Harcourt, Eugène d'. *La musique actuelle en Italie.* Paris: Durdilly, 1906.

Henstock, Michael. *Fernando De Lucia.* Portland, Ore.: Amadeus Press, 1990.

Hughes, S. *The Fall and Rise of Modern Italy.* New York: Macmillan, 1967.

Hulten, Pontus, and Germano Celant, eds. *Italian Art, 1900–1945.* New York: Rizzoli, 1989.

Huysmans, J. K. *Against the Grain.* English translation of *À Rebours.* New York: Dover Books, 1969.

Incagliati, Matteo. *Il Teatro Costanzi, 1880–1907: Note e appunte della vita teatrale a Roma.* Rome: Editrice Roma, 1907.

Iovino, Roberto. *Mascagni: L'avventuroso dell'opera*. Milan: Camunia, 1987.

Jeri, Alfredo. *Mascagni*. Milan: Garzanti, 1940.

Krehbiel, Henry. *A Second Book of Operas*. New York: Garden City Publishing, 1917.

LeNôtre, G. *Les Noyades de Nantes*. Paris: Perrin, 1914.

Leoni, Edilio. *Un medico e un teatro: Mezzo secolo all'Opera di Roma*. Milan: Electa, 1987.

Levi, Primo (L'Italico). *Paesaggi e figure musicale*. Milan: Treves, 1913.

Lualdi, Antonio. *Serate musicale*. Milan: Treves, 1928.

————. *Tutti vivi*. Milan: Dall'Oglio, 1955.

————. *Viaggi musicali in Italia*. Milan: Alpes, 1927.

Lyttleton, Adrian. *The Seizure of Power: Fascism in Italy, 1919–1929*. Princeton, N.J.: Princeton University Press, 1973.

Maehder, Jurgen, and Lorenza Guiot, eds. *Ruggero Leoncavallo nel suo tempo: Atti del 1°convegno di studi su Ruggero Leoncavallo*. Milan: Casa Musicale Sonzogno di Piero Ostali, 1993.

Magroni, Jacopo. *Del Maestro Cav. Pietro Mascagni— Memorie*. Livorno: Stab. Giuseppe Meucci, 1890.

Mannino, Franco. *Genii . . . VIP e gente commune*. Milan: Bompiani, 1987.

Mantovani, Tancredi. *"Iris" di Pietro Mascagni: Guida musicale*. Rome: Formiggini, 1929.

Marangoni, Guido, and Carlo Vanbianchi. *La Scala*. Bergamo: Istituto Italiano d'Arti Grafiche, 1922.

Mariani, Renato. *Verismo in musica e altri studi*. Florence: Olschki, 1976.

Marotti, G., and F. Pagni. *Giacomo Puccini intimo*. Florence: Vallechi, 1926.

Mascagni, Emy. *S'inginocchi la più piccina*. Milan: Treves, 1936.

Mascagni, Pietro. *Per le opere dell'ingegno*. Rome: Officina Poligrafica Italiana, 1905.

I Mascagni di San Miniato. San Miniato: Accademia degli Euteleti della Città di San Miniato, 1986.

Monaldi, Gino. *Pietro Mascagni: L'uomo e l'artista*. Rome: Voghera, 1898.

Monnesi, Antonio, ed. *I cento anni del Teatro Verdi, 1867–1967*. Pisa: Giardini, 1967.

Montale, Eugenio. *Prime alla Scala*. Milan: Mondadori, 1981.

Morini, Mario, ed. *Pietro Mascagni*. 2 vols. Milan: Casa Musicale Sonzogno di Piero Ostali, 1964.

————. *Studi su Pietro Mascagni: Atti del 1°convegno di studi su Pietro Mascagni*. Milan: Casa Musicale Sonzogno di Piero Ostali, 1987.

————. *Umberto Giordano*. Milan: Casa Musicale Sonzogno di Piero Ostali, 1968.

Morini, Mario, Roberto Iovino, and Alberto Paloscia, eds. *Pietro Mascagni: Epistolario*. 2 vols. Lucca: Libreria Musicale Italiana, 1997.

Morini, Mario, Nandi Ostali, and Piero Ostali Jr., eds. *Casa Musicale Sonzogno: Cronologie, saggi, testimonianze*. 2 vols. Milan: Casa Musicale Sonzogno di Piero Ostali, 1995.

Morini, Mario, and Piero Ostali, eds. *Mascagni e "l'Iris" fra simbolismo e floreale: Atti del 2° convegno di studi su Pietro Mascagni*. Milan: Casa Musicale Sonzogno di Piero Ostali, 1989.

Muro, Bernardo de. *Quando ero Folco*. Milan: Gastaldi, 1955.

Nicastro, Aldo. *Il melodramma e gli italiani*. Milan: Rusconi, 1982.

Nicolodi, Fiamma. *Gusti e tendenze nel novecento musicale in Italia*. Florence: Sansoni, 1982.

————. *Musica e musicisti nel ventennio fascista.* Fiesole: Discanto, 1984.

————, ed. *Musica italiana del primo novecento "la generazione dell'80."* Florence: Olschki, 1981.

Opicelli, Ernesto. *L'operetta da Hervé al musical.* Genoa: Sagep, 1985.

Orselli, Cesare. *Le occasioni di Mascagni.* Siena: Barbablù, 1990.

Orsini, Giovanni. *. . . di Pietro Mascagni.* Milan: Americana, 1912.

————. *Parisina, Parisina.* Florence: Bemporad, 1919.

————. *Vangelo d'un mascagnano.* Milan: Vecchi, 1926.

Ostali, Piero, and Nandi Ostali, eds. *"L'Amico Fritz" nel centenario della prima rappresentazione: Atti del 4°convegno di studi su Pietro Mascagni.* Milan: Casa Musicale Sonzogno di Piero Ostali, 1994.

————. *"Cavalleria rusticana," 1890–1990: Centi anni di un capolavoro.* Milan: Casa Musicale Sonzogno di Piero Ostali, 1990.

————. *"Il Piccolo Marat": Storia e revoluzione nel melodramma verista: Atti del 3°convegno di studi su Pietro Mascagni.* Milan: Casa Musicale Sonzogno di Piero Ostali, 1990.

Pasi, Mario. *Mascagni.* Long Island City, N.Y.: Treves, 1989.

Pellizzi, Camillo. *Le lettere italiane del nostro secolo.* Milan: Libreria d'Italia, 1929.

Pietro Mascagni 1890–1920: Dalla "Cavalleria" al "Piccolo Marat." Milan: Casa Musicale Sonzogno, 1920.

Piccini, G. ["Jarro"]. *Attori, cantanti, concertisti, acrobati: Ritratti, macchiette, anneddoti.* Florence: Bemporad, 1897.

Pistone, Daniele. *L'Opéra italien au XIX siècle de Rossini à Puccini.* Paris: Champion, 1986. Subsequently published in English translation by Amadeus Press in 1995.

Platen, Baron Charles de. *Souvenirs musicaux et dramatiques.* Rome: La Fiamma, 1911.

Pompei, Edoardo. *Pietro Mascagni nella vita e nell'arte.* Rome: Nazionale, 1912.

Prolo, Maria Adriana. *Storia del cinema muto italiana.* Milan: Poligono, 1957.

Rensis, Raffaelo de. *Musica vista.* Milan: Ricordi, 1961.

Ricci, Luigi. *34 anni con Pietro Mascagni.* Milan: Curci, 1976.

Rinaldi, Mario. *Musica e verismo.* Rome: De Santis, 1932.

Roselli, John. *Music and Musicians in Nineteenth-Century Italy.* Portland, Ore.: Amadeus Press, 1991.

Rossellini, Renzo. *Pagine di un musicista.* Milan: Cappelli, 1964.

Rubboli, Daniele. *Ridi pagliaccio.* Lucca: Fazzi, 1985.

Sachs, Harvey. *Music in Fascist Italy.* London: Weidenfeld & Nicolson, 1987.

————. *Toscanini.* New York: Harper & Row, 1978.

Salvetti, Guido. *Storia della musica: Il novecento I.* Turin: EDT, 1977.

Sanmartino, Enrico, Conte di. *Ricordi.* Rome: Danesi in Via Margutta, 1943.

Santini, Aldo. *Mascagni viva e abbasso.* Livorno: Belforte, 1985.

Scardovi, Stefano. *L'opera dei bassifondi: Il melodramma "plebeo" nel verismo musicale italiano.* Lucca: Libreria Musicale Italiana, 1994.

Schoumacker, L. *Erckmann-Chatrian, étude biographique et critique d'après des documents inédits.* Paris: Les Belles Lettres, 1933.

Scuderi, Gaspare. *"Iris": Guida attraverso il dramma e la musica.* Milan: Bottega di Poesia, 1924.

Stivender, David, ed. *Mascagni*. White Plains, N.Y.: Pro/Am Music Resources, 1988.

Stone, Marla Susan. *The Patron State: Culture and Politics in Fascist Italy*. Princeton, N.J.: Princeton University Press, 1998.

Tambling, Jeremy. *Opera and the Culture of Fascism*. Oxford: Clarendon Press, 1996.

Taylor, Joshua. *Futurism*. New York: Museum of Modern Art, 1961.

Tedeschi, Rubens. *Addio, fiorito asil: Il melodramma italiano da Boito al verismo*. Milan: Feltrinelli, 1978.

———. *D'Annunzio e la musica*. Scandicci: La Nuova Italia, 1988.

Terenzio, Vincenzo. *La musica italiana nell'ottocento*. Milan: Bramante, 1976.

———. *La musica tra romanticismo e avanguardia*. Bari: Adda, 1980.

Tintori, Giampietro. *Duecento anni di teatro alla Scala: Cronologia opere-balletti-concerti 1778–1977*. Milan: Grafica Gutenberg, 1979.

Tosi, Bruno. *Pertile: Una voce, un mito*. Venice: CGS, 1985.

Trezzini, Lamberto, and Angelo Curtolo. *Oltre le quinte*. Venice: Marsilio, 1973.

Venturi, Fulvio. *L'opera lirica a Livorno, 1847–1999*. Livorno: Circolo Musicale Amici dell'Opera Galliano Masini, 2000.

———, ed. *"Iris," 1898–1998: Il centenario*. Livorno: Circolo Musicale Amici dell'Opera Galliano Masini, 1998.

Viti, Giovanni Maria. *Teatro Reale dell'Opera*. Rome: Menaglia, 1941.

Weaver, William. *The Golden Century of Italian Opera*. New York: Thames & Hudson, 1980.

Zorzi, E., ed. *Le Maschere: Album-Ricordo*. Milan: Martinelli, 1901.

Zurletti, Michelangelo. *Catalani*. Turin: EDT/Musica, 1982.

ARTICLES

Abse, Tobias. "The Rise of Fascism in an Industrial City: The Case of Livorno, 1919–1922." In David Forgacs, ed., *Rethinking Italian Fascism*, pp. 52–82. London: Lawrence & Wishart, 1986.

Bacherini, Maria Adelaide Bartoli. "Pietro Mascagni direttore dimenticato." In Ostali, ed., *L'Amico Fritz*, pp. 139–53.

Baldacchi, Luigi. "Forzano drammaturgo." In Morini and Ostali, eds., *Il Piccolo Marat*, pp. 81–92.

———. "I libretti di Mascagni." *Nuova Rivista Musicale Italiana* 3 (July–September 1985): 395–410.

Barini, Giorgio. "*Isabeau* di Pietro Mascagni." *Nuova Antologia* 47 (February 1, 1912): 550–57.

———. "Pietro Mascagni." *Il Pianoforte* 4 (February 1923): 35–40.

Bernardini-Marzolla, Ugo. "Spunti di storia delle opera di Pietro Mascagni da un carteggio perduto." Comitato Onoranze, ed., *Contributi*, pp. 59–190.

Bonaventura, Arnaldo. "Pietro Mascagni." *Liburni Civitas* 1 (1928): 49–63.

Botteghi, Carlo. "*Iris:* Studio critico di un capolavoro." *Quaderni della Labronica* 7 (1979).

Budden, Julian. "La partitura del *Piccolo Marat* collegata alla grande tradizione dell'opera storico-patriottica dell'ottocento italiano." In Morini and Ostali, eds., *Il Piccolo Marat*, 47–56.

Businelli, Mariella. *"Sì,* l'operetta di Pietro Mascagni." *Rassegna Musicale Curci* 41 (May 1988): 13–18.

Capri, Antonio. "Verismo nell'opera di Mascagni." *La Scala* 65 (April 1955): 29–33.

Casini, Claudio. "Il verismo musicale italiano." In Casini, ed., *Mascagni*, pp. 9–30.

Cavalcabò, Claudio Fratta. "Mascagni e Puccini: Battaglie, vittorie, distrazioni." Selected articles from *La giovane montagna* 3–5 (March–May 1942).

Cella, Franca. "Policromia letteraria dei libretti mascagnani." In Casini, ed., *Mascagni*, pp. 111–94.

Celletti, Rodolfo. *"L'Amico Fritz* conferma il talento di Mascagni," *Musica e Dischi*, nos. 206, 207, 211 (August, September 1963, January 1964) (article in three installments).

———. "La *Cavalleria rusticana* e il mito di Mascagni." *Musica e Dischi*, nos. 199–205 (January–July 1963) (article in seven installments).

———. "La vocalità mascagnana." In Morini, ed., *Studi su Pietro Mascagni*, pp. 39–45.

Celli, Teodoro. "La *Cavalleria* et otto lettere." *La Scala* 47 (June 1951): 32–36.

Chiarelli, Luigi. "Mascagnana San Remo Aprile anno XI." *San Remo* 2 (May 5, 1933): 26–28.

Ciampelli, G. M. *"Le Maschere* di Mascagni alla Scala." *Musica d'Oggi* (March 1931).

Conati, Marcello. "Mascagni, Puccini, Leoncavallo &c. in Germania." *Discoteca alta fedeltà* 17 (August 1976): 18–25.

D'Arcais, Francesco. "La musica italiana e la *Cavalleria rusticana* del Maestro Mascagni." *Nuova Antologia* 25 (June 1, 1890): 518–39.

Favia-Artsay, Aida. "Did Mascagni Write *Cavalleria?" Opera Quarterly* 7 (summer 1990): 83–89.

Ferrero, Lorenzo. "Vecchia e nuova drammaturgia nel *Piccolo Marat.*" In Morini and Ostali, eds., *Il Piccolo Marat*, pp. 69–80.

Gallini, Natale. "Altri inediti mascagnani." *Martinella del Milano* 14 (August 1960): 295–99.

———. "Mascagni a Milano." In Morini, ed., *Pietro Mascagni*, 2:75–92.

———. "La metamorfosi di un idillio." *La Scala* 65 (April 1955): 39–42.

Gara, Eugenio. "Cantanti mascagnani tra pregiudizio e verità." In Morini, ed., *Pietro Mascagni* 1:203–49.

Gatti, Guido M. "Gabriele D'Annunzio and the Italian Opera Composers." *Musical Quarterly* 10, no. 2 (April 1924): 263–88.

———. "Il fenomeno Pietro Mascagni." *Musica* 10, no. 13 (July 10, 1916).

Gavazzeni, Gianandrea. "Il teatro di Mascagni nel suo tempo e nel nostro." *Rivista di Livorno* 6 (July–August 1956): 205–21.

Gelati, Giovanni. *"Cavalleria* in tribunale." In Ostali, ed., *"Cavalleria rusticana,"* 1890–1990, 115–22.

Giazotto, Remo. "Quattordici lettere inedite di Pietro Mascagni." *Nuova Rivista Musicale Italiana* 4 (1970): 493–513.

Goetz, Helmut. "Die Beziehungen zwischen Pietro Mascagni und Benito Mussolini." *Analecta musicologia* 17 (1976): 212–53.

Gori, Gianni. "Il fascino perverso della piovra nel 'teatro di poesia' post-romantico." In Morini and Ostali, eds., *Mascagni e "l'Iris" fra simbolismo e floreale,* pp. 71–80.

Gragnani, Emilio. "Mascagni a Livorno." In Morini, ed., *Pietro Mascagni* 2:45–74.

———. "Miscellanea mascagnana." *Rivista di Livorno* 2 (July–August 1956): 195–214.

———. "Prospetto cronologico della vita e delle opere di Pietro Mascagni." In Comitato Onoranze, ed., *Contributi,* pp. 565–692.

Iovino, Roberto. "Mascagni e D'Annunzio: *Parisina.*" *Rassegna Musicale Curci* 41 (May 1988): 19–23.

Kestner, Joseph. "Out of the Tinder Box." *Opera News,* April 8, 1978, pp. 11–14.

Klein, John W. "Mascagni and His Operas." *Opera* 6 (October 1955): 623–31.

———. "Pietro Mascagni and Giovanni Verga." *Music and Letters* 44 (October 1963): 350–57.

Labroca, Mario. "Il musicista del 'cantar continuo.'" *Radiocorriere* (May 1955).

Lancellotti, Arturo. "Mascagni a casa sua." *Noi e il mondo* 7 (July 1917): 477–84.

Lorena, Claudio. "L' 'opera nuova' e le 'opere perdute' di Pietro Mascagni." *Noi e il mondo* 14 (July 1924): 433–38.

Lualdi, Adriano. "Mascagni, D'Annunzio e *Parisina.*" *Quaderni d'annunziani* 30–31 (1965): 63–100.

———. "Mascagni, direttore d'orchestra." *L'Opera* 2 (1966): 24–27.

Luparello, Maria Ada. "Fiori nell'incanto sonoro." *La Scala* (October 1960): 47–50.

Maehder, Jürgen. "The Origins of Italian *Literaturoper: Guglielmo Ratcliff, La figlia di Iorio, Parisina,* and *Francesca da Rimini.*" In Arthur Gross and Roger Parker, eds., *Reading Opera,* pp. 92–128. Princeton, N.J.: Princeton University Press, 1988.

Mandelli, Alfred. "Armonia e colore nell'*Iris.*" In Morini and Ostali, eds., *Mascagni e "l'Iris" fra simbolismo e floreale,* pp. 23–34.

Mariani, Renato. "Quella piovra è il piacere." *La Scala* 47 (June 1951): 37–41.

———. "Socialità nel gusto di Mascagni." *La Scala* 65 (April 1955): 34–38.

Martignoni, Clelia. "Mascagni e D'Annunzio: una collaborazione difficile." In program book for production of *Parisina,* Teatro dell'Opera, Rome, 1978–79 seasons, pp. 36–43.

Mascagni, Pietro. "A proposito di critica." *La Cronaca Musicale* 4 (1899): 87–89.

——— [writing as "l'infognato"]. "A proposito di un discorso." *La Cronaca Musicale* 3 (1898): 17–25.

———. "Alle fonti della melodia." *Il Mondo,* November 7, 1915.

———. "Amilcare Ponchielli." *La Lettura,* August 1, 1934.

———. "Come nacque *Parisina.*" *Musica,* December 15, 1921, p. 2.

———. "Come si scrive un'opera." *La Lettura,* January 1, 1907, pp. 27–36.

———. "L'evoluzione della musica." Lecture published as a pamphlet. Rome: Società Editrice Dante Alighieri, 1900.

———. "Perchè ho scritto il *Nerone.*" *La Lettura,* November 1, 1933.

McPherson, Jim. "Bessie Abott and the Naked Lady." *Opera Quarterly* 17, no. 2 (spring 2001): 218–34.

Miller, Marion S. "Wagnerism, Wagnerians, and Italian Identity." In David C. Large and William Weber, eds., *Wagnerism in European Culture and Politics*, pp. 167–97. Ithaca, N.Y.: Cornell University Press, 1984.

Morini, Mario. "Attribuivano a Mascagni le barzellette antifasciste." *Nazione Sera*, October 3, 1953.

———. "Faville polemiche intorno a P. Mascagni." *Viator* 3 (January–February 1949): 23–25.

———. "Il 'fenomeno Mascagni' tra pubblicità e mito." In Criscione and Andalò, eds., *Mascagni ritrovato*, pp. 11–18.

———. "Formiggini e Mascagni erano l'incubo di Mussolini." *Il Tirenno*, March 25, 1952.

———. "*Iris* e i progetti non realizzati." In Comitato Onoranze, ed., *Contributi*, pp.191–286

———. "Lettere inedite a Luigi Illica." *La Scala* 65 (April 1955): 43–49.

———. "Mascagni al traguardo del centenario." In *Pietro Mascagni: Mostra documentale.* Milan: Biblioteca comunale di Milano, 1963.

———. "Mascagni e Illica nell'esperienza dell'*Iris*." In program book for production of *Iris*, Teatro di Villa Mimbelli. Livorno, 1988.

———. "Mascagni e Rossini." *L'Opera* 4 (1968): 12–13.

———. "Mascagni prima della *Cavalleria*: Da *In filanda* a *Pinotta*." *Rassegna Musicale Curci* 41 (May 1988): 3–7.

———. "Mascagni umorista." *La Scala* 69 (August 1955): 15–19.

———. "Mascagni vent'anni dopo." *L'Opera* 12 (January–March 1966): 21–23.

———. "Mascagni, Verga e *Cavalleria rusticana*." In Criscione and Andalò, eds., *Mascagni ritrovato*, pp. 89–98.

———. "Nascita dell'*Amico Fritz*." In Ostali, ed., *L'Amico Fritz nel centenario della prima rappresentazione*, pp. 9–14.

———. "Nascita e vicenda di *Parisina*." *Rassegna Musicale Curci* 32 (1979): 3–8.

———. "Ojetti librettista per una volta." *La Scala* (January 1960): 28–32.

———. "*Il Piccolo Marat*: L'inno della sua conscienza." In Morini and Ostali, eds., *Il Piccolo Marat*, 19–24.

———. "Pietro Mascagni e la 'Maria Antonietta' di Illica." *La Scala* 104 (July 1958): 16–25.

———. "Preparazione dei sette fiaschi delle *Maschere*." *La Scala* 75 (February 1956): 49–56.

———. "Profilo di Illica." *La Scala* (October 1956): 42–48.

———. "Profilo di Mascagni." In Morini, ed., *Pietro Mascagni* 2:9–44.

Nencini, Bianca Flury. "Giovanni Targioni-Tozzetti." *Liburni Civitas* 10 (1937): 105–23.

Nicastro, Aldo. "Melodramma e scommessa (appunti su *Parisina*)." *Chigiana: Rassegna annuale di studi musicologi* 17 (1980): 63–71.

Nicolodi, Fiamma. "La giovane scuola di fronte al fascismo: Puccini e Mascagni musicisti 'popolari.'" *Antologia Vieusseux* (October–December 1982): 2–26.

——. "Mascagni e il potere." In Casini et al., eds., *Mascagni*, pp. 195–226.

Oliver, Stephen. "*Cav*: Is It Really 'Verismo'?" *Opera* 37 (October 1986): 1130–35.

Orselli, Cesare. "*In filanda, Cavalleria rusticana, Guglielmo Ratcliff*: Nascita della morfologia mascagnana." In Morini, ed., *Studi su Pietro Mascagni*, pp. 61–70.

——. "Mascagni coglie l'occasione cinematografica." *Rassegna Musicale Curci* 38 (January 1985): 7–12.

——. "Paneggi medievali per la donna decadente: *Parisina* e *Francesca*." *Chigiana: Rassegna annuale di studi musicologi* 17 (1980): 135–50.

Paloscia, Alberto. "Mascagni e l'idillio: La nascita della 'commedia lyrica.'" In Ostali, ed., *L'Amico Fritz*, pp. 15–34.

——. "Opera ed esotismo: Per un drammaturgia del funerario." In Morini and Ostali, eds., *Mascagni e "l'Iris" fra simbolismo e floreale*, pp. 81–88.

——. "Verismo e opera storica." In Morini and Ostali, eds., *Il Piccolo Marat*, pp. 57–68.

Pannain, Guido. "*Cavalleria rusticana*." *Rassegna Musicale Curci* 17 (December 1963): 2–4.

Pasi, Mario. "Parisina Malatesta, dalla tragedia all'opera lirica." In program book for production of *Parisina*, Teatro dell'Opera, Rome, 1978–79, pp. 26–28.

Pastura, Francesco. "Pietro Mascagni e la vocalità del popolo italiano." *Realtà Nuova* (September 1963): 836–47.

Pescetti, Luigi. "*Cavalleria rusticana* dalla novella al dramma, al libretto." *Liburni Civitas*, special commemorative issue (1940): 29–41.

Piccardi, Carlo. "Mascagni e l'ipotesi del 'dramma musicale cinematografico.'" *Musica Realtà* 11 (August 1991): 87–109.

Ricci, Luigi. "Un bauletto magico." *La Scala* 126 (May 1960): 44–46.

Rinaldi, Mario. "L'addio di Palamidone." *La Scala* 50 (January 1954): 48–50.

——. "Mascagni a Roma." In Morini, ed., *Pietro Mascagni* 2:93–126.

——. "Mascagni salvò il Costanzi." *Il Messaggero*, December 7, 1963.

——. "Perchè Mascagni compose *Parisina*, e perchè Puccini non la scrisse." *Rassegna Musicale Curci* 32 (1979): 9–14.

Romagnoli, Ettore. "D'Annunzio e la musica." *Musica d'Oggi*, April 1938.

Roncaglia, Gino. "Mascagni operista." In Comitato Onoranze, ed., *Contributi*, pp. 19–58.

——. "Ricordo di Pietro Mascagni." In *Le Celebrazioni del 1963 e alcune nuove indagini sulla musica italiana del XVIII e XIX secolo*. Florence: Olschki, 1963.

——. "Il tribunale di Busseto." *La Scala* 6 (April 1950): 11–12.

Sachs, Harvey. "La Scala durante il ventennio fascista." *Nuova Rivista Musicale Italiana* 23, nos. 1–2 (1989): 99–109.

Salfi, Francesco Saverio. "L'opera di Pietro Mascagni nella storia della musica." *Rivista di Livorno* 9 (September–December 1959): 294–312.

Salvetti, Guido. "Dalla scapigliatura a *Cavalleria rusticana*." In Ostali, ed., *Cavalleria rusticana, 1890–1990*, pp. 65–74.

————. "Mascagni: La creazione musicale." In Casini et al., eds., *Mascagni*, pp. 31–110.

————. "La tentazione decadente in Pietro Mascagni." In Morini, ed., *Studi su Pietro Mascagni*, pp. 49–58.

Sansone, Matteo. "Verga and Mascagni: The Critics' Response to *Cavalleria rusticana*." *Music and Letters* 71 (May 1990): 198–214.

Santi, Piero. "Il linguaggio di Mascagni e *Il piccolo Marat*." In Morini and Ostali, eds., *Il Piccolo Marat*, pp. 25–46.

Simoni, Renato. "Il diario musicale di Renato Simoni." *La Scala* 5 (March 1950): 26–29.

Stivender, David. "The Genesis of a Masterpiece: Notes on *Guglielmo Ratcliff*." Brochure for Pietro Mascagni, *Guglielmo Ratcliff*. LP. MRF Records, MRF 57, n.d.

————. "Illica, Mascagni and the writing of *Isabeau*." Brochure for Pietro Mascagni, *Isabeau*. LP. MRF Records, MRF 97, 1973.

————. "Mascagni's *Lodoletta*." Brochure for Pietro Mascagni, *Lodoletta*." LP. MRF Records, MRF-110, 1974.

Stocchetti, Agostino. "La fede nella vita e nell'arte di P. Mascagni." *L'Italia*, December 25, 1934.

Tabanelli, Nicola. "Ancora la questione Mascagni." *Rivista Musicale Italiana* 11 (1904): 573–77.

————. "La questione Mascagni–Liceo di Pesaro dal punto di vista giuridico." *Rivista Musicale Italiana* 9 (1902): 903–22.

————. "La questione Mascagni–Liceo di Pesaro dinanzi al consiglio di stato." *Rivista Musicale Italiana* 10 (1903): 779–90.

Taddei, Adolfo. "Pietro Mascagni." *Liburni Civitas* 13 (1940): 3–28.

Targioni-Tozzetti, Giovanni. "Da *Cavalleria* a *Vistilia*." *Rivista di Livorno* 1 (1926): 118–25.

————. "Mascagni prima della *Cavalleria*." *La Lettura* (March 1932): 220.

————. "Ricordi e rettificazioni mascagnani." *Liburni Civitas* 4 (1932).

Tedeschi, Rubens. "*L'Amico Fritz*: Romanzo, commedia, libretto." In Ostali, ed., *L'Amico Fritz*, 35–48.

Tintori, Giampiero. "Carteggio Mascagni-Eisner." *L'Opera* 2 (1966): 29–31.

Tommasi, Gioacchino Lanza. "Il gusto musicale di D'Annunzio e il dannunzianesimo musicale." In F. Nicolodi, ed., *Musica italiana del primo novecento "la generazione dell'80.*" Florence: Oschki, 1981.

Torchi, Luigi. "*Guglielmo Ratcliff* di Pietro Mascagni." *Rivista Musicale Italiana* 2 (1895): 287–311.

————. "*Iris* di Pietro Mascagni." *Rivista Musicale Italiana* 6 (1899): 71–118.

————. "*Le Maschere* di Pietro Mascagni." *Rivista Musicale Italiana* 8 (1901): 178–80.

Vlad, Roman. "Modernità di *Cavalleria rusticana*." In Ostali, ed., *Cavalleria rusticana, 1890–1990*, pp. 15–40.

————. "Novità del linguaggio in *Cavalleria rusticana*." In Morini, ed., *Studi su Pietro Mascagni*, pp. 25–34.

Index